LABOR AND EMPLOYMENT

RELATIONS ASSOCIATION SERIES

Employee Ownership and Shared Capitalism

New Directions in Research

EDITED BY

Edward J. Carberry

First Edition

ISBN 978-0-913447-03-1

Price: $29.95

LABOR AND EMPLOYMENT RELATIONS ASSOCIATION SERIES
    Proceedings of the Annual Meeting (published electronically beginning in 2009)
    Annual Research Volume (published in the summer/fall)
    LERA Online Membership Directory (updated daily, member/subscriber access only)
    LERA Newsletter (published electronically 3-4 times a year)
    Perspectives on Work (published once a year in the summer/fall)
    Perspectives on Work Online Companion (published twice a year as a supplement)

Information regarding membership, subscriptions, meetings, publications, and general affairs of the LERA can be found at the Association website at www.lera.illinois.edu. Members can make changes to their member records, including contact information, affiliations, and preferences, by accessing the online directory at the website or by contacting the LERA national office.

LABOR AND EMPLOYMENT RELATIONS ASSOCIATION
University of Illinois at Urbana-Champaign
School of Labor and Employment Relations
121 Labor and Employment Relations Building
504 East Armory Ave., MC-504
Champaign, IL 61820
Telephone: 217/333-0072   Fax: 217/265-5130
Websites: www.leraweb.org   www.employmentpolicy.net
E-mail: leraoffice@illinois.edu

For John Logue . . . a practical idealist who helped tens of thousands share in ownership of the companies where they worked.

CONTENTS

Section III: Assessing the Experience of
Shared Capitalism in Different National Contexts

Chapter 1

Employee Ownership and Shared Capitalism: Assessing the Experience, Research, and Policy Implications

Edward J. Carberry
Erasmus University

One of the most persistent and important, but often ignored, trends of contemporary market economies continues to be the ownership of firms by their employees. Since the emergence of different experiments with employee ownership in the early 20th century, a consistently growing group of companies and expanding set of institutions have opened the door for firms to share the financial returns of economic production with broad groups of employees. The growth of various forms of "shared capitalism" (a term that I will use interchangeably with "employee ownership") has meant that, currently, a little under half of all employees in the private sector own stock in the companies in which they work or receive cash-based bonuses linked to different measures of corporate performance (Freeman, Blasi, and Kruse 2010). Although a number of careful academic studies have provided ample evidence that shared capitalism holds significant potential for creating more productive, stable, and equitable companies, the topic remains remarkably absent from policy and popular discussions about the workplace, employment, compensation and benefits, economic productivity, and competitiveness. In fact, employee ownership is often viewed as a fringe phenomenon among policy makers, managers, journalists, academics, and the general public.

Over the last three decades, however, a large, multidisciplinary academic literature has revealed that employee ownership is, in fact, a remarkably common phenomenon that can be found in a diverse group of firms and industries. This literature also provides persuasive evidence that shared capitalism can have significant and positive impacts on employee well-being, employee wealth accumulation, firm

1

productivity, and long-term firm stability and growth. Although a common assumption is that these positive outcomes are the consequence of employees being more motivated in their work by owning stock, the research consistently suggests that, in order to generate these positive outcomes, firms and managers need to structure and implement shared capitalism in specific ways—namely, by combining employee ownership with increased decision-making opportunities for employees and other HR practices associated with the high-performance work systems model (Appelbaum, Bailey, Berg, and Kalleberg 2000), such as extensive training on how firms work and extensive sharing of financial information. In addition, the literature has also demonstrated that, for shared capitalism to produce these positive effects, it needs to be offered as an additional reward on top of existing wages and other benefits rather than as a replacement. If implemented under the right conditions, shared capitalism offers a model of economic production based on the shared effort of all employees in creating productive, efficient, innovative, and stable organizations, as well as shared financial rewards for such effort. This model offers a stark alternative to the dominant one based on the primacy of short-term shareholder value and the concentration of the wealth generated by corporations into the hands of a few top managers.

Although the research on the positive effects of certain forms of shared capitalism for employees and firms is fairly conclusive, our understanding of the full range of causes, characteristics, and consequences of shared capitalism remains underdeveloped, particularly considering the persistent growth in the number of firms using shared capitalism, the growing sophistication with which firms approach implementing shared capitalism, and the emergence of new forms of shared capitalism, such as broad-based stock options in the 1990s. Employee ownership is a complex phenomenon that can be and has been fruitfully analyzed from a number of different social scientific perspectives.

This book showcases the diverse state of cutting-edge academic work on shared capitalism. More specifically, this book attempts to illuminate a representative cross section of current research about shared capitalism, enliven academic debates about it, and embolden new research initiatives. The works in this volume do not provide a complete picture of the current state of employee ownership or research about it, but by showcasing a representative sample of work, they illuminate shared capitalism's complexity as an organizational, psychological, sociological, and economic phenomenon that requires deep interdisciplinary understanding.

Another goal of this volume is to demonstrate to broader groups of policy makers, shareholder activists, journalists, business intellectuals, economic and social justice activists, and citizens the ongoing relevance of shared capitalism and its potential for improving broader social and economic outcomes beyond employee well-being and firm productivity, such as promoting economic growth, innovation, and employment stability, as well as addressing the alarming growth in wealth inequality that has occurred in the last two decades. Although this book and its introduction focus primarily on employee ownership in the United States and, to a lesser extent, western Europe, it is important to note that shared capitalism can be found in all parts of the globe, from broad-based employee stock options in Korea, to the privatization of formerly state-owned industries in eastern Europe, to worker cooperatives in Argentina that were created in response to the financial crisis of the early 2000s. This diversity provides a rich set of experiences on which we can draw to assess the potential offered by shared capitalism and to inform policies to encourage it. This volume represents a modest step in that direction.

In this introduction, I briefly describe the historical context and current landscape of employee ownership and shared capitalism in the United States, drawing on a number of existing studies that have capably mapped out this terrain. I then turn to a discussion of the history of academic research, highlighting what we know and how we know it, as well as what we still need to know. This provides a context in which I place the current studies featured in this book. I close with a discussion of what the rich social scientific literature on shared capitalism means for public policy.

Historical Context and Current Landscape

This book examines a variety of forms of shared capitalism, including worker cooperatives, employee stock ownership plans (ESOPs), 401(k) plans, broad-based employee stock option plans, employee stock purchase plans, profit-sharing plans, and gain-sharing plans. Each type of plan is characterized by a specific legal structure that defines a mechanism through which employees receive or purchase stock from their employers or receive a cash-based bonus. In worker cooperatives, for example, each employee usually owns an equal share of the firm and makes either a one-time or periodic investment to acquire this share. In ESOPs and 401(k) plans, employees receive employer stock in a retirement account. In ESOPs, firms make annual contributions of stock to employee accounts. What distinguishes ESOPs from other plans is that employees typically do not pay for the stock with their savings or with wage concessions; instead, the stock is granted to them. The company's grants of stock are made out of company profits or are financed by a loan with federal tax incentives. Furthermore, for firms to receive these and other tax benefits associated with ESOPs, all employees must be included in the plan, although there are some exceptions. In 401(k) plans, employer stock can be one of many investments in a diversified portfolio that employees buy using their savings. In many cases, companies match employee contributions to 401(k) plans with company stock matches. Since 401(k) plans are also tax qualified, all employees must be included in the plan.

There are also plans that provide shorter-term ownership opportunities (although employees can hold onto the shares for as long as they wish). Broad-based employee stock option plans (BBSOPs), for example, give employees the right to purchase a fixed amount of shares at a fixed price for a fixed period of time. Often, employees have to work at a company for a minimum length of time, usually three to five years, to get the right to exercise their stock options (i.e., purchase the shares). Although there is no legal definition of a "broad-based" stock option plan (and no legal requirements regarding the number and type of employees who must receive stock options), the common definition within the academic literature is that a broad-based plan is one that grants options to 50% or more of a firm's employees. Employee stock purchase plans (ESPPs) allow employees to defer part of their salary in order to buy discounted stock on specific purchase dates. The law requires that all employees be given the opportunity to participate in these plans, although there are a few exceptions. Profit-sharing and gain-sharing plans do not provide employees with a way to acquire stock directly but instead provide cash bonus payments based on corporate profits (in the former) and group-based performance (in the latter). There is, however, a plan called a deferred profit-sharing plan in the United States whereby workers receive cash profit sharing and can invest some of it in company stock contributed to a retirement plan, such as a 401(k) or a separate profit-sharing retirement plan.

In certain plans, such as ESOPs, the law requires that all employees participate (although there are some exceptions), while in BBSOPs, profit sharing, and gain sharing, management decides which employees participate. In ESPPs and 401(k) plans, all employees are eligible (again, with some exceptions), but they can choose whether to participate. Different forms of shared capitalism define specific legal rights for employees regarding treatment under the plan and access to specific types of plan information. Some plans also require that employees have a role in governance. Worker cooperatives are not legally required to give employees a significant role in governance, but since these organizations are set up to promote workplace democracy, they are often structured to provide all employees with an equal, and sometimes direct, role in governance decisions. In ESOPs in publicly traded firms, employees receive the same rights as any shareholder pertaining to stock allocated to their accounts, while in ESOPs in privately held firms, a trustee votes the shares for employees. Companies can, however, extend full voting rights to ESOP participants. In BBSOPs and ESPPs, employees receive voting rights only if they work for a publicly traded company and hold onto their shares after purchase. Most employees in these plans, however, sell their shares immediately upon purchase. Since employees do not receive stock in cash profit-sharing and gain-sharing plans, there are no legal requirements for employees to have any governance role. Beyond these fairly limited voting rights in ESOPS, no laws require firms to create structures for employee participation in decision making in conjunction with the implementation of any form of shared capitalism. In essence, therefore, most types of shared capitalist plans are primarily mechanisms for employees to acquire a financial stake in their employers, although no laws restrict firms from implementing structured ways for employees to participate in management or governance. In fact, a growing number of companies with employee ownership do expand the traditional employer–employee relationship by fostering employee participation in daily work decisions, broader management of the firm, and corporate governance.

Firms establish different forms of shared capitalism for a variety of reasons, such as deep ideological commitments to workplace democracy, the desire to provide employees with a short-term financial stake or offer competitive benefits as part of a broader human resource strategy, or the need to create a market for the shares of owners of firms that are not publicly traded. Shared capitalism of many types has existed in the United States since the 19th century (Blasi and Kruse 2006). Variations on profit sharing and gain sharing, for example, have been in place since at least the last century. These plans are flexible and provide straightforward ways for companies to share the financial benefits of improvements in productivity and profitability with employees. Worker cooperatives, which most fundamentally alter traditional systems of capitalist ownership and control of the firm, also have a long history in the United States (Logue and Yates 2001). They have been most common in specific industries (such as service and retail) and smaller firms and are often created because of ideological commitments of their founders to economic democracy. In addition to the long-term presence of these two types of plans, there have been waves of adoption of other types of plans. The first significant growth of shared capitalism occurred in the mid- to late 19th century in the United States (Blasi, Kruse, and Bernstein 2003)

and then later in the early 20th century within the then-new population of large, publicly traded companies (Blasi and Kruse 2006). These
plans, which included variations on direct ownership and profit sharing,
as well as employee involvement in governance through works councils,
were in part created to temper the radicalization of the broad movement
for workers' rights that emerged in lock step with industrial capitalism
(Rosen, Case, and Staubus 2005). This wave of diffusion of shared capitalism, however, ended with the Depression (Blasi and Kruse 2006).

Despite subsequent experiments with different forms of welfare capitalism (Jacoby 1997) and interest in human relations after the Depression (Rosen, Case, and Staubus 2005) and the growth in the number of
worker cooperatives in the 1960s (Jackall and Levin 1984), the next wave
of significant shared capitalist diffusion did not begin until the mid-
1970s with the passage of the Employee Retirement Income Security
Act (ERISA) in 1974, which created the legal structure for ESOPs. The
IRS created the legal structure for 401(k) plans in 1980. The number
of both plans has grown or held steady with the growing popularity of
defined contribution retirement plans since the 1980s. Later amend-
ments to ESOP regulations provided more tax benefits for companies
establishing them and, therefore, made the plans more attractive, particularly as a mechanism of business continuity in privately held firms.
Although 401(k) plans provide a way for employees to acquire stock,
they are predominantly viewed as retirement vehicles and not as a way
for employees to acquire a significant ownership stake.

More recently, the rise to prominence of knowledge-based industries associated with personal computers, the Internet, and biotechnology during the 1990s brought with it the diffusion of BBSOPs and, to
a lesser extent, ESPPs. The growth in these plans mirrored the growth
of the sector in general, beginning as far back as the 1950s in the semi-
conductor industry (Blasi, Kruse, and Bernstein 2003), continuing in the
1980s in the personal computer and software industries, and diffusing
widely in the 1990s with the emergence of a set of new industries related
to the Internet. BBSOPs were used primarily as a way for start-up firms
to attract and retain employees while conserving cash, although the sharing of capital ownership also stemmed in part from nontraditional ideas
about hierarchy and authority among some corporate leaders in these
sectors (Blasi, Kruse, and Bernstein 2003; Saxenian 1996). By the mid-
1990s, the practice had become institutionalized among high-tech firms
simply as "the way things are done." This evolution occurred in both
private and publicly traded companies, and, by the late 1990s, had even
started to spread to nontech firms. The bursting of the high-tech bubble
in 2000 and the subsequent corporate scandals that began with the

collapse of Enron, however, challenged the legitimacy of stock options and brought regulatory changes that negatively affected their accounting treatment. Anecdotal evidence suggests that, although private start-ups are still using these mechanisms, larger public companies have turned away from such plans, largely as a consequence of the changes in the accounting treatment of stock options. However, stock options remain a common component of executive compensation.

All of these developments have produced the current landscape of shared capitalism, which can be characterized as a diversity of forms in a diverse group of companies and industries. There are, however, five common manifestations of shared capitalism that can be classified as primary types: (1) ESOPS in privately held firms that own a minority of stock and function as retirement plans, (2) ESOPs that own a majority of stock and combine the plan with significant decision-making opportunities for employees, (3) small start-ups with BBSOPs and decentralized authority structures, (4) public firms in which one or many types of shared capitalism are implemented and function similar to shorter term, cash-based bonuses, and (5) worker cooperatives, which, by their nature, are unique organizational forms. This typology does not cover all firms, but it highlights the most common examples.

Like any organizational phenomenon, gaining an accurate picture of the overall incidence of plans is a difficult task due to a lack of available data, and, in the particular case of the United States, the regrettable lack of a national, longitudinal, representative survey of corporations. Kruse, Blasi, and Park (2010) provide the most recent estimates, using data from the General Social Survey (GSS) of individuals collected in 2002 and 2006. The GSS is a nationally representative sample of individuals (not organizations), but it asks questions about whether individuals own employer stock, have stock options, or participate in profit sharing or gain sharing. The most recent data (from 2006) indicated that a little less than half of the respondents (47%) participate in some form of shared capitalism. About a fifth (18%) own stock in their companies through an ESOP, 401(k), or ESPP; 38% participate in a profit-sharing plan, and 27% in a gain-sharing plan. The GSS does not collect data on worker cooperatives. The National Center for Employee Ownership (NCEO) provides the most reliable estimates of the number of firms using different types of plans. In early 2010, the NCEO estimates that there were approximately 10,500 companies with ESOPs (with 12.7 million participants and $900 billion in assets); 800 companies with 401(k) plans that are primarily invested in company stock (with 5 million participants and $200 million in assets); 3,000 firms with BBSOPs covering 10 million employees; and 4,000 firms with ESPPs covering about 11 million employees (NCEO 2010). Finally, there are approximately 300 worker cooperatives in the United States covering over 3,500 employees and with $400 million in annual revenues (U.S. Federation of Worker Cooperatives 2010).

This section provided an overview of the different forms of shared capitalism and their incidence in the U.S. economy. The evidence shows that the phenomenon is not limited to specific parts of the economy but is present in a number of industries (Freeman, Blasi, and Kruse 2010). Since shared capitalism comes in different forms in different types of firms, the motivations for the implementation of plans and their effects on employees, corporate performance, and broader social and economic outcomes are likely to be varied and complex. In the next section, I examine the findings from the academic literature regarding the causes and consequences of shared capitalism.

Academic Research on Shared Capitalism

Academic attention to shared capitalism has waxed and waned in the last four decades, mostly responding to the diffusion of different types of plans. Research on cooperatives, for example, began to appear in the 1970s as a response to a number of trends, including the emergence of experiments in worker self-management in the former Yugoslavia, the discovery of long-existing co-ops in Western Hemisphere capitalist countries, and the emergence of a new cohort of cooperatives in the United States in the 1960s (e.g., Jackall and Levin 1984; Jones 1977, 1979; Vanek 1975). Academic studies of ESOPs began to appear in the late 1970s following the creation of the legal structure for ESOPs in 1975 (e.g., Hammer and Stern 1980; Long 1979), and research on BBSOPs emerged in the late 1990s following the high-tech boom (e.g., Blasi, Kruse, and Bernstein 2003). The primary streams of academic research on shared capitalism have focused on the effects of shared capitalism on employees, the consequences for firm performance, and the consequences for firm stability and employment growth. However, this categorization by no means covers all studies on shared capitalism, which has been the focus of scholars in a diverse range of disciplines including economics, psychology, sociology, industrial and labor relations, human resource management (HRM), and organizational behavior.

Academic work on shared capitalism has employed a diverse range of methodologies, analyzing quantitative and qualitative data collected through surveys, interviews, ethnographies, case studies, and archival data. In this section, I provide a brief overview of the primary findings of this research. It is not an exhaustive treatment of the hundreds of studies that have been done, but it is intended to provide a high-level overview of three primary research streams. I mainly draw upon a number of comprehensive reviews of the literature, including Kruse and Blasi (1997), Kruse (2002), Kaarsemaker (2006), and Caramelli (Chapter 7 in this volume). Also, although research has been conducted on shared capitalism in all parts of the world, in this review, I focus chiefly on research on the U.S. experience.

Employee Outcomes

A common research topic has been the effect of shared capitalism on employee outcomes, such as standard employee attitudes in organizational psychology (e.g., job satisfaction, organizational commitment, turnover intention, motivation, and company loyalty); economic consequences such as wealth acquisition (Buchele, Kruse, Rodgers, and Scharf 2010); and sociological outcomes such as class identification (Meyers, Chapter 5 in this volume) and inequality (Carberry 2010). In his comprehensive review of 31 studies of the impact of shared capitalism on employee attitudes and behavior, Kruse (2002) finds that the evidence reveals that shared capitalism is usually associated with more commitment to and identification with organizations, that most studies found either a positive or neutral effect of shared capitalism on job satisfaction and motivation, and that most employees like being owners. Kruse (2002) is careful to note, however, that employee ownership does not automatically lead to improvements in attitudes—however, when it does, it is not a function of how much stock employees own but of the simple fact that they are owners.

In a similarly exhaustive review of 58 studies examining the relationship between shared capitalism (mostly ESOPs and cooperatives) and a range of HRM outcomes (e.g., job satisfaction, organizational commitment, psychological ownership) in different countries, Kaarsemaker (2006) found that 38 studies found a clear positive association, 12 found no effect, and only 8 studies found direct negative effects. Kaarsemaker (2006:36) observes that "although negative effects are relatively rare . . . favorable effects do not come about automatically," highlighting that managerial commitment to ownership and psychological ownership seem to be important moderating variables, as is participation in decision making, information sharing, and profit sharing.

Finally, in summarizing an extensive set of studies using a data set of over 40,000 employees in 14 companies with shared capitalism, Freeman, Blasi, and Kruse (2010:12) find that "shared capitalism is associated with greater participation in decision-making, higher pay, more job security, more job satisfaction, and better management labor practices. These relationships are stronger when shared capitalism is combined with employee involvement and decision-making and with other advanced personnel and labor policies."

Although most of the research on employee outcomes has focused on psychological measures, other work has concentrated on socioeconomic outcomes. In reviewing the research on the effect of shared capitalism on wages and wealth, Kruse (2002) notes that, in contrast to popular beliefs, shared capitalism is usually provided to employees as an additional benefit. In a recent study comparing wealth outcomes of over 40,000 employees in 14 companies with any form of shared capitalism, Buchele, Kruse, Rodgers, and Scharf (2010) found that employees accumulate significantly more wealth than employees in companies without shared capitalism and that shared capitalism does not come at the expense of wages. They also find, however, that the wealth of non-managers in these firms is only about one third that of managers. These results are in line with those found by Carberry (2010) using the same sample. That study also found that women and nonwhite workers are, on average, less likely to participate in shared capitalism programs and acquire significantly lower levels of financial wealth through these plans. Although many of these effects were the result of existing mechanisms of occupational and educational segregation, there was evidence that some plans were structured in ways that appear to systematically exclude women and nonwhite employees. Our understanding of the ultimate impacts of shared capitalism on broad patterns of economic inequality, however, remains very incomplete.

Corporate Performance

Another common topic of academic attention has been the effects of shared capitalism on corporate performance, and most of this attention has focused on ESOPs. The first large-scale study on the effect of ESOPs on firm performance was done in the mid-1980s by the U.S. General Accounting Office (GAO 1987). The findings indicated that ESOPs are associated with improvements to performance, but only when these plans are combined with employee involvement in job-level decision making. An early study by Rosen and Quarrey (1987) on a different sample of ESOP firms found similar results. Kruse (2002) reviewed the existing evidence from 30 studies on shared capitalism (mostly ESOPs) and observed that most research has found a positive or neutral relationship between shared capitalism and firm performance. In terms of ESOPs, productivity improves by an average of 4% to 5% in the year of ESOP adoption and continues after adoption. Kruse (2002:6) points out that this is "more than twice the annual productivity growth of the U.S. economy over the past 20 years." In another exhaustive review,

Kaarsemaker (2006) examined 70 studies and found that 48 provided evidence of a positive relationship between shared capitalism and corporate performance, while only 6 studies found negative effects and 12 found no effects.

Scholars have also examined the effect of profit-sharing plans on firm performance. In a rigorous longitudinal analysis of a representative sample of U.S. firms with profit-sharing plans, Kruse (1993) found that these plans improve firm productivity but only when they are structured as cash payouts (vs. payouts made in stock), when payouts are larger, and in smaller firms. In their review of the literature, Weitzman and Kruse (1995) find that most studies have found a positive connection between profit sharing and worker productivity. Our understanding of the connections between profit sharing and performance, however, needs to be brought up to date, especially considering the wide incidence of these plans in the U.S. economy. There have been fewer studies examining the impacts of BBSOPs on corporate performance (although the number is growing) and none on ESPPs. In a comprehensive review of existing work on BBSOPs, Aldatmaz and Ouimet (Chapter 8 in this volume) conclude that, although many studies find a positive relationship between BBSOPs and performance, there is insufficient evidence of a causal link or of specific mechanisms that may be driving such a causal link. However, existing studies of BBSOPs have suggested some logical mechanisms that might be driving the performance effect, such as the enhanced productivity of individual employees, the ability of firms to conserve cash in the start-up phase, and better employee retention, which can lead to lower turnover costs (Aldatmaz and Ouimet, Chapter 8 in this volume).

Although a number of studies have found evidence of a positive effect of ESOPs on performance, there is still a lack of evidence about the mechanisms driving performance gains. As Caramelli observes in his chapter in this volume, most work on the effect of shared capitalism on corporate performance has been theoretically thin. The common wisdom is that if employees become owners or receive cash-based bonuses based on productivity gains, they will work harder to improve company performance. However, Blasi (1988) observed that such thinking amounts to a "fallacy of performance," that is, getting employees to work harder and smarter will not necessarily lead to better firm performance, which is contingent on a number of complex factors. In fact, most in-depth explanations of the shared capitalism–performance link suggested by academic researchers have focused on sociological mechanisms, such as the reduction of management–labor conflict, and a "collective incentive to improve workplace cooperation, information sharing, and organizational citizenship behavior" (Kruse 2002:6). This observation would certainly be in line with the important finding of the GAO study (1987) that only when ESOPs are combined with participative decision-making structures do they improve corporate performance. These types of explanations have been echoed by Kaarsemaker (2006:44) in his comprehensive review, in which he points out that the existing literature provides significant evidence that the performance effects occur only in combination with "HRM practices like information-sharing, profit-sharing, and particularly participation in decision-making."

Moreover, in a rich set of recent studies based on both the General Social Survey and a unique sample of over 40,000 employees in 14 companies with shared capitalism, Freeman, Blasi, and Kruse (2010:23) observe that "shared capitalism works best when it combines monetary incentives with employee decision-making and personnel and labor policies that empower and encourage employees." Finally, extensive case study research by experienced practitioners in the field has offered very strong evidence that the combination of financial participation and an "ownership culture" drives the long-term success of shared capitalist companies (Rosen, Case, and Staubus 2005). A number of firms have effectively created such cultures of ownership by combining ownership with participation by employees in decision making, extensive information sharing about the business, and in-depth training and education about ownership and financial literacy (Rosen, Case, and Staubus 2005). Despite the persuasive balance of evidence regarding the role of more sociological explanations of the connections between employee ownership and corporate performance, we could still benefit from additional academic studies that more precisely illuminate the mechanisms driving the positive relationship.

Organizational Stability and Growth

A smaller number of studies have examined the influence of shared capitalism on employment growth, stability, and firm survival. In a large, longitudinal study of U.S. public companies, Blair, Kruse, and Blasi (2000) found that firms in which employees held more than 17% of company stock had more stable employment and that it did not come at the expense of efficiency or stock market performance. Furthermore, from the beginning of their observation period in 1983, they found that ESOP firms were 20% more likely to survive past 1995 than their industry peers. In a survey of a large population of ESOPs in Ohio, Logue and Yates (2001) found that firms with ESOPs grew faster than similar non-ESOP firms in their industries. In an update of their study using a larger data set, Logue and Yates (Chapter 10 in this volume) compare two groups of ESOPs who survived at least 17 and up to 25 years with those who did not survive as long. They found that longer-lasting ESOP firms were more likely to use more employee involvement practices, provide employees with a voice in governance, and engage in more extensive training and communication around business literacy. In addition, longer-surviving ESOPs were also more fiscally prudent in terms of taking on debt and being more willing to make sacrifices in the present for survival in the future. Finally, in an analysis of the longevity of the famous group of cooperatives founded in Mondragón, Spain, in 1956, Arando, Freundlich, Gago, Jones, and Kato (Chapter 9 in this volume) demonstrate that this network of co-ops has been able to realize constant employment and economic growth in the face of intensive market pressures relating to globalization and ongoing financial shocks.

What Does the Research Tell Us and What Do We Need to Know?

In assessing the substantial body of academic research, some well-supported conclusions can be drawn. Shared capitalism of different kinds, when implemented under certain conditions, can have positive effects on psychological and economic outcomes of employees at all occupational and organizational levels, as well as positive effects on firm performance, growth, and long-term stability. However, these gains are much more likely to occur when shared capitalism is implemented as a way to fundamentally enhance an existing culture based on shared commitment, sacrifice, information, and rewards, or as a way to transform more-traditional top-down cultures and authority structures along these lines. In short, shared capitalism appears to work well only when it is used as a way to promote workplaces that distribute power and authority more broadly.

The effects of shared capitalism on employee outcomes, corporate performance, and organizational survival represent only the three largest streams of research. Although researchers in a range of disciplines have looked at a number of other outcomes, it is beyond the scope of this introduction to review them in depth. Despite the impressive progress of researchers studying employee ownership, important gaps remain. First, we still lack in-depth longitudinal analyses of how shared capitalism has influenced long-term trends in income and wealth inequality. Despite the potential of shared capitalism to mitigate the dramatic increase in economic inequality in the United States since the 1980s, there are no academic studies that examine this effect directly. Most work studying broader patterns of wealth accumulation has focused on how the increased use of executive stock options has concentrated wealth at the top, but no studies have examined how shared capitalism writ large has affected the wealth of other groups or altered economic inequality (for a notable exception, see Morgan and Cha 2007).

Second, although we know that systems of participative management and ownership cultures seem to unlock the potential of shared capitalism, it would be helpful to have more studies that examine these connections in more detail and that attempt to discover exactly why this combination seems to be so important. What role do individual attitudes and behavior play? Do the performance gains emerge from the ways in which decentralized decision-making structures capitalize on the knowledge and experience of all employees? Is it about the creation of a cohesive collectivist culture? While we have extensive case study evidence that the combination of employee ownership and participative management is what matters (e.g., Rosen, Case, and Staubus 2005), we lack longitudinal, large-N studies testing this finding in a large sample of firms. In addition, few studies have examined why more companies that implement shared capitalism do not embrace employee participation in decision making and employee involvement in governance.

A third notable gap is the lack of sociological analyses of the diffusion of different forms of shared capitalism. Organizational sociologists have developed sophisticated tools for analyzing diffusion of a range of organizational practices (Strang and Soule 1998), but we are missing similar studies for shared capitalism, which would help us understand why firms adopt shared capitalism and help us identify potential barriers to adoption. It is notable that, despite the apparent benefits of shared capitalism for employees, firms, and shareholders, more firms do not adopt such plans. Moreover, we know that stock-based compensation has become a more common part of executive compensation in the last two decades. Why has a similar boom not occurred with broad-based equity compensation plans?

Finally, two prominent criticisms leveled at employee ownership have been that it promotes free riding in the workplace and that it creates too much financial risk for employees. In a set of recent studies, Freeman, Blasi, and Kruse (2010) examine these criticisms empirically and find that workers who received shared capitalism are more likely to engage in co-monitoring of employees, which potentially mitigates free riding. They also found that most employees in companies with shared capitalism have not taken on undue financial risk by excessively investing in company stock, and that shared capitalism can provide a financial asset that is part of a diversification strategy of the type advised by portfolio theory in economics if the level of stock funded by worker savings is kept within reasonable parameters. These empirical studies by Freeman, Blasi, and Kruse were the first to engage directly with the common criticisms of employee ownership, and additional work needs to be done to help us better understand the potential negative consequences of shared capitalism and the conditions under which these negative consequences are more likely to occur.

These gaps are just a few of the most obvious ones among many in the current literature. We could also benefit, for example, from studies that use a pre- and post-implementation design to more robustly analyze the impact of shared capitalism on the individual and organizational outcomes already discussed. Another important phenomenon relates to what happens when firms with significant employee ownership become publicly traded. Do the demands of a broader and more diverse group of outside shareholders, often focused on short-term profits, put employee ownership at risk? In addition, we need more research on newer forms of shared capitalism, such as BBSOPs and ESPPs. Despite a dramatic growth in the number of these plans in the 1990s, there remains a lack of scholarly understanding on their diffusion, characteristics, and consequences. Moreover, we know next to nothing about how the recurring scandals and crises in the last ten years have influenced the use of BBSOPs. We know that stock option and similar types of plans have continued for executives, but have firms scaled back on these new forms of shared capitalism under economic strain? In a related vein, what is the continuing role of BBSOPs among knowledge-based firms? A number of scholars have suggested that egalitarian organizational cultures and broad-based stock options were key to the development and success of the high-tech sector (Saxenian 1996; Blasi, Kruse, and Bernstein 2003). However, were BBSOPs only a convenient form of compensation in a booming economy or are they integral to the long-term success of these firms? Finally, although shared capitalism is a global phenomenon, we still need to better integrate lessons from cross-national experiences. Advancing research on all of these fronts would deepen our understanding of shared capitalism and the conditions under which it works best.

The Chapters in This Book

The chapters in this volume help address some of these gaps while illuminating others. The book is organized into three broad sections. Section I addresses the relationship between shared capitalism and organized labor, a topic likely to be of key interest to readers of this volume. Unions have historically been skeptical of employee ownership, seeing it as a way for management to co-opt employees and prevent the formation of unions, or to diminish the power of existing ones. However, since a wave of union-led employee buyouts of firms in old-line manufacturing industries such as steel in the 1980s, unions have maintained a less ambivalent stance toward employee ownership, preferring to evaluate it on a case-by-case basis. The three chapters in this first section explore the relationship between organized labor and shared capitalism in more depth.

In Chapter 2, McCarthy, Voos, Eaton, Kruse, and Blasi first provide an enlightening examination of the historical context of both unions and employee ownership and the existing literature on the two, highlighting that "unions have a mixed relationship—both ideologically and pragmatically—with shared capitalism." To examine this relationship in more depth, the authors analyze a unique cross-sectional sample of over 17,000 employees in 11 companies with shared capitalism, finding that the relationship between the two "appears to be complementary rather than oppositional."

In the next chapter, Berry and Schneider provide further support for a complementary relationship through their in-depth case study of Cooperative Home Care Associates (CHCA), a worker cooperative that is unionized by the Service Employees International Union (SEIU). This chapter demonstrates that, in situations where employee owners have a direct role in governance, unions still have opportunities to improve the quality of jobs and help employees develop leadership skills. Their analysis also highlights the importance of understanding the motivations for employee-owned firms in unionizing for the development of an effective relationship between labor and management, as well as the importance of formal structures that facilitate collaboration among executives, employee owners, and union representatives.

In Chapter 4, Bova approaches the union–shared capitalism relationship from a very different perspective, namely that of accounting and finance, examining the unintentional benefits of shared capitalism in unionized settings. Drawing upon a large sample of publicly traded ESOP companies, Bova reveals that shared capitalism can lead to better financial transparency in unionized settings by reducing the incentive for corporate managers to keep their books opaque. Employee ownership, therefore, may lead to positive outcomes for shareholders through this mechanism. This chapter is representative of an emergent literature within accounting and finance analyzing shared capitalism.

Section II provides a snapshot of the broad diversity of current research on shared capitalism in terms of topics, theoretical approaches, and research methods. In Chapter 5, Meyers examines the potential of shared capitalism to empower working-class employees, which has been one of the key ideological rationales for shared capitalism. Despite the centrality of the empowerment of employees in the discourse surrounding employee ownership, academic studies on this topic have been remarkably lacking. Through ethnographic and archival methods, Meyers examines working-class empowerment in two worker cooperatives. Her analysis demonstrates that employee ownership has the potential to empower working-class employees, but that empowerment is not an automatic consequence of shared capitalism, even in cooperatives (the form of shared capitalism that is the most egalitarian in terms of how ownership is shared and the most far-reaching in terms of providing employees with a role in governance). Meyers's chapter shows that empowerment only emerges in conjunction with formal, but nonhierarchical, organizational structures, and, since class always intersects with gender and race, with organizational narratives that recognize how gender and race interact with class in the workplace. Surprisingly, Meyers's chapter represents one of the few sociological studies of contemporary worker ownership—a gap that will hopefully be addressed in the near future, since sociology is distinctive in its recognition of the central role that power, social stratification, and gender and ethnoracial identities play in all social settings, especially organizations. This theoretical terrain has been relatively unexplored with respect to shared capitalism.

In Chapter 6, Kurtulus, Kruse, and Blasi examine a very different set of worker outcomes relating to attitudes about compensation risk and how the match between an employee's view of risk and the riskiness of employee compensation packages influences standard psychological outcomes of workers. One of the primary criticisms of employee ownership leveled by economists is that it creates too much risk for the average worker. The cross-sectional data set analyzed in this chapter provides a rare way to test contentions about risk and risk preferences and how they influence worker attitudes and behavior. The authors find that a match between compensation risk and risk preferences has a positive impact on a range of workplace attitudes and that risk-averse workers do not react negatively to shared capitalism. This chapter is the first academic study on the topic and also contributes to the broader literature on risk preferences and compensation in the HR literature.

Section II concludes on a more theoretical note. In Chapter 7, Caramelli takes on a core topic within existing academic work on shared capitalism: the influence of shared capitalism on corporate performance. In assessing the vast literature, Caramelli observes that this work has been very thin on explaining exactly why there is a relationship between shared capitalism and firm performance. Taking a different approach from existing work, he employs an inductive, qualitative methodology in the context of France to illuminate several new mechanisms through which employee ownership affects performance. In the final chapter of Section II, Aldatmaz and Ouimet provide an exhaustive review of the existing work on broad-based stock options in the economics and finance literature. Their careful and original synthesis of this growing body of work focuses on explanations for why firms adopt BBSOPs and the impact of BBSOPs on firm performance. The emergence of BBSOPs in the 1990s represents the latest development of a new form of shared capitalism, and our academic understanding of the contours and implications of this form remains very underdeveloped. This chapter provides a timely and important contribution to our knowledge.

The last section includes three chapters that each examine the broad experience of employee ownership in a specific geographic context. Such analyses, by linking the experience of shared capitalism to specific institutional, economic, and cultural environments, provide a unique perspective that is representative of a range of cross-national work (see Poutsma, de Nijs, and Poole 2003). In Chapter 9, Arando, Freundlich, Gago, Jones, and Kato provide a broad assessment of one of the most well-known examples of shared capitalism—the network of cooperative firms in the Mondragón region of Northern Spain. Using a unique set of new data collected from the cooperatives and archival sources, this chapter analyzes the reasons why the group of Mondragon cooperatives has survived and grown in the face of globalization and recurring financial crises while maintaining its original ideals of workplace democracy. Although these ideals have been compromised to some extent, the authors attribute the overall success of this network of firms to its institutional flexibility and innovation.

In Chapter 10, Logue and Yates assess the experience of ESOP firms in Ohio over a 21-year period. Drawing on a unique longitudinal data set of a representative sample of ESOP firms in Ohio, a type of data set that is rare, the authors examine the development of ESOP companies over time and the characteristics associated with ESOPs that endure for long periods. The authors find that ESOP firms that survive the longest are more committed to creating significant employee involvement in management and are more fiscally cautious and willing to make sacrifices. Long-lived ESOPs also experienced significant growth in the number of participants and had an increase in better-paying jobs with good benefits.

In the final chapter, Pendleton examines the experience of shared capitalism in the United Kingdom over the last two decades. The United Kingdom, along with the United States, has been one of the pioneers of laws to promote shared capitalism. Taking a broad, historical approach using archival data, Pendleton not only provides an elegant and engaging descriptive analysis of different types of shared capitalism in the United Kingdom, but he also makes an important theoretical contribution by emphasizing the necessity for researchers to pay careful attention to the different types of ownership. This insight is applicable to shared capitalism in any national context. In assessing the determinants of adoption of shared capitalism, Pendleton finds that different theoretical perspectives are salient for explaining the diffusion of different forms of it.

Taken together, the ten chapters in this book provide a sample of the diverse currents of contemporary academic research on shared capitalism. While they of course leave many questions unanswered and raise many new ones, they each address important and enduring gaps in our understanding of the experience of shared capitalism, offer innovative research designs and theoretical contributions, and open up many new lines of inquiry for additional research.

Promoting Shared Capitalism Through Public Policy

While the primary goal of this volume is to highlight current research on shared capitalism, the academic literature offers a number of implications for public policy, and I end this introduction with a deeper discussion of these implications. The consistency in the findings regarding the positive effects that shared capitalism can have on employee and firm outcomes should be more than sufficient evidence for the desirability of policies to encourage more companies to not only adopt such plans, but to do so in combination with other human resource practices, particularly broad-based employee participation in decision making. Moreover, it is likely that the positive effects on employee well-being, corporate performance, and organizational stability may also have broader economic and social consequences. For example, better-performing firms that are more likely to survive in the long term are the ones best positioned to foster sustained economic growth and employment stability. In addition, by more broadly distributing the financial gains of production of all kinds and supplementing wages that continue to stagnate for most occupations, shared capitalism might also help mitigate the alarming expansion of income and wealth inequality that has occurred over the last two decades in the United States. In fact, a key driver in this expansion of inequality has been the broad diffusion of shared capitalism for the upper echelon of top managers in publicly traded firms (Morgan and Cha 2007; DiPrete, Eirich, and Pittinsky 2010). These employees have benefited handsomely from having stock options and restricted stock units. More broadly distributing the opportunity of stock ownership to most or all employees would help reconnect the link between productivity improvements and the income of all employees—a link that prior to the 1980s was made through gradual increases in wages but has since been severed. In addition, shared capitalism, by putting more income into the hands of more people and dispersing purchasing power more broadly, could help promote economic growth and create a robust foundation of economic activity to spur new investment. Finally, by creating incentives for corporate managers to create more participative workplaces (since the research is clear that this is when shared capitalism has the most potential), policies to promote shared capitalism could help foster the development of organizational structures that allow more people to have input into decisions relating to economic production, investment, and distribution—a breadth of participation that is notably absent in the current shareholder value model, which is based on the concentration of rewards and decision making into a small group of people.

Although research on the broader social and economic effects of shared capitalism remains at a very early stage, such consequences do not seem far-fetched or fantastical. When viewed together with the persuasive academic evidence about the positive effects of shared capitalism on individual and organizational outcomes, a compelling case for policy initiatives to promote the adoption of shared capitalism by more companies emerges. Certainly, it is an unusual type of policy issue that could (and has) gained support from a broad range of the political spectrum, from those on the right, such as Ronald Reagan and Representative Dana Rohrabacher (R-Calif.), who see it as creating a population of capitalists, to those on the left who see it as a way to promote more democratic workplaces. A number of academics and practitioners have offered suggestions for policies to promote shared capitalism. In the rest of this section, I review these and offer a few new suggestions.

The most obvious type of policy would be to provide corporations with tax incentives to implement shared capitalism and to ensure that these plans are structured in ways that benefit most or all employees, not just a select few. Current laws on ESOPs provide an instructive and useful model. Firms that establish ESOPs can deduct from their taxable income contributions to the ESOP (up to 15% of payroll if the plan does not borrow money and up to 25% of payroll if a plan is leveraged). In addition, owners who sell to an ESOP can defer capital gains taxes on all proceeds from the sale, provided that the ESOP owns at least 30% of the firm's shares after the sale. However, ESOPs must meet specific conditions regarding participation (typically all full-time employees who have been with the company at least one year) and allocation (highly compensated employees cannot receive a disproportionately large percentage of stock). The ESOP laws provide a model for promoting the adoption of other types of plans, such as stock options, through similar policies. Three of the most prominent academics studying shared capitalism (Freeman, Blasi, and Kruse), in conjunction with the Center for American Progress, a major policy think tank in Washington, DC, have developed more specific policy proposals along these lines. In particular, these scholars suggest that the legal infrastructure of ESOPs could be implemented for all forms of shared capitalism so that, in order to receive a tax deduction for any form of performance-based compensation, firms must make the benefit available to a majority of their employees. For example, firms currently receive tax deductions for stock options granted to any employee (the deduction is realized during the year when an employee exercises the option), but these laws do not attach any broad-based conditions to this deduction. Hence, firms can currently receive tax deductions for stock option plans that cover only a small group of top managers. Attaching a condition that firms receive such deductions only if a large percentage of the workforce receives stock options would bring this type of plan in line with ESOPs, as well as with qualified retirement and health care plans, which currently require similar tests for nondiscrimination and broad coverage to receive preferential tax treatments. It is important to emphasize that implementing similar laws for all types of shared capitalism would not prevent firms from offering shared capitalism, but it would not provide companies with a tax deduction if this benefit were not made available to a broad group of employees. Large, publicly traded corporations currently receive substantial tax deductions for cash profit- and gain sharing plans (called long-term incentive plans), some restricted stock plans, and various other profit-sharing and equity compensation plans, which are typically aimed at only a thin slice of people at the top.

Such a policy suggestion is not entirely radical, and it builds on existing legislative structures and experience. Proposals based on these ideas would likely receive broad bipartisan support. However, in the current political climate defined by strong resistance to government spending to promote economic growth and social stability, any policy initiatives of this type are likely to face either strong resistance or be cut out of final legislation. More far-reaching initiatives, such as stricter, direct requirements for firms to implement shared capitalism, would face even lower chances of passage. Certainly, the history of different policies aimed at promoting shared capitalism has not been encouraging. The most substantial piece of legislation relating to the promotion of shared capitalism has been ESOP legislation. Its implementation was in large part due to its support by an extremely influential and powerful senator, Russell Long, who at the time was chairman of the Senate Finance Committee. However, there is a wealth of academic research telling us that shared capitalism can have very significant impacts on employee outcomes and firm performance, and can likely promote economic growth and employment stability, and reduce economic inequality. The social scientific record and its logical extensions present a strong case for policy makers and citizens to be much more interested in the further development of shared capitalism. In addition, there is a growing population of firms with vast experience implementing and developing shared capitalism, as well as an existing institutional infrastructure of professional advisors and associations that could help shape legislation and ensure its effective implementation and practice. In addition to directly encouraging firms to establish shared capitalism, tax incentives could also be created to encourage firms to implement participative decision making, information sharing, and business literacy training.

The federal government could take other, less direct steps to promote adoption by helping make information about shared capitalism (and what makes it work best) more broadly available to business owners, managers, and human resource professionals. Such information includes the technical details of establishing and maintaining plans, techniques for communicating and educating employees about ownership, and approaches to creating more participative organizations. One of the best ways to disseminate information is through organizations dedicated to this purpose. For example, a small number of states, including Massachusetts, Michigan, New York, Ohio, Oregon, and Washington, established employee ownership programs in the 1980s to help advise firms on setting up and managing employee ownership. Currently, only Ohio and Vermont (the latter's program was founded more recently) have dedicated offices of employee ownership, although other states continue to provide funding to support employee ownership. It would be relatively easy to revive former state offices and promote the founding of new ones through federal funds. A related idea is to establish a federal center for shared capitalism within an existing agency such as the Department of Labor. Currently, there are three national, private, nonprofit organizations (the National Center for Employee Ownership, the ESOP Association, and the Beyster Institute) that could serve as models for such an organization or even bypass the need to establish a new one and themselves serve as the primary recipients of federal funds. These organizations have been in operation for decades, disseminating information about how firms can establish and maintain shared capitalist practices, conducting research and training, and building networks of companies and consultants. These organizations have been essential to the broader diffusion of shared capitalism, and, although they have been very successful, their continued survival is always in potential danger. A steady stream of supplemental federal support could help ensure their longevity and help them expand their activities and reach.

Another policy initiative could be to help promote the integration of knowledge about shared capitalism into university and graduate curriculums, particularly MBA programs. There are broad efforts already under way to promote integration into MBA programs through groups such as the Aspen Institute and the Beyster Institute. The former has developed extensive resources for educators, such as case studies and sample curricula through the online Curriculum Library on Employee Ownership (CLEO). Direct federal aid for such initiatives through the Department of Education could dramatically broaden their range and deepen their impact. Logue and Yates (2001) have gone a step further in suggesting the creation of a federally funded land-grant university teaching and research program dedicated to shared capitalism.

A related issue is the capacity of both higher education and the business world to create adequate space for studying the emerging phenomenon of shared capitalism. One can certainly make the case that, in business schools and the popular media, a vision of the corporation is being presented that focuses on a "winner take all" model with rewards, power, and prestige concentrated at the top. This phenomenon may represent more of a myth than a reality. As the empirical evidence indicates, there are serious pockets of shared capitalism in the economy, among publicly traded and closely held firms, among some of the signature high-technology firms of the economy, and among both union and nonunion firms. Interestingly enough, many of those are strongly represented in *Fortune's* annual list of the 100 Best Companies to Work for in America. Nevertheless, the resources of higher education and the business world seem disproportionately reserved for studying the old paradigm. A concrete move in the other direction has been the recent creation of a set of fellowship programs to promote a wide interdisciplinary network of scholars to analyze shared capitalism. Indeed, some of the contributors to this volume are past recipients of such fellowships, which include the Beyster, Carey, Huber, and Louis O. Kelso fellowships. Continued funding of all of these educational efforts, through a variety of sources, would help expose new and existing generations of scholars, managers, and policy makers to the experience and potential of shared capitalism.

In this final section, I have highlighted the potential of shared capitalism for improving a range of individual, organizational, economic, and societal outcomes. Indeed, based on over 30 years of academic attention to employee ownership in a range of contexts, the conclusions and evidence are quite persuasive. Firms that implement shared capitalism and that do so in conjunction with formal structures that promote employee involvement in decision making, broad sharing of information, training and communication efforts around business literacy, and the promotion of a broader culture of shared responsibility and rewards, without substituting shared capitalism for existing wages and benefits, position themselves for improvements in a range of employee outcomes, better firm performance, and more long-term and stable employment and economic growth. These effects are not guaranteed, and shared capitalism is by no means a panacea for a number of deeper economic and social problems. Taken together, the vast experience of firms with different forms of shared capitalism, however, represents a compelling example of a very real alternative to the current short-term shareholder value economic model—an alternative that does not require a vast restructuring of current organizational and legal systems that govern economic production and distribution. Moreover, this model does not rely on redistributive policy initiatives that stand very little chance of becoming a reality in today's political climate, nor does it require firms to set up shared capitalism or take away the possibility of firms creating more narrowly targeted plans. The proposals here represent a reasonable, gradual way to make capitalist firms more productive, innovative, and equitable in how they organize and produce goods, and how they distribute the rewards from improvements they might realize in today's global economy.

Conclusion

In this introduction, I have provided an overview of the recent historical context of shared capitalism, reviewed the academic research on it, and highlighted the implications for public policy. Despite the persistent growth in the incidence of different forms of employee ownership and profit sharing since the late 1970s, key societal actors such as policy makers, regulators, investors, unions, journalists, and academics often consider it to be a fringe phenomenon. From its historical roots to its current incidence, however, shared capitalism runs very much in the mainstream of the contemporary U.S. economy. Moreover, over three decades of rigorous academic literature has given us strong evidence that shared capitalism provides significant untapped potential for creating more productive, stable, and equitable capitalist organizations. However, harnessing this potential requires continued careful social scientific research to inform policy and management practice. The diverse scholarship showcased in this volume will hopefully help move various conversations about shared capitalism forward as well as inspire new academic research on the topic.

References

Appelbaum, E., T. Bailey, P. Berg, and A. Kalleberg. 2000. *Manufacturing Advantage: Why High-Performance Work Systems Pay Off.* Ithaca, NY: ILR Press.

Blair, M.M., D. Kruse, and J. Blasi. 2000. "Employee Ownership: An Unstable Form or a Stabilizing Force?" In M.M. Blair and T.A. Kochan, eds., *The New Relationship: Human Capital in the American Corporation.* Washington, DC: Brookings Institution.

Blasi, J. 1988. *Employee Ownership: Revolution or Ripoff?* Cambridge, MA: Ballinger Publishing.

Blasi, J., and D. Kruse. 2006. "The Political Economy of Employee Ownership in the United States: From Economic Democracy to Industrial Democracy?" *International Review of Sociology,* Vol. 16, pp. 127–47.

Blasi, J., D. Kruse, and A. Bernstein. 2003. *In the Company of Owners: The Truth About Stock Options.* New York: Basic Books.

Buchele, R., D. Kruse, L. Rodgers, and A. Scharf. 2010. "Show Me the Money: Does Shared Capitalism Share the Wealth?" In Douglas Kruse, Richard Freeman, and Joseph Blasi, eds., *Shared Capitalism at Work: Employee Ownership, Profit and Gain Sharing, and Broad-Based Stock Options.* Chicago: University of Chicago Press.

Carberry, E. 2010. "Who Benefits from Shared Capitalism? The Social Stratification of Wealth and Power in Companies with Employee Ownership." In Douglas Kruse, Richard Freeman, and Joseph Blasi, eds., *Shared Capitalism at Work: Employee Ownership, Profit and Gain Sharing, and Broad-Based Stock Options.* Chicago: University of Chicago Press.

DiPrete, T., G. Eirich, and M. Pittinsky. 2010. "Compensation Benchmarking, Leapfrogs, and the Surge in Executive Pay." *American Journal of Sociology,* Vol. 16, no. 6, pp. 1671–1712.

Freeman, R., J. Blasi, and D. Kruse. 2010. "Introduction." In Douglas Kruse, Richard Freeman, and Joseph Blasi, eds., *Shared Capitalism at Work: Employee Ownership, Profit and Gain Sharing, and Broad-Based Stock Options.* Chicago: University of Chicago Press.

General Accounting Office. 1987. *Employee Stock Ownership Plans: Little Evidence of Effects on Corporate Performance.* Washington, DC: Government Printing Office.

Hammer, T., and R. Stern. 1980. "Employee Ownership: Implications for the Organizational Distribution of Power." *Academy of Management Journal,* Vol. 23, pp. 78–100.

Jackall, R., and H. Levin. 1984. *Worker Cooperatives in America.* Berkeley: University of California Press.

Jacoby, S. 1997. *Modern Manors: Welfare Capitalism Since the New Deal.* Princeton: Princeton University Press.

Jones, D. 1977. "The Economics and Industrial Relations of American Producer Cooperatives, 1791–1939." *Economic Analysis and Workers' Management,* Vol. 11, pp. 295–317.

Jones, D. 1979. "U.S. Producer Cooperatives: The Record to Date." *Industrial Relations,* Vol. 18, pp. 342–57.

Kaarsemaker, E. 2006. *Employee Ownership and Human Resource Management: A Theoretical and Empirical Treatise with a Digression on the Dutch Context.* Doctoral dissertation, Radboud University, Nijmegen, the Netherlands.

Kruse, D. 1993. *Profit Sharing: Does It Make a Difference?* Kalamazoo, MI: Upjohn Institute.

Kruse, D. 2002. "Research Evidence on Prevalence and Effects of Employee Ownership." Testimony presented before the Subcommittee on Employer–Employee

Relations Committee on Education and the Workforce, U.S. House of Representatives, Washington DC.

Kruse, D., and J. Blasi. 1997. "Employee Ownership, Employee Attitudes, and Firm Performance: A Review of the Evidence." In D. Lewin, D.J.B. Mitchell, and M.A. Zaidi, eds., *The Human Resource Management Handbook, Part 1.* London: JAI Press.

Kruse, D., J. Blasi, and R. Park. 2010. "Shared Capitalism in the U.S. Economy: Prevalence, Characteristics, and Employee Views of Financial Participation in Enterprises." In Douglas Kruse, Richard Freeman, and Joseph Blasi, eds., *Shared Capitalism at Work: Employee Ownership, Profit and Gain Sharing, and Broad-Based Stock Options.* Chicago: University of Chicago Press.

Logue, J., and J. Yates. 2001. *The Real World of Employee Ownership.* Ithaca, NY: ILR Press.

Long, R. 1979. "Desires for and Patterns of Worker Participation in Decision-Making after Conversion to Employee Ownership." *Academy of Management Journal,* Vol. 22, pp. 611–7.

Morgan, S., and Y. Cha. 2007. "Rent and the Evolution of Inequality in Late Industrial United States." *American Behavioral Scientist,* Vol. 50, pp. 677–701.

National Center for Employee Ownership. 2010. A Statistical Profile of Employee Ownership. http://www.nceo.org/main/article.php/id/2. [December 12, 2010.]

Poutsma, E., W. de Nijs, and M. Poole. 2003. "The Global Phenomenon of Employee Financial Participation." *International Journal of Human Resource Management,* Vol. 14, no. 6, pp. 855–62.

Rosen, C., J. Case, and M. Staubus. 2005. *Equity: Why Employee Ownership Is Good for Business.* Boston: Harvard Business School Publishing.

Rosen, C., and M. Quarrey. 1987. "How Well Is Employee Ownership Working?" *Harvard Business Review,* Vol. 65, no. 5, pp. 126–30.

Saxenian, A. 1996. *Regional Advantage: Culture and Competition in Silicon Valley and Route 128.* Boston: Harvard University Press.

Strang, D., and S. Soule. 1998. "Diffusion in Organizations and Social Movements: From Hybrid Corn to Poison Pills." *Annual Review of Sociology,* Vol. 24, pp. 265–90.

U.S. Federation of Worker Cooperatives. 2010. *About Worker Cooperatives.* http://www.usworker.coop/aboutworkercoops. [December 10, 2010.]

Vanek, Y. 1975. *Self-Management: Economic Liberation of Man.* New York: Penguin.

Weitzman, M., and D. Kruse. 1995. "Profit Sharing and Productivity." In A.S. Binder, ed., *Paying for Productivity.* Washington, DC: Brookings Institution.

CHAPTER 2

Solidarity and Sharing: Unions and Shared Capitalism

JOHN E. MCCARTHY
PAULA B. VOOS
ADRIENNE E. EATON
DOUGLAS L. KRUSE
JOSEPH R. BLASI
Rutgers University

Introduction: Capitalism, Shared Capitalism, and Unions

In classical Marxism, capitalism is defined as an economic system in which there is private ownership of the means of production. Ownership implies both rights to the profits generated by a business and rights to control the activities of employees and to direct the business itself, that is, governance. In large contemporary corporations, the ultimate owners—the shareholders—have only an indirect relationship, via the board of directors, over the managers who make many business decisions. Agency theory addresses the ways that owners can ensure that top executives act in their interests by aligning executives' financial incentives with those of the owners. For instance, executive compensation may be made contingent on financial success measures, or top executives may be required to hold large blocks of stock, or they may be provided with stock options that vest at a particular date, or their pensions may be tied to financial performance.

In short, in contemporary business organizations, the relationship among ownership, control, and financial gain from business success can be much more complex than envisioned in classic definitions of capitalism. For instance, financial incentives for employees to act in the interests of owners may extend far below the top executive level, to middle managers, professionals, and sometimes even lower-level employees. Examples of such incentives include employee ownership, profit sharing, gain sharing, and broad-based stock options. These programs have been labeled "shared capitalism" because they presumably broaden ownership

27

of economic enterprises enough to make employees "capitalists" in the sense that they reap some of the financial gains from ownership. Sometimes (but not always), the financial programs that are part of shared capitalism are paired with mechanisms that give employees involvement in some business decisions—typically ones related to their own job or department. These may or may not be the business decisions that lead to financial success or failure for the enterprise.

Between 2001 and 2006, the National Bureau of Economic Research (NBER) sponsored a major research project on shared capitalism—a project designed to investigate a number of the implications of employee ownership, profit sharing, gain sharing, and broad-based stock options (Kruse, Freeman, and Blasi 2010a). Various scholarly studies have been based on the NBER survey of organizations with such programs, which was a focused data set rather than a random sample of firms. One of the issues not explored in any depth to date in the research based on this survey is the relationship between American unions and shared capitalism. That is the subject of this chapter.

Before delving into the issue of how contemporary unions relate to employee ownership, profit sharing, gain sharing, and broad-based stock options, it is useful to step back and consider the way that union representation itself provides a degree of shared capitalism to employees— how all successful unions modify the nexus among ownership, control, and profits. Most obviously, unions raise employee compensation—they ensure that employees receive a greater share of the total revenues earned by the business. Unions also modify unilateral management decisions and management's right to direct employees—union contracts contain numerous clauses that limit, constrain, or channel how employees may be treated and what managers may do without consulting the union.[1] And, finally, unions have pushed governments to provide social benefits for ordinary people, ranging from Medicare to paid family leave. These, too, are an aspect of shared capitalism in the wider sense that "social benefits" or a government-provided "social safety net" represents a distribution of the wealth generated by the underlying economic system to people who are not owners.

In short, shared capitalism could be argued to be conceptually different from the specific financial participation programs examined in the NBER data set. Nonetheless, we will use that term in the rest of this chapter to refer to that narrower, specific set of financial participation programs. Given the extent of financial participation throughout the U.S. economy and its documented effects on firm performance and employment, it is important to probe more deeply into the relationship between these specific programs and unions. Indeed, this relationship has been neglected in the focus of academics in recent years on unions and high-performance systems. At the same time, financial participation is one of the elements of a high-performance work system. We begin by reviewing studies of how high-performance systems, per se, interact with collective representation. Then we turn to the smaller collection of literature on how unions interact with financial participation programs—either individual ones or the more systematic approaches that constitute shared capitalism.

High-Performance Work and HR Systems: Relevant Prior Research

Numerous scholarly studies of high-commitment or high-performance work and HR systems in the 1990s and early 2000s have by now generated a set of consensus conclusions—despite the fact that different studies evaluated somewhat different sets of practices and used somewhat different methodological approaches. One meta-analysis (Combs, Liu, Hall, and Ketchen 2006) found 13 practices that were common to most studies: incentive compensation, training, above-average compensation level, participation, hiring selectivity, internal promotion, HR planning, flexible work, performance appraisal, grievance procedures, teams, information sharing, and employment security. A more recent survey of the relationship between high-performance work practices and unions (Liu, Guthrie, Flood, and MacCurtain 2009:109) identified "rigorous staffing procedure, employee participation, job redesign, investments in training and alternative approaches to compensation (skill-based pay and group incentive compensation)" as key aspects of these systems.

Group incentive compensation overlaps, of course, with the shared capitalism that is the focus of the NBER study: profit sharing, gain sharing, and stock options are all group incentive compensation programs in the sense that they are based on collective rather than individual performance. Of course, these programs are sometimes paired with individual merit pay.[2]

We draw five main conclusions from the existing large collection of research literature on high-performance work systems in the United States. These conclusions are all echoed in the existing research using the NBER shared capitalism data set:

1. Isolated individual practices have less effect on firm performance, employee productivity, or other positive outcomes than a systemic approach that combines employee participation in decisions, financial participation, employment security, and supportive HR practices

(Combs, Liu, Hall, and Ketchen 2006; Appelbaum, Bailey, Berg, and Kalleberg 2000; Ichniowski et al. 1996). This core finding is also true for shared capitalism:

> The single overriding empirical result in this volume, which shows up in virtually all outcomes and data sets, is that combinations of policies—shared capitalism, employee involvement, and other positive labor practices—are complementary. (Freeman, Blasi, and Kruse 2010:22)

2. High-performance work systems (HPWPs) do improve firm performance according to most studies, although some studies have failed to find effects (Cappelli and Neumark 2001). One recent meta-analysis of the research literature indicates that

> increasing use of HPWPs by one standard deviation increases performance by .20 of a standard deviation. . . . Thus, HPWPs' impact on organizational performance is not only statistically significant but managerially relevant. (Combs, Liu, Hall, and Ketchen 2006:517–8)

Organizational performance was not directly measured in the NBER study, but a number of related matters were, and the impact of financial participation was positive.

> Shared capitalism was found to be "associated with greater attachment, loyalty, and willingness to work hard; lower chances of turnover; worker reports that co-workers work hard and are involved in company issues; and worker suggestions for innovations." (Freeman, Blasi, and Kruse 2010:12)

3. The mechanisms whereby high-performance work systems improve firm performance are not fully understood at this time. Much of the research fails to look inside the "black box" of the firm, or it is riddled with a variety of methodological limitations (Godard 2004). As Paul Thompson and Bill Harley (2007:156) point out, "It is common in the HRM [human resource management] literature to *assume* that performance gains from new forms of work organization accrue by virtue of their positive impact on employees."

> The studies that have been based on the NBER data set to date have the virtue of specifying and evaluating many individual pathways of potential effect (e.g., likely turnover, willingness to work hard, willingness to take action when fellow

workers are not working hard or well). Still, the pathways available in this data set are probably not all the ones that matter.

4. Experimentation with a variety of these practices is widespread among large U.S. corporations, but a full systemic implementation is less common (Osterman 2000; Handel 2007). One of the only nationally representative surveys of high-performance work practices, the National Employer Survey conducted in 1994 and repeated in 1997, found that only 1.10% of all U.S. establishments use a systematic approach that "bundles" a number of high-performance work practices consistent with the consensus conclusions already noted in this discussion. The surveys indicate that 1.74% of all unionized and 1.07% of all nonunion establishments adopted the most systematic approach (Blasi and Kruse 2006:565). Recent nationally representative surveys in 2002 and 2006 using the General Social Survey indicate that financial participation, however, is widespread. According to the NBER study:

> Almost half of American private-sector employees participate in "shared capitalism"—employment relations where the pay or wealth of workers is directly tied to workplace or firm performance. (Freeman, Blasi, and Kruse 2010:1)

5. High-performance work systems apparently improve overall employee well-being (Freeman and Rogers 1999). The body of evidence here is less extensive than that on performance, and much of it was published somewhat later. One exception is Hodson (1996), who did a statistical analysis based on a variety of earlier ethnographic studies of forms of work organization. He found that job satisfaction and pride were higher in workplaces with employee participation than in those that were bureaucratic or characterized by assembly lines, but lower than in those with craft organization.

In a special issue of *Industrial Relations* devoted to the matter, Michael Handel and David Levine (2004:1) point out that, theoretically, "involvement inherently makes work more interesting and enjoyable, thus increasing intrinsic satisfaction and motivation." However, some critical observers of early innovations alleged that involvement increases stress by increasing worker co-monitoring of performance, something that is exacerbated to the extent that pay is at stake (Parker and Slaughter 1997; Grenier 1988).

Appelbaum, Bailey, Berg, and Kalleberg (2000) found little evidence that high-performance systems generally increased stress. They conclude that such systems typically enhanced job satisfaction, organizational commitment, and trust in management (pp. 201–2). On the other hand, Brenner, Fairris, and Ruser (2004) report that cumulative trauma disorders were increased by some forms of workplace transformation. A recent study (Kruse, Freeman, and Blasi 2010b:271) found that, with shared capitalism, employees are more likely to say that they are treated with respect, that management–employee relations are good, that promotions are handled fairly, and that worker safety is a high priority with management. They note, "A measure that relates directly on the 'management by stress' theories is the employee's perception of stress at work, which is not significantly related to the shared capitalism index."

Evidence on whether employee involvement in itself increased employee earnings is mixed (Handel and Levine 2004). This demonstrates the potential importance to employees of having explicit financial incentives as part of a comprehensive system.

American Union Experience with Financial Participation

Unions have a long history with financial participation that has yet to be systematically examined—a history that involves acceptance of financial participation at times, and, in other contexts, suspicion of financial participation as an anti-union device. The National Civic Federation espoused widespread profit sharing in the early 1900s; Samuel Gompers was a prominent leader in the Federation, although his participation was criticized by more radical portions of the labor movement (National Civic Federation 1921; for a history, see also Cyphers 2002). On the other hand, the "welfare capitalism" of the 1920s used employee stock ownership and profit sharing as a way to insulate workers from trade unions—contributing to union leaders' rejection of such programs (Jacoby 1998; Foerster and Dietel 1927).

In considering the impact of unions on financial participation—both the likelihood of its implementation and outcomes where it is implemented—we first look at how unions have approached these programs in the more recent period. Probably the most important union principle is that these forms of compensation should not replace adequate and stable base pay levels. As John Zalusky, a former AFL-CIO research department staffer, once put it (1986:181), "For most workers, their debts and cash flow allow little or no room for risk-taking. Thus gainsharing and profit-sharing are useful to workers only when they contribute to basic security goals." Similarly, past AFL-CIO guidelines on ESOPs indicated that "replacement of an ESOP for a pension plan should be avoided" (McElrath and Rowan 1992:102). In short, unions prefer financial participation programs that provide a "bonus" over an adequate level of base pay and pension; they attempt to avoid ones that put a large portion of pay or retirement income at risk. Interestingly, Kruse, Freeman, and Blasi (2010b) find that the financial participation programs that are more effective are precisely the ones that meet this standard, whether or not the employees involved are represented by a labor union.

Unions also worry a great deal about employer manipulation of financial reporting so as to avoid paying bonuses to workers; this is more often a concern in profit sharing where bonuses are based on the "bottom lines" in an income statement from which items far out of the average worker's control, including executive compensation, have already been deducted (see, for instance, Zalusky 1990).

This distance between worker effort and control and payout, frequently referred to today as "line of sight," along with the issue of financial manipulation, causes unions to prefer programs that link financial participation to outcomes that the employees involved can actually influence. Gain sharing does that. Profit sharing often does not. Zalusky explains that gain sharing is a type of productivity bargaining familiar to unions:

> Most union members view these gainsharing plans as basic, although complex, wage bargains. They are an exchange of worker shortcuts, ideas, and higher levels of production for money. The bargainers weigh extra money against the downside features of peer-group pressure, potentially greater safety risks, and lost personal time protections. The parties design these plans to produce stable earnings related to worker performance rather than to factors beyond their control. (1986:176)

Productivity bargaining, of course, is something that organized workers can engage in, but that is often not possible in a nonunion context (Eaton and Voos 1994).

Financial participation of all kinds raises other issues for unions as well. For many labor leaders and activists, the differential payments that are made possible by bonuses based on facility or firm performance undermine the labor movement's commitment to equal pay for equal work (Zalusky 1990; Parker and Slaughter 1997; Nissen 1997). This isn't mere ideology: for instance, the UAW was subject to sharp criticism from members at General Motors in the late 1980s and early 1990s when they received tiny or even no bonuses while members at Ford, traditionally operating under identical collective bargaining agreements but at the time under different profit-sharing arrangements, received substantial bonuses. Closely tied to the issue of equality are the intertwined issues of union commitment and solidarity. McElrath and Rowan (1992:103), for instance, report that union leaders tend to believe that ESOPs "result in workers identifying more closely with the firms' interests, which would undermine trade union organization efforts and power and, thus, the union's role." Similarly, Parker and Slaughter (1997:220) argue that "drawing workers into 'sharing' the successes and failures of the firm reinforces worker identity with the firm. It undermines union efforts to create industry-wide standards, portability of benefits, or political action to restrict corporate power." Indeed, financial sharing is widely viewed as pushing workers toward an "enterprise" logic in which the success of their firm is valued over taking labor costs out of competition across firms.

Such factors all contribute to union opposition to these kinds of financial participation, all other things being equal. They lead to a hypothesis that unionization will be negatively associated with financial participation. At the same time, unions have found financial participation appropriate and even desirable under some circumstances. An employer's problematic financial position is one such circumstance. An employer promoting other forms of union and worker participation is another.

A prominent type of gain sharing, the Scanlon plan, is actually named after a United Steelworkers activist and local president and was developed by that union to supplement base wages for members working in companies that, typically for reasons of size or product, could not pay the union pattern in base wages without undermining the competitiveness of the business.

Zalusky notes that some financial participation programs in the union sector arise in the context of financially failing organizations in times of economic duress. The union may negotiate an ownership stake for members as an exchange for significant concessions made in collective bargaining designed to improve the chances for financial survival of the firm. He cites experience in the airline industry in the early 1980s and the Chrysler loan guarantee package of 1981 (Zalusky 1986, 1990). Others have surveyed the use of ownership stakes to restructure wages and benefits in the airline, trucking, and steel industries, and particularly in failing firms (Blasi and Kruse 1991:88–138). Similarly, the General Motors and Ford profit-sharing plans previously referenced were negotiated as part of the major concessionary agreements of the early 1980s.

The auto industry rescue package and concession bargaining that occurred in the deep recession of 2008–2009 is a more recent example. The United Auto Workers accepted major concessions in exchange for large ownership stakes in GM, Ford, and Chrysler to be held by a voluntary employee benefit association (VEBA) set up to administer retiree health insurance for former UAW members. Shared capitalism in this instance was indirect, but it resulted in a very substantial economic benefit to ordinary workers that was not available to the higher-level nonunion retirees of the same automakers—the former engineers and middle managers who simply lost significant benefits. Nor was this benefit available to the nonunion workers in the financial and insurance sector when the federal government bailed out the likes of AIG and Fannie Mae. When and if the U.S. auto industry fully recovers and becomes steadily profitable, UAW members and former members will benefit from a program of shared capitalism brokered by the union.

While a number of widely publicized cases of shared capitalism in unionized corporations have involved corporations under severe competitive pressures and outright "failing firms," and while media coverage of these practices is more common in high-profile unionized firms with competitive weaknesses, there is no evidence that shared capitalism in unionized settings is adopted mainly by failing firms. Indeed, shared capitalism as a rule is overwhelmingly a phenomenon of successful firms. An authoritative study by the U.S. General Accounting Office found that only 4% of ESOPs were adopted to save a failing company (U.S. General Accounting Office 1986:20, 39; see also Blasi and Kruse 1991:11, 73, 97).

The second circumstance in which unions may promote financial participation is when there is nonfinancial participation in managerial decisions. The AFL-CIO's landmark 1994 publication, *The New American Workplace* (AFL-CIO:46), for instance, argued that workers should participate financially in the gains realized through the transformation to more participative models of work organization: "This may be achieved through increases in base wages or, in other cases, through agreements providing for some form of *supplementary* contingent compensation (such as gain sharing, profit sharing, stock ownership, or the like)" [emphasis added].

The flip side of this argument is that, when firms propose forms of financial participation alone, unions typically push for nonfinancial participation. Scanlon plans, for instance, are characterized by a particular productivity gain-sharing formula *and* an employee involvement scheme through which to produce improved productivity. Interestingly, this argument parallels the "bundling" approach in the HR academic community and raises the hypothesis that, to the extent unions are successful in encouraging or forcing bundling, they may be associated with improvements in firm performance that are associated with these bundles of practices.

All these considerations lead to the hypothesis that unions may be complementary to financial participation. As will be reviewed in the next section, this hypothesis is directly contrary to the idea developed in earlier academic research that the overall relationship between the two will be negative. Certainly, the empirical relationship between unions and financial participation in the United States is an open research question at this time.

Prior Research on Financial Participation and Unions

A number of studies have examined how unions interact with high-performance work systems or with some of the individual financial participation programs included in the shared capitalism study. There is prior research on unions and gain sharing, profit sharing, or employee ownership but very little with regard to unions and broad-based stock options—probably because such options arose in nonunion high-technology companies and are still uncommon in union contexts (Beyster and Economy 2007). We draw on several recent literature reviews (Liu, Guthrie, Flood, and MacCurtain 2009; Verma 2005) as well as our own prior survey of earlier research—research that was more typically about individual programs than the systems approach that characterizes much research in the last 15 years (Eaton and Voos 1994). Here are the primary findings:

1. *Financial participation programs vary in distribution by union status.* Some research has reported that gain-sharing programs were more common in union companies and, while profit sharing was not unknown, it is less common in union than nonunion environments (Verma 2005; Eaton and Voos 1994).

   In contrast, according to a recent nationally representative survey *of individuals* on these issues (the 2002 and 2006 General Social Survey, or GSS), proportionally more union members than nonunion workers own company stock (24.2% compared with 19%), more union members than nonunion workers hold company stock options (12.4% compared with 10.9%), and fewer union members are eligible for either profit sharing or gain sharing (14% compared with 38%) (Kruse, Blasi, and Park 2010:56, 57; Kruse and Blasi 2007: Tables 2a and 2b). However, gain sharing in the GSS does not refer to formal gain-sharing programs—rather it is "eligibility for bonuses based on department or plant performance"—a more general concept that probably explains why such a large number of nonunion employees answered in the affirmative.

   The researchers attribute the greater incidence of company stock ownership on the part of union workers in the GSS to "the greater likelihood of retirement plans among union employees, many of which invest in company stock" (Kruse, Blasi, and Park 2010:57). The auto-industry VEBA would be another example of an indirect form of employee stock ownership tied to retirement. Obviously, the precise wording of the survey and the way it conceptualizes financial participation heavily influence the results with regard to unions.

2. *Only a few studies focus on whether financial participation benefits employees overall (apart from union status),* although there are somewhat more studies about whether it typically increases compensation. Handel and Levine (2004:34) report that, of 11 studies that evaluated "alternative pay" systems, about 27% had positive and significant effects on wages, but the majority had positive and insignificant effects. Kruse, Freeman, and Blasi (2010b) found that shared capitalism appears to benefit employees overall through higher pay and benefits, more participation in decisions, more positive evaluations of management and co-worker relations, more training, lower levels of supervision, and higher levels of job security.

Kruse, Freeman, and Blasi (2010:262b) also found that employees of companies with shared capitalism had higher job satisfaction, although the authors report that evidence has been mixed in earlier studies with regard to the impact of employee ownership, per se. We know of no study evaluating whether financial participation provides greater benefits to employees in union settings than in nonunion contexts, although we hypothesize that union programs should yield greater positive outcomes for employees to the extent the union is powerful and able to influence the design of programs in bargaining (see point 5).

In our analysis, we add to the evidence on how financial participation influences the job satisfaction of employees and the complex ways it interacts with union representation in this regard. We also examine the same relationships using a holistic score ("grade") that employees give their employer with regard to such intangibles as trustworthiness, honesty, and sense of common purpose.

3. *High-performance work systems increase firm performance in both union and nonunion settings,* and there is no convincing evidence to date of a larger effect in one context or the other (Liu, Guthrie, Flood, and MacCurtain 2009; Eaton and Voos 1994). However, in union settings, high-performance systems are more effective when they are supported by the union and the union is involved in the program (Kizilos and Reshef 1997; Cooke 1992). Union security and a high degree of labor organization contribute to a positive outcome (Kizilos and Reshef 1997).

We know less about the effectiveness of financial participation in increasing firm performance in union companies than we know about the effectiveness of high-performance work systems. For instance, Kim (1999) found that gain-sharing plans are more likely to survive in a union environment but are slightly less effective in such environments in increasing performance. Eaton and Voos (1994) concluded that union companies were more likely to adopt the relatively more effective programs—for instance, gain sharing rather than profit sharing—but that there was insufficient evidence to draw any conclusions about relative effectiveness.

We add to the evidence about relative effectiveness in this chapter. Our best variable in this regard is the employee's stated willingness to work hard. Employee loyalty—hence, a lower likelihood of turnover—is a second outcome variable that we are able to examine.

4. *Employment security is an important moderating variable, both theoretically and empirically* in the high-performance work system literature (Eaton and Voos 1994; Levine and Tyson 1990; Liu, Guthrie, Flood, and MacCurtain 2009). Workers who are more secure are typically more willing to make suggestions to increase productivity. Employees in union workplaces are individually more secure in some respects: just-cause provisions in union contracts reduce the likelihood of unfair discharge, and seniority systems protect the jobs of many union workers (at the same time they make new hires less secure). However, management may be more willing to close union establishments, either because of anti-union animus or because they are older, on average, than other workplaces in the United States, and closing may make union workers less secure, although the evidence indicates that union establishments are no more likely than nonunion establishments to close (Freeman and Kleiner 1999). So how this factor interacts with unionization is muddled—it may depend on the perceptions of the employees involved.

In this chapter, we add to the evidence about the importance of perceived job security for the effectiveness of financial participation.

5. Finally, *there is a small amount of evidence that unions have an impact on the way financial participation is structured,* and conceptually it would make sense that unions negotiate program characteristics so as to minimize the potentially negative effects we describe. McHugh, Cutcher-Gershenfeld, and Polzin (1997) examined characteristics of ESOPs and concluded that unions were

associated with a higher level of ESOP control of voting stock, allocations of stock based on hours worked, and increased levels of worker participation in both governance and the design of the ESOP itself.

We provide some evidence on this interesting issue by looking at components of shared capitalism across different levels of unionization.

It is clear to us from our review of existing studies that, while there has been some empirical exploration of the relationship between unions and financial participation, much remains unknown, and there have been fewer studies in recent years, in part because of the academic focus on high-performance work *systems*. The evidence reported in this chapter is an initial attempt to fill part of the gap in knowledge.

Assessing the Relationship Between Financial Participation and Unions

It should be clear at this point that American unions have a mixed relationship—ideologically and pragmatically—with financial participation.[3] In this section, we present analyses using the NBER data set on shared capitalism that help to further close the gap in knowledge about the contemporary relationship between unions and shared capitalism. Our spirit was not one of hypothesis testing but rather one of initial exploration of the empirical relationships.

The NBER project created a rich, cross-sectional data set, but it focused on firms with shared capitalism, rather than a random sample. Survey questions were answered by individuals. However, in our research, we focused not just on any particular individual's union status, but on the degree to which the establishment in which he or she works is unionized. We did so because we conceive of unionization as influencing what financial participation programs are available to individuals, how those programs operate "on the ground," and, hence, how individuals react to them. For a description of the data set and the analytic sample, please see the appendix to this chapter.

Analytic Strategy

We begin with an examination of the relationship between unionization and the components of shared capitalism. It is important to do so because, as discussed previously in this chapter, unions attempt to shape financial participation in various ways but particularly to reduce the amount of member compensation at risk. We then look at the relationship among unions, shared capitalism, and four key outcomes, beginning with the outcomes that are most important to unions—member outcomes. An additional outcome—the employee's perception of the degree of involvement in decision making—is used both as a control variable and a dependent variable in its own right. We begin with outcomes most important to workers and their representatives and move on to outcomes that are of concern to employers. The outcomes we were able to evaluate are as follows:

- *Job satisfaction.* This item measures the degree to which employees are satisfied with their jobs. Our work was based on the single question related to this important outcome because only a single item was available in the data set.[4]
- *Overall employer grade.* This item is an index of the grades the employees would give their employers in three areas: the employers' overall relationship with employees, the employers' trustworthiness, and the employers' creation of a sense of common purpose. Factor analysis was used to create a single measure from three underlying survey questions.[5]
- *Work hard.* This item measures the degree to which employees report that they are willing to work hard. This was based on a single question in the survey.[6]
- *Loyalty/plan to stay.* This item measures the degree to which employees express feelings of loyalty to their employer and demonstrate that loyalty through plans to stay with that employer in the future rather than seek another job. Factor analysis was used to create a single measure from two underlying questions.[7]
- *Employee involvement.* This item measures the degree to which employees perceive themselves to be involved in decision making. Factor analysis was used to create a single measure from four underlying questions.[8] We examined employee involvement as an outcome in its own right and used this variable as a control in other parts of the analysis because earlier research has indicated that employee involvement in decision making itself has positive impact on employee satisfaction, loyalty, and willingness to work hard.

For each of the dependent variables, we first determined the relationship between each outcome and both shared capitalism and unionization entered as linear variables. For shared capitalism, we used the shared capitalism index created by Kruse, Blasi, and Freeman (2010b).[9] For unionization, we focused on the percentage of all employees unionized in a particular establishment, while simultaneously controlling for individual union membership, occupation, tenure with the employer, race, and gender.[10] We used an estimating strategy that corrects for the fact that all employees in a single establishment have the same level of overall union organization.[11]

To the estimating equation we added an interaction term between shared capitalism and the percentage of unionization. The coefficient on this variable indicates whether shared capitalism and unionization act in a complementary fashion to improve employee or employer outcomes (a positive coefficient), act at cross-purposes (a negative coefficient), or simply are independent influences that are neither substitutes nor complements.

Finally, we re-estimated the same equation, controlling for three important contextual variables that are potentially influenced by organizations seeking to improve job satisfaction, employee loyalty, and the willingness to work hard. These controls are (1) employee perceptions of job security, (2) employee perception of the degree to which they are closely supervised (the antithesis of involvement in decision making), and (3) employee perception of involvement in decision making. Here our purpose was to evaluate the extent to which relationships between unionization and shared capitalism maintained their importance in the presence of these possibly confounding influences.

Descriptive Statistics

Table 1 presents the descriptive statistics for the key independent variables. Four of the eleven companies used in this analysis had some level of unionization. Unionization rates across all of the establishments in the data set ranged from totally nonunion to 95% union represented for nonmanagerial and nonsupervisory workers. Approximately 39% of employees were women, their tenure averaged a little more than ten years, and about 17% were nonwhite. The average level of shared capitalism was 2.8 on a scale from 0 to 10, where higher numbers on the scale correspond to greater coverage, greater financial stake, and, hence, greater shared capitalism (Kruse, Freeman, and Blasi 2010b).

Components of Shared Capitalism by Levels of Unionization

Table 2 contains information on particular components of the shared capitalism index, along with bonus pay as a percentage of total pay by levels of unionization in the various establishments.[12] One thing to note is that, where unions exist, they typically represent either a very small fraction of employees (most likely the skilled trades) or more than 40% (the industrial union pattern). Only a small number of the establishments in our study have intermediate levels of unionization. As predicted from the literature, sites with no unionization generally report

TABLE 1
Descriptive Statistics; NBER Shared Capitalism Project, 2001–2006.

	N	Mean	SD	Min	Max
Independent variables					
Shared capitalism index	14,037	2.846	1.727	0	10
Union membership (individual level)	17,261	0.081	0.274	0	1
Percent unionized (establishment level)	17,261	0.082	0.217	0	0.946429
Production, delivery or maintenance employee	17,261	0.671	0.470	0	1
Professional/technical employee	17,261	0.197	0.398	0	1
Administrative support employee	17,261	0.070	0.256	0	1
Job security	17,031	3.066	0.782	1	4
Close supervision	17,148	3.415	2.551	0	10
Nonwhite	16,027	0.167	0.373	0	1
Female	15,797	0.393	0.488	0	1
Tenure	17,055	10.622	9.350	0	51

Note: Mean values indicate the average survey response across all survey respondents. For example, the .081 value for union membership indicates that roughly 8% of survey takers indicated belonging to a union.

greater levels of profit sharing and employee ownership compared with sites with unionization rates greater than 40%. Strangely, and probably an idiosyncratic result of the characteristics of the two establishments in this category, establishments with medium levels of unionization have particularly high levels of most of the components of shared capitalism. However, shared capitalism is less common in the establishments with more than 40% unionization. Gain sharing is the least common program, but, again as expected, it is disproportionately available in sites with medium or high levels of unionization.

Unionized establishments, especially the more heavily unionized ones, are also less likely to have above-the-median payouts from the various kinds of financial participation programs, probably reflecting the union strategy of minimizing risk. Further, the bonus as a percentage of base pay is lowest in the heavily unionized establishments. These results do support the notions that unions shape the details of financial participation and that unionized establishments are associated with reduced levels of the aggregate measure of shared capitalism used in the NBER data set.

Regression Results

Job Satisfaction. Kruse, Freeman, and Blasi (2010b) found that the shared capitalism index was positively related to job satisfaction but

TABLE 2
Shared Capitalism by Percentage of Unionized Workers Within Establishments
(N = 17,261); NBER Shared Capitalism Project, 2001–2006.

	Percent unionized				
	0	1–5	11–40	>40	Total
Individual N	9,179	6,061	319	1,702	17,261
Establishment N	92	47	2	14	155
Company N	9	1	1	3	11
% with profit sharing	76.9	81.1	62.1	33.7	73.8
(N in parentheses)	(7,055)	(4,916)	(198)	(574)	(12,743)
% with gain sharing	11.8	8.6	27.3	13.7	11.1
(N in parentheses)	(1,084)	(519)	(87)	(234)	(1,924)
% with employee ownership	71.4	66.2	84.0	40.2	66.7
(N in parentheses)	(6,554)	(4,011)	(268)	(684)	(11,517)
% holding stock options	8.9	0.2	35.1	0.1	5.5
(N in parentheses)	(818)	(11)	(112)	(2)	(943)
% receiving a profit-sharing bonus either last year or this year	66.0	71.4	43.3	31.5	64.0
(N in parentheses)	(6,055)	(4,326)	(138)	(536)	(11,055)
% receiving a gain-sharing bonus either last year or this year	9.8	7.0	18.2	13.0	9.3
(N in parentheses)	(901)	(422)	(58)	(222)	(1,603)
% receiving a grant of stock options from company in last year	7.0	0.1	18.5	0.1	4.1
(N in parentheses)	(643)	(8)	(59)	(2)	(712)
Bonus as percent of base pay	5.1	1.0	4.9	1.3	

Note: The "6–10%" category is excluded because no establishments fell within that range.

that the coefficient lost its significance once they controlled for human resource policies. They concluded, "The strong association between shared capitalism and these human resource policies indicates that there may be important complementarities" (p. 273). Interestingly, we find that once we control for individual union membership and the percentage of unionization in the establishment, along with our standard set of controls for occupation, tenure, and demographics, the positive shared capitalism measure is insignificant (Model 1, Table 3). The interaction term is positive and significant; however, in the presence of high unionization and considerable shared capitalism, job satisfaction increases (Model 2).[13] The interaction term loses significance in Model 3, suggesting that the positive interaction is sensitive to the inclusion of job security, close supervision, and perceived involvement, which are strong predictors of satisfaction. The base shared capitalism coefficient

TABLE 3
Predicting Job Satisfaction; NBER Shared Capitalism Project, 2001–2006.

	Model 1	Model 2	Model 3
Shared capitalism index	0.00264	0.00207	–0.0197°°
	(0.0109)	(0.0109)	(0.00979)
Union membership (individual level)	0.00290	0.0128	0.0195
	(0.0151)	(0.0159)	(0.0144)
Percent unionized (establishment level)	–0.0219	–0.0133	0.00803
	(0.0213)	(0.0218)	(0.0184)
Shared capitalism index × percent unionized		0.0196°°	0.00355
		(0.00988)	(0.00870)
Job security		0.163°°°	
		(0.00880)	
Close supervision		–0.0219°°	
		(0.00849)	
Employee involvement factor score		0.445°°°	
		(0.00879)	
Constant	0.0616	0.0612	0.0154
	(0.0424)	(0.0413)	(0.0341)
N	12,114	12,114	11,689
Deviance	40,567.9	40,568.9	28,830.7
Decrease in deviance		.99	–1,281.68
Chi–square	96.73	100.74°	–1,281.68°°°
Df	9	10	13

° $p < .1$, °° $p < .05$, °°° $p < .01$.
Notes: Standardized coefficients are presented. All models control for tenure, race, gender, and occupation. Deviance tests were based on the comparison between the model and its previous model.

becomes negative when controlling for these variables. However, this does not account for complementarities among shared capitalism and these variables. Kruse and his colleagues (2010a) find that shared capitalism is linked to higher job satisfaction when it is combined with low supervision, employee involvement, training, and job security.

Overall Grade. An interesting alternative measure of employee overall "happiness" with the employer (as opposed to the job) is the grade given the employer with regard to its overall relationship with employees, trustworthiness, and development of a sense of common purpose. Here we anticipated that shared capitalism would be positive and unionization negative, and we were particularly concerned with evaluating the interaction among these factors. In fact, other things equal, shared capitalism was positive and union membership was generally negative, but only the individual-level union variable was typically significant (Model 1, Table 4). In Model 2, the interaction is positive and significant. Again, there is apparently a complementarity—establishments with both a high level of unionization and above-average shared capitalism have employees who give their employers a higher grade than those with low levels of the same two items (Model 2). The addition of the important controls for job security, close supervision, and perceived employee involvement does not alter this conclusion (Model 3). Job security and employee involvement are again extremely important explanatory variables, although here close supervision actually contributes to a high grade—a puzzling outcome at best.

If one considers the results in Tables 3 and 4 as reflecting outcomes that are good for employees (satisfaction with the job itself; a more positive view of the employer and the employer-employee relationship), there is evidence that a combination of high levels of shared capitalism and high levels of unionization produces better outcomes for employees

TABLE 4
Predicting the Grade Employees Give Employers; NBER Shared Capitalism Project, 2001–2006.

	Model 1	Model 2	Model 3
Shared capitalism index	0.0229°°	0.0227°°	0.00484
	(0.0105)	(0.0105)	(0.00926)
Union membership (individual level)	−0.0626°°°	−0.0427°°°	−0.0372°°°
	(0.0144)	(0.0152)	(0.0136)
Percent unionized (establishment level)	−0.0507°	−0.0298	−0.0106
	(0.0263)	(0.0271)	(0.021)
Shared capitalism index × percent unionized		0.0396°°°	0.0187°°
		(0.00998)	(0.00867)
Job security			0.155°°°
			(0.00829)
Close supervision			0.0376°°°
			(0.00793)
Employee involvement factor score			0.451°°°
			(0.00822)
Constant	0.145	0.146	0.0745
	(0.0791)	(0.0799)	(0.0651)
N	11,890	11,890	11,506
Deviance	32,039.7	32,029.5	27,630.3
Decrease in deviance		−10.282	−4,399.19
Chi–square	408.04	421.75°°°	4,523.76°°°
Df	9	10	13

° p < .1, °° p < .05, °°° p < .01.
Notes: Standardized coefficients are presented. All models control for tenure, race, gender, and occupation. Deviance tests were based on the comparison between the model and its previous model.

than the presence of one alone. At the same time, job security and a sense of involvement in decision making may be even more important in producing good outcomes.

Now we turn to the variables that are more closely related to outcomes for the employer.

Willingness to Work Hard. Blasi, Freeman, Mackin, and Kruse (2010) report that workers are more willing to work hard for the employer in the presence of higher levels of shared capitalism. Does this result hold in the presence of high levels of unionization? In fact, what is the relationship between unionization and the willingness to work hard (a relationship that we believe is unexplored by scholars— although one that certainly elicits comments in the popular press)? Results in Table 5 are interesting. Unionization either at the individual

TABLE 5
Predicting Willingness to Work Hard; NBER Shared Capitalism Project, 2001–2006.

	Model 1	Model 2	Model 3
Shared capitalism index	0.0424°°°	0.0424°°°	0.0298°°°
	(0.0108)	(0.0108)	(0.0105)
Union membership (individual level)	−0.00471	−0.0031	0.00264
	(0.0149)	(0.0156)	(0.0154)
Percent unionized (establishment level)	−0.0228	−0.0209	−0.0116
	(0.0206)	(0.0210)	(0.0202)
Shared capitalism index × percent unionized		0.0031	−0.00856
		(.744)	(0.00948)
Job security			0.0723°°°
			(0.0121)
Close supervision			−0.0299°°°
			(0.00910)
Employee involvement factor score			0.280°°°
			(0.00942)
Constant	0.0530	0.0523	−0.188
	(0.0435)	(0.0425)	(0.0588)
N	12,087	12,087	11,684
Deviance	30,881.3	30,886.9	28,824.1
Decrease in deviance		5.59	−2,062.42
Chi–Square	354.54	354.42	1,443.93°°°
Df	9	10	13

° $p < .1$, °° $p < .05$, °°° $p < .01$.

Notes: Standardized coefficients are presented. All models control for tenure, race, gender, and occupation. Deviance tests were based on the comparison between the model and its previous model.

level or at the level of the establishment is not significantly related to the willingness to work hard. Union workers and nonunion employees are equally willing to work hard. And the interaction of unionization and shared capitalism is also insignificant, although financial participation itself is positively related to willingness to work hard, even in the face of the important factors of job security, close supervision, and employee involvement. Insecure employees are less willing to work hard—another interesting finding in and of itself; once again, employee involvement is very strongly related to positive outcomes. Closely supervising employees has negative implications for their willingness to work hard.

Loyalty/Plan to Stay (Organizational Commitment). Greater loyalty to the employer and a lesser turnover intention have both been associated with greater levels of shared capitalism in earlier studies using this data set. We combined these two items into one factor to explore the further relationship with unionization, which we presume will increase loyalty because union members have been found in earlier studies to be less likely to quit their jobs (Hammer and Avgar 2007). The results in Table 6 indicate that, while unionization itself has a somewhat unclear relationship with these outcomes, the combination of high levels of unionization and greater shared capitalism is clearly positive and significant (Models 2 and 3). People with more-secure jobs, less supervision, and greater involvement in decision making are all more loyal or less likely to voluntarily leave the employer (Model 3).

Employee Involvement. The employee's perception of involvement in decision making can be thought of in two ways—as an outcome in its own right and as something that might be included as a control variable. We have been using it in the latter way up to now. But the bundling literature suggests that financial participation and employee involvement are complements. How do shared capitalism and unionization interact to influence this important perception, presumably by influencing the type of employee involvement programs put in place in the organization or how those programs operate? Results are presented in Table 7.

It would appear from Models 1 and 2 that shared capitalism is positively associated with the perception of employee involvement in decision making and that union representation may be negatively related to that same perception (although both union variables are only sometimes significant), but that the combination of high levels of unionization and shared capitalism is positive. Again, we see evidence that shared capitalism and unionization complement one another. That result holds in Model 3—the interaction is again

TABLE 6
Predicting Employee Loyalty Factor Score; NBER Shared Capitalism Project,
2001–2006.

	Model 1	Model 2	Model 3
Shared capitalism index	0.0564°°°	0.0558°°°	0.0338°°°
	(0.0108)	(0.0108)	(0.00977)
Union membership (individual level)	–0.00508	0.0198	0.0305°°
	(0.0148)	(0.0156)	(0.0143)
Percent unionized (establishment level)	–0.0531°°	–0.0312	–0.00848
	(0.0252)	(0.0253)	(0.0204)
Shared capitalism index × percent unionized		0.0506°°°	0.0326°°°
		(0.01000)	(0.00889)
Job security			0.254°°°
			(0.00879)
Close supervision			–0.0171°°
			(0.00843)
Employee involvement factor score			0.347°°°
			(0.00873)
Constant	0.0502	0.0478	0.0175
	(0.0440)	(0.0373)	(0.0314)
N	11,817	11,817	11,447
Deviance	32,467.2	32,448.3	28,830.7
Decrease in deviance		–19.914	–3,617.65
Chi–square	503.54	531.92°°°	3,704.94°°°
Df	9	10	13

° $p < .1$, °° $p < .05$, °°° $p < .01$.

Notes: Standardized coefficients are presented. All models control for tenure, race, gender, and occupation. Deviance tests were based on the comparison between the model and its previous model.

positive and significant. And, once again, job security seems to be a highly significant variable with a positive sign—although it is not clear whether those with greater job security perceive that they have greater involvement in decision making; whether those with more actual involvement in decision making have, or perceive themselves to have, more job security; or whether some unknown third factor (e.g., employer HR strategy) produces both outcomes.

What Does It All Mean?

One purpose of this chapter was to present research on American unions' participation in shared capitalism. An important union tenet with respect to compensation is that financial participation should not jeopardize stable base income (Zalusky 1986). Consistent with this belief, it appears that, in highly unionized establishments in the NBER shared

TABLE 7
Predicting Employee Involvement Factor Score; NBER Shared Capitalism Project,
2001–2006.

	Model 1	Model 2	Model 3
Shared capitalism index	0.0289°°°	0.0287°°°	0.0159
	(0.0105)	(0.0105)	(0.0104)
Union membership (individual level)	–0.0243°	–0.0105	–0.00984
	(0.0145)	(0.0154)	(0.0152)
Percent unionized (establishment level)	–0.0419°	–0.0283	–0.0151
	(0.0226)	(0.0234)	(0.0219)
Shared capitalism index × percent unionized		0.0270°°°	0.0172°
		(0.00988)	(0.00961)
Job security			0.197°°°
			(0.00911)
Close supervision			–0.0568°°°
			(0.00890)
Constant	0.101	0.102	0.0714
	(0.0641)	(0.0648)	(0.0629)
N	11,883	11,883	11,736
Deviance	32,088.5	32,086.5	31,174.6
Decrease in deviance		–1.95	–911.9
Chi–square	828.45	833.22°	1,410.74°°°
Df	9	10	12

° p < .1, °° p < .05, °°° p < .01.

Notes: Standardized coefficients are presented. All models control for tenure, race, gender, and occupation. Deviance tests were based on the comparison between the model and its previous model.

capitalism data set, less compensation is put at risk by way of profit sharing and employee ownership more generally (Table 2). This may reflect the caution of the American labor movement with regard to these programs—caution that comes from their desire to protect members from undue financial risk. It would appear that unions provide shared capitalism primarily in other ways than through financial participation programs. One notable exception here came with gain sharing, which perhaps reflects unions' predilection for financial participation packages that draw a clear "line of sight" between worker effort and variable pay. All union workplaces, except the ones that are only minimally organized (less than 5% union), are more likely to have gain sharing than are non-union workplaces.

A second but related aim was to explore the interaction of shared capitalism and union establishments on outcomes that are important to employers and employees. Here, the NBER data suggest that, when organized workplaces do have high levels of shared capitalism, the outcomes are generally positive for both employees and employers and that financial participation programs have a greater impact on outcomes than they would have in a nonunion environment. Significant, positive interactions were observed in models predicting the organizational commitment of employees, the grade employees give employers overall, and job satisfaction.

Thus, overall, the relationship between unions and financial participation appears to be complementary rather than oppositional. Union establishment effects on our various outcomes are generally either more positive or less negative than they otherwise would be when establishments also have strong programs of shared capitalism.[14] Although more research is needed, one implication of this finding may be that workers in unionized environments are, in fact, typically open to, and positively influenced by, variable income. An alternative interpretation is that the shared capitalism programs in the heavily unionized establishments are ones that better meet the interests of ordinary workers given the union role in shaping those programs and that this, in turn, leads them to be more effective.

There are, of course, important limitations to this research. One limitation is that we used a single item for some of our dependent variables, instead of an empirically validated factor. Wanous, Reichers, and Hudy (1997) suggest that single-item measures are acceptable if the psychological construct in question is sufficiently narrow and unambiguous to the respondent. The potential weaknesses in our dependent variable items are nonetheless noted. A further limitation comes in using the shared capitalism index as a measure for financial participation. The advantage of the shared capitalism index is that it provides a quick proxy for coverage and stake in shared capitalism. However, the index is limited in that its different forms of shared capitalism are conflated in one measure, when they are, in fact, different and could potentially have different effects. Therefore, it is not possible to gauge from our study how different *types* of shared capitalism programs influence workers across establishments with varying levels of union representation. Still, our research points toward important interactions between financial participation and unionism, which affect outcomes of interest to both workers and firms.

What seems to matter most in our analysis, however, are job security and employee involvement in decision making. These are the variables that not only typically have large coefficients but also have larger ones than shared capitalism—indicating that a change of one standard deviation yields a larger effect on outcomes of importance to employers (such as willingness to work hard and organizational commitment) as well as on the outcomes of importance to employees (such as job satisfaction). If one were to pick only one or two policies to emphasize, it would be employee participation in decision making and job security. It appears to make more sense, however, to implement these policies in conjunction with shared capitalism and other elements of a high-performance workplace, in order to take advantage of synergy between these policies and financial participation.

The importance of job security and employee involvement in this analysis may reflect the "voice" role of unions (Freeman and Medoff 1984), which may be complemented by shared capitalism. In this view, unions can enhance workplace productivity by providing voice mechanisms that (1) decrease turnover by giving dissatisfied workers an alternative to quitting, thereby preserving firm-specific skills and avoiding turnover costs; and (2) give workers the means and incentives to speak up about ways to improve performance and company survival. Voice theory provides one explanation for the higher average productivity of unionized workplaces (Doucouliagos and Laroche 2003).

Job security is a crucial ingredient in the voice perspective, since the job security provided by the typical union contract (establishing that workers can be fired only for just cause) gives workers assurance that they will not be fired for exercising voice. With this disincentive for voice removed, union workers are more likely to speak up when they have complaints or ideas, using both formal and informal mechanisms. Shared capitalism may provide an added incentive for workers to use voice mechanisms, particularly when they have ideas that can improve performance and, consequently, the size of the shared capitalism reward. The results of this study indicate that shared capitalism does in fact improve several outcomes in unionized workplaces, suggesting that shared capitalism can complement the voice role of unions and further increase productivity in unionized workplaces.

Appendix: Sample and Sampling Procedure

The NBER shared capitalism data set marks the most ambitious study on shared capitalism to date. The survey was administered to over 100,000 employees across 14 companies from 2001 to 2006. Roughly 56% of the surveys were administered by a paper instrument, while the remainder were administered over the Internet. In all, 46,907 surveys were returned, for an overall response rate of 45%. Of these surveys, 31,994 were completed by employees working in the United States. The companies included in the survey spanned the manufacturing, services, technology, and financial industries. The sample sizes across the

14 organizations ranged from 200 to 32,000. The response rates within companies ranged from 10% to 80%.

Because our interests in this study were on the distribution and effects of shared capitalism programs in American companies on the lower, nonmanagerial workforce, our analytic sample excluded employees working outside of the United States, as well as those in managerial or formal supervisory roles. We also required that survey takers answer at least half of the questions on basic job information and demographics. Surveys were dropped if the data set failed to indicate the establishment in which the employees worked, as this variable was used to develop the establishment-level predictor for the percentage of unionized workers at each work site. With these criteria in place, establishments were required to contain at least 30 representative surveys in order to have a sufficient number of observations to create a valid estimate of the percentage of unionization. Establishments providing fewer than 30 surveys were not retained. A total of 17,261 records remained across 155 establishments and 11 companies. Eight of these companies were manufacturers, with total employee populations ranging from 250 to 70,000. Two companies came from the service sector, and one was a large financial services company with a total employee population between 10,000 and 20,000 (Kruse, Freeman, and Blasi 2010b).

Endnotes

[1]Almost all U.S. union contracts contain "just-cause" provisions limiting the reasons why an employee may be dismissed to those situations in which there either is an economic reason for layoffs or one in which there is a valid reason for discharge.

[2]The HR systems approach largely overlaps with the high-performance approach in terms of practices, although sometimes the focus is on "performance appraisal–based compensation" or individualized merit pay rather than group incentive compensation. One study using this approach (Machin and Wood 2005) reports no relationship, positive or negative, in Britain between unions and firms with developed HR systems.

[3]At times, unions have welcomed these programs and have used them to enhance outcomes for members; in other contexts, they have viewed them as undermining independent employee representation.

[4]The question read, "How satisfied are you in your job?" For this study, responses were re-coded on a scale from 1 to 7, where 7 represented completely satisfied and 1 indicated completely dissatisfied.

[5]A group of survey items asked survey takers, "If you were to rate how well this company takes care of workers on a scale similar to school grades, what grade would you give in these areas? (C is an average grade.)" We used confirmatory factor analysis on three of these graded areas: overall relations with employees, trustworthiness in keeping its promises, and creating a sense of common purpose in the company. Responses were coded on a scale from 0 to 4, where 4 represented an A, and 0 an F.

We used principal components analysis with orthogonal rotation for validation. The factor's eigenvalue was 2.45, with a minimal loading of .89. The Cronbach's reliability coefficient for this factor was .88.

[6]The survey question read, "To what extent do you agree or disagree with this statement? 'I am willing to work harder than I have to in order to help the company I work for succeed.'" Responses were re-coded for this study on a scale from 1 to 5, where 5 indicated strong agreement and 1 indicated strong disagreement.

[7]The first question asked respondents, "How much loyalty would you say you feel toward the company you work for as a whole?" Responses were re-coded on a scale from 1 to 4, where 4 indicated a lot of loyalty and 1 indicated no loyalty. The other item asked, "How likely is it that you will decide to look hard for a job with another organization within the next twelve months?" Responses were re-coded on a scale from 1 to 4, where 4 indicated not at all likely and 1 indicated that the respondent was already looking. Principal components analysis produced an eigenvalue of 1.43 and loadings of .846 on our single factor.

[8]The survey questions read as follows: "How much involvement and direct influence do YOU have in deciding HOW to do your job and organize the work?"; "How much involvement and direct influence do YOU have in setting GOALS for your work group or department?"; "How much involvement and direct influence do YOU have in overall company decisions?"; and "Overall, how satisfied are you with the influence you have in company decisions that affect your job and work life?" Responses for all questions were coded on a scale from 1 to 4, with 1 representing very little influence or satisfaction and 4 representing a lot. We used principal components analysis with orthogonal rotation for validation. The factor produced an eigenvalue of 2.23, with a minimal loading of .71. The Cronbach's reliability coefficient was .74.

[9]This is a thermometer type index of shared capitalism "which assigns points based on coverage by shared capitalism programs and the size of the financial stakes" (Blasi, Freeman, Mackin, and Kruse 2010:143). Higher values in the index correspond to a greater stake of employee ownership.

[10]We controlled for occupation because attitudes and levels of employee involvement are likely to vary by one's functional position within the organization. We included 0-1 variables for three occupational classifications included in the data set: (1) *production, maintenance, or delivery workers*; (2) *professional technical workers* (combining engineers, scientists, and marketing and finance workers); and (3) *administrative support*. The omitted occupational category was *customer support personnel*.

[11]We adopted hierarchical linear modeling (HLM), using the xt mixed command in Stata 9.0, to test the effects of *percent unionized* on our dependent variables because of its ability to model nested, multilevel relationships (Raudenbush and Bryk 1992). Employees were nested within establishments; therefore, attitudes might co-vary within establishments, which violates a key assumption of ordinary least squares regression (Bliese 2000). To calculate intraclass correlation coefficients, we ran a null hierarchical model for each dependent variable, where no level-2 predictor was specified. An intraclass correlation coefficient signifies how much additional variance in a given dependent variable can potentially be explained away by higher-level predictors (Bliese 2000). For example, the intraclass correlation coefficient for our *employee involvement factor*, at .072 (p < .05), indicates that roughly 7% of the variance in the *employee involvement factor* could be attributed to higher-level as opposed to individual-level phenomena. Our results supported the use of HLM across all of our

dependent variables (for *employee loyalty factor*, ICC1 = .067, p < .05; for *employer grade factor*, ICC1 = .096, p < .10; for *job satisfaction*, ICC1 = .035, p < .05; and for *willingness to work hard*, ICC1 = .046, p < .05). The intraclass correlation coefficients for the company level fell below 2% for all of our outcome variables. Therefore, we present HLM models using two levels as opposed to three. Running models at three levels did not alter the direction of significance of any coefficient.

[12]We also looked at differences in these variables by union status at the individual rather than establishment level. There were no major differences in the results at the individual as opposed to the establishment level.

[13]A negative relationship between unionization and job satisfaction is widely reported in the literature (Hammer and Avgar 2007). We interpret this as indicating that making employees conscious of things on the job that are problematic so that these issues can be raised with the employer is an important component of voice or effective representation, but it also could be something that arises from processes of selection (bad jobs being more likely to become unionized) or simple ineffectiveness of union representation.

[14]There are some regressions for which the interaction term is insignificant, but it usually is not negative and never is negative and significant.

References

AFL-CIO. 1994. *The New American Workplace.* Washington, DC: AFL-CIO Committee on the Evolution of Work.

Appelbaum, Eileen, Thomas Bailey, Peter Berg, and Arne Kalleberg. 2000. *Manufacturing Advantage: Why High-Performance Work Systems Pay Off.* Ithaca, NY:ILR Press.

Beyster, J.R., and P. Economy. 2007. *The SAIC Solution: How We Built an $8 Billion Employee-Owned Technology Company.* New York: John Wiley.

Blasi, Joseph R., Richard B. Freeman, Christopher Mackin, and Douglas L. Kruse. 2010. "Creating a Bigger Pie? The Effects of Employee Ownership, Profit Sharing, and Stock Options on Workplace Performance." In Douglas L. Kruse, Richard B. Freeman, and Joseph R. Blasi, eds., *Shared Capitalism at Work: Employee Ownership, Profit and Gain Sharing, and Broad-Based Stock Options.* Chicago: University of Chicago Press, pp. 139–65.

Blasi, Joseph R., and Douglas L. Kruse. 1991. *The New Owners: The Mass Emergence of Employee Ownership in Public Companies and What It Means for American Business.* New York: HarperCollins.

Blasi, Joseph R., and Douglas L. Kruse. 2006. "High Performance Work Practices at Century's End." *Industrial Relations*, Vol. 45, no. 4, pp. 547–78.

Bliese, Paul D. 2000. "Within-Group Agreement, Non-Independence, and Reliability: Implications for Data Aggregation and Analysis." In Katherine J. Klein and Steve W.J. Kozlowski, eds., *Multilevel Theory, Research and Methods in Organizations.* San Francisco: Jossey-Bass, pp. 349–81.

Brenner, Mark D., David Fairris, and John Russer. 2004. "'Flexible' Work Practices and Occupational Safety and Health: Exploring the Relationship between Cumulative Trauma Disorders and Workplace Transformation." *Industrial Relations*, Vol. 43, no. 1, pp. 242–66.

Cappelli, Peter, and David Neumark. 2001. "Do 'High-Performance' Work Practices Improve Establishment-Level Outcomes?" *Industrial and Labor Relations Review*, Vol. 54, no. 4, pp. 737–75.

Combs, James, Youngmei Liu, Angela Hall, and David Ketchen. 2006. "How Much Do High-Performance Work Practices Matter? A Meta-Analysis of Their Effects on Organizational Performance." *Personnel Psychology*, Vol. 59, no. 3, pp. 501–28.

Cooke, William N. 1992. "Quality Improvement Through Employee Participation." *Industrial and Labor Relations Review*, Vol. 46, no. 1, pp. 119–34.

Cyphers, Christopher J. 2002. *The National Civic Federation and the Making of a New Liberalism*. Westport, CT: Praeger.

Doucouliagos, Christos, and Patrice Laroche. 2003. "What Do Unions Do to Productivity? A Meta-Analysis." *Industrial Relations*, Vol. 42, no. 4, pp. 650–91.

Eaton, Adrienne E., and Paula B. Voos. 1994. "Productivity-Enhancing Innovations in Work Organization, Compensation, and Employee Participation in the Union Versus the Nonunion Sectors." In David Lewin and Donna Sockell, eds., *Advances in Industrial and Labor Relations*, Vol. 6. Greenwich, CT: JAI Press, pp. 63–109.

Foerster, R., and E. Dietel. 1927. *Employee Stock Ownership in the United States*. Princeton: Industrial Relations Section, Department of Economics, Princeton University.

Freeman, Richard, and Morris Kleiner. 1999. "Do Unions Make Enterprises Insolvent?" *Industrial and Labor Relations Review*, Vol. 52, no. 4, pp. 510–27.

Freeman, Richard B., Joseph R. Blasi, and Douglas L. Kruse. 2010. "Introduction." In Douglas L. Kruse, Richard B. Freeman, and Joseph R. Blasi, eds., *Shared Capitalism at Work: Employee Ownership, Profit and Gain Sharing, and Broad-Based Stock Options*. Chicago: University of Chicago Press, pp. 1–38.

Freeman, Richard B., and James Medoff. 1984. *What Do Unions Do?* New York: Basic Books.

Freeman, Richard B., and Joel Rogers. 1999. *What Do Workers Want?* Ithaca, NY: ILR Press.

Godard, John. 2004. "A Critical Assessment of the High-Performance Paradigm." *British Journal of Industrial Relations*, Vol. 42, no. 2, pp. 349–78.

Grenier, Guillermo. 1988. *Inhuman Relations: Quality Circles and Anti-Unionism in American Industry*. Philadelphia: Temple University Press.

Hodson, Randy. 1996. "Dignity in the Workplace under Participative Management: Alienation and Freedom Revisited." *American Sociological Review*, Vol. 61, no. 5, pp. 719–38.

Hammer, Tove Helland, and Ariel Avgar. 2007. "The Impact of Unions on Job Satisfaction, Organizational Commitment, and Turnover." In James T. Bennett and Bruce E. Kaufman, eds., *What Do Unions Do?: A Twenty-Year Perspective*. New Brunswick, NJ: Transaction Publishers.

Handel, Michael J. 2007. *A New Survey of Workplace Skills, Technology, and Management Practices (STAMP): Background and Descriptive Statistics*. Unpublished paper, Department of Sociology, Northeastern University.

Handel, Michael J., and David I. Levine. 2004. "Editors' Introduction: The Effects of New Work Practices on Workers." *Industrial Relations*, Vol. 43, no. 1, pp. 1–43.

Ichniowksi, Casey, Thomas A. Kochan, David Levine, Craig Olson, and George Strauss. 1996. "What Works at Work: Overview and Assessment." *Industrial Relations*, Vol. 35, no. 3, pp. 400–22.

Jacoby, Sanford M. 1998. *Modern Manors*. Princeton: Princeton University Press.

Kim, Dong-one. 1999. "Determinants of the Survival of Gainsharing Programs." *Industrial and Labor Relations Review*, Vol. 53, no. 1, pp. 21–42.

Kizilos, Mark, and Yonatan Reshef. 1997. "The Effects of Workplace Unionization on Worker Response to HRM Innovation." *Journal of Labor Research*, Vol. 17, no. 4, pp. 643–56.

Kruse, Douglas L., and Joseph R. Blasi. 2007. *Report on the 2002 and 2006 General Social Survey.* New Brunswick, NJ: School of Management and Labor Relations, Rutgers University.

Kruse, Douglas L., Joseph R. Blasi, and Rhokeun Park. 2010. "Shared Capitalism in the U.S. Economy: Prevalence, Characteristics, and Employee Views of Financial Participation in Enterprises." In Douglas L. Kruse, Richard B. Freeman, and Joseph R. Blasi, eds., *Shared Capitalism at Work: Employee Ownership, Profit and Gain Sharing, and Broad-Based Stock Options.* Chicago: University of Chicago Press, pp. 41–75.

Kruse, Douglas L., Richard B. Freeman, and Joseph R. Blasi. 2010a. "Do Workers Gain by Sharing?: Employee Outcomes under Employee Ownership, Profit Sharing and Broad-Based Stock Options." In Douglas L. Kruse, Richard B. Freeman, and Joseph R. Blasi, eds., *Shared Capitalism at Work: Employee Ownership, Profit and Gain Sharing, and Broad-Based Stock Options.* Chicago: University of Chicago Press, pp. 257–89.

Kruse, Douglas L., Richard B. Freeman, and Joseph R. Blasi, eds. 2010b. *Shared Capitalism at Work: Employee Ownership, Profit and Gain Sharing, and Broad-Based Stock Options.* Chicago: University of Chicago Press.

Levine, David, and Laura S. Tyson. 1990. "Participation, Productivity and the Firm's Environment." In Alan S. Blinder, ed., *Paying for Productivity.* Washington, DC: Brookings.

Liu, Wenchuan, James P. Guthrie, Patrick C. Flood, and Sarah MacCurtain. 2009. "Unions and the Adoption of High Performance Work Systems: Does Employment Security Play a Role?" *Industrial and Labor Relations Review*, Vol. 63, no. 1, pp. 109–27.

Machin, Stephen, and Stephen Wood. 2005. "Human Resource Management as a Substitute for Trade Unions in British Workplaces." *Industrial and Labor Relations Review*, Vol. 58, no. 2, pp. 201–18.

McElrath, Roger G., and Richard L. Rowan. 1992. "The American Labor Movement and Employee Ownership: Objections to and Uses of Employee Stock Ownership Plan." *Journal of Labor Research*, Vol. 12, no. 1, pp. 99–119.

McHugh, Patrick P., Joel Cutcher-Gershenfeld, and Michael Polzin. 1997. "Employee Stock Ownership Plans: Whose Interests Do They Serve?" In *Proceedings of the Forty-Ninth Annual Meeting of the Industrial Relations Research Association*, Madison, WI, pp. 23–32.

National Civic Federation. 1921. *Profit Sharing by American Employers: Examples from England and France. A Report of the Profit Sharing Department of the National Civic Federation.* New York: E.P. Dutton.

Nissen, Bruce, ed. 1997. *Unions and Workplace Organization.* Detroit: Wayne State University Press.

Osterman, Paul. 2000. "Work Reorganization in an Era of Restructuring: Trends in Diffusion and Effects on Employee Welfare." *Industrial and Labor Relations Review*, Vol. 53, no. 2, pp. 179–96.

Parker, Mike, and Jane Slaughter. 1997. "Advancing Unionism on the New Terrain." In Bruce Nissen, ed., *Unions and Workplace Reorganization.* Detroit: Wayne State University Press, pp. 208–25.

Raudenbush, Stephen W., and Anthony S. Bryk. 1992. *Hierarchical Linear Models: Applications and Data Analysis Methods.* Newbury Park, CA: Sage.

Thompson, Paul, and Bill Harley. 2007. "HRM and the Worker: Labor Process Perspectives." In Peter Boxall, John Purcell, and Patrick Wright, eds., *The Oxford*

Handbook of Human Resource Management. Oxford: Oxford University Press, pp. 147–65.

U.S. General Accounting Office. 1986. *Employee Stock Ownership Plans: Benefits and Costs of ESOP Tax Incentives for Broadening Stock Ownership*. Washington, DC: U.S. General Accounting Office.

Verma, Anil. 2005. "What Do Unions Do to the Workplace? Union Effects on Management and HRM Policies." *Journal of Labor Research*, Vol. 26, no. 3, pp. 415–49.

Wanous, John P., Arnon Reichers, and Michael Hudy. 1997. "Overall Job Satisfaction: How Good Are Single-Item Measures?" *Journal of Applied Psychology*, Vol. 82, no. 2, pp. 247–52.

Zalusky, John L. 1986. "Labor's Collective Bargaining Experience with Gainsharing and Profit Sharing." In *Proceedings of the 39th Annual Meeting, Industrial Relations Research Association*. New Orleans, pp. 174–82.

Zalusky, John L. 1990. "Labor–Management Relations: Unions View Profit Sharing." In Myron J. Roomkin, ed., *Profit Sharing and Gain Sharing*. Metuchen, NJ: Scarecrow Press, pp. 65–78.

CHAPTER 3

Improving the Quality of Home Health Aide Jobs: A Collaboration Between Organized Labor and a Worker Cooperative

DAPHNE PERKINS BERRY
University of Massachusetts, Amherst

STU SCHNEIDER
Cooperative Home Care Associates

It became apparent in the beginning that the union was going to have to change their approach and that we, at the cooperative, were going to have to change ours. . . . They had to understand that they were not the only ones who represent the best interests of the workers and we had to let them in to accept that they could bring situations to our attention.

Michael Elsas, president of Cooperative Home Care Associates, August 2010[1]

Introduction

In their report on global aging, Kinsella and He 2009) addressed the significant consequences that an aging population has on a nation's labor supply and the sustainability of its social programs. They pointed out that soon after 2010, for the first time in recorded human history, the number of people over the age of 65 will outnumber those below the age of 5, with the greatest increases occurring among those over the age of 80. Their report also noted that views of caring for elders are changing to favor home-based and community-based services instead of institutionalization.

In the United States, home care workers (also referred to as home health aides or home attendants) provide services to elders and individuals with physical disabilities to help them to live independently in their homes and communities. These services include ostomy care and monitoring vital signs; assistance in using medical equipment, such as a Hoyer lift in trans-ferring a patient from the bed to a wheelchair; accompaniment to medical appointments; and light housekeeping and preparation of meals. Without this essential support, many individuals who rely on a home care worker would require services from a nursing home.

According to the Paraprofessional Healthcare Institute (PHI),[2] between the years 2000 and 2030, the number of elders in the United States will increase by 104%, while the pool of women in the age group from which direct-care workers are usually drawn (ages 25 to 44), will increase by only 7%. Yet fewer women within this age cohort are pursu-ing jobs as home care workers. In the United States, home health aide jobs are characterized by poverty-level wages, part-time hours, minimal benefits such as health insurance or paid earned leave time, a high rate of occupational injury, limited opportunities for career advancement, and high turnover. Nationally, nearly 52% of all personal and home care aides reside in households with incomes less than 200% of the federal poverty line,[3] and annual turnover among these positions is estimated nationally at 60%. Dresser's study (2008) of work performed in the home (including home health aide work) examined the harsh working conditions and challenges to initiatives designed to improve the quality of jobs traditionally performed in the home by women for little or no pay. Dresser linked the limited financial compensation associated with such work in the past to the poor wages earned by those—disproportion-ately minority women—who currently fulfill these responsibilities.

In 1985, in response to the poor quality of home health aide jobs, Cooperative Home Care Associates (CHCA) was created as a worker cooperative to model the implementation of innovative workforce and compensation practices in the sector. By improving the quality of home health aide jobs, CHCA developed the capacity to provide its clients (elders and individuals living with disabilities) with enhanced quality of services. In fulfilling this dual mission, CHCA has grown to become the nation's largest worker cooperative, with more than $40 million in annual revenues and 1,700 employees. CHCA also allocates 80% of annual revenue to the wages and benefits earned by its home care work-ers—including dividends to worker-owners and contributions to the 401(k) accounts of all employees in profitable years.

Interestingly, the worker-owners of CHCA are represented by the 1199SEIU, United Healthcare Workers East, an affiliate of the Service Employees International Union (SEIU), and referred to in this chapter as 1199SEIU. The union organizes home care workers to improve the quality of their jobs. This organizing work has catalyzed a significant expansion of 1199SEIU, which now represents 300,000 members and retirees in New York, Maryland, Massachusetts, and the District of

Columbia. 1199SEIU's 70,000 home care workers belong to one of its largest and fastest-growing divisions. It advocates for higher wages and improved working conditions, educates and empowers workers to seek social and economic justice, and encourages its members to acquire greater knowledge and skill in the health care sector.

CHCA presents an interesting research case for examining in more depth the relationship between employee ownership and unions. Academics, labor, and business practitioners have documented tensions in these relationships, often related to the implementation of employee ownership without participation, but with reductions in employee compensation by firms experiencing financial challenges. In their study of employee-owned firms and unions, for example, Whyte and Blasi (1984) identified reactions of union leaders to the concept of employee ownership, ranging from indifference to hostility, and interest tempered by skepticism and ambivalence. Most studies exploring relationships between worker-owned enterprises and unions examined cases that involved the transfer of ownership through an employee stock ownership plan (ESOP). In those cases, ownership did not always provide employees with the right to participate in organizational decision making (Kruse and Blasi 1997; Logue and Yates 2001; Whyte and Blasi 1984). Additionally, since many firms created ESOPs after experiencing severe financial difficulties, the decisions that managers and union leaders made often included significant wage and benefit concessions from workers. Thus, workers often experience the implementation of ESOPs as preceding reductions in the quality of their jobs. However, Whyte and Blasi (1984:137) recognized that a union could "play an indispensable role, with management, in organizing and implementing quality of working life (QWL)[4] or other participatory programs." Other studies (Addison and Belfield 2007; Bennett and Kaufman 2007; Freeman 2007) focused on the outcomes achieved by unions, citing enhancements in wages and benefits as well as worker voice (i.e., representation, participation in workplace decision making, and a mechanism for communicating with management and/or collective bargaining power). However, Bell (2006) noted potential similarities in the goals of certain employee-owned firms and unions despite different strategies used to achieve objectives.

In 2003, 1199SEIU organized CHCA's 1,600 home care workers, which provided an opportunity to study the evolution of the relationship between the two organizations into a successful partnership toward creating better jobs for CHCA's workers. Building on previous research on unions in worker-owned firms, we explored the role of a union in expanding opportunities for employees to participate in organizational decision making and develop the skills necessary to realize expanded opportunities relating to wealth, power, and personal development. The relationship between CHCA and 1199SEIU has also created the opportunity to explore these topics among a cohort of low-income African American and Latina women, who tend to be underexamined in the literature on employee ownership. Based on findings from this study, we propose areas of future research on the relationship between unions and worker ownership, employee participation, and improving the quality of home health aide jobs. We also suggest further exploring the role of unions in creating new opportunities for home care workers to pursue educational and career advancement.

We began our study by reviewing the theory and research related to worker-owned firms and unions, as well as the history of the CHCA and 1199SEIU partnership. Next, through an in-depth case study using qualitative and quantitative data, we examine key elements of the relationship between CHCA and 1199SEIU, highlighting the benefits of a close relationship between worker-owners within the home care industry and their union.

Employee-Owned Firms and Unions

Academics and practitioners have often focused on whether there is a real or perceived *need* for unions in employee-owned firms. Whyte and Blasi's (1984) study of unions and worker-owned companies examined various circumstances in which firms became employee owned, various types of ownership, and a range of relationships and outcomes in different business, financial, legal, and industry environments. In many cases, union support of employee ownership came with buyouts in exchange for saving jobs. In many of these cases, ownership was accompanied not by meaningful participation in organizational decision making but by reductions in pay and benefits. Negotiating contracts aimed at protecting the jobs with stock that conferred different types of voting rights presented union leaders with difficult problems. As unions experienced both successes and failures regarding quality jobs and participation in workplace decisions, they developed both negative and positive attitudes toward employee ownership. Examining whether workers in such companies would still need a union, Whyte and Blasi (1984) found that some did feel in need of representation. And despite persistent struggles in relationships between unions and employee-owned firms, the study noted interest by some union leaders in alternative management structures, but this was not supported by policy initiatives. Whyte and Blasi (1984:137) foresaw "a major role for unions in employee-owned firms" with union support of participatory decision making in QWL and other programs vital, even in cases in which management has an interest in worker participation.

In another study, which includes a review of research on employee ownership, employee attitudes, and firm performance, Kruse and Blasi (1997) assessed attitudes toward unions in employee-owned firms. Although the firms studied were primarily conversions to employee ownership through buyouts, Kruse and Blasi found that, while results varied, several of the studies also indicated an increase in perceived need for union representation. For example, in one study with a sample of 38 nonmanagerial union workers in a firm that had been recently purchased by its employees, Long (1980) reported favorable views of union–management cooperation. More specifically, this study focused on the perceived fear that employee ownership might reduce the allegiance of workers to their union. Exploring the potential of a situation of worker-owners bargaining with themselves, Long noted that "the fundamental conflict of interests between labour and capital on which many labour theorists have based the need for labour unions would seem to disappear" (1980:238). He also noted, however, that some theorists criticize such an argument as simplistic and as failing to fully consider the complexities of different situations. Long found that more than 82% of employees surveyed felt that there was no reason the union and the owners could not work well together, while a few respondents (less than 30%) thought it difficult to be loyal to a union and to the employee-owned company, and even fewer perceived dissimilar goals between the two groups. In other words, while most felt that they would be treated fairly without a union, they thought that having a union would pose no divided loyalty problems and, overall, preferred one.

Long's speculation regarding the need for a union, particularly where employee ownership and control are involved, has been examined in other studies. Logue and Yates (2001), for example, addressed the notion that it would be difficult to conceptualize how a union, established to oppose and bargain with firm owners, could represent workers who were also owners. Like other studies mentioned earlier in this chapter, they noted tensions rooted in past experiences but concluded that many current union leaders recognize a place for unions in the world of employee-owned firms, as unions seek to unionize workers in organizations that, citing an AFL-CIO director, see the "high road of mutual support and block the low road to the sweatshop" (2001:112).

Turning to other recent research on what unions bring to workers of a firm, Addison and Belfield's (2007) study of a range of voice mechanisms reveals conflicting evidence about the levels of voice among union and nonunion workplaces. More specifically, they noted that research performed in the United States and other countries indicates that reports of the effects of union voice in firms depends on the measures of voice examined, the measure of productivity or profitability, and the focus on collective- or individual-level effects. In addition, a focused look at studies from the United Kingdom provided empirical results across union and nonunion workplaces that indicate greater voice in both unionized and nonunionized workplaces. Addison and Belfield's (2007) study did, however, identify key aspects of voice for unions, including participation in various workgroups; input into grievance procedures; communication with management regarding pay, training, and promotion; management's understanding of family issues; and worker input in company decisions on work practices.

In two related studies, Freeman (2007) and Bennett and Kaufman (2007) conducted a reassessment of the research of Freeman and Medoff's *What Do Unions Do?*, which was published in 1984 and examined the economic, political, and social effects of unions on workplaces and on society. The more recent text re-examined the assessments and conclusions of earlier research. Both Freeman's (2007) and Bennett and Kaufman's (2007) studies identified themes in the original text related to unions and benefits (or detriments) to workers or business output in general (not specific to worker-owned companies). Referencing attention in the original text to the effects of democratization of the workplace, Freeman (2007) reminded us that collective bargaining requires the efforts of at least two participants and that management's response to worker voice is critical in determining the outcomes. Like Whyte and Blasi (1984), Freeman (2007) noted that even in firms with mechanisms to facilitate worker participation, those who are represented by a union have a greater ability to influence outcomes because voice without power is often ignored by senior management in organizations. Freeman also highlighted subsequent work (Freeman and Rogers 1999) related to union-facilitated employee voice in which workers can participate in workplace decisions via various workgroups or committees. Bennett and Kaufman (2007:4) highlighted both negative and positive effects of unions, emphasizing that, for the latter to occur, a "spirit of cooperation and mutual gain" must exist. Finally, Kaufman's (2007) assessment that the primary economic functions for unions in the workplace also included those of increasing worker involvement in workplace practices, and of protecting them from managerial abuse and substandard wages and working conditions.

These studies draw attention to several topics that we encounter in our study of CHCA and 1199SEIU. Kruse and Blasi's (1997) review highlighted no decrease in the perceived need for a union after employees became owners due to a buyout, and in some cases, an increase in the perceived need for union efforts. Logue and Yates (2001) recognized that despite skepticism about the ability to collaborate successfully, "high-road" employers[5] and unions shared some common goals and values. Addison and Belfield's (2007) attention to the multiple meanings and outcomes of worker voice drew attention to the environment in which voice is operative. Freeman's (2007) and Bennett and Kaufman's (2007) emphasis on the critical importance of management response and Kaufman's (2007) highlighting that the primary function of unions is to increase participation were, as we will see later in this chapter, also significant for this study. Finally, Whyte and Blasi's (1984) big-picture study reiterated these findings and highlighted gaps in research in which the current study of CHCA and 1199SEIU might be placed.

Hence, prior research on firms in which worker participation was not a desired outcome focuses on a decidedly challenging environment for a union to improve the quality of jobs for its members. However, in our setting, the value placed on augmenting the voice of workers by both a union and the ideologically driven founders of a cooperative represents a situation characterized by space for conversations and the development of strategies for achieving critical, common goals. Hence, we might expect this to be a productive setting for a positive relationship between employee ownership and unions. Our case study also examines more closely the role of a union in organizing a worker-owned cooperative operating within an industry characterized by low-paying jobs and employing a large workforce of minority women—a group with historically limited access to quality jobs or democratic workplaces. We identify areas of tensions between the organizations as well as key strategies and structures that have shaped their collaboration and cooperation. Our research also highlights the motivations of both organizations as they pursue different strategies for achieving similar goals, which include securing quality jobs for workers and their participation in organizational decision making.

CHCA and 1199SEIU

Cooperative Home Care Associates

In 1985, Rick Surpin and Peggy Powell co-founded CHCA as a worker cooperative to provide quality home health aide jobs to low-income South Bronx residents and to improve the quality of these jobs (Inserra, Conway, and Rodat 2002). One of the primary ways CHCA attempted to achieve this goal was through the development of a four-week home health aide training program in 1987, which currently helps 400 low-income New York City residents each year to earn the credentials needed to work in New York State as both personal care assistants and home health aides. While earning home health aide certification in New York State requires only 75 hours of training, CHCA believes that more time is necessary for individuals to learn the many critical clinical and interpersonal skills involved in providing clients with quality services. In 2009, the year before enrolling in this training, 66% of participants in CHCA's training program earned less than $5,000 per year, 53% lacked a high school or general equivalency degree, and 60% were immigrants to the United States (including those born in Puerto Rico).

CHCA directly employs most graduates from its training program in home health aide positions and provides them with the following retention-support services:

- A guaranteed hours program (implemented in 1993), which provides home care workers who have been employed at CHCA for at least three years with pay for working at least 30 hours each week, regardless of their actual schedule, as long as they do not refuse any client assignment.
- A peer mentor program (implemented in 2003) through which six experienced home care workers received promotions to full-time administrative staff members who now assist new training program graduates in successful transition to employment.
- Coaching supervision (fully implemented in 2008), where supervisors at CHCA use a nonpunitive management approach to help employees address problems while ensuring accountability for their decisions.

After working at CHCA for three months, employees attend a three-hour workshop about purchasing an ownership stake in the cooperative. This workshop begins with a brief history of cooperation and cooperatives within an economic context before describing the process of accumulating equity within CHCA. Specifically, employees who opt to become worker-owners authorize deductions totaling $50 from their paychecks as a down payment toward a $1,000 share of stock in the cooperative. CHCA then loans the employee the remaining amount, which is repaid through small weekly payroll deductions. The ownership stake provides the worker with all rights, privileges, and responsibilities of worker ownership, including one vote in elections for 8 of 13 members on the cooperative's board of directors. After working for one year at CHCA, worker-owners are eligible to be nominated as candidates in elections to the cooperative's board of directors.

Similarly, after working at CHCA for three months, all home care workers become union members and have weekly dues of 1.2% of their earnings deducted from their paychecks. As union members, all home health aides currently receive an individual health insurance benefit, with no required contribution, through a Taft-Hartley plan administered by 1199SEIU. When needed, they also receive support from a union organizer assigned by 1199SEIU to CHCA, who advocates for grievances, and are represented by eight home care workers selected as union delegates. After one year of union membership, the 1199SEIU Bill Michelson Homecare Education Fund (hereafter referred to as the education fund) defrays the cost of CHCA home care workers to attend specific classes or earn additional credentials in the health care sector.

1199SEIU and Industry Context

Since its creation in 1935, 1199SEIU has grown to represent more than 300,000 members and retirees including nurses, social workers, those working in mental health and substance clinics, nursing home workers, and home care workers. In addition to higher wages and improved working conditions, 1199SEIU advocates for job security, health insurance, childcare services, and pensions for its members. In addition, through its grievance process, the union helps home care workers who have been unfairly discharged or disciplined by their employers and those who may have experienced discrimination. Within the home health aide industry, strong union representation has proven an effective strategy for improving the quality of home care jobs. Due in part to advocacy efforts by 1199SEIU, the City of New York enacted a living wage law in 2002, which today ensures that home care workers who are paid by contracts administered by New York City receive an hourly base wage of $10—regardless of their employer.

Home care workers in New York City receive different titles and levels of compensation depending on the funding source from which they are paid to provide services for a particular client. Home care workers who are paid with Medicaid funds administered by the City of New York are called home attendants and receive an hourly base pay of $10. Other home care workers in New York City, who are paid from other public programs, are called personal care assistants or home health aides, and they earn an hourly base wage that rarely exceeds $8.50. In 2007, Cooperative Home Care Associates received a contract from the City of New York to provide 400 Bronx residents with home care services and began hiring home attendants in July 2008. Currently, CHCA employs 350 home attendants and 1,250 home health aides, and both groups of home care workers are represented by 1199SEIU.

Previous Collaborations

CHCA began collaborating with 1199SEIU in 1987—just two years after CHCA's incorporation—as the union began a campaign to increase the wages of one type of home care worker (referred to as "home attendant"). CHCA's senior managers encouraged its worker-owners to support this effort by attending rallies and volunteering their time. Since CHCA only employed one other type of home care worker (referred to as "home health aide") at the time, worker-owners realized that 1199SEIU's efforts would not increase their own compensation as home health aides. However, a small group of home health aides from CHCA volunteered with 1199SEIU to support the general principle that home care workers deserved greater compensation. Ultimately, 1199SEIU's efforts resulted in home attendants receiving an increase in wages and benefits that totaled 42% during a three-year period (Inserra, Conway, and Rodat 2002).

CHCA's initial collaboration with 1199SEIU continued in 1989, when the union provided representatives to serve on a New York City Home Care Workgroup, which was organized by CHCA staff. The workgroup conducted research about job quality for home health aides and recommended providing higher reimbursement rates for home care services as a strategy for improving New York State's home care system. This effort contributed to New York State (through its Medicaid program) providing home care employers with a labor market adjustment determined by the wages and benefits provided to home health aides. However, although the specific amount of the funds received by home care agencies was determined by their labor costs, New York State did not require that this money be used to increase the compensation earned by home care workers. CHCA was one of the few employers in the sector to use the funds received from this source to increase the compensation of its home health aides (Inserra, Conway, and Rodat 2002).

Until 2001, 1199SEIU focused its efforts within New York City's home care industry on organizing only home attendants, but then began planning a campaign to unionize home health aide employers. After learning of the union's goals, CHCA's senior managers initiated conversations with home care workers in leadership positions at the cooperative about the benefits of formally collaborating with 1199SEIU. These conversations helped CHCA's home health aides understand 1199SEIU's role in advocating for New York City's living wage law, which increased the hourly base wage of home attendants to $10. As a result of these conversations, 1199SEIU negotiated a card-check neutrality agreement with CHCA before organizing its home care workers.

This allowed CHCA's home care workers to vote on the question of unionization by signing an authorization card instead of participating in a lengthy ballot process. In 2003, CHCA's home health aides officially voted to unionize through 1199SEIU.

The literature on employee ownership and unions suggests the need for further exploration of collaborations between employee-owners and unions. We capitalize on 1199SEIU's recent unionization of CHCA to conduct an empirical examination of the impact on the quality of jobs for low-income home health aides. The evidence presented in this section reveals the potential for employee-owners and unions to collaborate effectively in achieving their common goals and that employee-owners were amenable to union representation. It is also important to note that CHCA viewed 1199SEIU's organizing of its home care workers as another key strategy to achieve its mission of creating quality jobs for its 1,250 home health aides, especially given the union's success in increasing the wages for home attendants. We now present our detailed analysis of the relationship between CHCA and the 1199SEIU.

Methodology

To examine the collaboration between CHCA and 1199SEIU in more depth and explore the related issues of home care worker compensation, participation, and other dynamics of the partnership, we used qualitative and quantitative data collection methods. Through interviews, observation, a survey, and archival data, we first collected background and contextual data. We then solicited the perspectives of home care workers and administrative personnel at both the cooperative and the union. The first co-author of this chapter conducted seven 45-minute, open-ended and semi-structured interviews with administrative staff from CHCA and 1199SEIU, including CHCA's president, the union organizer assigned by 1199SEIU to CHCA, organizationally active home care workers who are also owners of the cooperative, and members of 1199SEIU. Based on this work, the second co-author conducted a 15-minute focus group with five additional home care workers and one former home care worker promoted to a full-time administrative position. These conversations focused on 1199SEIU's role in encouraging participation in organizational decision making and pursuing continuing education opportunities.

The first co-author also participated in over 40 hours of observation in four regional meeting/information sessions (home care worker information dissemination, participation, and feedback sessions), two Labor/Management Committee (LMC) meetings, and two 1199SEIU home care worker support sessions. The second co-author serves on CHCA's management team and on the LMC created between the cooperative and 1199SEIU. Information from several documents prepared as part of his work output was also analyzed for this paper. These documents included reports and presentations about CHCA's initial experiences following 1199SEIU's unionization of its home health aides, CHCA's workforce development practices, the LMC's work, and home care worker participation in organizational decision making. Both co-authors also reviewed data from 1199SEIU's Homecare Education Fund about the participation of CHCA home care workers in pursuing opportunities for continuing education.

Finally, to examine the attitudes of a larger sample of CHCA's home health aides, we used data collected from a survey originally designed to examine the effects of ownership and participatory decision making on outcomes for home health aide workers and, by extension, their clients.[6] For this chapter, we included a question asking whether membership in the union had impacted the quality of a home health aide's job. Our overall collection effort extended for 18 months, with a focused period of six months, to generate much of the data presented in this chapter.

Data and Findings

In this section, we present the results of our research. In Table 1, we summarize key topics addressed by respondents through participant observation, interviews, and survey data. The primary, recurrent themes from all sources included support and representation received from 1199SEIU,

TABLE 1
Topics and Sources of Data for CHCA–1199SEIU Collaboration

		Cited in		
		Participant observation	Interviews	Survey
Compensation	Wages	✓		✓
	Health insurance	✓	✓	✓
	Paid sick leave	✓	✓	✓
Participation and leadership development	Labor/Management Committee	✓	✓	✓
	Union delegates	✓	✓	✓
	Education	✓	✓	✓
Worker voice, empowerment	Grievances	✓	✓	✓
	Terminations	✓	✓	
	Support and representation	✓	✓	✓
Other	Tensions over wages and organizational motivation for collaboration	✓	✓	

grievances, the education benefit administered by 1199SEIU, home health aide participation in organizational decision making, and wages.

We first provide an overview of significant initiatives and challenges in 1199SEIU's relationship with CHCA following the unionization of its 1,600 home care workers. We then present the results from interviews with key actors regarding their views of the collaboration, followed by a review of the survey results. Finally, we conduct a more detailed treatment of the topics most often cited by participants in the study as important to the collaboration: wages, benefits, and participation by home health aides in the organization's decision-making processes.

We begin by describing key phases in the relationship between CHCA and 1199SEIU, starting with initial challenges, progressing through ongoing collaboration, and concluding with the partnership through a formal LMC.

Initial Challenges and Outcomes

Initial Challenges: Health Insurance and Paid Sick Leave. After home health aides voted to unionize, 1199SEIU was skeptical of the degree to which CHCA actually created higher-quality jobs for its home health aides, since their hourly base wage did not significantly exceed that paid by other New York City home care agencies. However, the union soon recognized the essential differences in choices made by CHCA's management toward this goal. For example, 1199SEIU realized that CHCA paid extra money to its Taft-Hartley health insurance plan to help home care workers who worked just under 120 hours in two consecutive months maintain their coverage. Given the requirements of this health insurance plan, without CHCA's supplemental payments, home health aides with inconsistent client assignments would experience months-long lapses in their insurance coverage.

However, many of CHCA's home health aides experienced challenges in transitioning to an 1199SEIU-managed health insurance plan. Before CHCA's unionization, all employees were eligible to receive health insurance free from CHCA (with no required contribution). But many home care workers managed their hours to maintain eligibility for Medicaid, which was accepted by most health care providers in New York City and did not require co-payments for services. Following CHCA's unionization, all home health aides (after 90 days of employment) who worked at least 120 hours for two consecutive months were required to receive health insurance from an 1199SEIU-managed Taft-Hartley plan. Thus, for the first time, a number of home care workers were responsible for co-payments and experienced limitations on the health care providers who would accept their insurance.

In another early experience, 1199SEIU worked to overturn a decision approved by CHCA's board of directors that reduced the number of paid sick leave received by home care workers from 12 days to 6 days. This occurred after CHCA's senior managers projected a decrease in the amount by which its revenue would expand and therefore recommended that all home care workers receive only the number of sick days that were actually *used* by most home care workers. However, 1199SEIU viewed this action as a reduction in employee compensation and advocated strongly against it. Ultimately, CHCA and 1199SEIU reached a compromise whereby existing employees would maintain their current level of paid sick days while new employees would receive six days their first year and two additional paid days in each of the next three years.

1199SEIU–CHCA Collaboration. In support of the union's objectives to provide support to workers and to enhance their knowledge and participation, CHCA's union representative, Guadalupe Astacio, spends each Friday at CHCA, when hundreds of home health aides pick up their weekly paycheck or pay stub. She uses this opportunity to share information about both the union and the cooperative. The union has also selected eight home care workers to serve as delegates to assist in the work of disseminating information among CHCA's 1,600 home care workers. These union delegates also build relationships with their peers in order to solicit their feedback and communicate concerns to CHCA's senior executives.

As a union representative, Ms. Astacio, on a case-by-case basis, helps home care workers resolve workplace challenges by helping them access internal and external resources. She promotes 1199SEIU's Member Assistance Program, which offers CHCA's home care workers bereavement counseling, as well as support in resolving alcohol or substance abuse, landlord–tenant disputes, and parenting challenges. Ms. Astacio has secured the conditional reinstatement of several home care workers who failed a random annual drug screen after they brought CHCA documented proof of completing a substance abuse program and passed a new random drug screen. She has also advocated for the reinstatement of home care workers who have experienced tension with clients or co-workers after they have completed an anger management class.

Partnership Between the Cooperative and the Union: A Labor/Management Committee. CHCA and 1199SEIU have also developed a formal LMC—the first by a home care agency in New York City. This LMC has created new opportunities for home care workers, union delegates, managers, administrative staff members, and union organizers to collaborate in addressing key organizational challenges. CHCA and

1199SEIU retained a consulting firm to facilitate the design process, which resulted in the creation of six workgroups, each focusing on addressing a distinct organizational challenge. The purposes of the first three workgroups are as follows:

- *Service delivery:* Improves relationships between coordinators and home care workers in providing quality services to elders and individuals living with physical disabilities. This workgroup has arranged for coordinators to spend time with CHCA's union organizer to hear complaints about schedules and client assignments directly from home care workers.

- *Communications:* Improves the process by which CHCA disseminates essential information about its finances and policies to its home care workers. The workgroup has experimented with restructuring CHCA's offsite quarterly meetings by conducting a highly successful onsite "Information Fair," at which the company disseminated information to triple the number of home care workers who had typically attended offsite meetings.

- *Childcare:* Identifies and addresses unmet childcare needs among home care workers. However, after conducting extensive research that revealed that home care workers spend nearly one third of their take home pay on childcare services, the workgroup realized that they could not effectively reduce this expense and decided to disband.

  With a grant in 2009 from the Federal Mediation and Conciliation Service, CHCA and 1199SEIU have extended their contract with their LMC consultant, the Praxis Consulting Group, to create three additional workgroups:

- *Health care:* Encourages employees to use key health services and promote opportunities for accessing free mammography services; low-cost, farm-fresh produce, and CHCA's dental benefits and preventive services.

- *Employee morale:* Pursues efforts to track and enhance the morale of CHCA's employees.

- *Cooperative's Home Attendant Program (CHAP) integration:* Works toward consistent benefits among CHCA's 350 home attendants and 1,250 home health aides.

Given the hourly base wage differential between its newly hired home attendants and many home health aides ($10 compared with $8), CHCA decided to delay the opportunity for home attendants to purchase an ownership stake in the cooperative and participate in its TransitChek® benefit (CHCA's home health aides may purchase discounted public transportation trips using pretax income). Therefore, CHCA managed two distinct home care workforces, with two rates of pay and benefits eligibility. The LMC began the work of planning to integrate CHCA's home attendants into the cooperative's culture. In part, through the efforts of this workgroup, home attendants are now eligible to participate in CHCA's worker ownership and TransitChek benefits.

In addition, each LMC work group requests feedback about its recommendations from all LMC members during bimonthly meetings. The LMC's leadership team, composed of five senior executives from CHCA and 1199SEIU, approves all workgroup recommendations during meetings scheduled approximately every six months. However, depending on their scope, some workgroup recommendations are considered for implementation by specific managers or members of CHCA's operations team, which comprises all managers.

Finally, unique among the few unionized cooperatives in the United States, 1199SEIU does not recruit union members to participate as candidates in an "organized slate" during annual elections for positions on CHCA's board of directors. Instead, 1199SEIU supports efforts by CHCA staff in informing worker-owners about opportunities to pursue board positions and managing the cooperative's election process.

In this section, we examined the initial challenges to these two organizations working together, as well as the strategies used in overcoming these issues and pursuing specific collaborations. In the next section, we present data from interviews with the company president, the union organizer assigned by 1199SEIU to CHCA, and several organizationally involved home health aides to explore the dimensions and consequences of this collaboration in more detail.

The Union and Home Health Aide Jobs at CHCA: In the Words of . . .

The interview excerpts presented in this section focus on key themes raised by the respondents regarding the relationship between CHCA and 1199SEIU. We begin with excerpts of the open-ended interview by this chapter's first co-author with CHCA's president, who addressed all themes explored in this study, followed by an analysis of interviews with CHCA's union representative, and home health aides at CHCA.

CHCA's President. The president of CHCA, Michael Elsas, has been in the home care business for several decades and has worked within conventional for-profit and not-for-profit organizations. He has been involved in the struggle for better wages for home care workers during much of that time. We asked Mr. Elsas to comment on, in general, the need for a union in a worker cooperative, the particular reasons for the unionization of CHCA's home care workers, the nature of the working relationship between the organizations, outcomes, and whether he had advice to give others at worker cooperatives regarding unionization. His perspective addressed themes from previous research, such as the need for a good working relationship between managers of the business organization and the union, worker voice, and increased participation from workers. He also brought additional benefits, particularly in the context of a worker cooperative organization, to light.

Mr. Elsas is careful to position his view of the six-year collaboration between CHCA and 1199SEIU as a view from within a particular context, which does not necessarily represent advice for specific decisions that should be made by other companies. The union's success at securing wage increases for a segment of the home care workforce—in the context of the difficulties of achieving this goal—was a key factor in Mr. Elsas's support for the decision to unionize at CHCA. So, even though he felt that CHCA's worker-owners may not have needed many of the benefits for which unions are known—such as improved work environments, medical benefits, and worker voice—the possibility of better wages for CHCA's workers was pivotal. "The union was very strong in New York in 2004. They had been very successful in raising wages and benefits for those segments of our industry that were unionized. . . . At that time, our workers were making $7.50, and this segment (unionized) of home attendants were soaring past us with the union. . . . We have to do what's best for the workers."

Another motivation for the union affiliation was the possibility of influencing the industry toward CHCA's model of creating better jobs for home care workers. "We absolutely believed that our company uses the best practices and is a model of how workers should be trained, supervised, motivated, etc."

His experience of day-to-day working with his union counterparts and the union representative to CHCA indicates a close working relationship and flexibility between the leaders in both organizations. An indication of the type of shared goals, values, and early cooperation between the cooperative and the union has been the outcomes following negotiation about a formal grievance process. According to Mr. Elsas, "When we were negotiating our first contract, CHCA's grievance procedure became the grievance procedure that was incorporated into our contract, not the union's. Ours was already a user-friendly, transparent process."

Mr. Elsas's articulation of positive outcomes from the unionization of CHCA's home care workers highlighted an overall increase in home care worker participation in organizational functions, higher interest in participation with the LMC, and use of the union-sponsored education benefit:

> "It's [the LMC] an important new addition to the company because one of the big challenges that we've had is keeping participation at a high level. . . . This is a big cooperative, 1,700 workers. We had been losing effectiveness in terms of participation. . . . The LMC has raised workers' awareness. . . . Now with the union's involvement [through the LMC], we address workplace issues 365 days a year, . . . as opposed to waiting for a contract to end and at negotiation time finding out that something's not working. . . . Participation in decision making and industry advocacy is one way in which CHCA develops leaders, so the resulting increase in participation through working with the union is a welcome, if unexpected, benefit."

A final advantage of affiliation with the union identified by Mr. Elsas is the education benefit. "It's about tapping resources that we have never been able to provide at the current reimbursement rate. There's no way with our current wage and benefit structure that we could have also provided an education benefit to our home care workers. So this is very positive." He noted that the education fund was starting to be used in preparing home care workers for administrative positions and that CHCA has hired a licensed practical nurse who was formerly a home health aide and who had attended school paid for by the union's education fund. Information from this interview with Mr. Elsas led us to seek additional information regarding effects of unionization on CHCA worker-owners, specifically changes in the amount and nature of participation at the cooperative as well as use of the 1199SEIU Homecare Education Fund.

CHCA's 1199SEIU Union Representative. Like CHCA's president, the representative to CHCA from 1199SEIU, Guadalupe Astacio, has been in the home care business for many years. Since she began working in the industry as a home health aide, she understands the efforts of home care workers, their work environment, and challenges encountered while working with clients. We asked Ms. Astacio if she felt that workers at a cooperative such as CHCA needed union representation and to describe the working relationship between both organizations. She first made it clear that CHCA is among the best home care agencies that she has encountered in her years in the business and that the home care workers at the cooperative already had many benefits. However, she also emphasized that CHCA workers still need a union for "representation," noting that the union "always has something that benefits the home care workers. Like representation, education, and always being there for the worker." She provides the example of a worker having someone to represent him or her during CHCA's termination process, but also points out that from her experience, if CHCA terminated someone, it was because they really felt that it was the right (and only) decision left to make. "But," Ms. Astacio said, "I look for a way to fight for that person, to see if there is an opportunity for the worker to make a change in her life. Sometimes there might be family problems, abuse. Sometimes . . . a mistake." She said that CHCA is willing to listen and works with her in trying to help home care workers however possible.

Like Mr. Elsas, she referenced the cooperation by all parties in attempts to resolve problems. In addition, the union provides benefits and knowledge about how they can be accessed (i.e., medical screenings, disability or worker's compensation, education benefits). Ms. Astacio emphasized that 1199SEIU respects CHCA's rules and that much has changed since CHCA management and workers first began working with 1199SEIU staff—that both sides have grown together in working for the benefit of the home care workers.

Home Health Aides. We interviewed five actively participating CHCA home health aides[7] about their jobs, their benefits, participatory decision making, and LMC workgroups, as well as six other home health aides more specifically about their participation in decision making and use of the education fund. These home care workers have a high level of participation in organizational decision making. They appreciate the differences in their benefits (better) and pay (sometimes not higher compared to those of other agencies) and specifically appreciated their training (more than the 75 hours required by New York State to earn a home health aide credential). They also have an appreciation for the incremental value of the union to themselves and home health aides in the industry. The home health aides, when asked what they thought of CHCA as a place to work, immediately identified the company's focus on training, education benefits, and facilitated access to these benefits in the context of wages. One had been on public assistance for a time and indicated that she just needed a job, so was surprised to find that a position with CHCA also provided very good training. "When I started here, . . . I just needed a job. . . . I went through the training, which was four weeks (in a) classroom and then on-the-job training until I was certified. . . . The training was awesome."

Another health care aide, having worked at a different home care agency prior to CHCA, emphasized that, despite not having perhaps the very highest wages in the industry, CHCA provided benefits that she found valuable:

> In the other agency the only thing you had was *a job*. You have nothing (else) at all. *No medical plan . . . no benefits. . . .* Here we have family leave. When you return you get everything the same way as when you left . . . if you continue as a student and you want to be a licensed nurse. They don't do reimbursement. They *pay* . . . depending on your income. . . . In the long run, it's better for you to have benefits.

Still other home care workers focused on ownership, participation, and advocacy, citing their appreciation of owning part of the company, understanding of company finances, work-related concerns of home care workers such as safety when visiting clients, and advocating for their industry:

> We [the Policy Action Group] advocate for ourselves and for our clients. We go to lobby in Albany every year and we're just about the only home care agency that goes all the time without the home care association. . . . On the Quality Improvement Group, we find ways to improve conditions and safety issues. . . . [S]ome places [neighborhoods] are not that good.

Our study's second co-author conducted a focus group with five home health aides at CHCA and a peer mentor who worked as a home care worker until February 2010. All serve on the LMC's Health Care Workgroup and volunteered to participate in a focus group about their use of 1199SEIU's education benefit and the union's role in their leadership development. Of the six employees participating, four had taken classes paid for by 1199SEIU's education fund: three to learn computer skills and one to improve her English proficiency. Completion of 1199SEIU's computer course was credited by the peer mentor as effective preparation for fulfilling the responsibilities of her new position. The two home care workers cited scheduling conflicts as a reason for completing only the first part of 1199SEIU's two-part computer class. Yet one of these two workers expressed pride in the skills learned, as she had previously had to rely on her son to use the computer and was now able to complete specific tasks on her own. Another home care worker stated that enrollment had closed for 1199SEIU's computer class at the time that she wanted to participate in this course.

All four members of the LMC's Health Care Workgroup who participated in a course funded by 1199SEIU's education fund praised their instructors for their skill and encouragement. One home care worker said that completing 1199SEIU's English as a second language (ESL) program had given her the confidence to join the LMC and enabled her to feel more comfortable communicating with others in English.

Home care workers also described 1199SEIU's impact on their leadership development by creating the opportunity for them to serve on the Labor/Management Committee. All six noted that through this work, they learned to feel more comfortable and confident in expressing their opinions—with one noting that this experience helped her to "come out of my shell—and there was a lot in my shell." Two of the home care workers also explained that working on the LMC had taught them to share their opinions effectively and appropriately within meetings. (We believe that this resulted in part from a workshop on effective meeting participation completed by all LMC members.) Another expressed pride in CHCA for creating leadership development opportunities for home care workers. She said that whenever she heard other home care workers complain about CHCA, she asked them if they ever got involved with the cooperative or why they never accepted invitations from others at CHCA to attend specific meetings or join committees.

Overall, these caregivers feel that CHCA is a better place to work than most home care agencies because of CHCA's dedication to providing benefits to workers and that the cooperative's relationship with 1199SEIU has helped in achieving that goal. However, our survey revealed that some home health aides (nearly 40%) felt different about their relationship with 1199SEIU, likely because of stalled progress on realizing an across-the-board increase for home health aides.

Survey Results

To access the views of a broader group of home health aides, we invited all CHCA home care workers who picked up their paychecks on two consecutive Fridays to complete a survey about their employment tenure with the cooperative. We administered this survey to 259 people and collected 257 usable surveys (two surveys were excluded from this analysis because there were not enough items completed to be useful). One of the survey questions asked if the union had impacted the quality of their jobs. The responses to that question are shown in Table 2.

TABLE 2
Home Health Aide Responses to "Has the union made a difference in the quality of your job?"

	N	%
	257	
Yes	122	48
No	99	38
No response	36	14

Thirty-six respondents did not answer the question about the union's impact on job quality—a rate of nonresponse five times higher than the average rate of nonresponse for a question on the survey. Approximately 26% of those who answered the question provided additional comments in response to a supplemental question about the specific impacts of 1199SEIU on their job quality. Comments of those who responded were largely positive, such as "They have helped us a lot" and "They help me get the things I need." However, others submitted comments with an alternate view, such as "They've done nothing for us" and "Things are the same." Other responses referenced the following issues:

- *Voice:* "We have the medium that helps us to express ourselves" and "I understand the union job better, my rights as a home attendant. I now am able always to make things easier for myself and for my client."

- *An understanding of the advocacy that the union does on behalf of the worker and support they can count on:* "I feel like I am part of a team that cares for my financial and work needs, so I can perform my job well"; "Because they look out for your interests"; "I can't take the time to really ask about things or take part. So they are here to fight harder for me"; and "I know people can count on benefits and services when they need them."

- *Attention to union impact to their pay and benefits:* These responses were mixed, with positive comments such as "They fight so we obtain better benefits of health, salaries, and education." However, disappointment with their pay is also evident: "For three years, I have not received the promised salary of $10 per hour"; "The paid rate is still the same. We need an increase"; "No, I have had no benefits"; and "The union doesn't represent us for a pay raise."

Overall, respondents commented about their participation in decision making, health and education benefits; overall support received; and their hourly wages. In the next section, we analyze in more depth some of these key themes identified in our study of the collaboration between CHCA and 1199SEIU.

Exploring Key Themes in More Depth

Tensions Between CHCA and 1199SEIU. Information from our interviews and observations reveal an initial wariness between administrators at CHCA and 1199SEIU regarding their ability to develop a productive working relationship. Some at the cooperative felt that CHCA's worker-owners did not need a union to represent their interests because the cooperative had successfully implemented unique practices to improve the quality of home care jobs (relative to other home health aide employers in New York City). As stated by CHCA's president in the epigraph to this chapter, "they are not the only ones who represent the best interests of the workers." Nevertheless, 1199SEIU's success in securing an hourly base wage of $10 for home attendants helped convince CHCA's senior managers and other home care workers to seek a closer collaboration with 1199SEIU.

From the perspective of 1199SEIU, they were interested in launching a comprehensive, industry-wide organizing campaign by first targeting employers who were already empowering their home care workers. Additionally, CHCA's president wanted to work with the union in improving the quality of home health aide jobs and model an effective collaboration with 1199SEIU to other home care employers in New York City. With respect to specific interactions between the two organizations, the union organizer assigned by 1199SEIU to the cooperative said that she respected CHCA's rules and policies while working to resolve problems experienced by home care workers. She also works with, not against, CHCA's administrative staff in advocating on behalf of home care workers.

Despite the positive relationships among CHCA's senior managers and administrative staff members with 1199SEIU, many home health aides recognized that the union has not achieved significant progress (to date) toward an hourly wage of $10, while continuing to deduct dues each week from their paychecks. Only 48% of the 221 respondents to the survey question specific to the union stated that 1199SEIU had improved the quality of their jobs. Although only seven home care workers skipped a typical question on this survey, 36 did not respond to the question asking whether the union had improved the quality of their jobs. We surmise that these workers were hesitant to express negative opinions about 1199SEIU's advocacy efforts in hopes that such work will eventually succeed.

Although the partnership between CHCA and 1199SEIU has created new opportunities for home care workers, tensions persist in this relationship—primarily among home health aides—given the challenge of securing the wage increase that represented a key motivation for joining 1199SEIU back in 2003.

Worker Voice and Participation. As indicated in discussions with CHCA's union representative, Ms. Astacio, 1199SEIU advocates for home care workers by communicating their concerns with CHCA's senior managers. Additionally, eight union delegates assist Ms. Astacio in achieving this goal. She also assists individual home care workers in resolving personal or job-related challenges by helping them identify and obtain resources available from the union, cooperative, or other community organizations. Ms. Astacio emphasizes that 1199SEIU represents and fights for whatever a worker might need and not have the resources or access to obtain.

CHCA's president, all of the home health aides interviewed, the second co-author, and some home health aides via comments on the survey identified worker voice as a key value of the cooperative, and one that is enhanced by CHCA's relationship with 1199SEIU. The home care workers noted that 1199SEIU had helped them to express themselves and understand their job as well as their rights. Mr. Elsas noted that the union has brought some situations experienced by home care workers to the attention of CHCA's administrative staff. For example, the Labor/Management Committee's Service Delivery Workgroup has arranged for CHCA's coordinators to sit with an 1199SEIU union organizer for several hours each payday to hear complaints directly from home care workers about their work schedule and client assignments.

CHCA's president and the second co-author of this chapter recognized an increased level of participation by home care workers in decision-making processes resulting from 1199SEIU's work. For example, CHCA's union delegates helped defuse one key complaint among home health aides about a $40 deposit on cell phones they were required to use in tracking their hours worked. In a scheduled meeting with CHCA's president, union delegates shared complaints by home care workers about this deposit requirement, which resulted in a policy change so that home care workers were charged $40 only if their cell phones from CHCA were lost or stolen.

Finally, while comparable pre-union data are not available, based on the qualitative data obtained for this study, we recognize a significant probability that 1199SEIU's work with CHCA impacted the responses of home care workers. Of 257 survey respondents, 95% stated that the company provides them with the information and training needed to improve the company, 92% felt that they were kept informed of important issues, 88% indicated that CHCA's culture encourages the sharing of ideas about improving the company, 84% were satisfied with the influence they had in decisions affecting their work, and 79% felt that their ideas count on the job. In addition, despite dissatisfaction with their pay, 88% indicated that they were satisfied with their jobs, and only 19% indicated that they were likely to look hard for a job somewhere else within the next 12 months.

Leadership Development and Access to Continuing Education Opportunities. One important finding of our analysis that has not been referenced in the literature on unionized employee-owned firms is that 1199SEIU's partnership with CHCA provided home care workers with new leadership development training and opportunities. Labor/Management Committee members have received training on effective communication and meeting participation skills. In turn, many LMC members are now helping to disseminate key information to other CHCA home care workers. For example, members of the LMC's Communications Workgroup have organized information fairs to help home care workers understand key CHCA financial data (such as quarterly revenue, expenses, and profit) and to receive other financial literacy services, such as information about their 401(k) accounts, the importance of opening checking and savings accounts, and preventing identity theft. Members of the LMC's Health Care Workgroup have also communicated the importance of receiving key preventive services—such as blood pressure, cholesterol, and blood glucose screenings; tests for body mass index, vision, and hearing; and annual dental exams and mammograms—to other home care workers.

Other LMC members have begun to complete tasks that were previously fulfilled by CHCA's administrative staff members. For example, members of the LMC's Employee Morale Workgroup recently accepted a request by CHCA's president to organize a regular Breakfast with the President series to facilitate communication with home care workers who currently do not participate in organizational decision-making opportunities. Previously, this work was completed on occasion by staff from CHCA's human resources department. 1199SEIU has also encouraged many home care workers to attend rallies to learn more about and to advocate for adequate resources for publicly funded home care programs. Mike Shay of the Praxis Consulting Group, which advised CHCA and 1199SEIU on the LMC, described the Labor/Management Committee between CHCA and 1199SEIU as one of the most effective he has observed during his 30 years of work within the field of employee ownership—particularly LMC's success in developing new leaders within the union and cooperative.

Finally, 1199SEIU's education fund has also created an opportunity for some home care workers to participate in continuing education opportunities—93 in the past two years. CHCA's home care workers have used this benefit to attend the following types of classes: ESL, general equivalency degree (GED) preparation, adult basic skills, certified nursing assistant (CNA) certification, gerontology, and licensed practice nurse (LPN) training. In his interview for this study, CHCA's president noted that the cooperative could not afford to defray the cost of employee participation in collegiate or continuing education courses without partnering with 1199SEIU.

Health Insurance. We conclude this section by describing an area of future work between CHCA and 1199SEIU, which illustrates the three key themes previously discussed: tensions, voice, and leadership development. When 1199SEIU first organized CHCA's home health aides, many preferred their Medicaid coverage to the health insurance benefit provided by a Taft-Hartley plan jointly managed by 1199SEIU and employer representatives. In 2011, many home health aides employed by CHCA will again be able to receive health insurance coverage through Medicaid and other publicly subsidized programs due to a provision of the recent federal Patient Protection and Affordable Care Act. This legislation precludes health insurance plans from limiting claims to less than $750,000 annually.

The Taft-Hartley plan managed by 1199 SEIU provides CHCA's home health aides with a health insurance benefit with an annual $6,500 limit on reimbursed health services at an approximate annual cost of $2,000 per beneficiary. The same plan without this now-prohibited service limitation will cost CHCA approximately $4,380 per beneficiary, each year. Therefore, CHCA will require a contribution from home care workers toward the cost of this benefit for the first time in its history (at a rate of $5 per week) and can afford to provide health insurance coverage to only 450 of its 1,250 home health aides.

Although CHCA and 1199SEIU will work together to help its remaining 800 home health aides obtain health coverage from Medicaid or other publicly subsidized insurance programs, both organizations recognize that these changes will likely create additional tensions among home care workers. In response, CHCA and 1199SEIU have asked members of the Labor/Management Committee's Health Care Workgroup to assume a key role in explaining these changes to other home care workers as well as the reasons for these changes. Toward that end, two home care workers who serve on this workgroup attended a half-day seminar with three CHCA administrative staff members to learn more about federal health reform legislation.

Discussion and Conclusion

The prior studies of employee ownership and unions identified in the first section of this chapter focused on identifying the sources of uneasy relationships between worker-owned companies and unions as well as the benefits of collaboration between such entities. In those studies, workers became owners when their companies encountered severe financial difficulties. The case of CHCA and 1199SEIU is different. CHCA has worked to provide its employees with quality jobs and a supportive work environment since its establishment in 1985. 1199SEIU also seeks quality jobs and a participative work environment for its members. Therefore, collaboration between the organizations toward common goals created an environment that increased the probability of developing an effective partnership, capable of providing home care workers with tangible benefits. Indeed, our research provides strong evidence of a cooperative relationship, although tensions were also evident.

The results of our study of the relationship between CHCA and 1199SEIU confirmed the findings articulated by previous researchers. For example, Long's (1980) research identified no expected problems with divided loyalties or divergent goals; such problems were also not encountered in our study. As found by Logue and Yates (2001), the union sought unionization of businesses seeking the "high road of mutual support" such as CHCA when they began working to organize home care agencies in New York City. As indicated by CHCA's president, the decision to unionize was specific to the business environment in which the cooperative operated, which was characterized by very low wages and low levels of benefits for home health care workers. Because low wages were a key reason for partnering with the union, the particular business environment was important for considering the applicability of findings from this case study to other relationships between unions and employee-owned firms.

Additionally, Whyte and Blasi (1984), Addison and Belfield (2007), and Freeman (2007) highlighted the importance of a firm's response to the unionization of its employees. In our case study, CHCA's motivation for 1199SEIU's organizing of its home care workers, and CHCA management's open response to the union's initiatives, were key factors shaping the positive outcomes described in this chapter. Kaufman (2007) recognized that one specific purpose of unions is to enhance worker participation, and Freeman and Rogers (1999) found that workgroups and committees are important mechanisms for participation. We noted both of these outcomes in our study.

Our research has also confirmed a key assertion of Whyte and Blasi's (1984) research: unions might be indispensable in organizing and implementing participatory programs within an employee-owned firm. The cooperative's unique motivation in viewing the unionization of its employees as a critical strategy for achieving an essential element of its mission ultimately resulted in a relationship that helped to enhance other important organizational objectives for CHCA. CHCA's objectives related to poverty alleviation represent another unique characteristic of this study of a worker-owned enterprise and a union. Most studies within the field of employee ownership have not focused on the experiences of very low-wage, historically disenfranchised workers and thus have not identified the importance of even modest steps to help such employees gain access to education.

Perhaps the most important finding of our study are the strategies used by CHCA and 1199SEIU to work through initial challenges to create a successful partnership, although the two groups pursued different approaches for achieving similar goals. As referenced early in this chapter, the union organizer assigned by 1199SEIU to CHCA has devoted a significant portion of her time to building relationships with the cooperative's home care workers and encouraging their participation in organizational decision making. The creation of eight union delegate roles has complemented the eight elected worker-owners to CHCA's board of directors and effectively doubled the number of leadership opportunities available to home care workers. A new Labor/Management Committee has also enabled more home care workers to collaborate with CHCA's administrators and 1199SEIU's organizers in addressing key challenges.

The partnership between 1199SEIU and CHCA has also created new leadership development opportunities for home care workers. As mentioned earlier, during the past two years, 93 home care workers pursued continuing education and advancement opportunities paid for by the union's education fund. Additionally, LMC members have learned new skills for disseminating information to other home care workers and communicating their concerns back to administrators within CHCA and 1199SEIU. Therefore, in addition to benefits relating to cooperative ownership and involvement in decision making, we believe that 1199SEIU's unionization of CHCA's home care workers has also created opportunities for them to pursue career advancement, and hence economic mobility. Interviews with home care workers, the union organizers, and CHCA's president have all highlighted the importance of 1199SEIU's education benefit. CHCA's president noted that the cooperative could not afford to defray the cost of its employees to complete collegiate or continuing education courses without its partnership with 1199SEIU. For the many home care workers earning less than $8.50 per hour (excluding the value of their benefits), the cost of continuing their education represents an additional obstacle toward career advancement.

In closing, initial skepticism between CHCA and 1199SEIU has dissipated among key administrators from both organizations as they have worked together toward common goals. Our findings within an industry characterized by poor-quality jobs held by a large number of minority women suggest topics for useful future research. We highlight the importance of additional research on the potential of expanded involvement among home care workers in organizational decision making toward reducing turnover within these positions, and on the role of unions in assisting home care workers to achieve educational and occupational advancements. CHCA's success in improving the quality of its home health aide jobs—with assistance and support from 1199SEIU—highlights the potential for new collaborations between unions and employee-owned firms in addressing the quality of jobs for home health aide workers, the labor market shortages within the industry, and the quality of home care services needed by millions of elders and people with disabilities.

Acknowledgments

We would like to thank the many caring home care workers at Cooperative Home Care Associates who were willing to share their time and thoughts, as well as Guadalupe Astacio, 1199SEIU's organizer to CHCA; Michael Elsas, CHCA's president; Denise Hernandez, CHCA's director of operations; and many more CHCA administrative staff for their support of this effort.

Endnotes

[1] Michael Elsas (August 2010) in a discussion with the first co-author on the relationship between workers from Cooperative Home Care Associates and their union, 1199SEIU.

[2] The Paraprofessional Healthcare Institute (PHI), a research, policy, and training organization that works toward improving the quality of elder care and disability services by improving the jobs of direct-care workers.<http://phinational.org/>. [September 24, 2010].

[3] PHI analysis of U.S. Census Bureau, Current Population Survey, 2009 Annual Social & Economic (ASEC) Supplement, with statistical programming and data analysis provided by Carlos Figueiredo.

[4] Quality of working life (QWL) is a term used to refer to a conceptually broad group of working conditions including adequate and fair compensation, safe working conditions, opportunities to develop capabilities, free speech and the right to privacy, and socially relevant work. See Walton (1973).

[5] A high-road employer supports worker quality of life generally through, at a minimum, support for decent wages, benefits, and leave policies.

[6] The survey used in this study is an adaptation (for applicability to the home health aide job) of the National Bureau of Economic Research Shared Capitalism Survey (Kruse, Freeman, Blasi 2010). Our adaptation was intended to explore the dynamics of quality care in a worker cooperative compared to home care agencies structured as nonprofit and conventional for-profit organizations.

[7] These home health care workers may not necessarily be representative given that they were chosen since they could provide information about home health aide participation in organizational decision making and working with the union.

References

Addison, John, and Clive Belfield. 2007. "Union Voice." In James T. Bennett and Bruce E. Kaufman, eds., *What Do Unions Do?: A Twenty-Year Perspective*. New Brunswick, NJ: Transaction Publishers, pp. 238–74.

Bell, Dan. 2006. Worker-Owners and Unions: "Why Can't We Just Get Along?" *Dollars & Sense: The Magazine of Economic Justice*, September/October. <http://www.dollarsandsense.org/archives/2006/0906bell.html>. [September 24, 2010].

Bennett, James T., and Bruce E. Kaufman. 2007. "What Do Unions Do? A Twenty-Year Perspective" (preface). In James T. Bennett and Bruce E. Kaufman, eds., *What Do Unions Do?: A Twenty-Year Perspective*. New Brunswick, NJ: Transaction Publishers, pp. 1–11.

Dresser, Laura. 2008. "Cleaning and Caring in the Home: Shared Problems? Shared Possibilities?" In Annette Bernhardt, Heather Boushey, Laura Dresser, and Chris Tilly, eds., *The Gloves-Off Economy: Workplace Standards at the Bottom of America's Labor Market*. Champaign, IL: Labor and Employment Relations Association, pp. 111–35.

Freeman, Richard B. 2007. "What Do Unions Do? The 2004 M-Brane Stringtwister Edition." In James T. Bennett and Bruce E. Kaufman, eds., *What Do Unions Do?: A Twenty-Year Perspective*. New Brunswick, NJ: Transaction Publishers, pp. 607–36.

Freeman, Richard B., and James L. Medoff. 1984. *What Do Unions Do?* New York: Basic Books, Inc.

Freeman, Richard B., and Joel Rogers. 1999. *What Workers Want*. Ithaca, NY: Cornell University Press.

Inserra, A., M. Conway, and J. Rodat. 2002. *The Cooperative Home Care Associates: A Case Study of a Sectoral Employment Development Approach*. Queenstown, MD: The Aspen Institute.

Kaufman, Bruce E. 2007. "What Unions Do: Insights from Economic Theory." In James T. Bennett and Bruce E. Kaufman, eds., *What Do Unions Do?: A Twenty-Year Perspective*. New Brunswick, NJ: Transaction Publishers, pp. 12–45.

Kinsella, Kevin, and Wan He. 2009. *An Aging World: 2008, U.S. Census Bureau, International Population Reports*. P95/09-1. Washington, DC: U.S. Government Printing Office.

Kruse, Douglas, and Joseph R. Blasi. 1997. "Employee Ownership, Employee Attitudes, and Firm Performance: A Review of the Evidence." In D. Lewin, D.J.B. Mitchell, and M.A. Zaidi, eds., *Human Resources Management Handbook, Part 1*. Greenwich, CT: JAI Press, pp. 131–51.

Kruse, Douglas L., Richard B. Freeman, and Joseph R. Blasi. 2010. "Introduction." In Douglas L. Kruse, Richard B. Freeman, and Joseph R. Blasi, eds., *Shared Capitalism at Work: Employee Ownership, Profit and Gain Sharing, and Broad-Based Stock Options*. Chicago: National Bureau of Economic Research, pp. 1–37.

Logue, John, and Jacquelyn Yates. 2001. *The Real World of Employee Ownership*. Ithaca, NY: ILR Press.

Long, Richard J. 1980. "Job Attitudes and Organizational Performance Under Employee Ownership" *Academy of Management Journal*, Vol. 23, no. 4, pp. 726–37.

Walton, Richard. 1973. "Quality of Work Life: What Is It?"*Sloan Management Review,* Vol. 15, no. 1, pp. 11–21.

Whyte, William F., and Joseph R. Blasi. 1984. "Employee Ownership and the Future of Unions." *Annals of the American Academy of Political and Social Science,* Vol. 473, pp. 128–40.

CHAPTER 4

Shared Capitalism, Corporate Disclosure, and Management's Incentive to Signal a Positive Outlook

FRANCESCO BOVA
University of Toronto

Introduction

The accounting and finance literature has provided theory and evidence suggesting that higher-quality disclosure and more transparency can help a firm obtain higher firm values (i.e., stock prices), all else equal. For example, higher-quality disclosure and greater transparency have long been theorized to create shareholder value by reducing a firm's cost of capital. Separately, recent work by Bova, Dou, and Hope (2010) suggested that employee ownership may have a significant impact on improving a company's disclosure quality and overall transparency by mitigating a firm's incentive to keep information opaque in situations where its employees can use such information to extract rents from the firm (e.g., when employees are highly unionized). In this chapter, I combine the inferences from both literatures to test whether employee ownership, through its ability to improve a firm's transparency, leads to positive market outcomes for shareholders. This chapter departs from the existing literature that focuses on employee ownership as a vehicle that creates shareholder value through its ability to generate productivity gains (see, e.g., Kim and Ouimet 2009). Rather, my results suggest that employee ownership might also create shareholder value through its ability to improve the firm's transparency with not just its workers, but the market in general. This chapter therefore expands upon our understanding of the benefits of employee ownership that accrue to both the firm's employees and the firm's owners.

First, I provide a primer on voluntary disclosure, discuss its theorized effect on creating shareholder value, and describe some common metrics used to assess disclosure quality. Second, I review the literature that assesses the firm's incentive to reduce voluntary disclosures when contracting with an above-market-rent-extracting employee base (e.g., a unionized employee base) and how employee ownership can be used as a tool to both mitigate employees' ability to extract rents from the firm and improve voluntary disclosure quality. Finally, I conduct a new analysis that assesses whether employee ownership can create shareholder benefits through its ability to improve a firm's transparency. Specifically, I test whether the improved transparency that accompanies employee ownership aids financial analysts in developing expectations about future performance, and, in turn, whether firms are more likely to meet or beat those expectations, as a result. From a shareholder perspective, the implications are important because empirical evidence suggests that there are positive stock market consequences to meeting or beating financial analysts' expectations.

Consistent with my predictions, I find that unionized firms are more likely than a nonunionized control group to miss, and, in particular, just miss, analysts' expectations. The evidence suggests that this tendency to miss forecasts is driven by unionized firms providing less information to the market than their nonunionized counterparts. However, I find that unionized firms are more likely to meet or beat analysts' expectations as employee ownership increases. In contrast, I find no evidence that employee ownership causes a similar increase in the likelihood of meeting or beating expectations in a nonunionized control group. This collective evidence characterizes two novel benefits to firms utilizing employing stock ownership plans (ESOPs) in settings where employees have negotiation power. First, employee ownership appears to benefit the firm not only by aligning goals between the firm and its employees but also by increasing disclosure from the firm to all of its stakeholders by mitigating the firm's need to keep information opaque. Second, employee ownership, through its ability to improve disclosure quality, appears to generate market outcomes that benefit shareholders. Taken together, the combined results suggest a novel route through which employee ownership may satisfy the objectives of not only the firm's employees but also the firm's owners.

Voluntary Disclosure, Labor Unions, and Employee Ownership

Voluntary Disclosure

Higher-quality voluntary disclosure and increased transparency have long been theorized to create shareholder value by reducing a firm's cost of capital. Specifically, higher-quality disclosure is thought to reduce estimation risk and mitigate uncertainty regarding a firm's actual return distribution. If this estimation risk is nondiversifiable, investors require a premium to take on the extra risk. This premium should result in a higher cost of capital and lower stock prices for firms that are more opaque with the market, and a lower cost of capital and higher stock prices for firms that are more transparent with the market, all else equal. (e.g., see Coles, Lowenstein, and Suay 1995, and Lambert, Leuz, and Verrecchia 2007).

To illustrate how lowering a firm's cost of capital might improve a firm's value, I present the following commonly used discounted cash flow model:

$$X_0 = \sum_{t=0}^{N} \frac{CF_t}{(1+i)^t}$$

The variables are defined as follows: X_0 is the sum of discounted cash flows and represents the value of the firm (i.e., a firm's stock price), N is the total number of periods, CF_t is the expected cash flow in period t, i is the firm's cost of capital, and $(1 + i)^t$ is the discount factor in period t. It follows that any factor that lowers the firm's cost of capital, also lowers the firm's discount factor, $(1 + i)^t$, and in turn increases the value of the firm.

Interestingly, despite the theorized shareholder benefits to better disclosure quality, empirical evidence illustrates great variation in both the quantity and quality of voluntary disclosure across firms.[1] This variation implies that there may also be costs to full disclosure. One type of cost that may lead to variation in disclosure arises from firms' incentives to keep information opaque when various stakeholders can use firm-generated information to extract rents from the firm. The example commonly cited in the literature is that of a firm keeping information asymmetric in order to avoid revealing strategic advantages to its competitors (e.g., see Verrecchia 2001). However, other stakeholders may create a similar incentive for firms to keep information opaque. This chapter focuses on the firm's employees as a group of stakeholders who have the potential to extract above-market rents from the firm, and on management's incentive to have an opaque disclosure policy when contracting with employees who have significant negotiation leverage.

Before a discussion can begin as to why a firm might want to voluntarily disclose more information or less information, it is important to understand why researchers often focus on voluntary disclosure as opposed to mandatory disclosure as a proxy for a firm's transparency. First, researchers expect more variation in voluntary disclosure quality than mandatory disclosure quality because firms have more discretion in providing voluntary disclosure. This greater variation in voluntary disclosure quality should, in turn, lead to more powerful tests of any hypothesis that focuses on a firm's transparency. Second, evidence suggests that the stock market's response to voluntary disclosure is greater than its response to mandatory disclosure. Specifically, Beyer, Cohen, Lys, and Walther (2009) found that less than 3% of the stock return variance in a quarter occurred immediately surrounding mandatory earnings announcements and SEC filings, while just under 16% of the variance occurs around management guidance—a prominent type of voluntary disclosure. These results imply that firms disclose a large amount of information voluntarily. For readers who are unfamiliar with the voluntary disclosure literature, I provide some examples of voluntary disclosure measures that are commonly used in the accounting literature.

The first set of voluntary disclosure measures is based on management-issued guidance. Management-issued guidance is issued directly from the firm via a news release or in conjunction with the release of an earnings report. There are several measures of guidance that proxy for higher-quality disclosure. Simple measures include using the number of times a firm issues guidance in a given year and whether the firm issues any guidance in a given year. More complex measures attempt to measure both the quantity and quality of guidance. For example, Chen, Chen, and Cheng (2008) tested whether a firm's guidance contains good or bad news by assessing the market's reaction to guidance. Additionally, Francis, Nanda, and Olsson (2008) measured the specificity of the information provided in a firm's guidance, where more-specific guidance is deemed to be of higher quality. Moving to a related class of measures, researchers have also assessed conference calls as a measure of higher-quality voluntary disclosure (e.g., Brown, Hillegeist, and Lo 2004; Frankel, Mayhew, and Sun 2009), as the literature has found that firms that initiate a system of periodic conference calls exhibit a noticeable reduction in information asymmetry with the market. Finally, researchers have also focused on the readability of various disclosures as a proxy for the quality of the firm's voluntary disclosures. A commonly used measure to assess readability is the Fog index. The Fog index first creates a reading complexity score as a function of syllables per word and words per sentence and then converts the score into the average education level needed for someone to understand the prose in the document. Li (2008) showed that annual reports with a large Fog index (i.e., less readable reports) are associated with firms that observe lower earnings persistence and lower future profitability. The implicit takeaway from Li's evidence is that firms with weaker prospects for growth and profitability appear to obfuscate this information from the market by making their disclosures more complex.

Labor Unions and Disclosure

Having discussed the merits to assessing voluntary disclosure as a proxy for a firm's transparency, I review the evidence related to firms' incentives to keep information opaque when contracting with a unionized employee base. I focus on unionized employees because they are conjectured to have the ability to extract above-market rents from the firms they work for due to the collective nature of their bargaining groups. If the firm's employees have the ability to extract above-market rents from the firm (i.e., obtain wage premia above the competitive market wage), then managers may have an incentive to reduce disclosure in order to prevent those rents from being extracted. This conjecture is supported anecdotally and empirically from a variety of sources. For example, Reynolds, Masters, and Moser (1998) stated that "an important feature of the (labor) negotiations is an effort to conceal or even misrepresent one's true position." Additionally, Kleiner and Bouillon (1988) found evidence that information sharing is associated with increased bargaining power for American unions. They interpreted this result as evidence that more information enables unions to bargain more effectively and extract higher rents during negotiation. Empirical tests conducted on samples composed of publicly traded firms additionally support this hypothesis. For example, Hilary (2006) provided evidence suggesting that information asymmetry between the firm and the market is greater for firms that work in industries with higher union density. Moreover, Scott (1994) provided evidence that Canadian firms facing a higher likelihood of strikes reduce the amount of information provided on pension-related issues.

Employee Ownership and Disclosure

Finally, I discuss employee ownership's potential role in mitigating firms' incentives to have an opaque disclosure policy when contracting with a unionized employee base. Bova, Dou, and Hope (2010) posited that employee ownership may alleviate management's incentive to keep information asymmetric with a unionized employee base and, more broadly, the market in general. The hypothesis is motivated by analytical and empirical findings in Cramton, Mehran, and Tracy (2008)—an article that modeled the impact of employee ownership in a unionized setting. The Cramton, Mehran, and Tracy (2008) model demonstrated that an increase in employee stock ownership leads to a weaker bargaining position for the union, the firm becoming more amenable to initial wage demands, and a smaller number of labor disputes involving strikes. The decrease in union bargaining power arises as employee compensation becomes more closely linked to the stock returns of the firm. Thus, as employee ownership increases, any costly negotiation frictions (e.g., extended negotiations, strikes) also impact employee compensation to a greater extent.

Given this evidence, Bova, Dou, and Hope (2010) conjectured that employee ownership, through its ability to reduce both a union's bargaining power and a union's ability to extract above-market rents, should both decrease the negative consequences to disclosing information to unionized employees and mitigate the incentive for management to keep information asymmetric with the market in general. Bova, Dou, and Hope (2010) tested these conjectures using a novel set of test variables and multiple voluntary disclosure proxies. Specifically, they compared all U.S. publicly traded firms with employee stock ownership plans (ESOPs) to a sample of non-ESOP firms, matched on parameters that proxy for a firm's incentive to adopt an ESOP. As a proxy for employee ownership, their study used a binary indicator variable in which all ESOP sample firms were denoted with a 1, while all non-ESOP control firms are denoted with a 0. To proxy for employee negotiation leverage, and correspondingly the employee base's ability to extract above-market rents from the firm, the researchers utilized the unionization density of the firm's industry. Finally, the study interacted the ESOP and unionization density variables to test whether employee ownership has a larger effect on improving voluntary disclosure quality as the negotiation leverage of the employee base increases. Running multivariate tests in which voluntary disclosure proxies are separately regressed on the test variables and applicable controls produced evidence consistent with the authors' conjectures. Specifically, the authors found that, as a firm's union density increases, the firm is less likely to (1) issue management forecasts, (2) produce more forecasts on average, (3) issue more good news and bad news forecasts, (4) have higher-quality management guidance, (5) initiate and provide more conference calls, and (6) have more-readable annual reports. The results implied that firms that operate in highly unionized settings have an incentive to keep information opaque with the market. Conversely, the study found that firms with ESOPs are more likely to have higher-quality disclosure for all of the aforementioned disclosure proxies. This evidence is consistent with the finding that employee ownership reduces employee negotiation leverage and, in turn, reduces the firm's incentive to keep information opaque. Finally, the interaction between unionization rates and employee stock ownership generally revealed that, as the unionization rates of the firm's industry become greater (and implicitly, the employees' ability to extract above-market rents becomes greater), the role of employee ownership in improving disclosure quality becomes economically and significantly larger.

The collective results suggest that employee ownership may benefit the firm not only by aligning goals between the firm and its employees but also by improving transparency from the firm to all of its stakeholders, by mitigating the firm's need to keep information opaque.

Employee Ownership, Disclosure, and Market Outcomes

The results of Bova, Dou, and Hope (2010) suggested that employee ownership leads to a firm providing a richer external information environment for all of its stakeholders. For the remainder of the chapter, I hypothesize and test whether specific capital market benefits accrue to the firm following this improvement in a firm's information environment.

To start, if highly unionized firms provide less information to the market than their nonunionized counterparts then, presumably, market participants will have a more difficult time setting expectations for unionized firm performance (e.g., expected earnings or cash flows). I focus on how this information asymmetry in a unionized setting impedes a particularly important group of market participants—namely, financial analysts—from developing expectations of a firm's earnings for a quarter.

I focus on financial analysts because they play a very important role in disseminating information in capital markets. In particular, evidence suggests that the most important earnings thresholds for firms to meet or beat are the mean consensus quarterly earnings expectations set by financial analysts (see Brown and Caylor 2004, and Herrmann, Hope, Payne, and Thomas 2010). The analysts' consensus of expected earnings is defined as the average of all analyst earnings estimates for a given firm in a given quarter. Consensus analysts' earnings estimates are valued by the market because they are considered to be less obsolete than other proxies for a firm's expected earnings, such as the firm's earnings from the same quarter in the previous year. Analysts' consensus expectations are considered to be less obsolete estimates of future earnings for two reasons. First, the consensus is usually taken shortly before earnings are reported. Second, analyst expectations, unlike the other most prominent threshold—earnings from the same quarter in the previous year—are determined by more than just historical earnings information.

Specifically, evidence suggests that historical earnings, publicly available information, and privately collected information all play a role in developing analysts' expectations (Cotter, Tuna, and Wysocki 2006). Perhaps the most important factor in developing an analyst's expectation of earnings is the information provided by the firm via guidance or other disclosures. Evidence in Richardson, Teoh, and Wysocki (2004) suggests that managers know this and often voluntarily provide guidance (via various forms of disclosure) in an attempt to "walk down" analyst earnings expectations to a point where the firm can meet or beat those expectations (for brevity, I simplify "meet or beat analysts' expectations" as "MBE" for the remainder of the chapter).

The walking down of analyst expectations, also known as expectations management, is one method that managers use to MBE. Another method that managers use to MBE is to manipulate earnings higher, a process called earnings management. Evidence in DeGeorge, Patel, and Zeckhauser (1999) provides support for the notion that managers utilize either expectations management, earnings management, or a combination of the two in order to MBE, as they found evidence of a right-middle asymmetry in the distribution of analyst forecast errors. A right-middle asymmetry in the distribution of analyst forecast errors is characterized by a dearth of small negative errors (i.e., instances of reported earnings that just miss analysts' consensus estimates) and a surplus of 0 and small positive errors (i.e., instances of reported earnings that meet or just beat analysts' consensus estimates). For increased clarity, I provide an example of how a right-middle asymmetry in the distribution of forecast errors might develop. Let's assume that the analyst consensus for a firm's quarterly earnings is $1 per share. The firm knows that it will fall short of this threshold and achieve earnings per share of $0.98. Furthermore, if things stay as they are, the firm will most likely be punished by the stock market for reporting earnings that miss the consensus threshold. The firm has three options to meet or beat expectations: it can attempt to guide analysts' expectations (via some form of disclosure) to a consensus equal to or less than $0.98; it can choose, for example, less conservative accounting choices in an attempt to achieve earnings of $1 per share or greater; or it can apply a combination of the first two options. If any of these strategies succeed, the result will be that the firm generates a 0 or slightly positive analyst forecast error as opposed to a slightly negative forecast error. If the majority of firms engage in this kind of behavior, then we should observe the aforementioned right-middle asymmetry in the distribution of analyst forecast errors across all firms. The implication of this asymmetry is that managers whose reported earnings would have otherwise just missed analysts' consensus expectations will employ a combination of earnings or expectations management in order to MBE.

However, I hypothesized (Bova 2009) that there is a competing incentive for managers with unionized employees to miss earnings estimates. Specifically, I suggested that managers of unionized firms may intentionally miss analysts' estimates in order to signal a negative outlook to their unions. Interestingly, a natural outcome to unionized firms keeping information opaque with the market is that financial analysts have less information with which to construct their earnings expectations. Additionally, if nonunionized firms attempt to deflate analysts' expectations to a point where they can just meet or beat them and unionized firms do not similarly attempt to bias expectations lower, then, by construction, unionized firms should miss consensus estimates more often than their nonunionized counterparts. To summarize, a natural consequence to an opaque disclosure policy, all else equal, should be an increased propensity to miss consensus estimates; hence, we should observe highly unionized firms missing consensus estimates more often than their nonunionized counterparts.

Consistent with these predictions, I found (Bova 2009) that unionized firms were more likely than a nonunionized control group to miss, and, in particular, just miss, mean consensus analysts' earnings forecasts. The evidence also suggests that the increased tendency for unionized firms to miss consensus estimates relative to their nonunionized counterparts is driven by unionized firms providing less information to the market as opposed to unionized firms manipulating their earnings. Specifically, managers of unionized firms appear to take less action than their nonunionized counterparts to guide forecasts downward when estimates are too high—a result that is consistent with unionized firms providing less information to the market in general.

I extend this result by hypothesizing that employee ownership, through its conjectured ability to drive better disclosure in unionized firms, should aid firms in managing analysts' expectations. Specifically, if an increase in employee ownership allows unionized firms to provide more guidance to the market, it should then become easier for unionized firms to manage analysts' expectations to a point where expectations are beatable. As a result, we should expect to observe an increased propensity for unionized firms with high employee ownership to MBE relative to unionized firms with low levels of or no employee ownership. Evidence consistent with this hypothesis would be important from a capital market perspective, as the literature suggests many positive market consequences of MBE. For example, MBE has been shown to lead to not only positive abnormal stock returns on the days surrounding the firm's earnings announcement but also to higher subsequent returns (Bartov, Givoly, and Hayn 2002) and higher valuation premia (Kasznik and McNichols 2002) for those firms that MBE more often.

In the next section, I describe the sample and methodologies used to conduct the test of this hypothesis. I follow these descriptions with a discussion of the empirical results. Finally, I suggest avenues for future research based on both the collective results of the tests and the existing literature on the subject.

Data and Methodology

The primary data source I used to construct the sample was obtained from the National Center for Employee Ownership (NCEO). The NCEO ESOP Public Companies Database, created from NCEO-sponsored surveys, contains firm-specific information on types of ownership plans, number of employees, and employee ownership percentages. The database was last comprehensively updated in August 1991. Although several firms have had their data updated more recently, there are not enough data points in the periods following 1991 to conduct an effective cross-sectional analysis in those periods. Thus, my sample of firms comprised those NCEO firms with employee ownership data that had their records updated as of August 1991. By using a sample of employee ownership companies that are either unionized or nonunionized, I was able to turn two "dials" while conducting my tests. First, I could test whether different levels of employee ownership affect a unionized firm's likelihood of MBE. Second, I could assess whether employee ownership has a similar effect on a nonunionized firm's propensity to MBE. The latter test is a form of robustness check for the hypotheses discussed in this chapter. Specifically, employee ownership should have an influence on improving a firm's transparency only in the unionized setting because a firm should not have an incentive to keep information opaque in a nonunionized setting. Thus, employee ownership should lead to more guidance and an increased propensity to MBE for only the unionized subgroup. If I observe evidence of employee ownership having a similar effect in a nonunionized setting, then the results would suggest that there is another economic phenomenon at work than the one conjectured in this chapter. Finally, because my sample in 2009 (Bova 2009) spanned from the late 1990s to 2006, and Bova, Dou, and Hope (2010) spanned from 1999 to 2007, the NCEO sample, which is centered on the early 1990s, allowed for an opportunity to retest prior assertions with a different sample in a different time period.

For the NCEO firms that have data for 1991, I generated consensus quarterly forecasts and reported quarterly earnings per share (EPS) from the Institutional Brokers' Estimate System (I/B/E/S) unadjusted database.[2] I defined forecast error, FE_{iq}, as the I/B/E/S unadjusted actual EPS, E_{iq}, for firm i in quarter q less the unadjusted consensus analyst EPS forecast, F_{iq}, for firm i in quarter q. The consensus forecast is the average of analysts' most recent EPS forecasts prior to the earnings announcement for quarter q (Brown and Kim 1991).

I increased the sample size to include forecast errors from 1992 and 1993, so that the final sample spanned both periods of recession (1991) and economic recovery (1992–1993). I did not increase the sample past 1993 to mitigate the impact of obsolete employee ownership data over time.[3] Finally, if the most recent consensus forecast did not occur at least 60 days prior to the report date, I discarded the observation to mitigate the effect of obsolete estimates on the analysis. The final sample comprised 2,773 quarterly observations for 279 firms—107 of which were classified as unionized and 172 of which were classified as nonunionized. Additionally, the median level of employee ownership for the unionized (nonunionized) subsample was 9% (10%). The main empirical model was a pooled logistic regression, as follows:

$$\ln\left(\frac{p_{iq}}{1-p_{iq}}\right) = \alpha_{iq} + \beta_1 \circ UNION_i + \beta_2 \circ PCT\_OWN_i$$
$$+ \beta_3 \circ UNION_i \circ PCT\_OWN_i + \beta_4 \circ COVER_{iq} + \beta_5 \circ SIZE_i$$
$$+ \beta_6 \circ EPS\_STD_i + \beta_7 \circ GROWTH_i + \beta_8 \circ PREV\_MRE_{iq}$$
$$+ \beta_9 \circ \Delta EPS_{iq} + industry\ fixed\ effects + year\ fixed\ effects + \varepsilon \quad (1)$$

where p represents the likelihood of MBE for firm i in quarter q. MBE is equal to 1 if the forecast error for firm i in quarter q is 0 or positive and 0 if the forecast error is negative. UNION is an indicator variable that takes a value of 1 if there is evidence that a firm is at least partially unionized. I determined whether a firm had unionized employees via two routes. First, using the Lexis/Nexis and Factiva databases, I searched for news articles from 1988 onward by keying on the terms "collective bargaining," "labor union," "unionized," "unions," and "labor" with every firm in the NCEO sample. Second, I searched a database from the Bureau of Labor Statistics (the Collective Bargaining Agreement Public File), which contains over 2,000 collective bargaining agreements (CBAs) for matches with the NCEO sample. Altogether, I found evidence of 107 firms in the NCEO sample that have workforces that are at least partially unionized. Given my evidence in Bova (2009), I expected the coefficient on UNION to be signed negatively (i.e., unionized firms should be more likely to miss consensus expectations than their nonunionized counterparts). PCT_OWN is the percentage of employee ownership for firm i taken from the NCEO database. I did not have any expectation regarding its sign. UNION°PCT_OWN is an interaction variable between UNION and PCT_OWN. As per this chapter's prediction, I expected employee ownership to mitigate the incentive for unionized firms to have an opaque disclosure policy. That should, in turn, increase the likelihood of MBE in a unionized setting. Thus, I expected the coefficient on UNION°PCT_OWN to be positive.

COVER is the natural log of the number of analysts covering firm i in quarter q. Lim (2001) found that firms with greater analyst coverage were more likely to MBE. Hence, I expected the coefficient on *COVER* to be positive. *SIZE* is the natural log of the number of employees employed by firm i as listed in the NCEO database. Lim (2001) also found that bigger firms were more likely to MBE; hence, I expected *SIZE*'s coefficient to be positive. *EPS_STD* is the coefficient of variation for firm i's reported quarterly EPS from 1991 through 1993. Here, rather than divide simply by the mean, I divided by the absolute value of the mean so as not to exclude firms for which the mean was negative. *EPS_STD* is not calculated for firms with less than eight quarters of data. Lim (2001) found that the more volatile the firm-specific earnings, the more likely the firm will miss estimates; hence, I expected the coefficient on *EPS_STD* to be negative. *GROWTH* is the one-year forward price-to-earnings ratio for firm i taken by dividing the 1991 fiscal year end stock price by the 1992 I/B/E/S annual mean consensus EPS estimate, taken one year before. *GROWTH* was not calculated for any firm with negative annual mean consensus EPS estimates. Brown (2003) and Skinner and Sloan (2002) found larger negative stock price responses to missing estimates for firms with higher growth prospects. Thus, growth firms appeared to have an extra incentive to MBE. As a result, I expected the coefficient on *GROWTH* to be positively signed. *PREV_MBE* is an indicator variable that equals 1 if firm i meets or beats analyst consensus estimates in quarter q-1. ΔEPS is an indicator variable that equals 1 if firm i has 0 or positive differences in EPS between quarter q and quarter q-4. Abarbanell and Lehavy (2003) and Myers, Myers, and Skinner (2007) provided evidence of a positive link between prior performance and prior MBE and the likelihood of MBE in a current quarter. Thus, I expected the coefficients on both variables to be positively signed. Finally, I included industry-fixed effects and year-fixed effects to complete the model.

Table 1 partitions the sample by unionization/nonunionization and tests for differences between the means and medians of the variables in each subgroup. Perhaps most notably, unionized firms in the NCEO sample are significantly larger than their nonunionized counterparts. Interestingly, this should bias the sample away from finding evidence of an increased propensity for unionized firms to miss estimates, as firm size is a positive determinant of a firm's propensity to MBE. Additionally, consistent with Abarbanell and Lehavy (2003), the median forecast error for the nonunionized group is 0. Interestingly, however, the median forecast error for the unionized group is negative. Finally, untabulated results reveal that the largest sectors represented in the unionized sample are electrical utilities and oil, while the largest sectors of the nonunionized sample are banking and technology.

TABLE 1

Descriptive Statistics of the NCEO Sample Partitioned by Union/Nonunion Firms.

Variable	Full sample				Union sample				Nonunion sample				Test for differences of the means (p-value)	Wilcoxon tests (p-value)
	N	Mean	Median	Std. Dev.	N	Mean	Median	Std. Dev.	N	Mean	Median	Std. Dev.		
FE	2773	-0.022	0.000	0.383	1168	-0.023	-0.010	0.344	1605	-0.022	0.000	0.409	0.9777	0.0069
PCT_OWN	2773	0.114	0.090	0.072	1168	0.116	0.090	0.076	1605	0.114	0.100	0.068	0.4779	0.1365
COVER	2773	1.538	1.609	0.921	1168	1.992	2.197	0.767	1605	1.208	1.099	0.883	<.0001	<.0001
SIZE	2763	8.738	8.700	1.739	1168	9.665	9.898	1.576	1595	8.060	8.006	1.527	<.0001	<.0001
EPS_STD	2594	1.660	0.468	5.240	1149	1.741	0.473	6.222	1445	1.595	0.468	4.303	0.4962	0.0026
GROWTH	2612	9.580	6.705	11.725	1101	11.257	7.774	13.038	1511	8.358	5.930	10.505	<.0001	<.0001
PREV_MBE	2692	0.516	1.000	0.500	1135	0.479	0.000	0.500	1557	0.543	1.000	0.498	0.0011	0.0012
ΔEPS	2756	0.549	1.000	0.498	1164	0.511	1.000	0.500	1592	0.576	1.000	0.494	0.0007	0.0001

Variable Definitions: FE is the firm quarter-specific forecast error, taking the I/B/E/S unadjusted reported EPS for firm i in quarter q and subtracting the most recent I/B/E/S unadjusted mean consensus forecast estimate for firm i in quarter q. PCT_OWN is the percentage of firm i owned by its employees taken from the NCEO database. $COVER$ is the natural log of the number of analysts covering firm i in quarter q. $SIZE$ is the natural log of the number of employees employed by firm i as listed in the NCEO database. EPS_STD is the standard deviation of firm i's I/B/E/S unadjusted reported EPS values over the sample period divided by the absolute value of the mean of the reported EPS values. EPS_STD is constructed only for firms with at least eight quarters of data. $GROWTH$ is the forward price-to-earnings ratio for firm i taken by dividing firm stock price (from the CRSP tapes) taken at the firm's 1991 fiscal year end by the 1992 I/B/E/S unadjusted mean consensus annual EPS estimate, taken one year before. $PREV\_MBE$ is an indicator variable that equals 1 if firm i meets or beats analyst consensus estimates in quarter $q-1$. ΔEPS is an indicator variable that equals 1 if firm i has zero or positive differences in EPS between quarter q and quarter $q-4$. The Tests for Differences of the Means and Wilcoxon Tests columns provide the p-values for each test.

Distribution of Analyst Forecast Errors

The median value for employee ownership for the whole NCEO sample is 9%. Thus, I classified firms with between 0% and 9% employee ownership as having low employee ownership. I labeled the group of unionized and nonunionized firms with low employee ownership, Union/Low and Nonunion/Low, respectively. I classified firms with employee ownership of greater than 9% as having high employee ownership. I labeled the group of unionized and nonunionized firms with high employee ownership, Union/High and Nonunion/High, respectively.

Table 2 contains an assessment of the statistical significance of any asymmetries in each group's distribution of analyst forecast errors. Table 2, column A, illustrates that unionized firms in the sample have a significantly higher proportion of negative forecast errors to positive forecast errors than their nonunionized counterparts. Thus, unionized firms appeared to miss analysts' consensus estimates more often than their nonunionized counterparts. Table 2, columns B and C, display evidence of a significant left-middle asymmetry in the distribution of

TABLE 2

Ratios of Positive to Negative Analyst Forecast Errors for the NCEO Sample Along Different Subsets of the Forecast Error Distribution.

		A	B	C	D
Group	N	Ratio of positive to negative forecast errors [Min, 0) & (0, Max]	Ratio of positive to negative forecast errors [−.02, 0) & (0, .02]	Ratio of positive to negative forecast errors [−.01, 0) & (0, .01]	Ratio of positive to negative forecast errors [Min, −.30] & [.30, Max]
Union	1168	0.851°°°	0.793°°	0.647°°°	0.685°
Nonunion	1605	1.084°°	0.969	0.896	0.851
Union/Low	605	0.822°°°	0.633°°°	0.479°°°	0.692
Union/High	563	0.883°°	1.033	0.865	0.679
Nonunion/Low	789	1.096°	1.055	1.030	0.684
Nonunion/High	816	1.072	0.893	0.768	1.069

Variable Definitions: *Forecast errors* are calculated by taking the I/B/E/S unadjusted reported EPS for firm i in quarter q and subtracting the most recent I/B/E/S unadjusted mean consensus estimate for firm i in quarter q. *Union/Low* represents all forecast errors for unionized firms with 9% or less employee ownership. *Union/High* represents all forecast errors for unionized firms with more than 9% employee ownership. *Nonunion/Low* represents all forecast errors for nonunionized firms with 9% or less employee ownership. *Nonunion/High* represents all forecast errors for nonunionized firms with more than 9% employee ownership. °, °°, °°° indicate significance at the 10%, 5%, and 1% level, respectively, for a two-tailed z-test that tests the difference in proportions.

the unionized subgroup, illustrating that unionized firms were also more likely to just miss consensus estimates than their nonunionized counterparts. However, when the distribution of forecast errors is partitioned by both unionization and employee ownership, there is a significant left-middle asymmetry in the distribution of only the Union/Low subgroup. Thus, the results shown in Table 2, columns B and C, provide preliminary evidence to support the hypothesis that managers of unionized firms have an incentive to just miss estimates, but that this tendency is mitigated as employee ownership increases. Finally, Table 2, column D, illustrates that, while a left tail asymmetry exists in the distribution of errors for three of the four subgroups, none of the left tail asymmetries are significant at the 5% level.

Regression Results

Moving from the preliminary analysis of asymmetries in the forecast error distribution, I assessed the impact of unionization and employee ownership on a firm's likelihood of MBE by conducting multivariate tests using the logistic regression specified in Equation (1). As shown in Table 3, Models 1 and 2, I tested multivariate models incorporating UNION and UNION°PCT_OWN, my variables of interest. In Model 1, the coefficient on UNION is significantly negative, suggesting that, on average, unionized firms are less likely to MBE than their nonunionized counterparts. Additionally, the coefficient on UNION°PCT_OWN is positive, significant, and of a greater magnitude than the coefficient on PCT_OWN, indicating that, as employee ownership increases in a unionized context, the probability of MBE also increases.

Model 2 provides a more refined test for earnings or expectations management by truncating the distribution of forecast errors used for the analysis to include only those forecast errors between [−.02, .02]. I truncated the distribution, as the analyst error literature found a right-middle asymmetry in the distribution of forecast errors right around 0 and not in the left and right tails of the distribution. The implication is that managers often manage earnings or expectations so that earnings that would otherwise just miss hitting expectations instead meet or just beat them. Model 2 continues to exhibit a significant negative coefficient on UNION and a positive coefficient on UNION°PCT_OWN at the 1% and 5% level, respectively, with all controls signed as predicted.

Using the parameter estimates in Model 2, I assessed the marginal effect of the variables of interest on the likelihood of MBE relative to the baseline probability of MBE.[4] The marginal effect of unionization is the change in the likelihood of MBE relative to the baseline probability when UNION is increased from 0 to 1. The marginal effect of employee ownership in a unionized setting is the change in the likelihood of MBE relative to the baseline probability when PCT_OWN is increased from one standard deviation below its mean value to one standard deviation above its mean value and where UNION equals 1. The marginal effect of switching UNION from 0 to 1 decreases the likelihood of MBE by 7.86%. When UNION equals 1, the marginal effect of a one-standard-deviation increase in PCT_OWN about its mean increases the likelihood of MBE by 15.69%.

Taken together, the results imply that managers of unionized firms are more likely to miss, and in particular just miss, analyst forecasts than their nonunionized counterparts and that this tendency is substantially mitigated by employee ownership. These results are consistent with both Bova (2009) and the conjectures of this chapter.

Earnings Management to Meet or Beat Other Thresholds and an Implicit Test of Expectations Management

Finally, I constructed a test to explore whether unionized firms have a higher propensity to miss two other important thresholds and whether the propensity to miss them is mitigated by employee ownership. While analysts' consensus estimates are the most important threshold for firms to meet or beat, DeGeorge, Patel, and Zeckhauser (1999) also found that managers have an incentive to meet or beat two other thresholds: an EPS of 0 and quarterly earnings from four quarters previous. I categorized these two thresholds as strictly earnings-based thresholds. While MBE can arise as a function of either earnings or expectations management, manipulations used to meet or beat the strictly earnings-based thresholds can be achieved only as a function of earnings management. I suggest that assessing the impact of unionization and employee ownership on the likelihood of meeting or beating the strictly earnings-based thresholds is important for two reasons.

First, if earnings management plays a role in the MBE test results of Table 3, Models 1 and 2, we may also expect to observe earnings management around the two strictly earnings-based thresholds. If there is evidence of both unionized firms having an incentive to miss thresholds other than analysts' consensus estimates and employee ownership mitigating this tendency, then my collective results may simply illustrate that unionized firms are more likely to miss important thresholds in general, as opposed to analyst estimates in particular. Second, if I do not find evidence of unionized firms missing the strictly earnings-based thresholds, then implicitly, I suggest that the results in Table 3, Models 1 and 2, are consistent with unionized firms providing less guidance and disclosure to the market, and employee ownership mitigating this incentive to provide less guidance.

TABLE 3
Logit Regression of the Likelihood of Firms Meeting or Beating Various Thresholds.

| | Pred. | Thresholds | | | | | |
| | | Analyst estimates | | EPS = Zero | | Seasonally differenced earnings | |
		Model 1	Model 2	Model 3	Model 4	Model 5	Model 6
Intercept		−0.522	−0.676	3.073°°°	−0.238	−0.517°°°	−0.546
(std. error)		(0.409)	(0.678)	(0.729)	(2.224)	(0.384)	(0.616)
UNION	−	−0.510°°	−0.907°°°	0.206	−0.577	0.206	0.821°°
(std. error)		(0.200)	(0.350)	(0.369)	(1.063)	(0.189)	(0.290)
PCT_OWN	?	−2.168°°	−1.585	0.457	6.052	0.330	1.116
(std. error)		(0.967)	(1.419)	(1.964)	(7.163)	(0.910)	(1.290)
UNION° PCT_OWN	+	2.679°°	5.123°°	−1.364	−2.008	−1.185	−4.122°°
(std. error)		(1.323)	(2.150)	(2.514)	(8.922)	(1.245)	(1.828)
COVER	+	0.091	0.024	0.750°°°	0.529	−0.143°°	−0.072
(std. error)		(0.073)	(0.120)	(0.129)	(0.413)	(0.070)	(0.104)
SIZE	+	0.051	0.143°°	−0.210°°°	−0.244	0.061°	0.059
(std. error)		(0.039)	(0.066)	(0.071)	(0.198)	(0.037)	(0.056)
EPS_STD	−	−0.024°°	−0.016	−0.069°°°	−0.004	0.001	0.003
(std. error)		(0.009)	(0.019)	(0.012)	(0.075)	(0.009)	(0.015)
GROWTH	+	−0.010°°	0.008	−0.045°°°	0.018	−0.003	−0.005
(std. error)		(0.005)	(0.009)	(0.007)	(0.022)	(0.005)	(0.007)
PREV_MBE	+	0.414°°°	0.040	0.751°°°	0.742	0.667°°°	0.581°°°
(std. error)		(0.091)	(0.148)	(0.184)	(0.512)	(0.086)	(0.132)
ΔEPS	+	1.487°°°	0.371°°	1.257°°°	0.288	—	—
(std. error)		(0.092)	(0.152)	(0.192)	(0.441)		
Year fixed effects		yes	yes	yes	yes	yes	yes
Industry fixed effects		yes	yes	yes	yes	yes	yes
Pseudo R₂		12.62%	3.13%	21.00%	21.28%	5.01%	4.20%
N		2405	824	2405	254	2405	1108

Variable Definitions: In Models 1 and 2, the binary dependent variable equals 1 if firm i meets or beats analyst mean consensus estimates in quarter q. In Model 2, I truncate the sample to include only those firm quarters with forecast errors in the range [−.02, .02]. In Models 3 and 4, the binary dependent variable equals 1 if firm i has zero or positive earnings in quarter q. In Model 4, I truncate the sample to include only those firm quarters with EPS in the range [−.10, .10]. In Models 5 and 6, the binary dependent variable equals 1 if firm i has zero or positive seasonal differences in quarter q. In Model 6, I truncate the sample to include only those firm quarters with seasonal EPS differences in the range [−.10, .10]. UNION is an indicator variable that equals 1 if there is evidence that firm i has at least a partially unionized employee base, post-1988. PCT_OWN is the percentage of firm i owned by its employees, taken from the NCEO database. COVER is the natural log of the number of analysts covering firm i in quarter q. SIZE is the natural log of the number of employees employed by firm i as listed in the NCEO database. EPS_STD is the standard deviation of firm i's I/B/E/S unadjusted reported EPS values over the sample period divided by the absolute value of the mean of the reported EPS values. GROWTH is the forward price-to-earnings ratio for firm i taken by dividing firm stock price (from the CRSP tapes) taken at the firm's 1991 fiscal year end by the 1992 I/B/E/S unadjusted mean consensus annual EPS estimate, taken one year before. PREV_MBE is an indicator variable that equals 1 if firm i meets or beats analyst consensus estimates in quarter q-1. ΔEPS is an indicator variable that equals 1 if firm i has zero or positive differences in EPS between quarter q and quarter q-4. Year fixed effects incorporate indicator variables for 1991 and 1992. Industry fixed effects incorporate indicator variables for each I/B/E/S sector name. °, °°, °°° indicate significance at the 10%, 5%, and 1% level, respectively.

In two separate tests, I re-ran the logit model specified in Equation (1) but with redefined dependent variables. For the first test, p is the probability that firm i generates 0 or positive EPS in quarter q. For the second test, p is the probability that firm i meets or beats quarterly EPS from four quarters previous.

Table 3, Models 3 and 4, shows the likelihood of a firm in the NCEO sample reporting 0 or positive quarterly EPS. Model 3 tested the full sample, while Model 4 truncated the distribution to incorporate errors where EPS falls between [–.10, .10].[5] I truncated the EPS distribution in Model 4, because, much like the analyst error distribution, there tends to be a right-middle asymmetry in the distribution of EPS around 0. This right-middle asymmetry implies that managers often manage earnings so that EPS that would otherwise be slightly negative becomes 0 or slightly positive. Models 3 and 4 reveal that the coefficient on UNION is insignificant, while the coefficient on UNION*PCT_OWN is insignificant and signed incorrectly relative to the hypotheses in this chapter.

Table 3, Models 5 and 6, demonstrates the likelihood of a firm in the NCEO sample observing a 0 or positive change in seasonally differenced earnings. Model 5 tested the full sample, while Model 6 truncated the distribution to incorporate errors where seasonal differences fall between [–.10, .10]. As above, I truncated the seasonally differenced earnings distribution in Model 6 because there tends to be a right-middle asymmetry in the distribution of seasonally differenced earnings around 0. This right-middle asymmetry implies that managers often manage earnings so that earnings that would otherwise be slightly less than the earnings the firm reported for the same quarter in the previous year become 0 or slightly greater. Models 5 and 6 reveal that the coefficients on UNION and UNION*PCT_OWN, although both statistically significant in Model 6, are both signed incorrectly relative to the hypotheses in this chapter.

The collective evidence from Table 3, Models 3 through 6, suggests that unionized firms are neither more likely to miss strictly earnings-based thresholds nor more likely to meet or beat them as employee ownership increases. The results are consistent with the previous literature and consistent with the claim that the results of the MBE tests in Models 1 and 2 are at least partially driven by the impact of unions and employee ownership on shaping management's incentive to provide information to the market. The latter point is consistent with evidence in Bova (2009), which found that unionized firms display an increased propensity to miss estimates due to an absence of guidance provided to analysts, and not due to the manipulation of earnings.

Conclusion

Consistent with my findings in 2009, I found that unionized firms are more likely to miss, and, in particular, just miss, analyst estimates when compared with a nonunionized control group. The evidence suggests that the missed estimates arise due to a lack of expectations management as opposed to earnings management. Incremental to the contribution in Bova (2009), I also found that a unionized firm's likelihood of missing estimates is mitigated by an increase in employee ownership and that employee ownership does not have a similar effect on nonunionized firms. These results are consistent with employee ownership mitigating a firm's incentive to maintain an opaque disclosure policy in a unionized setting.

The results of this chapter and those of Bova (2009) and Bova, Dou, and Hope (2010) provide evidence of positive links between employee stock ownership and the quantity of disclosure, the quality of disclosure, and the likelihood of producing positive profitability signals through an increased propensity to MBE. Having drawn these links, I now combine them with other inferences from both the finance and accounting literature to suggest several avenues for research into employee stock ownership's role in creating shareholder value.

To begin, I revisit the discounted cash flow model discussed earlier. When valuing a company's stock, asset pricers will often use a discounted cash flow model as follows:

$$X_0 = \sum_{t=0}^{N} \frac{CF_t}{(1+i)^t}$$

Any factor that affects expected cash flows, CF_t, is thought of as having a "numerator effect" on the sum of discounted cash flows. Alternately, any factor that affects the discount factor, $(1+i)^t$, is thought of as having a "denominator effect" on the sum of discounted cash flows. Traditionally, when considering an ESOP's effect on discounted cash flows, an asset pricer might point to an ESOP's role in generating higher employee loyalty, lower turnover, or higher productivity as factors that will increase the future cash flows accruing to shareholders. Thus, the adoption of an ESOP has historically been thought to increase shareholder value via productivity gains that increase expected cash flows or, in other words, through a positive numerator effect on the valuation model.

As I suggest previously in this chapter, the accounting literature has also theorized and found evidence that higher-quality disclosure leads to a decrease in a firm's cost of capital by reducing the firm's information asymmetry with the market (see, e.g., Francis, LaFond, Olsson, and Schipper 2004, 2005). Thus, it is also possible that employee ownership may have a positive denominator effect on the valuation model through its impact on improving disclosure quality and, in turn, a firm's cost of capital. Additionally, the accounting literature has conjectured that higher-quality disclosure has a real effect in that it improves a firm's action space for possible investments (see Gao 2010). If we further assume that a firm's expected cash flows are increasing in its opportunity for investment, then employee ownership may subtly provide another positive numerator effect on the valuation model by improving the firm's investment opportunities.

Disentangling these novel routes through which employee ownership potentially creates shareholder value should not only provide interesting paths for future research but also continue to inform the ongoing debate as to the merits of employee ownership. Building on the latter point, the results presented to date and the avenues for future research discussed in this chapter provide more fodder for the argument that employee ownership remains a unique tool that increases the welfare of not only the firm's employees but also its shareholders and other, non-shareholder stakeholders.

Endnotes

[1] Beyer, Cohen, Lys, and Walther (2009) provided an extensive review of this literature.

[2] The I/B/E/S database provided analyst estimate dates, actual earnings, and report dates for all firms with analyst coverage. I used unadjusted quarterly data to mitigate the effect of I/B/E/S-related rounding errors discussed in Payne and Thomas (2003).

[3] The potential for obsolescence in the employee ownership data is exacerbated by the effect of regulatory changes in the 1990s that led to leveraged ESOPs becoming more costly on the income statement. This regulatory change led to many firms finding ESOPs less attractive and, presumably, affected the NCEO employee ownership percentages over time (Case, Staubus, and Rosen 2005).

[4] The baseline probability of MBE is the probability of MBE when all continuous independent variables are held at their means and indicator variables are held at 0.

[5] I used a wider range of errors for Table 3, Models 4 and 6, than I did in Table 3, Model 2, because the distribution of analyst forecast errors is less tightly concentrated around 0 for the EPS and seasonally differenced EPS distributions. Thus, by widening the range, I allowed for more observations in each strictly earnings-based threshold test. However, all results for the strictly earnings-based threshold tests remain robust to including only those errors that fall in the range between [−.02, .02].

References

Abarbanell, Jeffrey, and Reuven Lehavy. 2003. "Biased Forecasts or Biased Earnings? The Role of Reported Earnings in Explaining Analyst Bias and Over/Underreaction in Analysts' Earnings Forecasts." *Journal of Accounting and Economics*, Vol. 36, pp. 105–46.

Bartov, Eli, Dan Givoly, and Carla Hayn. 2002. "The Rewards to Meeting or Beating Earnings Expectations." *Journal of Accounting and Economics*, Vol. 33, pp. 173–204.

Beyer, Anne, Daniel Cohen, Thomas Lys, and Beverly Walther. 2009. "The Financial Reporting Environment: Review of the Recent Literature." *Journal of Accounting and Economics*, forthcoming.

Bova, Francesco. 2009. *Labor Unions and Management's Incentive to Signal a Negative Outlook*. Unpublished paper, University of Toronto.

Bova, Francesco, Yiwei Dou, and Ole-Kristian Hope. 2010. *Employee Ownership and Firm Disclosure*. Unpublished paper, University of Toronto.

Brown, Lawrence. 2003. "Small Negative Surprises: Frequency and Consequence." *International Journal of Forecasting*, Vol. 19, pp. 149–59.

Brown, Lawrence, and Marcus Caylor. 2004. "A Temporal Analysis of Quarterly Earnings Thresholds: Propensities and Valuation Consequences." *The Accounting Review*, Vol. 80, pp. 423–40.

Brown, Lawrence, and Kwon-Jung Kim. 1991. "Timely Aggregate Analyst Forecasts as Better Proxies for Market Earnings Expectations." *Journal of Accounting Research*, Vol. 29, pp. 382–85.

Brown, Stephen, Stephen Hillegeist, and Kin Lo. 2004. "Conference Calls and Information Asymmetry." *Journal of Accounting and Economics*, Vol. 37, pp. 343–66.

Case, John, Martin Staubus, and Corey Rosen. 2005. *Equity: Why Employee Ownership Is Good for Business*. Boston: Harvard Business School Press.

Chen, Shuping, Xia Chen, and Qiang Cheng. 2008. "Do Family Firms Provide More or Less Voluntary Disclosure?" *Journal of Accounting Research*, Vol. 46, pp. 499–536.

Coles, Jeffrey, Uri Loewenstein, and Jose Suay. 1995. "On Equilibrium Pricing Under Parameter Uncertainty." *Journal of Financial and Quantitative Analysis*, Vol. 30, pp. 347–74.

Cotter, Julie, Irem Tuna, and Peter Wysocki. 2006. "Expectations Management and Beatable Targets: How Do Analysts React to Explicit Earnings Guidance?" *Contemporary Accounting Research*, Vol. 23, pp. 593–628.

Cramton, Peter, Hamid Mehran, and Joseph Tracy. 2008. *ESOP Fables: The Impact of Employee Stock Ownership Plans on Labor Disputes*. FRB of New York Staff Report. No. 347. New York: Federal Reserve Bank.

DeGeorge, Francois, Jayendu Patel, and Richard Zeckhauser. 1999. "Earnings Management to Exceed Thresholds." *Journal of Business*, Vol. 72, pp. 1–33.

Francis, Jennifer, Ryan LaFond, Per Olsson, and Katherine Schipper. 2004. "Costs of Equity and Earnings Attributes." *The Accounting Review*, Vol. 79, pp. 967–1010.

Francis, Jennifer, Ryan LaFond, Per Olsson, and Katherine Schipper. 2005. "The Market Pricing of Accruals Quality." *Journal of Accounting and Economics*, Vol. 39, pp. 295–327.

Francis, Jennifer, Dhananjay Nanda, and Per Olsson. 2008. "Voluntary Disclosure, Earnings Quality, and Cost of Capital." *Journal of Accounting Research*, Vol. 46, pp. 53–99.

Frankel, Richard, William Mayhew, and Yan Sun. 2009. "Do Pennies Matter? Investor Relations Consequences of Small Negative Earnings Surprises." *Review of Accounting Studies*, Vol. 15, pp. 220–42.

Gao, Pingyang. 2010. "Disclosure Quality, Cost of Capital, and Investors' Welfare." *The Accounting Review*, Vol. 85, pp. 1–29.

Herrmann, Don, Ole-Kristian Hope, Jeff Payne, and Wayne Thomas. 2010. "The Market's Reaction to Unexpected Earnings Thresholds." *Journal of Business, Finance, and Accounting*, forthcoming.

Hilary, Gilles. 2006. "Organized Labor and Information Asymmetry in the Financial Markets." *Review of Accounting Studies*, Vol. 11, pp. 525–48.

Kasznik, Ron, and Maureen McNichols. 2002. "Does Meeting Expectations Matter? Evidence from Analyst Revisions and Share Prices." *Journal of Accounting Research*, Vol. 40, pp. 727–9.

Kim, E. Han, and Paige Ouimet. 2009. *Employee Capitalism or Corporate Socialism? Broad-Based Employee Stock Ownership.* Unpublished paper, University of Michigan and University of North Carolina.

Kleiner, Morris, and Marvin Bouillon. 1988. "Providing Business Information to Production Workers: Correlates of Compensation and Profitability." *Industrial and Labor Relations Review*, Vol. 41, pp. 605–17.

Lambert, Richard, Christian Leuz, and Robert Verrecchia. 2007. "Accounting Information, Disclosure, and the Cost of Capital." *Journal of Accounting Research*, Vol. 45, pp. 385–420.

Li, Feng. 2008. "Annual Report Readability, Current Earnings, and Earnings Persistence." *Journal of Accounting and Economics*, Vol. 45, pp. 221–47.

Lim, Terence. 2001. "Rationality and Analysts' Forecast Bias." *The Journal of Finance*, Vol. 56, pp. 369–85.

Myers, James, Linda Myers, and Douglas Skinner. 2007. *Earnings Momentum and Earnings Management.* Unpublished paper. Available at SSRN<http://ssrn.com/abstract=741244>.

Payne, Jeffrey, and Wayne Thomas. 2003. "The Implications of Using Stock-Split Adjusted I/B/E/S Data in Empirical Research." *The Accounting Review*, Vol. 78, pp. 1049–67.

Reynolds, Lloyd G., Stanley H. Masters, and Colletta H. Moser. 1998. *Labor Economics and Labor Relations* (11th ed.). Upper Saddle River, NJ: Prentice Hall.

Richardson, Scott, Siew Hong Teoh, and Peter Wysocki. 2004. "The Walk-Down to Beatable Analyst Forecasts: The Role of Equity Issuance and Insider Trading Incentives." *Contemporary Accounting Research*, Vol. 21, pp. 885–924.

Scott, Thomas. 1994. "Incentives and Disincentives for Financial Disclosure: Voluntary Disclosure of Defined Benefit Pension Plan Information from Canadian Firms." *The Accounting Review*, Vol. 69, pp. 26–43.

Skinner, Douglas, and Richard Sloan. 2002. "Earnings Surprises, Growth Expectations, Stock Returns, or Don't Let an Earnings Torpedo Sink your Portfolio." *Review of Accounting Studies*, Vol. 7, pp. 289–312.

Verrecchia, Robert. 2001. "Essays on Disclosure." *Journal of Accounting and Economics*, Vol. 32, pp. 97–180.

CHAPTER 5

Employee Ownership, Democratic Control, and Working-Class Empowerment

JOAN S.M. MEYERS
Rutgers University

Introduction

Organizational scholars and workplace equality advocates have largely dismissed the ability of democratic employee ownership to deliver power and autonomy to working-class employees.[1] This chapter addresses this gap by investigating how two 100% employee-owned and democratically governed worker-owned cooperatives (businesses where employees are both the owners and the directors of their workplaces) succeeded and failed to give working-class people control over their workplaces. This study addresses the ability of democratic employee ownership to create working-class empowerment, to extend power and autonomy within a context of the necessary economic enfranchisement to enjoy it. The chapter reveals that democratic employee ownership *can* create working-class empowerment, but it requires formal and nonhierarchical organizational structures supported by organizational narratives that recognize the legitimate and intersecting importance of both race/ethnicity and gender with class in the workplace.

Shared capitalism's goal of aligning worker and owner interests, in industries ranging from elite high-tech companies to blue-collar manufacturing and service organizations, has tended to focus exclusively on *wealth* despite the urging from some quarters to focus equally on worker power and autonomy issues in developing "ownership culture" (Rosen, Case, and Staubus 2005). Prior to the 1950s, worker *control* was just as important to labor and other social movements as increased *wages* (Polletta 2002). Most shared capitalist firms, however, ignore this history and reproduce the typical workplace stratification of power: managers have it, and nonmanagers do not. While worker cooperatives—a small subset of employee ownership (EO) companies—offer their employees far more equitable distributions of power and autonomy as well as wealth, they have historically been unable to recruit and/or retain working-class employees. The reasons are varied (including an inability to compete in the market leading to substandard wages, a rejection of new members by founders leading to a two-tiered system more like a limited partnership, and cultural differences among classes that affect how power is shared), but this has largely rendered worker cooperatives incapable of extending their empowerment benefits to the working class. Thus, worker cooperatives, like other forms of EO, have seemed unfeasible sites from which to advance working-class empowerment.

This chapter demonstrates, however, the potential of worker cooperatives for greater working-class enfranchisement by analyzing the experience of two successful and stable companies doing business for over a quarter century. More specifically, this chapter reveals that empowerment is not only a matter of increasing the proportion of working-class employees, more equitably distributing profits across positions or levels within the firm, or even having a more explicit class mission. Both the industrial-scale organic bakery and the natural foods supermarket worker cooperatives on which this study focuses had a majority of working-class employees performing working-class jobs, and both developed egalitarian profit-sharing across differences of skill, responsibility, and tenure. Yet the bakery's managerial control combined with its organizational narratives about race, class, and gender stratified rewards, while the grocery's worker control and its organizational narratives distributed these rewards far more broadly. This chapter outlines how the interaction of each company's (1) direction of power (horizontal or vertical); (2) degree of organizational formality (the use of standardized and usually written documents to effect processes, procedures, and policies); and (3) organizational narratives, or internal discursive constructions about its workers, significantly shaped how power and autonomy were distributed within class and across race/ethnicity and gender, resulting in profoundly different degrees of working-class inclusion.

The analysis presented in this chapter draws upon and expands the work of Joan Acker, who has argued that all organizations have *inequality regimes*—"loosely interrelated practices, processes, actions, and meanings that result in and maintain class, gender, and racial inequalities within particular organizations"(Acker 2006b:443)—that vary in intensity. She theorized that *hierarchy* bolsters workplace inequality by assigning more value (and resulting wealth, power, and autonomy) to some skills than others, regardless of companies' need for all levels of skills. Further, workplace hierarchies obscure the larger social processes that unequally develop or allow recognition of such skills across class, race/ethnicity, and gender. The findings presented here support her theory, revealing that social inequalities are increased or minimized by the degree to which control is organized vertically or horizontally, and the findings further illuminate the effect of *formal rules and procedures* on the direction of power. As an earlier generation of scholars of democratic and social justice organizations have argued, the degree to which power is formalized through explicit rules about who can use it, and how, affects the organization's ability to disrupt pre-existing class (Freeman 1970, 1984; Mansbridge 1980), ethnoracial (Mansbridge 1980; Sirianni 1993), and gender inequalities (Kleinman 1996). In those earlier studies as in this one, informal power is found to be too easily appropriated by those whose classed, raced, and/or gendered cultural capital—in the form of research and writing abilities, public speaking skills, or simply confidence—trumps that of subordinated others. Yet formality *in itself* does not create greater equality: this research indicates that, when paired with hierarchy, formality can create further disparities of power and autonomy. Only when formality institutionalizes democratic and broadly distributed power does it positively affect working-class empowerment.

Yet organizational structure cannot be viewed in isolation. Organizational narratives are critical to an understanding of working-class empowerment in light of demographic changes: the American working class is increasingly composed of men and women of color and white women (Bettie 1995), despite entrenched and hegemonic beliefs about the whiteness and maleness of "the working class" (Rose 1997). I extend Acker's theory by examining organizational narratives about ethnicity/race, class, and gender, rather than focusing only on organizational demographics. That is, rather than assuming that gender, race, or class have an inherent meaning across time and space, I focus on the ways in which they become salient in the workplace. This research shows that organizational narratives legitimate and naturalize different firm-level structures of power in similar demographic settings. Narrower organizational conceptions of workers support hierarchical managerial control and make it seem inevitable, which concentrates power in the historically dominant white male sector of the working class. More expansive narratives demand a broader distribution of worker control across mixed-gender and mixed race/ethnicity working-class organizational populations, and make such distributions appear necessary to achieve both democratic and economic organizational goals.

In the sections that follow, I outline histories of workplace attempts to deliver economic and social empowerment across class, and I describe my methods and the backgrounds of the two cases compared in this study, "People's Daily Bread Bakery" and "One World Natural

Grocery."[2] I examine the class effects of differences in organizational structure and the way formality interacts with both managerial and worker control in these two bureaucracies. I then describe the supporting role of organizational narratives before outlining interconnections between organizational power, formal practices and policies, and organizational narratives. I conclude with a series of challenges this research raises for studies of EO, participatory democracy, and class in the workplace.

Worker Ownership and Working-Class Empowerment

From its earliest days, one of the goals of worker ownership has been to improve the opportunities of working-class people. However, class is not instantly transformed when employees assume ownership. An *individual* change in relationship to the means of production—from employed to co-owner—does not transform the larger *social* and *cultural orders* that assign individuals particular status and material possibilities. Class continues to have material effects in how it shapes access to housing, residential stability, and education, all of which affect ability to attain and keep a job. It also has pernicious effects that are less material and more cultural: a sense of confidence, of belonging, and of entitlement that combine to create *cultural capital* (Bourdieu 1986). Class stratification includes not only inequalities of wealth but also of access to, and enjoyment of, power and autonomy over key aspects of one's life. To be working class, then, is to have less access to wealth, power, and autonomy—inequalities that worker ownership can only address on an individual rather than societal level. Such inequalities are also outcomes of gendered and ethnoracialized social processes, but it would be a mistake to view class stratification as separable from these other forms. Class inequality is always achieved *through* inequalities of gender and ethnicity/race. This intersectional approach to class (P.H. Collins 1990), therefore, demands that class be seen as both subjective and objective, as well as deeply interpenetrated by (but not reducible to) gender and ethnoracial inequality.

Given the inroads made by shared capitalism into industries employing high numbers of working-class employees, EO studies potentially offer a wealth of insight about working-class empowerment. Twenty percent of the U.S. workforce participated in EO by the first decade of the 21st century (Kruse, Blasi, and Park 2010). EO, however, is typically confined to partial ownership, does not necessarily incorporate group decision-making or governance aspects, and does not necessarily extend to a company's entire workforce. Further, minimal inequality research has been conducted on these firms. That is, it is unclear which workers are more or less involved and how that involvement translates into workplace rewards such as job satisfaction, wealth, or power. What research exists indicates that EO does little to mitigate effects of occupational segregation on job access, wealth accumulation, and access to power, and, in some cases, exacerbates the effects of other workplace inequality mechanisms (Carberry 2010). While more studies of the relationship between EO and inequality are needed, it seems clear that ownership alone (particularly when stratified within companies) has little positive effect on class inequalities.

Despite the overt concentration of ownership and control into employee hands, worker-owned cooperatives—companies entirely owned and operated by their employees—have also historically fallen short of success in working-class empowerment. North American and European socialist, populist, utopian, and labor social movements advocated worker ownership to promote humane working conditions and equal access to the fruits of workers' labor and helped to develop thousands of businesses in diverse industries (Holyoake 1918; Jones 1979; Curl 1980; Goodwyn 1981; Taylor 1983; Schneiberg, King, and Smith 2008). Largely due to their reliance on bank loans that could be withdrawn and markets that could become exclusionary where noncooperative firms banded together against them, most of these enterprises failed, leaving a cautious legacy in their wake. Those that did survive faced a different set of issues: the "degeneration" of worker control into two tiers of founding owners and newer, non-owning employees (Webb and Webb 1897; Grob 1969). Even the internationally famous Mondragon network of investor- and worker-owned companies in the Basque region of Spain has seen increasing stratification between higher-paid managers who have ever more control over business decisions and lower-paid workers who report increasing alienation and anomie (Kasmir 1996). Thus, worker cooperatives seem doomed to either keep their principles intact and fail, or succeed as businesses but lose broader social justice goals.

The rise of worker cooperatives in North America and western Europe in the 1960s and 1970s—the cohort of the companies in this study—was perhaps possible due to a *dis*connection from the previous history. Emerging from white, middle-class youth subculture instead of labor-oriented social movements, the new cooperatives sought no bargains with capitalism but instead rejected what were seen as the dehumanizing effects of commodified labor and bureaucracy (Jackall and Levin 1984; Santa Barbara Legal Collective 1982). Internal social control was exerted through interpersonal relationships established by recruiting on the basis of friendship or potential friendship, rather than rules or managerial direction (Rothschild and Whitt 1986). Eschewing material rewards—and indeed often paying far below subsistence level (Rothschild and Whitt 1986)—the benefits sought were largely social and interpersonal: control over one's destiny and equality with one's co-workers (Rothschild-Whitt 1979; Mansbridge 1980; Ferguson 1991; Kleinman 1996). The focus on emotional connection, sharing control among members, rotating jobs, flat pay scales, and integrating the "public" sphere of work with the "private" one of family and community theoretically counteracted the forces of deskilling, job and occupational segregation, unequal pay, and harassment that create organizational inequalities (Braverman 1974, 1998; Milkman 1987; Acker 1990; Reskin and Roos 1990; Padavic 1992; Tomaskovic-Devey 1993; Steinberg 1995; S.M. Collins 1997).

Yet the rejection of financial goals in favor of more emotional, social, and interpersonal ones had profound class (and intertwined ethnoracial) effects on employees of these organizations. First, obviously, only those with other sources of wealth can afford to stay at jobs that pay below subsistence level. Thus, workers who remained (and consequently came to influence cooperative culture and direction) were largely middle and upperclass (Mansbridge 1980). Second, however, was the insidious effect of friendship on these organizations. Not only did friendship-based social control limit growth to accommodate face-to-face interactions among all members (thus reducing competitive power with larger corporations and reproducing financial precariousness), but the emphasis on friendship situated recruitment and retention within social networks (Rothschild-Whitt 1979), which are typically segregated by race/ethnicity and class (McPherson, Smith-Lovin, and Cook 2001). Furthermore, resistance to bureaucracy and its formality fostered conditions of what Freeman termed "structurelessness" (1970, 1984), where the overt and explicit distribution of power is replaced by one that reiterates the larger social stratification of power along class, gender, and ethnoracial fault lines.

Together, these conditions produced demographically homogeneous organizations. That is, the financial instability due to small size skewed these organizations toward more elite workers, friendship-based organizational control reinforced this population's dominance, and structurelessness obscured advantages of cultural capital and thus cemented this dominance. Indeed, several democratic organizations' scholars (Mansbridge 1980; Hacker 1989; Loe 1999; Pencavel 2001) and even members themselves (Ferguson 1991) posited homogeneity as integral to economic stability and success in these flat, anti-bureaucratic organizations.

This cohort of democratic workplaces, therefore, seemed to be primarily valuable to elite members of the labor market, and these groups' structurelessness has been linked to additional workplace penalties for those from socially marginalized groups (Sirianni 1993).

Yet despite historic failures of both EO and worker cooperative firms to deliver power, autonomy, and wealth to working-class employees, there have been exceptions that can be instructive. Worker-owned cooperatives' democratic nature creates the possibility, if not the assurance, of working-class empowerment.

In the Store and On the Floor

My interest in this project arose when a friend who worked at One World Natural Grocery told me about complaints made by the CEO of the People's Daily Bread Bakery at a worker cooperative conference. The CEO claimed that the conference's focus on participatory democratic practices privileged the skills and knowledge of educated, middle-class employees and thus excluded or exploited the working-class people his company set out to empower. As this CEO later explained to me, he felt working-class people would rather give managers control than sit in "endless" meetings to work things out. He believed the primary needs of his working-class employees were material: stable jobs that provided a decent living. Management was necessary in a capitalist economy to compete efficiently and preserve these jobs. Only middle-class people could afford the luxury of the poor pay and instability that accompanied participatory democracy. Since the grocery's worker control seemed to create rewarding working conditions for its employees, I was initially dismayed to think that such organizations could only benefit an already privileged sector of the labor force. However, as I embarked on this project, I quickly found that there was very little difference in employee class background in the two worker-owned cooperatives (class was qualitatively measured based on questions about the respondents' and their parents' educational background; parents' occupations; whether the respondents' parents rented or owned the family home; the respondents' childhood family car, if any; and recollective stories that gave a sense of the family's wealth). Given what I could observe of the differences in workforce composition and levels of job segregation, my interest in how management might affect the distribution of resources across class, race/ ethnicity, and gender was piqued, and I began to seriously pursue these questions in these settings.

I therefore chose to compare One World Natural Grocery and People's Daily Bread Bakery, two relatively large worker-owned cooperatives (100 to 200 employees) with similar longevity (25 to 30 years at time of study) operating in the natural foods market niche, both located within the same "Golden Valley" geographic region of California. I collected data using ethnographic and archival methods: both nonparticipant and participant observation, interviews, and document analysis. Preliminary research conducted between November 2001 and October 2002 included 12 semistructured, formal interviews with employees at the two organizations, and visits to each of the sites. From July–September 2003, I engaged in intensive observation of both companies. During this period, I conducted 36 semistructured, informal interviews with employees of four teams at each site: office, production (baking and packaging), route sales, and shipping at the bakery; and office, produce, cashiers, and housewares at the grocery. I was thus able to contrast similar white-collar, blue-collar, and customer-oriented teams, as well as the team at each site identified as most conflictual and thus where organizational rifts might be best observed. I spent six weeks at each company, averaging nine hours per day and five days per week on site, where I would take constant notes as a nonparticipant observer (usually) or recollective notes in concentrated breaks during a few instances of participant observation. In both cases, I expanded my notes after shifts. In addition, I analyzed archival material at each organization: meeting minutes and agendas, advertising, promotional materials, training and policy manuals, internal communications, and internal financial documents including earnings for all members during the 2003–2004 fiscal year broken out by race, gender, team, and tenure (names removed). During this period, I also attended numerous meetings and orientations at both sites, official and informal social gatherings of both companies' employees, and conferences of worker-owners. In all, I spent approximately 800 hours engaged with members of the two companies.

The combination of recollective interviews, observation, and documents helped me triangulate the histories presented by members. By designing research to follow people and their narratives over time, I was better able to identify significant practices that reproduced and diminished class inequalities. All fieldnotes and interview transcripts were initially coded during the observation period using a mixture of inductive and deductive analysis. For instance, I began my project interested in inequality, but thought I was observing a bureaucratic organization (the bakery) and a nonbureaucratic one (the grocery). As it became clear during my fieldwork that the grocery was no less bureaucratic for all its rejection of hierarchy, recognition of the significance of bureaucratic practices emerged. Thus, the analytic process involved "asking questions of fieldnotes"—refining my approach as a field researcher, rather than simply an analyst of fieldnotes—before moving on to "focused" coding

(Emerson, Fretz, and Shaw 1995:146). This focused coding was done in 2005 with HyperRESEARCH qualitative data analysis software. The acknowledgment and ongoing refinement of my theoretical approach toward those I encountered in the field, as well as the reflexive practice of using my own experiences in the field as additional data, mark my methodological approach as one of the extended case method (Burawoy 1998).

The two worker-owned cooperatives I studied differed sharply from those studied in the 1960s and 1970s (Rothschild-Whitt 1979; Swidler 1979; Mansbridge 1980; Jackall and Levin 1984; Rothschild and Russell 1986), despite their roots in that cohort. Although plagued by rocky finances in their early years, both had matured into successful businesses capable of supporting a stable core of workers. Both were founded by white, educated, middle class workers, but the workforce of both companies was over 80% working-class and 40% people of color at the time of my study. However, despite retaining a similar commitment to democratic governance, the distributions of wealth, power, and autonomy varied. These specific similarities and differences made these ideal comparative cases from which to discover empowerment strategies for working-class employees.

The bakery and the grocery had many similarities with each other (cohort, geography, natural foods market, commitment to social justice), as well as similar differences from the cohort from which they emerged (growth, stability, capital, working-class, and ethnoracially diverse workforce). People's Daily Bread Bakery, located in a suburban business park in the southern part of the Golden Valley, was founded by three women and two men in the mid-1970s, all of whom borrowed start-up money from their white, middle-class families. The bakery was set up as a collectivist-democratic organization, a highly participatory form of management in which all employees discuss and make all decisions together (Rothschild-Whitt 1979). A series of serendipitous events permitted significant growth, but they struggled with internal accountability and profitability issues, including both shirkers and charismatic would-be leaders. In the late 1980s, the bakery had over 50 employees (making it larger than 85% of U.S. bakeries), and many members had financial responsibilities the founders never imagined. When an unofficial leader quit in response to criticism of his financial actions, they elected to transition from a participatory-democratic organizational structure to a managerial system with representative-democratic governance oversight in hopes of solving their problems. And in many ways it seemed that managerial control—accompanied by more typical hiring practices based on experience and skill; pay differentials for merit, experience, and responsibility;

and rejection of friendship as a basis for social control—had indeed been the best solution. At the time of my study, the workforce had expanded to just over 100 employees at a four-building plant, the company was generating $17.5 million in net revenues, and the reach of the company's organic sourdough baked goods was nationwide. People's *non*managerial employees had higher average annual earnings than the local median household annual earnings, and their injury rates were far below the average for their industry. That is, these were good working-class jobs: stable, well-paying, and safe. And the workforce had become almost entirely working class, including the managers. Greybo, the white, working-class female plant safety coordinator, explained to me that only two managers had more than a high school diploma, and pointedly said, "I don't know if managers in other firms that are 17- to 20-million dollar businesses get there without a degree."[3]

Yet, despite the unusual access to power held by (some) working-class members, gender and ethnicity/race shaped working-class access to jobs, wealth, power, and autonomy. For reasons that will become clear, where women had once formed the majority of employees and held positions across jobs, they were now only 15% of the workforce (see Table 1). Half were clustered in the office and none were in production, which employed 83% of the bakery's employees of color—or, more appropriately, *men* of color, as women of color were less than 2% of the workforce.

While the workforce had become far more ethnoracially diverse due to an increase in the employment of recent Mexican migrants, all of these workers were men and almost entirely in the lowest-paid and least autonomous production positions. These gender and ethnoracial inequalities of access manifested in stratified levels of earnings, as can be seen in Table 2. What is less visible are the inequalities of power and autonomy. As the rest of the chapter shows, because working-class women were largely excluded

TABLE 1
Workforce Demographics in 2003.[4]

Workforce demographics	People's Daily Bread Bakery Sample: 95 (100)	One World Natural Grocery Sample: 185 (234)
Whites	57%	61%
People of color	43%	39%
Men	85%	43%
Women	15%	56%
White men	44%	30%
White women	13%	32%
Men of color	41%	13%
Women of color	2%	25%

TABLE 2
Distribution of Resources in 2003.

Earnings[5]	People's Daily Bread Bakery Sample: 95 (100)	One World Natural Grocery Sample: 185 (234)
Mean annual earnings		
All employees	$61,374	$40,155
Managers	$90,135	n/a
Nonmanagers	$57,460	n/a
Whites	$67,955	$39,809
People of color	$54,080	$40,703
Men	$60,999	$43,400
Women	$68,104	$37,942
White men	$67,461	$43,409
White women	$69,687	$36,453
Men of color	$53,854	$43,381
Women of color	$58,606	$39,893
2003 county median individual earnings	$30,083	$37,498
2003 county median household income	$54,614	$57,833
2003 county mean household income	$71,320	$80,614
Mean hourly earnings		
All employees	$32.46	$30.14
Managers	$46.18	n/a
Nonmanagers	$30.22	n/a
Whites	$35.93	$30.55
People of color	$27.83	$29.49
Men	$31.80	$28.62
Women	$36.67	$31.41
White men	$35.59	$29.20
White women	$37.10	$31.81
Men of color	$27.53	$27.34
Women of color	$34.06	$30.91
2004 county mean hourly wage	$19.16	$24.37

and working-class men of color were largely relegated to nonmanagerial, lower-wage, restrictively supervised jobs, it was mostly white working-class men who benefited from the bakery.

One World Natural Grocery, located in the Golden Valley's main urban hub about 50 miles north of the bakery, was founded in the mid-1970s by the mostly young, white, and middle-class followers of a spiritual leader. After a smuggling scandal that cost the guru most of his disciples and created a wariness of charismatic leadership, the store's workforce transitioned from volunteers to a mix of waged former believers and nonbelievers. Unlike many other collective stores in the area, the grocery's spiritual commitment to "service to the community" spurred its growth. Thus, it gradually expanded until it evolved into a 40,000-square-foot natural foods and products supermarket, generating net revenues of $25 million. Despite financial crises similar to those of the bakery, the grocery continued to reject positional management and hired consultants to strengthen its democratic governance. This resulted in a mix of participatory and representative structures. Long-range decisions were made by elected committees and whoever attended the monthly membership meetings. Authority over most day-to-day decisions was located within 14 teams, including hiring and firing, allocation of raises, and vacation and leave allocations.

Table 2 shows that grocery employees did not have earnings as impressive as bakery employees, grossing less than 70% of the median annual household earnings for their county. However, grocery workers' lesser *annual* earnings largely resulted from choosing to work fewer than 40 hours (the bakery mandated a 40-hour work week); average grocery *hourly* earnings were nearly equal to those of nonmanagerial bakery employees and were higher for nonwhite employees. Like the bakery, the grocery was approximately 40% people of color and over 80% working class but, as shown in Tables 1 and 2, the grocery also had a female majority of employees and very little difference in earnings, power, or job autonomy among social groups.

As I demonstrate in the following section, these differences were largely produced by the bureaucratic arrangement and formalization of power, which were then buttressed by organizational worker discourses that made each kind of bureaucracy seem not only natural but particularly suited to the membership. I do not claim that the organization and formalization of power were a result of organizational narratives, or that these organizational narratives resulted from the structuring of power. Nor do I argue that any one aspect of these bureaucracies is the cause of the degree of inequality regime. Rather, the next section reveals how power, formality, and narratives interacted in specific (and mutually reinforcing) combinations to heighten or reduce workplace inequality.

Working-Class Inclusion and Empowerment: The Effects of Organizational Structure, Formalized Rules and Practices, and Organizational Narratives

Carberry's (2010) study of shared capitalism's inequality effects indicates that, in the main, most of the gendered and ethnoracial stratification of wealth and power in EO organizations can be chalked up to the larger social processes that create workplace inequalities (education, labor market and job segregation, and job tenure) and not to specific characteristics of shared capitalism plans. However, my analysis reveals that the bakery's class stratification of wealth and power was far less acute than that of typical corporations, and the grocery had only a few small variations of wealth, power, and autonomy across class *and* race/ethnicity and gender. That is, although research indicates that noncooperative forms of EO may not mitigate existing inequalities, both the bakery and the grocery were able to do so. This suggests that there are indeed ways in which organizational power structures can reproduce or reduce inequalities, and that democratic employee ownership might provide models of inequality reduction.

The bakery and the grocery organized power very differently: bakery management was vertical, although nominally directed by an all-employee board of directors, while the grocery created a hybrid horizontal and vertical democracy. As the next three subsections of this chapter show, the ability of each organization to distribute power and autonomy across class—including intraclass differences of race/ethnicity and gender—was deeply affected by the degree to which each company organized power horizontally or vertically; the extent to which each formalized this organization through rules, policies, and procedures; and the organizational narratives each deployed about what it meant to be a worker.

Managerial and Worker Control: Two Kinds of Bureaucracy

For most people, it is impossible to imagine a *bureaucratic* organization without *hierarchy*, without legitimate, fixed power inequalities. Yet, despite the grocery's lack of hierarchy, both organizations were indeed bureaucratic. Positions were separate from people, hiring was done on the basis of perceived skills and expertise rather than social ties, authority was legitimated either through election or position rather than personal charisma or family-based claims, and both companies were thoroughly permeated by formal documents specifying rules, policies, and procedures. In the bakery, this was accompanied by a hierarchy of power similar to that of most large workplaces. The grocery's bureaucracy, on the other hand, institutionalized a complex and nonhierarchical power structure. Comparing the two thus permits analysis of how different kinds of bureaucracies inhibit or enhance working-class empowerment.

At the bakery, hierarchy had both direct and indirect effects on working-class empowerment. Although most bakery managers were working class, the restriction of decision-making power to a subgroup reduced the power and autonomy of the working-class workforce. There were also more subtle effects. By creating an elected, all-employee board of directors, employees had been intended to have control over the CEO (and thus the managerial system). Yet, over the years, it had become almost entirely composed of managers who, because they were the only ones visibly making and implementing decisions, were widely perceived as smarter and more capable—and the only ones with suffi-cient time and wage flexibility to run for these meagerly stipended posi-tions. Even in the one remaining site of potential participatory worker power, the membership meeting, worker proposals were unlikely to be considered unless they had advance approval from the board of direc-tors. As Pam, the white, middle-class office team manager, explained, "The members would say, 'Do we want to waste our time? Is this lady off the wall? She didn't even go to the board!'" This made it almost impossible for nonmanagers to demonstrate independent capabilities. In addition, most of the managers and board members were white men, strengthening the cultural link between whiteness, masculinity, and leadership. This created observable problems with exercising authority for women and nonwhites, further reducing direct access to power for a large segment of the working class.

Job access at the bakery—and thus any chance at workplace power and autonomy—was also affected by the narrowing of hiring into the hands of a single manager whose individual beliefs and decisions created informal policies. For example, despite describing job applicants and even former workers of other genders, Pam, whose eight-person office team was entirely female, and Charlie, the Latino manager of the forty-person all-male production team, both explained this gender segregation as a result of the gendered preferences of job seekers. Disconnections such as those Pam and Charlie displayed—between their certainty that workers self-selected into jobs by gender and their own descriptions of mixed-gender applicants to both teams—reveal the submerged, stable beliefs held by those in charge of hiring. Pam's bias may have protected the one secure site of women's employment at the bakery, but most job openings were in production. As research has revealed, although people may have gender preferences, the effect of these on job choice is insignificant compared to economic need (Padavic 1992). Charlie's bias combined with the ethnoracialized local labor market funneling Latinos into production to effectively deny employment to Latinas. Thus, the bakery's creation of jobs for "the working class" effectively extended that welcome only to men.

Even where managers were not themselves the cause of inequality (as in cases of unequal job opportunities), the inequalities of the larger social world were quietly legitimated and incorporated into the bakery through the broader practice of unequally valuing managerial and non-managerial jobs. That is, once there was acceptance of autonomy and pay disparities between *levels* of work, it was easier to accept such disparities between *kinds* of work. Thus, it was not conspicuous to bakery employees that two teams with similar managerial control would have extremely different levels of power and autonomy. In the production team, with 69% employees of color, workers were subject to intense managerial surveillance: discipline for being more than 15 minutes late, varying manager-set weekly schedules, penalties for switching shifts with team members, and even regulation of leisure time through mandatory on-call days. In contrast, members of the 91% white route sales and delivery (RSD) team each drove their store routes alone and were subject to little regulation beyond the loss of commission if sales quotas were unmet. This was not because the work was inherently autonomous. Sales decisions could have been made by managers, and the technology they used could have created greater levels of surveillance. Instead, these differences were a result of the bargaining power held by white RSD employees in the larger labor market who could (and, when their autonomy was threatened, sometimes did) leave for lateral employment opportunities. In contrast, the once-prevalent food processing plants that competed for People's production labor were shrinking and disappearing. Yet, rather than suggesting that hierarchy merely follows inequalities, the disparity in autonomy revealed that managerial control was to be a tool that could be wielded against the less powerful. Instead of leveling the playing field, managerial control augmented privileges that were socially conferred to some workers and stripped from others.

In contrast, the grocery's hybrid participatory/representative-democratic worker control also had direct and indirect effects on class inequality, but they were effects that broadened rather than narrowed working-class empowerment. Direct effects included literal empowerment across organizational demographics by giving almost all major decision-making power to the 14 democratic teams into which all employees were organized. Indirectly, this use of participatory democracy prevented the dominance of middle-class and white interests on the two most powerful elected representative committees, the board of directors and the Intercooperative Concerns Committee (ICC), and strengthened bonds among potentially isolated members of socially marginalized groups. Like the bakery, the grocery had an elected, all-employee board of directors that consistently had more whites, more men, and more people from middle-class backgrounds than the membership as a whole.

However, the board's decisions could be, and at times were, vetoed by majority vote at the membership meeting. Further, the numerous smaller elected and voluntary committees had no such overrepresentations of whites, men, or people from middle-class backgrounds. These other committees not only provided space to showcase the knowledge, skills, and actions of working-class men and women of color, as well as white women, but also increased face-to-face interactions among the more than 200 employees. Decentralization of power thus repeatedly offered evidence against the dominant cultural linkages between whiteness, masculinity, knowledge, and capability, and increased sites through which claims to power could be made. This helped to account for the regular inclusion of working-class women of color on the lists employees offered me of "key grocery people" alongside three white men.

Another indirect effect was to preserve and increase access to grocery jobs by non-elites. As I witnessed during observation and was told in interviews, team hiring decisions were made by elected three-person committees, and discussion about candidates seemed to delegitimize any internalized ethnoracial and gender scripts grocery workers might privately hold. No team displayed any gender or ethnoracial skewing, and only one a class skew (surprisingly not the white-collar office, but the physically strenuous cheese team). The culture of regular democratic participation also led to intensified cross-worker surveillance, or a sense of "200 bosses," as Elena, a working-class Latina cashier, put it. At the grocery, though, these bosses were not simply concerned with the bottom line. When another employee discovered that Brian, a white, working-class male board member, had conducted business without prior board approval as required, he lost his bid for re-election despite his previous success and a general consensus that his actions were cost effective and beneficial. Any social correlation of Brian's whiteness and masculinity with financial acumen was surpassed by the culture of accountability combined with highly effective participatory management.

At both companies the direction of power—horizontal or vertical—had gender and ethnoracial effects, shaping the scope of working-class power and autonomy in the workplace. At the bakery, the way hierarchical management naturalized inequality and concentrated decision-making power into fewer hands effectively translated internalized individual beliefs about gender and ethnoracial needs and desires into unequal job access, power, and autonomy. This created a far steeper inequality regime than at the grocery, where inequalities were suspect and decisions were made in dialogue and across nodes of power. Although not entirely equal, the grocery's organization of power produced a highly and unusually egalitarian distribution of workplace rewards.

Subordinated and Protective Formality

As the previous section indicates, broader and more participatory power structures are necessary to produce working-class empowerment. However, such organizational structures are not *sufficient* for creating working-class inclusion and/or empowerment. In this section, I argue that the key to the grocery's ability to avoid class and ethnoracial homogeneity while preserving participatory democratic involvement lies in its embrace of bureaucratic formality, in its clear and documented codification of rules, policies, and procedures. However, as this section also demonstrates, formality cannot be treated as a discrete force of egalitarianism. Instead, it interacts with the structural arrangement of power to minimize *or* reinforce inequality regimes. While Acker (2006a) argues that hierarchy makes inequality regimes steeper, these cases suggest that where hierarchy is absent, formality is required to avoid the problems of "structurelessness" that Freeman (1970, 1984) identifies—the covert and unassailable usurpation of power by those with dominant cultural capital—and to create broader democratic worker control.

Both the grocery and the bakery were highly formal, with numerous written policy and orientation manuals, financial reports, disciplinary notices, team logs, clipboards holding inter-team communication, safety posters, agendas, and meeting minutes. At the grocery, however, formality *was* the mechanism through which power was distributed, protecting the interests of organizational minorities. It was not just Brian's violation of organizational norms that undermined his re-election, as previously described, but it was the formal practices of information sharing that made his specialized knowledge redundant: Brian's reports were part of the board minutes that were distributed across the organization (and, like all storewide documents, translated into Spanish); and employees were expected and paid to read the reports and then discuss them in team, membership, and Collective Concerns meetings. These practices undermined the tight coupling between white masculinity and financial leadership by integrating the consumption of business information across gender, race/ethnicity, and class.

The grocery's formality protected those with less cultural capital in two ways. First, it disseminated rules that mandated greater fairness and blocked subtle forms of inequality. Second, it backed these rules with formal training procedures including one-time orientations in organizational history, structure and process, and fiscal practices; a buddy system through which long-term workers guided the newly hired through their first year of meetings and advised as requested; and a committee providing assistance in research and writing to all employees, leveling the playing field among those with and without the educational training needed to produce and advocate for agenda items at the membership meeting. Both the formal rules and formal procedures fortified the hybrid democratic structure against charismatic or elite bids for power and compensated for inequalities in cultural capital that employees brought to the organization.

The critical nature of formality in reducing inequality was highlighted as much where it was absent as where it was present. Where formal rules and procedures had not been created, hybrid democracy did not prevent power from devolving to whites and men. Buying—the selection of a sales team's goods—was one such area. Buying was a coveted position that provided a greater autonomy as well as time off the shop floor. Buyers for the highly profitable teams were men, almost all white, and, as with managers at the bakery, they were largely perceived as superior individuals rather than as fortuitously placed, thus reproducing links between whiteness and maleness and financial wisdom. No policies had been created for how buyers were to be trained; instead, an informal system of skills sharing had been developed. Links between this practice and inequality had been noted by some employees. Jan, a middle-class white woman said,

> Buyers, the guys pass accounts off to each other. They do. There's definitely an old-boy buyer thing going on. You know, like Burgundy [the buyer for the most profitable team in the store], he's finding the young man of his choice to train up to his position. And the women aren't even in the same realm, you know. I mean, I don't think he considered it, and I don't think he knows he's not considering it.

That is, the grocery's greater egalitarianism cannot be attributed to something about this specific group of people. Without formality intervening to bring hybrid democratic practices into play, informal and unequal social patterns re-emerged, re-creating the "structureless" situations typical of the 1960s and 1970s collectives.

The bakery's formalized hierarchy created certain protections that were not present at the grocery but that simultaneously bolstered the bakery's inequality regimes. At the grocery, despite repeated reminders by the passionately class-conscious, white, working-class safety coordinator that working people's primary assets were their bodies, workers resisted being "policed," and, as a result, grocery worker injuries and resulting worker compensation claims harmed members' futures and the grocery's bank account. In contrast, the bakery was formidable in protecting workers' bodies, far surpassing industrial bakery averages. This was accomplished through the intersection of formality with managerial control. Formal documents included customized safety videos and training manuals, a blanketing of safety posters and signs in each team's work area noting the number of days without an accident, and a system of "near miss" documents that could be completed by any employee (and were heavily encouraged with rewards for teams with the most reports). These documents were then reviewed by all levels of management and the plant safety coordinator, and a description of the remedy was made to the reporting team. In addition, the plant safety coordinator regularly observed teams and created her own reports. This helped explain the remarkable wholeness of bakery employees' bodies, as well as their extremely low insurance payments. Yet these formal practices also augmented managerial control, as managers used safety documents to discipline employees through drug testing, written warnings, suspensions, and terminations. Safety culture was not simply protective of workers but also protective of power and autonomy inequalities, solidifying managers' greater power and autonomy. Thus, even here the subordination of formality to hierarchy was visible.

The bakery's use of English to formalize policies created less fairness, even where it might be expected, and preserved social and organizational inequalities. Orientations for new employees included similar levels of formality as those of the grocery, and similarly mind-numbing, three-hour blasts of information, but where these were followed up at the grocery with interlocking practices such as the formal buddy system, there were no formal options available for bakery employees seeking further information or explanation other than to go to a manager. Further, the effect of orientations was severely limited by the bakery's formalization of English proficiency policies. This meant that formality not only created managerial/nonmanagerial inequalities but also had insidious ethnoracial effects. The (white, English-speaking) manager-dominated board implemented an English proficiency requirement for employees, necessary not only for communicating with managers but also for comprehension of company English-only orientation materials, financial reports, and non-OSHA safety materials. Workers could be hired with minimal English but were required to take remedial community college courses. While there had been a brief experiment with on-site Spanish training for managers, resistance from some managers led to the quick demise of the program. Thus, even in production, where almost all of the primary Spanish speakers worked, the team with the most daytime hours had the highest number of primary English speakers (and also the highest number of white employees), while the teams with the least "social" hours employed most of the Spanish-speaking workers. The English-language requirement gave managers tools to reproduce occupational segregation, and it intimidated some primary Spanish speakers from becoming voting (and profit-sharing) members. Thus, formal rules implemented by managers through the democratic governance system limited power and created additional barriers and burdens for non-English-speaking working-class employees.

Formality was thus compatible with both managerial hierarchy and participatory democratic control but had very different effects. It might seem that participatory democracy requires far more freedom and fluidity than the rigidity imposed by formal rules, policies, and procedures would allow. Certainly, members of the participatory-democratic worker cooperatives of the 1960s and 1970s resisted formality for exactly this reason. However, as previously demonstrated in this chapter, formality can in fact strengthen the functioning of participatory democracy by clarifying expectations and lines of power and by leveling cultural capital inequalities among members, with training and protections. In contrast, formality does little to level these inequalities when combined with hierarchy, eroding democratic participation by solidifying the scope and nature of managers' power. While Freeman (1970, 1984) is no doubt correct that cultural capital inequalities are magnified by structurelessness, it seems that hierarchical structure transforms cultural capital into organizational capital. That is, while a lack of formality can indeed allow those with social advantage—whether from actual training or from entitlement due to the expectations of those around them—to exert dominance on particular jobs, organizational direction, or accrual of wealth, formalized hierarchy reifies those advantages of cultural capital in the people who occupy the limited positions of authority. Bakery managers, the only ones who could legitimately demonstrate decision-making power, seemed to hold their authority by virtue of essential and personal superiority rather than their organizational position. In contrast, where formality protected the broad distribution of power at the grocery, knowledge and authority was showcased across the typical divides of class, race/ethnicity, and gender, producing organizational capital in subjects who held and had access to far less power in the larger world than they did at work. The grocery's documentation of lines of power and methods of grievance and redress undermined the ability of those with cultural capital advantages to subtly affect organizational direction.

Organizational Narratives: Legitimating Inequality Regimes

Given their very similar origins, it was not inevitable that the bakery and the grocery should evolve into such different bureaucracies with different levels of inequalities. The bakery had adopted far more typical organizational practices, subordinating formal rules and policies to the discretion of a hierarchy of managers, which had devolved power largely to whites and severely limited opportunities for women. In contrast, the grocery had preserved the largely decentralized and direct-democratic practices of its founders but had created multiple and interlocking layers of formal rules and policies that appeared to preserve the ability of men and women of color and white women to have access to grocery jobs, wealth, and power. Why did these organizations evolve such different inequality regimes? Why should similar demographic groups support such different distributions of workplace rewards? Bakery employees— and particularly upper management—were not blind to class, gender, or ethnoracial inequality, and indeed prided themselves on providing a good livelihood to working-class people, including a disproportionately large number of Latinos. Nor was it inevitable that the white, middle-class founders of the grocery would have developed practices that disrupted their privileges. In this section I show that members made sense of and explained the differing degrees of their workplace inequality regimes by using *organizational narratives*—social stories and practices that define and solidify these stories that have traction and legitimacy among workers within an organization (both on an individual and group level) about the ways in which workers' sense of self and others *as workers* intersects with race/ethnicity, class, and gender. Organizational narratives promote certain aspects of workers' selves and minimize others, although, as the cases here reveal, the specific form these narratives take cannot always be predicted. Thus, despite their founders' similar whiteness and middle-class backgrounds, the bakery developed a highly classed narrative that minimized race/ethnicity and gender as central to defining a worker/member, while the grocery developed more multifaceted narratives that only weakly invoked class but legitimized race/ethnicity and gender.

As the bakery CEO's criticisms of participatory democracy at the conference noted earlier made clear, class was a highly legitimate referent at the bakery. This class discourse was evident not only in how employees identified themselves and each other but also in a variety of organizational practices. Two practices previously noted include the recruitment of nondegreed managers, sharply reducing class differences between managers and nonmanagers, and the stringent safety policies and procedures that protected workers' bodies to an unusual degree. Another was the distribution of profits not only to member-owners but also to the 30% of employees who were not yet eligible or had not chosen to become members,[6] recasting profit as the right of producers rather than owners—a practice unique to the bakery among North American worker-owned cooperatives. It was also evident in workers' self-presentation, where a singular class framework was echoed throughout my interviews with bakery employees. Such a framework was at best submerged into a category of "white trash" at the grocery but more commonly completely absent (most grocery employees seemed bewildered when asked to identify their class). This was starkly visible in the differences in self-presentations of Leslie, a bakery RSD team member, and Jennifer, a member of the grocery's cooler team. While both were working-class, suburban-raised, white women with terminal high school degrees, who had both held similar jobs to their current ones before coming to the worker-owned cooperative, and whose tasks involved similar levels of interface with the buying public and thus required similar commodification of emotions (Hochschild 1983), they drew on very different narratives to define their work choices and themselves as workers. Despite the significant degree of power and autonomy held by RSD drivers, Leslie described her job as a *well-paying* option for someone with only a high school diploma who needed help to support her family (which I later discovered to be her female partner and their children) rather than one with greater freedom from managerial, male, or heterosexual control. This typical class, and historically masculine (Acker 1990), framing was one I regularly encountered at the bakery.

In contrast, Jennifer, whose floor shifts put her at the mercy of customer demands and thus seemed to have diminished autonomy, used a typical grocery framework of an inherent need for autonomy—describing her inability to tolerate bosses with the gendered descriptive of herself as too "bitchy"—and pleasure in co-worker ethnoracial diversity to explain her job choice. Additional grocery practices articulated "workerness" around gender and ethnicity/race. Workers who were parents received an extra dollar per hour per child, thus legitimating family concerns as workplace ones. Meeting minutes were distributed verbatim, at one point including African American slang, "Don't be a hater, we're ballerz" in a summary statement exhorting the membership not to complain about a decision because the grocery was doing fine financially. Reproduction of nonstandard English, as well as the practice of regular translation of documents into Spanish by the company team of translators, legitimated a multivocal organizational voice. Where bakery workers mostly drew on class discourses of material rewards and ignored possible gender or sexuality frames, grocery workers more readily linked gender and ethnoracial discourses to ones of freedom in explaining their rewards as workers. In almost all cases, the bakery's strong class logic edged out gender or ethnoracial explanations for actions, while the weakness of class's explanatory power at the grocery permitted alternate workplace logics to emerge.

It would, however, be unfair and misleading to say that only grocery workers were concerned about gender and ethnoracial inequalities. Both companies took overt organizational steps to remedy gender and ethnoracial conflicts they acknowledged to exist within their walls. However, the difference between managerial and worker control affected these actions. When bakery conflicts arose in the early 1990s that were overtly religious, racial, and sexuality-based in nature, upper management and the board hired external "diversity trainers." The consultants engaged all employees over a series of days in a variety of workshops that were widely seen to be helpful in cooling emotions and creating better interpersonal relationships among diverse employees. They "just [let] people be who they are. You know, 'cause that doesn't have anything to do with business," as Keith, the middle-class Latino personnel manager explained. By presenting ethnoracial, religious, and sexual concerns as external struggles that had unfortunately made their way into the organization, could be managed with the psychotherapeutic techniques of identifying common humanity, and could be organizationally dealt with in one intensive intervention, the bakery effectively delimited these social inequalities as *external, interpersonal,* and *irregular.* This articulation was wholly different from the *internal* and *structural* class inequality that their policies attempted to remedy through such *ongoing* practices as promotion without educational credential and profit sharing among owning and non-owning employees alike. That is, the bakery clearly differentiated class workplace effects from those of gender, sexuality, religion, and ethnicity/race.

The grocery, on the other hand, identified its ethnoracial and sexual conflicts as part and parcel of their workplace. Instead of bringing in consultants for a single round of workshops, the grocery hired consultants to create internal trainers in an ongoing "Anti-Oppression Task Force" who thereafter conducted week-long annual trainings for small groups of grocery workers. As with all committee work, task force members and trainees were paid for the hours they spent in these activities, legitimating this as integral to the grocery's function. In the task force's biweekly meetings, they aimed to keep their work from becoming "more of a sensitivity training than an anti-oppression training," as white, middle-class member Sally explained. The task force also pointed out and raised awareness about organizational and interpersonal practices that reproduced inequalities. Employees pointed out how some of the task force's concepts were being incorporated into day-to-day interactions within and between teams, and trainees described having a robust and organizationally sanctioned language with which they could advocate for company policy changes. By literally making these practices part of doing business, by rejecting individualizing psychotherapeutic frameworks, and by institutionalizing the reproduction of challenge to inequality throughout the company, the grocery advanced gender and ethnoracial inequalities as *internally reproduced, structural,* and *ongoing* workplace issues that were the legitimate terrain of workplace intervention. In this way, the bakery and the grocery sharply diverged in their treatment of inequalities as *workplace* structures of meaning and action.

Interestingly, neither the bakery's "diversity" nor the grocery's "anti-oppression" trainings included explicit focus on class. At the bakery, a widespread and overt feeling of class homogeneity requiring less intervention than the clashes among a heterogeneous mix of ethnicities/races, genders, sexualities, and religions seemed to be the cause. At the grocery, the task force's lack of attention seemed more an outcome of a diffused class awareness. Yet, while the grocery's "class blindness" indicated absent class *cognizance*, it did not mean that class had no effect on the actions taken by the grocery.

Given the dominant class logic of the bakery, it would seem reasonable to expect strong class solidarity as an outcome. Certainly, those critical of the inclusion of gender and race/ethnicity as core workplace issues have argued that only a highly focused class framework can preserve the class solidarity necessary to winning power for the working class (Gitlin 1995). However, the cases of the grocery and the bakery suggest that such a singleness of focus does not necessarily promote such solidarity, nor that a multi-pronged approach erodes the possibility of solidarity or (broadly defined) working-class empowerment. This was readily apparent when a grocery workers' strike occurred in Southern California that threatened to spread to the Golden Valley in a few months. At the bakery, managers and the RSD team discussed using practices employed during an earlier strike: wearing large badges saying "worker-owned" to distinguish them from unionized delivery drivers, or coordinating with (presumably scab) loading dock receivers to minimize contact with picket lines. RSD team members reacted angrily when they felt my questions implied they should not cross the picket line. Frank, a working-class white man, snapped, "We're non-union, and the last time the Teamsters told us to deliver if you can." Sylvia, a working-class white woman, corroborated: "It's aimed at consumers, not vendors." Although, like the grocery, the bakery was not unionized, it surprised me that bakery employees had little sense of mutual interest with the unionized grocery workers in their surrounding community. At the bakery, a class organization narrative did not mobilize a sense of shared class interests leading to supportive action.

In contrast, the grocery almost immediately acted to set up a voluntary automatic payroll deduction to support the strike fund, utilized by 20% of grocery workers at the height of the strike. Some fund participants described their actions in class terms as, "We're all workers," but most noted how the supermarket boycott called by the union had increased their customer numbers and said they didn't want to profit from the struggles of "people like me," which, upon further inquiry, meant women with children, people of color, or people on a tight budget. What emerged were materially supportive class solidaristic actions based on identifications through gender, ethnicity/race, and consumer power. In these ways, the grocery reconfigured the meaning of class to level gender and ethnoracial inequalities embedded in a historically "classed" framework. This is significant in helping to understand how the grocery was able to create as much or more working-class access to jobs as the bakery: largely by promoting greater access to power and autonomous jobs across gender and ethnicity/race.

The bakery's narrowly classed organizational narrative authorized remedy of the most basic of class injustices: the exploitation of labor for someone else's profit. Yet, in relegating other aspects of workplace inequality to the external world for solutions, the bakery gave the advantages of safe, stable, and well-paying working-class jobs primarily to working-class people who were white and men. There were some advantages for working-class Latinos, as the classed masculinity of production extended them access to those jobs. However, without explicit ethnoracial dimensions of the bakery's workplace subjectivity, Latinos were left with no way to make legitimate claims on the organization's ethnoracial inequalities of autonomy (and pay). As sociologists who study the historical development of class discourse in the United States have noted, class has been and still is constructed through ethnoracial and gender structures of meaning. Stanley Aronowitz argues that, in bargaining with capital, the American labor movement sacrificed "ecology, feminism, and racial justice" (1992:24), while Acker (2006a) complements this history by noting that state efforts to level class inequalities, such as the postwar GI Bill provisions for education and home loans, were aimed at and of disproportionate benefit to white men. Thus, deployment of the historically developed idea of class—which is in fact particularistically white and male—works against the interests of people of color as well as white women.

On the other hand, the grocery's more diffuse organizational narrative—encompassing race/ethnicity, gender, and sexuality as well as class—permitted ethnoracial and gender inequality to be addressed as workplace issues, mitigating inequality across more of the working-class population who tried to access and benefit from grocery jobs. This indicates that an either/or struggle between class and "status identities" is not the central issue. Instead of viewing class as the base interest mediated by other forms of subjectivity, class may be as bounded and particularistic as critics contend "status identities" are. Class identity, as historically constructed, can be detrimental to the creation of class solidarity across ethnoracial and gender lines; thus, it can block access to power (and even to jobs) for men and women of color and white women. Instead, a multifaceted organizational narrative seems to reconfigure class as encompassing workplace struggles that occur through practices and processes of gender and ethnicity/race, linking the broad distribution of power to the needs of a heterogeneous workforce.

Links Between Power, Formality, and Organizational Narratives

The bakery switch to managerial hierarchy was intended to maximize profitability by fitting better into the capitalist world, under the assumption that its workers' interests were the "classed" ones of ownership of labor and its surplus. Thus, control of the company's direction, and indeed of the components of its workplace subjectivity, was put into the hands of its white, male, and fairly Marxist CEO at the same time as class emerged as a strong narrative. Managers pushed the assumption of shared and legitimate interests as a way to justify their actions, but, in so doing, imposed a homogeneous narrative on the workforce, relocating competing narratives—gendered ones about enjoyment of family, or ethnoracial ones about workplace and community empowerment—outside the organization's purview. While the typical nondemocratic corporation has no need to justify the control of a diverse workforce by a much more homogeneous managerial stratum, a democratic organization must be able to make congruence between members with more power and those with less. For the bakery, a classed organizational narrative performed this function by making managers *proxies* of workers' class interests. As the bakery's hierarchical bureaucracy achieved legitimacy in part by reflecting business practices around them, it reinforced inequality as a natural fact of workplaces just as Acker (2006a) has described: managers have power over the managed, men over women, whites over people of color, and so on. Because class is always enacted through gender and ethnicity/race, the bakery's unremarked use of class became marked by dominant operations of gender and ethnoracial status, producing perceptions of women as essentially unfit for production jobs and Latinos as essentially available for stern discipline regimes of scheduling. It was not inevitable that class should dominate the bakery's organizational narrative, but it was at least highly likely that People's transformation into a managerial hierarchy would narrow rather than expand this narrative so that the representative power structure could act as proxy for worker interests.

At the grocery, neither control nor subjectivity was constricted, but instead a multiplicity of subjects and policies and practices found space to grow. The gradual development of One World's organization-building efforts and its hybrid democratic control contrasted with the planned transformation of People's. These disconnected and decentralized policies were advantageous for creating wider access and empowerment, and the broader diversity had a reciprocal effect on organizational structure. Grocery policies protected and thus *articulated* a heterogeneity of subjects across class, gender, and ethnicity/race. Delegation of recruitment and retention power to the teams protected and increased this heterogeneity, and in turn the grocery's heterogeneous workforce enacted further policies and practices that increased the legitimacy of workers across categories of difference. The grocery's organizational narrative demanded multinodal access to power and the preservation of the possibility of conflict to accommodate an employee population that defined itself as internally dissimilar. Thus, a mutually reinforcing relationship between mostly decentralized but formalized power and a diverse workforce was ever more firmly entrenched: a multifaceted workplace subjectivity required multiple sites of empowerment to mute inequalities.

What this makes clear is that inequality regimes function through both visible and subtle mechanisms. The (always ethnoracialized and gendered) class outcomes of the inequality regimes in these two employee-owned workplaces are not due *only* to the arrangement of power. Instead, the organization of power, the formal processes and documents that codify power, *and* the organizational narratives that stabilize the flow and reach of power must be identified and analyzed in order to understand how EO might better empower the working class.

Conclusion

In the last 30 years or so, participatory democracy has fallen out of favor as a means to the end of workplace empowerment for a non-elite workforce. The few scholars who have focused on such organizations, as previously noted, often present pessimistic conclusions when it comes to inequality. Further, despite the larger proportion of the working class employed by EO companies, little research has been done on the class outcomes of these companies. This research fills an empirical gap in the literature by offering examples of how worker ownership can be utilized by a predominantly working-class workforce—and even of an organization with a high degree of participative democratic worker control. It offers workers both models and analysis of relations between EO and inequality, and it renews hope in the organizational potential of participatory democracy.

This research has presented several specific challenges to the scholarship on EO and class empowerment. First, it is clear that democratic employee ownership *can* create working-class empowerment. This should reawaken lines of inquiry for scholars, for workplace equity activists seeking to positively influence economically depressed working-class communities, and for EO firms seeking a competitive edge. While democratic managerial control such as that found at the bakery can offer stable, safe jobs to working-class people, the streamlining of power into fewer hands has stronger within-class inequality effects than does broadly distributed participatory democratic worker control. This chapter has come at the issue from a social justice perspective, but the "business case for diversity" (Cox 1993, 1994) could also be made here. Creating organizations that can recruit and retain talent and ability from a broader workforce might create more flexible and innovative firms that can appeal to a broader consumer base.

This leads to the second challenge: it is clear that neither homogeneity nor an elite workforce is necessary for functional participatory democracy. As scholars of other kinds of organizations have found, the formality of bureaucracy is effective in protecting minority interests from elite domination (Polletta 2002). While earlier structureless participatory democracy proved to either exclude or strip power from working-class members, bureaucratic participatory democracy seems able not only to include working-class employees but also to extend inclusion across race/ethnicity and gender. The evidence presented here indicates that working-class people are interested in and capable of managing their own businesses, and, when employees are paid for what are typically managerial functions (that is, the "endless" meetings decried by the bakery's CEO), they will take on that responsibility. This may have important implications not only for worker-owned cooperatives but also for firms (EO or not) with highly participative employee programs: the difficulty in eliciting tacit knowledge from employees may be less about their ability or willingness to share than about employers requesting donations of such participation from employees who see others being well compensated for their knowledge. It also supports the conclusions drawn by Rosen, Case, and Staubus (2005) about the need for formalized training and information sharing as part of fostering a firm's ownership culture to create successful EO.

However, third, this research challenges the conventional EO wisdom that participative management *generically* benefits employees. The examples here make clear that different forms of participation—work teams, governance committees, management councils—draw on classed, ethnoracialized, and gendered social and workplace practices, and thus have classed, ethnoracialized, and gendered outcomes, particularly when combined or not combined with educational and training efforts. Disregarding a workforce's multiplicity of differences, and the intersections of these differences, imperils the ability of participative EO to have egalitarian effects.

The fourth and final challenge is to the concept of class as external to other social statuses such as gender, ethnicity/race, sexuality, or ability. Typically, talk about "the working class" excludes men and women of color and white women, positing barriers they face as additional or external to class. As this chapter has shown, this approach obscures how issues affecting white, male working-class people are privileged, reproducing whiteness and maleness as a norm from which working-class men and women of color and white women deviate. That is, this research aims to turn this approach on its head: instead of asking how gender or race mathematically increases the inequality effects of class, this analysis has illustrated that class effects are always constituted through gender and race/ethnicity. This far more intersectional approach helps us understand how a "class" discourse helps to deliver advantages to a small (white, male) subgroup within the working class and how an intersectional discourse that acknowledges workplace power inequalities such as race/ethnicity, gender, sexuality, and ability can better deliver advantages to working-class people.

While a clear benefit of this kind of qualitative research is the exploration of the "black box" of how inequality effects are reproduced or reduced, it is limited by the small number of firms studied. In part, that is an effect of the small number of large, democratically governed firms that exist, and the even smaller number of those that use some degree of participatory democratic governance. Further investigation of some of these findings in fully employee-owned firms that are not worker-owned cooperatives would help us develop more robust understandings of inequality and EO.

Democratically governed, entirely employee-owned worker cooperatives comprise a tiny fraction of the minority of U.S. workplaces that employ shared capitalism, but they offer important lessons about balancing long-term profitability goals with the mitigation of inequality effects that could inform employee involvement practices in shared capitalist firms. By attending to the effects of organizational structure, levels of formalization, and narratives about workers, we are better able to understand the outcomes of shared capitalism.

Endnotes

[1] While it is beyond the scope of this chapter to fully engage with the debates regarding historical and contemporary definitions and uses of the concept of "the working class," use of "working class" here posits that class is a system of inequality and refers to a group socioeconomic status (occupational prestige, earnings, wealth, and education) and what has been described as "inherited cultural identit[y]" (Bettie 2000:10). That is, "the working class" in this chapter are people from families and communities who had access to low-wage and low-prestige work only, who themselves are constrained by similar levels of access, and who have consciously and unconsciously adopted specific (and differing by race/ethnicity and gender) norms of behavior and expectation based on experiences within families and communities shaped by class inequality.

[2] Names and identifying details of organizations, places, and people have been changed to protect confidentiality, although details that are crucial to the meaning of the work have not been changed.

[3] Class is, of course, not entirely measured by educational level, but education is a highly reliable marker of class. In these specific cases, the two managers exhibited other markers of the working class: parental education and occupation, and family wealth.

[4] The sample eliminates employees who worked less than five hours per week; worked insufficient hours to be eligible for membership; or were hired or terminated six months or more into the year. Total population follows sample size in parentheses. Note the bakery's labor statistics are somewhat obscured by hiring contingent labor, particularly in production, who aren't eligible for profit-sharing and aren't tracked by the bakery. Anecdotally, this labor force appeared to be almost entirely male and Latino. Also note that grocery employees self-report ethnoracially, while the bakery's personnel office labels all its workers centrally. The grocery also surveys and records transgender members, who are absent from the gender count.

[5] Annual earnings include wages or salaries, profit sharing (in cash and valued shares of the company), and dividends paid on accrued noncash shares. The comparison is somewhat problematic, as grocery employees also receive a 20% discount on food and their health care benefits are more generous than the bakery's. Hourly earnings are derived by dividing each employee's annual earnings by her or his recorded hours. (As required for profit sharing based on input of hours, even salaried bakery employees track annual hours.) Note that the earnings of women of color at the bakery are not very meaningful, as there were only two such employees. All annual county-level annual earnings data are from the U.S. Census Bureau's 2003 American Community Survey, but counties are not identified to protect the companies' confidentiality. County-level hourly earnings data are from the California Employment Development Department (2004).

[6] Although some might legitimately raise concern about the high proportion of nonmember employees, particularly given earlier cooperatives' unwillingness to extend membership beyond the founders (e.g., Perry 1978) and very early critics' concerns that cooperatives were likely to "degenerate" into separate tiers of owners and non-owning employees (Webb and Webb 1897), it was clear from interviews and observation that a no vote on membership was exceptional. Every employee who applied for membership was accepted during my three years of observation, and no one could remember more than one member who had been rejected for membership since management had been instated in 1989.

References

Acker, Joan. 1990. "Hierarchies, Jobs, Bodies: A Theory of Gendered Organizations." *Gender and Society,* Vol. 4, no. 2, pp. 139–58.

Acker, Joan. 2006a. *Class Questions: Feminist Answers.* Judith A. Howard, Barbara Risman, Joey Sprague, eds., Gender Lens Series. Lanham, MD: Rowman and Littlefield.

Acker, Joan. 2006b. "Inequality Regimes: Gender, Class, and Race in Organizations." *Gender and Society,* Vol. 20, no. 4, pp. 441–64.

Aronowitz, Stanley. 1992. *The Politics of Identity: Class, Culture, Social Movements.* New York and London: Routledge.

Bettie, Julie. 1995. "Class Dismissed? Roseanne and the Changing Face of Working-Class Iconography." *Social Text,* Vol. 14, no. 4, pp. 125–49.

Bettie, Julie. 2000. "Women without Class: Chicas, Cholas, Trash, and the Presence/Absence of Class Identity. *Signs,* Vol. 26, no. 1, pp. 1–35.

Bourdieu, Pierre. 1986. "The Forms of Capital." In J. Richardson, ed., *Handbook of Theory and Research for the Sociology of Education.* New York: Greenwood Press, pp. 241–58.

Braverman, Harry. 1974, 1984. *Labor and Monopoly Capital: The Degradation of Work in the Twentieth Century* (25th anniversary ed.). New York: Monthly Review Press.

Burawoy, Michael. 1998. "The Extended Case Method." *Sociological Theory,* Vol. 16, no. 1, pp. 4–33.

Carberry, Edward J. 2010. "Who Benefits from Shared Capitalism? The Social Stratification of Wealth and Power in Companies with Employee Ownership." In Douglas Kruse, Richard Freeman, and Joseph R. Blasi, eds., *Shared Capitalism at Work: Employee Ownership, Profit and Gain Sharing, and Broad-Based Stock Options.* Chicago: University of Chicago Press, pp. 317–49

Collins, Patricia Hill. 1990. *Black Feminist Thought: Knowledge, Consciousness, and the Politics of Empowerment.* Boston: Unwin Hyman.

Collins, Sharon M. 1997. "Black Mobility in White Corporations: Up the Corporate Ladder but Out on a Limb." *Social Problems,* Vol. 44, no. 1, pp. 55–67.

Cox, Taylor. 1993, 1994. *Cultural Diversity in Organizations: Theory, Research, and Practice.* San Francisco: Berrett-Koehler.

Curl, John. 1980. *History of Work Cooperation in America: Cooperatives, Cooperative Movements, Collectivity, and Communalism from Early America to the Present.* Berkeley, CA: Homeward Press.

Emerson, Robert M., Rachel I. Fretz, and Linda L. Shaw. 1995. *Writing Ethnographic Fieldnotes.* Chicago and London: University of Chicago Press.

Ferguson, Ann Arnett. 1991. "Managing without Managers: Crisis and Resolution in a Collective Bakery." In Michael Burawoy, ed., *Ethnography Unbound: Power and Resistance in the Modern Metropolis.* Berkeley, Los Angeles, London: University of California Press, pp. 108–32.

Freeman, Jo. 1970, 1984. "The Tyranny of Structurelessness." In *Untying the Knot: Feminism, Anarchism, and Organization.* London: Dark Star/Rebel Press, pp. 5–16.

Gitlin, Todd. 1995. *The Twilight of Common Dreams: Why America Is Wracked by Culture Wars.* New York: Metropolitan.

Goodwyn, Lawrence. 1981. *The Populist Movement: A Short History of the Agrarian Revolution in America.* Oxford, London, New York: Oxford University Press.

Grob, Gerald N. 1969. *Workers and Utopia: A Study of Ideological Conflict in the American Labor Movement, 1865–1900.* New York: Quadrangle/The New York

Times Book Company.

Hacker, Sally. 1989. *Pleasure, Power and Technology*. London: Unwin Hyman.

Hochschild, Arlie Russell. 1983. *The Managed Heart: Commercialization of Human Feeling*. Berkeley: University of California Press.

Holyoake, George Jacob. 1918. *The History of the Rochdale Pioneers, 1944–1992* (10th ed. rev. and enl. ed.). London: G. Allen and Unwin.

Jackall, Robert, and Henry M. Levin. 1984. *Worker Cooperatives in America*. Berkeley: University of California Press.

Jones, Derek. 1979. "U.S. Producer Cooperatives: The Record to Date." *Industrial Relations*, Vol. 18, no. 3, pp. 342–57.

Kasmir, Sharryn. 1996. *The Myth of Mondragón: Cooperatives, Politics, and Working-Class Life in a Basque Town*, June Nash, ed. Albany, NY: State University of New York Press.

Kleinman, Sherryl. 1996. *Opposing Ambitions: Gender and Identity in an Alternative Organization*. Chicago, London: University of Chicago Press.

Kruse, Douglas, Joseph R. Blasi, and Rhokeun Park. 2010. "Shared Capitalism in the U.S. Economy: Prevalence, Characteristics, and Employee Views of Financial Participation in Enterprises." In Douglas Kruse, Richard Freeman, and Joseph R. Blasi, eds., *Shared Capitalism at Work: Employee Ownership, Profit and Gain Sharing, and Broad-Based Stock Options*. Chicago and London: University of Chicago Press, pp. 41–75.

Loe, Meika. 1999. "Feminism for Sale: Case Study of a Pro-Sex Feminist Business." *Gender and Society*, Vol. 13, no. 6, pp. 705–32.

Mansbridge, Jane J. 1980. *Beyond Adversary Democracy*. New York: Basic Books.

McPherson, Miller, Lynn Smith-Lovin, and James M. Cook. 2001. "Birds of a Feather: Homophily in Social Networks." *Annual Review of Sociology*, Vol. 27, pp. 415–44.

Milkman, Ruth. 1987. *Gender at Work: The Dynamics of Job Segregation by Sex During World War II*. Urbana, IL: University of Illinois Press.

Padavic, Irene. 1992. "White-Collar Work Values and Women's Interest in Blue-Collar Jobs." *Gender and Society*, Vol. 6, no. 2, pp. 215–30.

Pencavel, John. 2001. *Worker Participation: Lessons from the Worker Co-Ops of the Pacific Northwest*. New York: Russell Sage Foundation.

Perry, Stewart E. 1978. *San Francisco Scavengers: Dirty Work and the Pride of Ownership*. Berkeley, CA: University of California Press.

Polletta, Francesca. 2002. *Freedom Is an Endless Meeting: Democracy in American Social Movements*. Chicago, London: University of Chicago Press.

Reskin, Barbara F., and Patricia Roos. 1990. *Job Queues, Gender Queues: Explaining Women's Inroads into Male Occupations*. Philadephia: Temple University Press.

Rose, Sonya. 1997. "Class Formation and the Quintessential Worker." In John Hall, ed., *Reworking Class*. Ithaca, NY: Cornell University Press, pp. 133–66.

Rosen, Corey, John Case, and Martin Staubus. 2005. *Equity: Why Employee Ownership Is Good for Business*. Boston: Harvard Business Press.

Rothschild, Joyce, and Raymond Russell. 1986. "Alternatives to Bureaucracy: Democratic Participation in the Economy." *Annual Review of Sociology*, Vol. 12, pp. 307–28.

Rothschild, Joyce, and Allen J. Whitt. 1986. *The Cooperative Workplace: Potentials and Dilemmas of Organisational Democracy and Participation*. Ernest Q. Campbell, ed., American Sociological Association Rose Monograph Series. Cambridge, UK: Cambridge University Press.

Rothschild-Whitt, Joyce. 1979. "The Collectivist Organization: An Alternative to

Rational-Bureaucratic Models." *American Sociological Review,* Vol. 44, no. 4, pp. 509–27.

Santa Barbara Legal Collective. 1982. "Is Anybody There? Notes on Collective Practice." In Frank Lindenfeld and Joyce Rothschild-Whitt, eds., *Workplace Democracy and Social Change.* Boston: Porter Sargent Publishers, pp. 247–56.

Schneiberg, Marc, Marissa King, and Thomas Smith. 2008. "Social Movements and Organizational Form: Cooperative Alternatives to Corporations in the American Insurance, Dairy, and Grain Industries." *American Sociological Review,* Vol. 73, pp. 635–67.

Sirianni, Carmen. 1993. "Learning Pluralism: Democracy and Diversity in Feminist Organizations." In Frank Fischer and Carmen Sirianni, eds., *Critical Studies in Organization and Bureaucracy.* Philadelphia: Temple University Press, pp. 554–76.

Steinberg, Ronnie J. 1995. "Gendered Instructions: Cultural Lag and Gender Bias in the Hay System of Job Evaluation." In Jerry Jacobs, ed., *Gender Inequality at Work.* Thousand Oaks, CA: Sage Publishers.

Swidler, Ann. 1979. *Organization without Authority: Dilemmas of Social Control in Free Schools.* Cambridge, MA: Harvard University Press.

Taylor, Barbara. 1983. *Eve and the New Jerusalem: Socialism and Feminism in the Nineteenth Century.* New York: Pantheon Books.

Tomaskovic-Devey, Donald. 1993. *Gender and Racial Inequality at Work: The Sources and Consequences of Job Segregation.* Ithaca, NY: ILR Press.

Webb, Sidney, and Beatrice Potter Webb. 1897. *Industrial Democracy.* London and New York: Longmans, Green and Co.

CHAPTER 6

An Empirical Analysis
of Risk Preferences,
Compensation Risk, and
Employee Outcomes

FIDAN ANA KURTULUS
University of Massachusetts, Amherst

DOUGLAS L. KRUSE
JOSEPH R. BLASI
Rutgers University

Introduction

Employee compensation packages often comprise both a fixed salary portion and a variable portion that is tied to firm, group, or individual output or performance. Examples of performance-based pay include profit sharing, company stock and stock option payments, and group-level or individual-level performance bonuses. The prevalence of employee participation in the financial performance of firms and other performance-based pay schemes has been growing in the past several decades in the United States and other advanced economies. According to the 2006 wave of the General Social Survey, which is a nationally representative survey of individuals conducted by the National Opinion Research Center, over a third of U.S. workers are covered by profit sharing, 27% are covered by department- or team-based bonuses, 18% own company stock, and 9% own company stock options. Coverage is similar in France, Great Britain, Italy, and Japan (Jones and Kato 1995; Del Boca, Kruse, and Pendleton 1999).

Firms use performance-based pay in employee compensation packages to induce greater worker effort and identification with the firm. However, performance-based pay introduces variability into compensation, which risk-averse workers dislike, and the greater the portion of compensation that is composed of performance-based pay as opposed to a fixed salary, the greater is the compensation risk faced by the employee. In this study, we use the NBER Shared Capitalism Database, consisting of more than 40,000 employee surveys from 14 firms, to analyze whether a close match between workers' risk preferences and the riskiness of their compensation packages is related to improved employee outcomes such as lower absenteeism, lower shirking, lower probability of voluntary turnover, greater worker motivation, and higher levels of job satisfaction and loyalty.

An advantage of our data is that they contain information on individual-level measures of risk aversion, which is often discussed as an important factor in worker attitudes toward variable pay, but is rarely measured. We use this information, coupled with measures of the riskiness, or variability, of workers' compensation packages, including the proportion of pay composed of various forms of shared capitalism such as ownership of company stock, profit and gain sharing, and bonus arrangements, to explore the consequences of alignment between risk preferences and compensation risk on worker outcomes. To our knowledge, this is the first study to empirically examine the implications of a preference–compensation risk match on employee outcomes. The primary finding of our study is that a match between the worker's risk preferences and the extent of risk in his or her compensation is associated with higher levels of motivation, job satisfaction, company attachment, and loyalty, but that risk-averse workers are generally less responsive than risk-loving workers to a preference–compensation match.

Theoretical Framework and Past Literature

A basic assumption in most theoretical models of the employee–employer relationship is that the worker is risk averse, deriving greater utility from fixed pay over variable pay of equal expected value (Milgrom and Roberts 1992; Holmstrom 1979; Shavell 1979). Furthermore, the more risk averse the worker, the greater the reduction in his or her utility generated by variability in pay. Workers who are very risk averse will prefer to have lower compensation risk than those who are less risk averse. Therefore, an alignment of risk preferences and compensation risk is likely to lead to improved utility, reflected in improved worker outcomes such as job satisfaction and company attachment.

A few previous studies have examined the relationship between risk preferences and attitudes toward variable pay, and a fairly large literature exists on the relationship between variable pay and worker outcomes, but there have not been any prior studies looking at how an alignment of risk preferences and compensation risk may lead to improved worker outcomes. This is the primary contribution of our paper to the literature. The few past studies on the role of risk preferences in shaping attitudes toward variable pay found that risk aversion reduced worker preferences for variable pay in laboratory experiments (Cadsby, Song, and Tapon 2007) as well as in actual work environments (Kurtulus, Kruse, and Blasi 2011; Cornelissen, Heywood, and Jirjahn 2008). On the other hand, there is a fairly large literature exploring the relationship between variable pay and worker outcomes. For example, Wilson and Peel (1991) and Brown, Fakhfakh, and Sessions (1999) found that employee participation in profit sharing and share ownership lowers absenteeism and quit rates; Bryson and Freeman (2010) found that employee ownership increases labor productivity; Blasi, Freeman, Mackin, and Kruse (2010) found that it increases worker motivation; and Green and Heywood (2008) found that profit sharing and bonuses increase job satisfaction. Our study links these two branches of the literature by examining how a preference–compensation risk match influences worker outcomes.

Data and Variables

We use the NBER Shared Capitalism Database, which consists of detailed information collected from more than 40,000 employee surveys from 14 firms, to explore whether a close match between workers' risk preferences and the riskiness of their compensation packages relates to improved employee outcomes including lower absenteeism, lower probability of voluntary turnover, greater worker motivation, and higher levels of job satisfaction, attachment to the company, loyalty, and innovation.

The NBER data comprise one of the largest worker-level data sets on labor practices and worker sentiment ever collected. The survey was conducted during the years 2002 through 2006 using a combination of web-based and paper survey methods. It had a high response rate, averaging 53% across the 14 companies. The firms participating in the survey included large multinationals with employment spanning North America, South America, Europe, and Asia, as well as smaller firms with mostly U.S. employees. The sample included eight firms in the manufacturing industry, two high-technology firms, and four in the service industry. Three of the fourteen companies exceeded 10,000 employees, five employed between 1,000 and 10,000 workers, and the remaining six employed fewer than 1,000 workers. All of the firms had employee ownership and variable pay programs, though of varying forms and degrees: thirteen had individual bonus plans, nine had workgroup-based or department-based performance bonus plans, eleven had broad-based profit-sharing plans, five had broad-based stock option plans, eight had standard employee stock owner-ship plans (ESOPs), one had a 401(k) employee stock ownership program, four had employee stock purchase plans, and three had 401(k)s with com-pany stock. Most had combinations of these plans.

The employees in the NBER Shared Capitalism Database, of course, may not be representative of the overall U.S. workforce—indeed, those employees work at firms that view shared capitalism favorably and may have joined the firms because those workers are more favorably inclined toward shared capitalism and less averse to the compensation risk it creates than other workers. Shared capitalism is, however, unlikely to be the determining factor for most employees in choosing whether to work at an organization, so, in these companies, we would expect to also find many employees who care little about shared capitalism and took the job for other reasons (e.g., pay, location, job fit, career opportunities). Consistent with this expectation, there is substan-tial variation within these companies in attitudes toward shared capital-ism (Kurtulus, Kruse, and Blasi 2011). Furthermore, the high incidence of shared capitalism across the U.S. economy (Kruse, Blasi, and Park 2010) provides an indication that the results may be generalizable to other firms and workers.

In order to explore whether a close match between workers' risk preferences and the riskiness of their compensation packages relates to improved employee outcomes, we must first define an appropriate mea-sure that captures a match between risk preferences and compensation risk. To do so, we make use of two variables in the NBER Shared Capi-talism Database. Our indicator of a worker's risk preference is:

> LOVERISK = Worker's self-assessment of his or her risk pref-erence on a 0–10 scale, with 0 indicating that the worker hates taking risk and 10 indicating the worker loves taking risk.[1]

Our indicator of how variable or risky is a worker's compensation package is:

> COMPRISK = Share of the worker's base salary that consists of performance-related pay including cash profit sharing and individual-based, workgroup-based, or department-based per-formance bonuses. [2,3]

We divide the distribution of COMPRISK into two halves: below the median (low COMPRISK) and at or above the median (high COMPRISK). LOVERISK takes on values 0, 1, 2, . . . , 10, with 0 indi-cating that the worker dislikes taking risks and 10 indicating that the worker enjoys taking risks, so we divide LOVERISK into two halves:

below the risk-neutral value of 5 (low LOVERISK) and at or above that value (high LOVERISK).[4] We then define the following indicators of match and nonmatch:

MATCH = 1 if LOVERISK is high and COMPRISK is high, or if LOVERISK is low and COMPRISK is low; 0 otherwise.

HIGHMATCH = 1 if LOVERISK is high and COMPRISK is high; 0 otherwise.

LOWMATCH = 1 if LOVERISK is low and COMPRISK is low; 0 otherwise.

NOMATCH = 1 if LOVERISK is high and COMPRISK is low, or if LOVERISK is low and COMPRISK is high; 0 otherwise.

NOMATCH10 = 1 if LOVERISK is high and COMPRISK is low; 0 otherwise.

NOMATCH01 = 1 if LOVERISK is low and COMPRISK is high; 0 otherwise.

Worker preference for risk has a mean of 5.6, but there is wide dispersion: LOVERISK equals 4 at the 25th percentile, 6 at the 50th percentile, and 7 at the 75th percentile. Variable pay comprises 13% of base salary for the typical worker, but again there is considerable variation: COMPRISK is 2% at the 25th percentile, 5% at the 50th percentile, and 15% at the 75th percentile. Forty percent of workers have a high preference for risk and a high level of compensation risk (HIGHMATCH = 1), 14% have a low preference for risk and low compensation risk (LOWMATCH = 1), 36% have a high preference for risk but low compensation risk (NOMATCH10 = 1), and the remaining 10% of workers have a low preference for risk but high compensation risk (NOMATCH01 = 1).

We examine the influence of alignment between risk preferences and compensation risk on the following worker outcome variables:

DAYSABS = Number of days absent in the last 6 months (non-vacation).

LOOKHARD = Worker reported likelihood that he or she will look hard for a job with another organization within the next 12 months, on a scale of 1 to 4, with 1 indicating not at all likely, 2 indicating somewhat likely, 3 indicating very likely, and 4 indicating that the worker is already looking.

MOTIVATION = The worker's willingness to work harder than he or she has in the past in order to help the company succeed, with 1 indicating strongly disagree, 2 indicating disagree, 3 indicating neither agree nor disagree, 4 indicating agree, and 5 indicating strongly agree.

JOBSATISFAC: Worker's job satisfaction at the company, on a scale of 1 to 7, with 1 indicating completely dissatisfied and 7 indicating completely satisfied.

LONGTIME: Dummy variable indicating whether the worker sees himself or herself working at the company for the foreseeable future, with 1 indicating yes and 0 indicating no.

LOYAL: Degree of loyalty the worker feels toward the company, on a scale of 1 to 4, with 1 for no loyalty at all, 2 for only a little loyalty, 3 for some loyalty, and 4 indicating a lot of loyalty.

SUGGESTIONS: Worker-reported frequency of suggestions to improve department or company effectiveness made to someone in the company in the past, with values 1 (never), 2 (occasionally), 3 (monthly), 4 (weekly), and 5 (daily).

Our regression specifications also include a wide array of worker characteristics as control variables that are likely to influence worker outcomes (such as motivation and attachment to the firm) and that may also be correlated with the worker's risk preferences and the riskiness of his or her compensation. For instance, past research has shown women, older workers, workers with greater tenure at the firm, and workers with lower education and salary levels to be more risk averse (Niederle and Vesterlund 2007; Dohmen et al., forthcoming; Dohmen and Falk, forthcoming; Kurtulus, Kruse, and Blasi 2011). Many of these variables are also correlated with our worker outcome variables, so not controlling for them would yield biased estimates of the relationship between a preference–compensation match and worker outcomes. We additionally control for whether the worker believes his or her pay is at or above market level since this is likely to influence the relationship between that worker's preference–compensation risk match and that worker's attachment to the firm, loyalty, motivation, and so on. A worker whose risk preferences and compensation risk are aligned may work longer hours because he or she derives greater enjoyment from the job, and this will also be reflected in his or her motivation, job satisfaction, and company attachment, so we also control for weekly hours worked. Lastly, in a few of the NBER firms, workers in specific occupations and those who are union members are not eligible to participate in certain profit-sharing and bonus programs, so we include controls for the worker's occupation and union status.

The control variables we include in all our regression models are defined as follows:

AGE = Worker age.

FEMALE = 1 if worker is female; 0 otherwise.

UNION = 1 if worker is a union worker; 0 otherwise.

TENURE = Worker's tenure at the firm, in years.

BASEPAY = Worker's annual base pay the previous year, excluding overtime, bonuses, and commissions.

HOURS = Worker's weekly hours worked.

ATMKT = 1 if the worker believes that his or her annual base salary at the firm is at or above the going market rate for employees in other companies with similar experience and job descriptions in the region; 0 otherwise.

Ethnicity Indicators

WHITE = 1 if worker is white; 0 otherwise.

HISPANIC = 1 if worker is Hispanic; 0 otherwise.

BLACK = 1 if worker is black; 0 otherwise.

ASIAN = 1 if worker is Asian; 0 otherwise.

NATIVE AMERICAN = 1 if worker is Native American; 0 otherwise.

OTHER = 1 if worker is other ethnicity; 0 otherwise.

Education Indicators

NO HIGH SCHOOL = 1 if worker does not hold a high school degree; 0 otherwise.

HIGH SCHOOL = 1 if worker's highest educational degree is a high school degree, including GED; 0 otherwise.

SOME COLLEGE = 1 if worker has attended some college but has not received a bachelor's degree; 0 otherwise.

ASSOCIATE DEGREE = 1 if worker's highest educational degree is an associate's degree; 0 otherwise.

COLLEGE = 1 if worker's highest educational degree is a bachelor's degree; 0 otherwise.

GRADUATE SCHOOL = 1 if worker's highest educational degree is a master's, professional, or doctoral degree; 0 otherwise.

Occupation Indicators

PRODUCTION: 1 if worker's occupation is production; 0 otherwise.

ADMINISTRATIVE SUPPORT = 1 if worker's occupation is administrative support; 0 otherwise.

PROFESSIONAL AND TECHNICAL = 1 if worker's occupation is professional and technical (including engineers and scientists); 0 otherwise.

SALES = 1 if worker's occupation is sales; 0 otherwise.

CUSTOMER SERVICE = 1 if worker's occupation is customer service; 0 otherwise.

MANAGEMENT = 1 if worker's occupation is management; 0 otherwise.

Descriptive statistics for all variables are provided in Table 1.

TABLE 1
Descriptive Statistics

	Mean	Std. Dev.	Min.	Max.	Obs.
loverisk	5.60	2.44	0	10	41,695
comprisk	0.13	0.88	0	125	27,437
daysabs	1.73	7.41	1	180	44,651
lookhard	1.57	0.83	1	4	46,202
motivation	4.02	0.90	1	5	45,832
jobsatisfac	5.03	1.30	1	7	43,413
longtime	0.82	0.39	0	1	46,061
loyal	3.33	0.80	1	4	42,350
suggestions	2.22	0.84	1	5	33,423
match	0.54	0.50	0	1	27,134
highmatch	0.40	0.49	0	1	27,134
lowmatch	0.14	0.35	0	1	27,134
nomatch	0.46	0.50	0	1	27,134
nomatch10	0.36	0.48	0	1	27,134
nomatch01	0.10	0.30	0	1	27,134
age	40.93	10.50	16	84	36,791
female	0.31	0.46	0	1	38,325
union	0.12	0.32	0	1	46,269
tenure	9.54	8.98	0	51.08	45,755
basepay	54,820.22	41,997.23	600	1,000,000	30,457
hours	45.79	8.14	0	100	45,696
atmkt	0.59	0.49	0	1	36,236
ethnicity:					
white	0.77	0.42	0	1	36,061
hispanic	0.07	0.26	0	1	36,061
black	0.05	0.21	0	1	36,061
asian	0.08	0.27	0	1	36,061
native american	0.01	0.11	0	1	36,061
other	0.02	0.15	0	1	36,061
education:					
no high school	0.04	0.19	0	1	35,758
high school	0.23	0.42	0	1	35,758
some college	0.22	0.41	0	1	35,758

Continued

TABLE 1
Descriptive Statistics (Continued)

	Mean	Std. Dev.	Min.	Max.	Obs.
associate degree	0.08	0.28	0	1	35,758
college	0.28	0.45	0	1	35,758
graduate school	0.14	0.34	0	1	39,436
occupation:					
production	0.43	0.50	0	1	45,816
administrative support	0.06	0.24	0	1	45,816
professional and technical	0.30	0.46	0	1	45,816
sales	0.06	0.23	0	1	45,816
customer service	0.03	0.17	0	1	45,800
management	0.13	0.33	0	1	45,816

Note: Based on the NBER Shared Capitalism Survey of N = 46,907 workers.

Results

Our hypothesis is that a match between the worker's risk preferences and extent of risk in his or her cash compensation will result in improved worker outcomes (lower absenteeism, lower likelihood of looking for a new job, higher motivation, greater job satisfaction, higher likelihood of staying with the company in the future, greater loyalty, and higher frequency of suggestions). This implies that MATCH, HIGHMATCH, and LOWMATCH should be associated with better worker outcomes, while NOMATCH, NOMATCH10, and NOMATCH01 should be associated with worse worker outcomes. Therefore, we expect the relationships between the match variables and the worker outcome variables to have the following signs (and the nonmatch variables to have the opposite of these signs): DAYSABS (–), LOOKHARD (–), MOTIVATION (+), JOBSATISFAC (+), LONGTIME (+), LOYAL (+), SUGGESTIONS (+).

As a first step in exploring whether a match between the worker's risk preferences and extent of risk in his or her compensation results in improved worker outcomes, we estimate regressions of each outcome variable on MATCH and worker controls. These results are presented in Table 2. We use OLS to estimate all except for the DAYSABS equation, where we estimate a Tobit model since that outcome variable is left-censored at zero, and for LONGTIME, where we estimate a Probit model (with table entries indicating the Probit marginal effects) since that outcome variable is a dummy variable.

The revealed relationships between MATCH and the various outcome measures overwhelmingly support our hypothesis that a match between the worker's risk preferences and extent of risk in his or her compensation will result in improved worker outcomes. The negative and statistically significant effects of MATCH on DAYSABS and

TABLE 2

Effect of MATCH (Against Omitted Base Group NOMATCH) on Worker Outcomes
(Using Compensation Risk Variable COMPRISK)

	daysabs (1)	lookhard (2)	motivation (3)	jobsatisfac (4)	longtime (5)	loyal (6)	suggestions (7)
match	−0.642°°°	−0.030°°	0.038°°°	0.075°°°	0.014°°	0.063°°°	−0.021
	(0.230)	(0.012)	(0.013)	(0.019)	(0.006)	(0.012)	(0.013)
age	−0.078°°°	−0.009°°°	0.004°°°	0.008°°°	0.000	0.008°°°	−0.004°°°
	(0.014)	(0.001)	(0.001)	(0.001)	(0.000)	(0.001)	(0.001)
female	2.818°°°	−0.092°°°	0.077°°°	0.109°°°	0.020°°°	0.100°°°	−0.119°°°
	(0.320)	(0.014)	(0.015)	(0.021)	(0.006)	(0.013)	(0.014)
union	0.549	0.266°°°	−0.117°°°	−0.191°°°	−0.086°°°	−0.134°°°	0.010
	(0.660)	(0.036)	(0.036)	(0.052)	(0.015)	(0.033)	(0.030)
tenure	−0.006	−0.005°°°	−0.007°°°	−0.007°°°	0.001°°	−0.000	0.003°°°
	(0.015)	(0.001)	(0.001)	(0.001)	(0.000)	(0.001)	(0.001)
basepay	0.000	−0.000	0.000°°°	0.000°°°	0.000°°°	0.000°°°	0.000°°°
	(0.000)	(0.000)	(0.000)	(0.000)	(0.000)	(0.000)	(0.000)
hours	−0.160°°°	0.002°°	0.008°°°	0.005°°°	0.001°°	0.006°°°	0.008°°°
	(0.020)	(0.001)	(0.001)	(0.001)	(0.000)	(0.001)	(0.001)
atmkt	−0.798°°°	−0.278°°°	0.181°°°	0.449°°°	0.092°°°	0.245°°°	−0.030°°
	(0.231)	(0.012)	(0.013)	(0.019)	(0.006)	(0.011)	(0.013)
ethnicity:							
hispanic	−1.389°°°	0.025	0.168°°°	0.225°°°	−0.034°°	0.123°°°	0.066°
	(0.458)	(0.028)	(0.029)	(0.045)	(0.013)	(0.025)	(0.035)
black	−0.626	0.170°°°	0.159°°°	0.061	−0.045°°°	−0.103°°	−0.182°°°
	(0.582)	(0.036)	(0.036)	(0.052)	(0.015)	(0.032)	(0.030)
asian	−3.266°°°	0.01	0.224°°°	0.017	−0.033°°°	0.054°°°	−0.021
	(0.453)	(0.022)	(0.022)	(0.032)	(0.010)	(0.019)	(0.036)
native american	0.515	−0.003	0.087	0.131	−0.040	−0.030	−0.068
	(1.102)	(0.059)	(0.067)	(0.093)	(0.029)	(0.057)	(0.054)
other	−0.425	0.160°°°	0.046	−0.082	−0.057°°°	0.01	0.050
	(0.766)	(0.050)	(0.045)	(0.063)	(0.021)	(0.040)	(0.059)
education:							
high school	−0.155	−0.048	−0.033	0.021	0.027°	−0.012	−0.044
	(0.840)	(0.040)	(0.046)	(0.071)	(0.016)	(0.040)	(0.040)
some college	0.806	0.051	−0.022	−0.122°	0.003	−0.002	0.053
	(0.844)	(0.040)	(0.046)	(0.071)	(0.017)	(0.039)	(0.041)
associate degree	−0.779	0.095°°	−0.041	−0.195°°°	−0.031	−0.023	0.060
	(0.876)	(0.043)	(0.049)	(0.075)	(0.020)	(0.042)	(0.043)
college	−1.414°	0.128°°°	−0.058	−0.223°°°	−0.035°	−0.030	0.154°°°
	(0.853)	(0.041)	(0.047)	(0.072)	(0.019)	(0.040)	(0.043)
graduate school 0.175°°°	−2.284°°	0.149°°°	−0.077	−0.227°°°	−0.058°°°	−0.025	
	(0.902)	(0.043)	(0.049)	(0.074)	(0.021)	(0.041)	(0.048)
occupation:							
administrative	−1.539°°°	−0.151°°°	0.296°°°	0.269°°°	0.046°°°	0.327°°°	−0.005
	(0.545)	(0.030)	(0.030)	(0.048)	(0.011)	(0.026)	(0.024)
prof. and tech.	−0.537	−0.132°°°	0.227°°°	0.253°°°	0.040°°°	0.293°°°	0.089°°°
	(0.333)	(0.019)	(0.020)	(0.028)	(0.008)	(0.017)	(0.020)
sales	−3.412°°°	−0.237°°°	0.300°°	0.439°°°	0.070°°°	0.450°°°	−0.052°
	(0.511)	(0.025)	(0.027)	(0.039)	(0.009)	(0.022)	(0.028)
customer service	−0.840	−0.136°°°	0.316°°°	0.030	0.027°	0.298°°°	0.067°°
	(0.616)	(0.037)	(0.040)	(0.062)	(0.015)	(0.035)	(0.032)

Continued

TABLE 2
Effect of MATCH (Against Omitted Base Group NOMATCH) on Worker Outcomes
(Using Compensation Risk Variable COMPRISK) (*Continued*)

	daysabs (1)	lookhard (2)	motivation (3)	jobsatisfac (4)	longtime (5)	loyal (6)	suggestions (7)
management	−1.935°°°	−0.196°°°	0.366°°°	0.422°°°	0.068°°°	0.432°°°	0.455°°°
	(0.399)	(0.022)	(0.024)	(0.034)	(0.008)	(0.020)	(0.028)
Constant	6.713°°°	2.146°°°	3.214°°°	4.071°°°	—	2.367°°°	1.901°°°
	(1.209)	(0.062)	(0.066)	(0.099)		(0.057)	(0.068)
Observations	19218	19566	19594	19618	19571	19307	13904
Pseudo R2	0.013	—	—	—	0.053	—	—
Adj. R2	—	0.074	0.081	0.066	—	0.114	0.122

Note: Equations are estimated using OLS, except for the DAYSABS equation, which is estimated using Tobit, and the LONGTIME equation, which is estimated using Probit (with Probit marginal effects presented in table entries). Robust standards are in parentheses. °, °°, °°° indicate significance at the 10%, 5%, and 1% levels, respectively. The omitted category for the ethnicity dummy variable group is WHITE, the omitted category for the education dummy variable group is NO HIGH SCHOOL, and the omitted category for the occupation dummy variable group is PRODUCTION.

LOOKHARD indicate that workers whose compensation risk matches their risk attitudes exhibit lower absenteeism and lower intention to leave the firm. Table 2 also reveals that a match between the worker's risk preferences and extent of risk in his or her compensation increases worker motivation, job satisfaction, company attachment, and loyalty. Frequency of suggestions to improve department or company effectiveness is the only outcome variable that is not statistically significantly associated with MATCH (last column).

The results in Table 2 support our hypothesis that a match between the worker's risk preferences and extent of risk in his or her compensation will result in improved worker out comes, but also of interest is the possibility that the way in which employees respond to a match will be different among the risk-loving than the risk-averse workers. A possible reason for this asymmetry is that workers who are more risk averse may be more reluctant to leave their job to seek another one when they don't have a preference–compensation match, since they may not want to bear the uncertainty associated with being unemployed or not knowing how much better their new job will suit them. To explore possible asymmetries in the match response among the risk loving and the risk averse, we regress our worker outcome variables on the more-specific match variables HIGHMATCH (which equals 1 if the worker is risk loving and faces high compensation risk; 0 otherwise) and LOWMATCH (which equals 1 if the worker is risk averse and faces low compensation risk; 0 otherwise) against the omitted category of NOMATCH (which equals 1 if the worker's risk preference does not match his or her compensation-risk level), controlling for the full set of worker characteristics.

The estimates presented in Table 3 reveal that the risk averse are generally less responsive to a match, while the risk loving respond

TABLE 3
Effect of HIGHMATCH and LOWMATCH (Against Omitted Base Group NOMATCH) on Worker Outcomes (Using Compensation Risk Variable COMPRISK)

	daysabs (1)	lookhard (2)	motivation (3)	jobsatisfac (4)	longtime (5)	loyal (6)	suggestions (7)
highmatch	−0.645°°	−0.010	0.090°°°	0.094°°°	0.015°°	0.094°°°	0.065°°°
	(0.261)	(0.014)	(0.015)	(0.021)	(0.006)	(0.013)	(0.016)
lowmatch	−0.637°	−0.071°°°	−0.070°°°	0.034	0.011	−0.002	−0.136°°°
	(0.332)	(0.018)	(0.020)	(0.029)	(0.008)	(0.018)	(0.016)
age	−0.078°°°	−0.009°°°	0.004°°°	0.008°°°	0.000	0.008°°°	−0.004°°°
	(0.014)	(0.001)	(0.001)	(0.001)	(0.000)	(0.001)	(0.001)
female	2.817°°°	−0.087°°°	0.088°°°	0.114°°	0.020°°°	0.107°°°	−0.103°°°
	(0.324)	(0.014)	(0.015)	(0.021)	(0.006)	(0.013)	(0.015)
union	0.549	0.269°°°	−0.110°°°	−0.188°°°	−0.086°°°	−0.129°°°	0.021
	(0.662)	(0.036)	(0.036)	(0.052)	(0.015)	(0.033)	(0.030)
tenure	−0.006	−0.004°°°	−0.007°°°	−0.007°°°	0.001°°	−0.000	0.003°°°
	(0.015)	(0.001)	(0.001)	(0.001)	(0.000)	(0.001)	(0.001)
basepay	0.000	−0.000°	0.000°°°	0.000°°°	0.000°°°	0.000	0.000°°°
	(0.000)	(0.000)	(0.000)	(0.000)	(0.000)	(0.000)	(0.000)
hours	−0.160°°°	0.002°°	0.008°°°	0.005°°°	0.001°°	0.005°°°	0.008°°°
	(0.020)	(0.001)	(0.001)	(0.001)	(0.000)	(0.001)	(0.001)
atmkt	−0.798°°°	−0.278°°°	0.181°°°	0.448°°°	0.092°°°	0.245°°°	−0.029°
	(0.231)	(0.012)	(0.013)	(0.019)	(0.006)	(0.011)	(0.013)
ethnicity:							
hispanic	−1.389°°°	0.024	0.165°°°	0.224°°°	−0.034°°	0.121°°°	0.059°
	(0.458)	(0.028)	(0.029)	(0.045)	(0.013)	(0.025)	(0.035)
black	−0.626	0.169°°°	0.156°°°	0.060	−0.045°°°	−0.104°°°	−0.186°°°
	(0.583)	(0.036)	(0.036)	(0.053)	(0.015)	(0.032)	(0.030)
asian	−3.265°°°	0.014	0.214°°°	0.013	−0.034°°	0.047°°	−0.037
	(0.454)	(0.022)	(0.022)	(0.032)	(0.010)	(0.019)	(0.036)
native american	0.515	−0.002	0.090	0.131	−0.040	−0.030	−0.064
	(1.101)	(0.059)	(0.068)	(0.093)	(0.029)	(0.057)	(0.054)
other	−0.424	0.157°°°	0.040	−0.084	−0.057°°°	0.016	0.045
	(0.766)	(0.050)	(0.045)	(0.063)	(0.021)	(0.040)	(0.059)

Continued

TABLE 3
Effect of HIGHMATCH and LOWMATCH (Against Omitted Base Group
NOMATCH) on Worker Outcomes (Using Compensation Risk Variable
COMPRISK) (*Continued*)

	daysabs (1)	lookhard (2)	motivation (3)	jobsatisfac (4)	longtime (5)	loyal (6)	suggestions (7)
education:							
high school	−0.155	−0.048	−0.033	0.02	0.027°	−0.012	−0.045
	(0.840)	(0.040)	(0.046)	(0.071)	(0.016)	(0.040)	(0.040)
some college	0.806	0.047	−0.032	−0.126°	0.003	−0.008	0.040
	(0.844)	(0.040)	(0.046)	(0.071)	(0.017)	(0.039)	(0.040)
associate degree	−0.779	0.091°°	−0.053	−0.199°°°	−0.031	−0.029	0.044
	(0.878)	(0.043)	(0.049)	(0.075)	(0.020)	(0.042)	(0.043)
college	−1.413°	0.121°°°	−0.076	−0.230°°°	−0.035°	−0.041	0.129°°°
	(0.856)	(0.041)	(0.047)	(0.072)	(0.019)	(0.040)	(0.043)
graduate school	−2.283°°	0.142°°°	−0.095°°	−0.234°°°	−0.058°°°	−0.036	0.153°°°
	(0.905)	(0.043)	(0.049)	(0.074)	(0.022)	(0.041)	(0.048)
occupation:							
administrative	−1.538°°°	−0.154°°°	0.288°°°	0.267°°°	0.046°°°	0.322°°°	−0.011
	(0.546)	(0.030)	(0.030)	(0.048)	(0.011)	(0.026)	(0.024)
prof. and tech.	−0.536	−0.140°°°	0.207°°°	0.245°°°	0.039°°°	0.281°°°	0.073°°°
	(0.340)	(0.019)	(0.020)	(0.029)	(0.008)	(0.018)	(0.020)
sales	−3.410°°°	−0.249°°°	0.269°°°	0.427°°°	0.070°°°	0.431°°°	−0.096°°°
	(0.522)	(0.026)	(0.027)	(0.040)	(0.009)	(0.022)	(0.028)
customer service	−0.839	−0.137°°°	0.313°°°	0.029	0.027°	0.296°°°	0.063°
	(0.616)	(0.037)	(0.039)	(0.061)	(0.015)	(0.035)	(0.032)
management	−1.934°°°	−0.205°°°	0.342°°°	0.413°°°	0.067°°°	0.417°°°	0.422°°°
	(0.407)	(0.022)	(0.024)	(0.035)	(0.008)	(0.020)	(0.028)
Constant	6.711°°°	2.161°°°	3.256°°°	4.086°°°	—	2.392°°°	1.948°°°
	(1.216)	(0.062)	(0.067)	(0.099)		(0.057)	(0.068)
Observations	19218	19566	19594	19618	19571	19307	13904
Pseudo R2	0.013	—	—	—	0.053	—	—
Adj. R2	—	0.074	0.084	0.066	—	0.115	0.128

Note: Equations are estimated using OLS, except for the DAYSABS equation, which is estimated using Tobit, and the LONGTIME equation, which is estimated using Probit (with Probit marginal effects presented in table entries). Robust standards are in parentheses. °, °°, °°° indicate significance at the 10%, 5%, and 1% levels, respectsively. The omitted category for the ethnicity dummy variable group is WHITE, the omitted category for the education dummy variable group is NO HIGH SCHOOL, and the omitted category for the occupation dummy variable group is PRODUCTION.

in the expected manner with improved outcomes: the coefficient on HIGHMATCH has the expected statistically significant sign in every equation except in the LOOKHARD equation, while the only outcome variables that have the expected relationship with LOWMATCH are DAYSABS and LOOKHARD. For example, the effect of a preference–compensation match on lowering absenteeism is stronger for risk-loving workers; and a match results in higher job satisfaction, firm attachment, and loyalty among risk-loving workers—as we would expect—but has no statistically significant effect among risk-averse workers. Also of note is the surprising result that, among the risk averse, the effect of a match on motivation and the frequency of innovative suggestions is lower in comparison to those with no preference–compensation match (the omitted group). At the end of this section, we say more on the finding that a match between the preferences of risk-averse workers and compensation risk does not necessarily improve outcomes.

We next turn to a closer analysis of workers whose risk preferences do not match their compensation risk—that is, those who either are risk loving but face low compensation risk (NOMATCH10 = 1) or those who are risk averse but face high compensation risk (NOMATCH01 = 1). We do this to explore the possibility that, among workers whose risk preferences do not match the extent of compensation risk they face (i.e., NOMATCH = 1), there may be asymmetries in behavior. For example, a lack of a match may result in inferior worker outcomes for the risk loving but not the risk averse, following the same reasoning introduced earlier (i.e., that the risk averse may be reluctant to leave their job and seek another, thereby incurring income uncertainty associated with unemployment). To investigate this, using the subsample of workers whose risk preferences do not match their compensation risk, we estimate regressions of our seven worker outcome variables on NOMATCH10 against the omitted category NOMATCH01, controlling for the full set of worker characteristics. The results in Table 4 reveal that, among workers with no match, the risk-loving workers look harder for another job, have higher motivation, lower job satisfaction, lower intention to stay at the firm, and are less loyal to the firm, but they offer more suggestions than those who are risk averse. Put differently, the risk averse are generally less negatively affected by a mismatch between their risk preferences and the compensation risk they face.

This echoes our earlier finding that, for risk-averse workers, a preference–compensation match does not necessarily improve outcomes and, in some cases, it may even lower worker performance. There are at least four possible explanations for this finding. One is that even risk-averse workers like having output-contingent compensation despite their aversion to the variability it creates in their pay, perhaps because seeing their risk-loving colleagues receive variable compensation creates a desire for it among them as well, or because profit sharing and bonuses instill a sense of ownership and cooperation that workers like, despite their disutility from the risk it imposes on their earnings. Both risk-loving and risk-averse workers seem to have a baseline appreciation of the notion of incentives tied to performance,

TABLE 4

In the Subsample of Workers with NOMATCH = 1 (i.e., MATCH = 0), Effect of NOMATCH10 (Against Omitted Base Group NOMATCH01) on Worker Outcomes (Using Compensation Risk Variable COMPRISK)

	daysabs (1)	lookhard (2)	motivation (3)	jobsatisfac (4)	longtime (5)	loyal (6)	suggestions (7)
nomatch10	−0.111	0.178°°°	0.045°	−0.110°°°	−0.062°°°	−0.097°°°	0.128°°°
	(0.414)	(0.022)	(0.023)	(0.034	(0.010	(0.021)	(0.022)
age	−0.091°°°	−0.010°°°	0.005°°°	0.008°°°	0.001°	0.009°°°	−0.003°°°
	(0.022)	(0.001)	(0.001)	(0.002)	(0.000)	(0.001)	(0.001)
female	3.198°°°	−0.102°°°	0.132°°°	0.154°°°	0.033°°°	0.148°°°	−0.110°°°
	(0.517)	(0.021)	(0.021)	(0.032)	(0.009)	(0.019)	(0.020)
union	0.909	0.175°°°	−0.103°°	−0.165°°°	−0.059°°°	−0.119°°°	0.012
	(0.925)	(0.042)	(0.043)	(0.064)	(0.019)	(0.039)	(0.036)
tenure	−0.023	−0.004°°°	−0.007°°°	−0.007°°°	0.001	−0.001	0.004°°°
	(0.028)	(0.001)	(0.001)	(0.002)	(0.001)	(0.001)	(0.001)
basepay	0.000	0.000	0.000°°°	0.000	0.000°°°	−0.000	0.000
	(0.000)	(0.000)	(0.000)	(0.000)	(0.000)	(0.000)	(0.000)
hours	−0.139°°°	0.002°	0.006°°°	0.002	0.001°	0.005°°°	0.007°°°
	(0.037)	(0.001)	(0.001)	(0.002)	(0.001)	(0.001)	(0.001)
atmkt	−0.604	−0.291°°°	0.182°°°	0.464°°°	0.098°°°	0.266°°°	−0.048°°°
	(0.395)	(0.019)	(0.020)	(0.029)	(0.009)	(0.018)	(0.018)
ethnicity:							
hispanic	−1.720°°	0.022	0.205°°°	0.277°°°	−0.008	0.142°°°	0.094°°
	(0.785)	(0.042)	(0.045)	(0.069)	(0.020)	(0.040)	(0.047)
black	−0.154	0.192°°°	0.151°°°	0.068	−0.040°	−0.126°°°	−0.155°°°
	(0.909)	(0.048)	(0.048)	(0.071)	(0.021)	(0.044)	(0.039)
asian	−6.438°°°	0.052	0.318°°°	−0.020	−0.045°°	0.039	−0.001
	(0.913)	(0.038)	(0.038)	(0.060)	(0.019)	(0.035)	(0.051)
native american	−1.559	−0.014	0.139°	0.133	−0.043	−0.032	−0.052
	(1.496)	(0.080)	(0.082)	(0.120)	(0.041)	(0.075)	(0.071)
other	0.566	0.113	0.078	0.000	−0.036	0.100	0.048
	(1.527)	(0.088)	(0.071)	(0.107)	(0.035)	(0.071)	(0.076)

Continued

TABLE 4

In the Subsample of Workers with NOMATCH = 1 (i.e., MATCH = 0), Effect of
NOMATCH10 (Against Omitted Base Group NOMATCH01) on Worker Outcomes
(Using Compensation Risk Variable COMPRISK) (*Continued*)

	daysabs (1)	lookhard (2)	motivation (3)	jobsatisfac (4)	longtime (5)	loyal (6)	suggestions (7)
education:							
high school	−0.665	−0.075	0.011	0.050	0.037	0.064	−0.082
	(1.436)	(0.056)	(0.065)	(0.102)	(0.024)	(0.059)	(0.057)
some college	0.806	0.017	0.024	−0.114	0.016	0.080	0.028
	(1.446)	(0.056)	(0.065)	(0.102)	(0.025)	(0.059)	(0.057)
associate degree	−1.313	0.097	0.008	−0.154	−0.032	0.052	0.030
	(1.520)	(0.062)	(0.069)	(0.109)	(0.030)	(0.063)	(0.062)
college	−1.679	0.117°	−0.067	−0.224°°	−0.048	0.034	0.125°°
	(1.493)	(0.060)	(0.068)	(0.106)	(0.029)	(0.062)	(0.061)
graduate school	−2.666	0.101	−0.093	−0.196°	−0.055	0.028	0.112°
	(1.655)	(0.064)	(0.072)	(0.112)	(0.034)	(0.065)	(0.068)
occupation:							
administrative	−1.353	−0.118°°°	0.226°°°	0.176°°°	0.039°°	0.243°°°	0.015
	(0.889)	(0.041)	(0.042)	(0.067)	(0.018)	(0.037)	(0.034)
prof. and tech.	−0.703	−0.100°°°	0.216°°°	0.231°°°	0.027°°	0.261°°°	0.069°°
	(0.581)	(0.029)	(0.029)	(0.043)	(0.013)	(0.027)	(0.027)
sales	−4.126°°°	−0.213°°°	0.296°°°	0.367°°°	0.070°°°	0.494°°°	−0.072°
	(0.922)	(0.046)	(0.049)	(0.075)	(0.017)	(0.038)	(0.042)
customer service	−1.231	−0.155°°°	0.320°°°	0.062	0.055°°°	0.301°°°	0.041
	(0.791)	(0.047)	(0.049)	(0.079)	(0.020)	(0.045)	(0.043)
management	−2.655°°°	−0.214°°°	0.392°°°	0.461°°°	0.089°°°	0.443°°°	0.428°°°
	(0.708)	(0.035)	(0.036)	(0.054)	(0.013)	(0.032)	(0.041)
Constant	5.645°°°	2.007°°°	3.196°°°	4.277°°°	°	2.378°°°	1.834°°°
	(2.105)	(0.096)	(0.102)	(0.153)		(0.093)	(0.098)
Observations	8237	8387	8386	8408	8379	8258	7209
Pseudo R2	0.009	°	°	°	0.053	°	°
Adj. R2	°	0.085	0.058	0.056	°	0.102	0.083

Note: Equations are estimated using OLS, except for the DAYSABS equation, which is
estimated using Tobit, and the LONGTIME equation, which is estimated using Probit
(with Probit marginal effects presented in table entries). Robust standards are in parentheses. °, °°, °°° indicate significance at the 10%, 5%, and 1% levels, respectively. The omitted category for the ethnicity dummy variable group is WHITE, the omitted category for
the education dummy variable group is NO HIGH SCHOOL, and the omitted category
for the occupation dummy variable group is PRODUCTION.

and, while the risk averse might prefer a less-intense version of this
scenario, it is not necessarily the case that they are not motivated by
incentives. This issue is explored in greater detail in another paper of
ours on worker attitudes toward different forms of employee ownership (Kurtulus, Kruse, and Blasi 2011).

To more fully explore the findings that a preference–compensation match does not always yield improved outcomes in the case of risk-averse workers, we use a subsample of employees who have a low tolerance for risk (i.e., low LOVERISK) to estimate regressions of our seven employee outcome variables on NOMATCH01 (i.e., the person is risk averse but faces high compensation risk) against the base group of workers who are risk averse and face low compensation risk, controlling for the full set of worker characteristics. Results are illustrated in Appendix Table A. There is indeed some evidence that risk-averse workers exhibit better outcomes when they face high compensation risk than when they face low compensation risk in the case of attachment to the firm, loyalty, and frequency of innovative suggestions; however, in the case of the remaining outcome variables, the results are not statistically significant at conventional levels.

A related potential explanation is that workers may respond favorably to having a choice in the composition of their compensation rather than the firm paternalistically choosing this for them. We find some evidence supporting this hypothesis, which we discuss in the next section.

Risk-averse workers may also not mind performance-related pay when it is "gravy" on top of regular base pay, rather than substituting for base pay, in which case it may be seen as an uncertain gift from the company rather than something that may harm one's economic position. The evidence from both national and company surveys indicates that shared capitalism pay tends to supplement rather than substitute for base pay (Kruse, Freeman, and Blasi 2010). The relationship between performance-related pay, base pay, and risk aversion is a valuable area for further research.

Finally, previous research has shown profit sharing, employee ownership, and other forms of variable pay to be most effective in increasing productivity and performance when implemented as part of a package of complementary high-performance workplace practices such as delegation of decision-making rights to workers, team production, and on-the-job training (Ichniowski et al. 1996; Ichniowski, Shaw, and Prennushi 1997; Becker and Huselid 1998; Blasi, Freeman, Mackin, and Kruse 2010). A match between risk preference and compensation risk may improve outcomes even for risk-averse workers when combined with complementary high-performance workplace practices. Though we do not explore this in the current paper, we view it as a fruitful avenue for future research.

Robustness Analysis

We also investigate an alternative compensation risk variable that includes further measures of employee ownership, in particular the value of stock and option holdings of the worker:

COMPRISK1 = Share of the worker's base salary that consists of performance-related pay (including profit sharing and individual-based, workgroup-based, or department-based performance bonuses); company stock held in ESOPs, 401(k) plans, and bought in the open market, and potential profit from exercising company options.[5]

The advantage of COMPRISK1 is that it is more inclusive of different forms of employee ownership and employee equity participation than COMPRISK. We estimate all our regressions using this alternative compensation risk measure COMPRISK1 and the associated match variables MATCH1, HIGHMATCH1, LOWMATCH1, NOMATCH101, NOMATCH011 (constructed exactly as before, except using COMPRISK1 instead of COMPRISK).[6] As seen in Tables 5 through 7, the estimated relationships of interest generally are qualitatively the same in sign and significance, but the magnitudes are slightly smaller when compared to the estimates from the regressions that used COMPRISK.

Nevertheless, we prefer COMPRISK over COMPRISK1 and treat it as our main compensation risk measure for two reasons. First, COMPRISK is a sharper measure of the share of salary that comprises variable pay in a given year, while COMPRISK1 includes cumulative forms of employee ownership and employee equity participation that have been amassed over several years. Specifically, COMPRISK pertains to the portion of the worker's base salary comprising profit sharing and performance bonuses in a given year, while the stock and option holdings included in COMPRISK1 pertain to cumulative holdings and not just stock and option grants in a given year. Second, while the workers have no choice over the portion of salary composed of profit sharing and bonuses captured in COMPRISK, some components of COMPRISK1 are subject to employee choice in a number of the firms in the NBER survey where workers had discretion over their investments in company stock. Using a compensation risk measure over which the worker has no choice, namely COMPRISK, helps prevent endogeneity bias in the regression estimates since the dependent variables are unlikely to affect COMPRISK (while they might plausibly affect worker decisions to purchase stock, so the COMPRISK1 specification might yield biased estimates due to reverse causality).[7]

TABLE 5
Effect of MATCH1 (Against Omitted Base Group NOMATCH1) on Worker
Outcomes (Using Compensation Risk Variable COMPRISK1)

	daysabs (1)	lookhard (2)	motivation (3)	jobsatisfac (4)	longtime (5)	loyal (6)	suggestions (7)
match1	−0.386°	−0.025°°	0.026°°	0.065°°°	0.012°°	0.059°°°	−0.053°°°
	(0.223)	(0.012)	(0.013)	(0.019)	(0.006)	(0.011)	(0.013)
age	−0.079°°	−0.009°°°	0.004°°°	0.008°°°	0.000	0.008°°°	−0.004°°°
	(0.014)	(0.001)	(0.001)	(0.001)	(0.000)	(0.001)	(0.001)
female	2.820°°°	−0.091°°°	0.080°°°	0.108°°°	0.020°°°	0.102°°°	−0.122°°°
	(0.323)	(0.014)	(0.015)	(0.021)	(0.006)	(0.013)	(0.015)
union	0.494	0.269°°°	−0.125°°°	−0.197°°°	−0.087°°°	−0.138°°°	0.009
	(0.661)	(0.036)	(0.036)	(0.052)	(0.015)	(0.033)	(0.030)
tenure	−0.003	−0.004°°°	−0.007°°°	−0.007°°°	0.001°°	−0.001	0.003°°°
	(0.015)	(0.001)	(0.001)	(0.001)	(0.000)	(0.001)	(0.001)
basepay	0.000	−0.000	0.000°°°	0.000°°°	0.000°°°	0.000°	0.000°°°
	(0.000)	(0.000)	(0.000)	(0.000)	(0.000)	(0.000)	(0.000)
hours	−0.160°°°	0.002°°	0.008°°°	0.005°°°	0.001°°	0.006°°°	0.008°°°
	(0.020)	(0.001)	(0.001)	(0.001)	(0.000)	(0.001)	(0.001)
atmkt	−0.787°°°	−0.277°°°	0.180°°°	0.451°°°	0.092°°°	0.245°°°	−0.032°°
	(0.232)	(0.013)	(0.013)	(0.019)	(0.006)	(0.011)	(0.013)
ethnicity:							
hispanic	−1.376°°°	0.027	0.166°°°	0.225°°°	−0.035°°°	0.124°°°	0.058°
	(0.461)	(0.029)	(0.030)	(0.046)	(0.013)	(0.026)	(0.035)
black	−0.574	0.171°°°	0.163°°°	0.057	−0.046°°°	−0.106°°°	−0.180°°°
	(0.587)	(0.036)	(0.036)	(0.053)	(0.015)	(0.032)	(0.030)
asian	−3.271°°°	0.018	0.228°°°	0.021	−0.034°°°	0.057°°°	−0.029
	(0.458)	(0.022)	(0.022)	(0.032)	(0.010)	(0.019)	(0.036)
native american	0.541	0.000	0.088	0.13	−0.041	−0.036	−0.062
	(1.100)	(0.059)	(0.068)	(0.093)	(0.029)	(0.057)	(0.054)
other	−0.373	0.164°°°	0.052	−0.085	−0.058°°°	0.017	0.054
	(0.769)	(0.050)	(0.045)	(0.064)	(0.021)	(0.040)	(0.060)
education:							
high school	−0.046	−0.052	−0.036	0.020	0.025	−0.018	−0.045
	(0.845)	(0.040)	(0.047)	(0.072)	(0.016)	(0.039)	(0.040)
some college	0.89	0.050	−0.025	−0.126°	0.00	−0.010	0.051
	(0.849)	(0.040)	(0.046)	(0.071)	(0.017)	(0.039)	(0.041)
associate degree	−0.711	0.091°°	−0.038	−0.202°°°	−0.032	−0.028	0.058
	(0.882)	(0.043)	(0.049)	(0.075)	(0.021)	(0.042	(0.044)
college	−1.402	0.126°°°	−0.058	−0.227°°°	−0.037°	−0.034	0.149°°°
	(0.859)	(0.041)	(0.047)	(0.072)	(0.019)	(0.040)	(0.043)
graduate school	−2.242°°	0.148°°°	−0.074	−0.230°°°	−0.060°°°	−0.028	0.172°°°
	(0.908)	(0.043)	(0.049)	(0.075)	(0.022)	(0.041)	(0.048)

Continued

TABLE 5
Effect of MATCH1 (Against Omitted Base Group NOMATCH1) on Worker
Outcomes (Using Compensation Risk Variable COMPRISK1) (*Continued*)

	daysabs (1)	lookhard (2)	motivation (3)	jobsatisfac (4)	longtime (5)	loyal (6)	suggestions (7)
occupation:							
administrative	−1.617°°°	−0.149°°°	0.290°°°	0.288°°°	0.046°°°	0.328°°°	−0.002
	(0.551)	(0.030)	(0.030)	(0.048)	(0.011)	(0.027)	(0.024)
prof. and tech.	−0.616°	−0.136°°°	0.228°°°	0.259°°°	0.041°°°	0.295°°°	0.085°°°
	(0.334)	(0.019)	(0.020)	(0.029)	(0.008)	(0.017)	(0.020)
sales	−3.457°°°	−0.242°°°	0.300°°°	0.450°°°	0.071°°°	0.455°°°	−0.053°
	(0.518)	(0.025)	(0.027)	(0.039)	(0.009)	(0.022	(0.028)
customer service	−0.933	−0.136°°°	0.313°°°	0.033	0.028°	0.303°°°	0.067°°
	(0.620)	(0.037)	(0.040)	(0.062)	(0.015)	(0.035)	(0.033)
management	−1.990°°°	−0.201°°°	0.368°°°	0.430°°°	0.069°°°	0.440°°°	0.454°°°
	(0.402)	(0.022)	(0.024)	(0.034)	(0.008)	(0.020)	(0.029)
Constant	6.605°°°	2.144°°°	3.234°°°	4.080°°°	—	2.381°°°	1.916°°°
	(1.214)	(0.062)	(0.066)	(0.100)		(0.058)	(0.068)
Observations	18974	19318	19346	19371	19324	19065	13732
Pseudo R2	0.013	—	—	—	0.053	—	—
Adj. R2	—	0.074	0.081	0.066	—	0.114	0.122

Note: Equations are estimated using OLS, except for the DAYSABS equation, which is estimated using Tobit, and the LONGTIME equation, which is estimated using Probit (with Probit marginal effects presented in table entries). Robust standards are in parentheses. °, °°, °°° indicate significance at the 10%, 5%, and 1% levels, respectively. The omitted category for the ethnicity dummy variable group is WHITE, the omitted category for the education dummy variable group is NO HIGH SCHOOL, and the omitted category for the occupation dummy variable group is PRODUCTION.

TABLE 6
Effect of HIGHMATCH1 and LOWMATCH1 (Against Omitted Base Group
NOMATCH1) on Worker Outcomes (Using Compensation Risk Variable
COMPRISK1)

	daysabs (1)	lookhard (2)	motivation (3)	jobsatisfac (4)	longtime (5)	loyal (6)	suggestions (7)
highmatch1	−0.460°	0.001	0.077°°°	0.091°°°	0.013°°	0.091°°°	0.027°
	(0.257)	(0.014)	(0.014)	(0.021)	(0.006)	(0.013)	(0.016)
lowmatch1	−0.242	−0.083°°°	−0.088°°°	0.004	0.009	−0.014	−0.158°°°
	(0.326)	(0.019)	(0.020)	(0.029)	(0.008)	(0.018)	(0.016)
age	−0.079°°°	−0.009°°°	0.004°°°	0.008°°°	0.000	0.008°°°	−0.004°°°
	(0.014)	(0.001)	(0.001)	(0.001)	(0.000)	(0.001)	(0.001)
female	2.807°°°	−0.086°°°	0.089°°°	0.113°°°	0.021°°°	0.108°°°	−0.109°°°
	(0.327)	(0.014)	(0.015)	(0.021)	(0.006)	(0.013)	(0.015)
union	0.477	0.276°°°	−0.112°°°	−0.190°°°	−0.087°°°	−0.130°°°	0.024
	(0.664	(0.036	(0.036)	(0.052	(0.015)	(0.033)	(0.030)
tenure	−0.002	−0.005°°°	−0.007°°°	−0.007°°	0.001°°	−0.001	0.002°°°
	(0.015)	(0.001)	(0.001)	(0.001)	(0.000)	(0.001)	(0.001)
basepay	0.000	−0.000°°	0.000°°°	0.000°°°	0.000°°°	0.000	0.000°°°
	(0.000)	(0.000)	(0.000)	(0.000)	(0.000)	(0.000)	(0.000)
hours	−0.160°°°	0.002°°	0.008°°°	0.004°°°	0.001°°	0.005°°°	0.008°°°
	(0.020)	(0.001)	(0.001)	(0.001)	(0.000)	(0.001)	(0.001)
atmkt	−0.785°°°	−0.278°°°	0.178°°°	0.450°°°	0.092°°°	0.243°°°	−0.032°°
	(0.232)	(0.013)	(0.013)	(0.019)	(0.006)	(0.011)	(0.013)
ethnicity:							
hispanic	−1.376°°°	0.027	0.166°°°	0.225°°°	−0.035°°°	0.124°°°	0.058°
	(0.461)	(0.029)	(0.030)	(0.046)	(0.013)	(0.026)	(0.016)
black	−0.570	0.170°°°	0.161°°°	0.056	−0.046°°°	−0.107°°°	−0.185°°°
	(0.587)	(0.036)	(0.036)	(0.053)	(0.015)	(0.032)	(0.030)
asian	−3.254°°°	0.012	0.217°°°	0.015	−0.034°°°	0.050°°°	−0.033
	(0.461)	(0.022)	(0.022)	(0.032)	(0.010)	(0.019)	(0.036)
native american	0.542	−0.000	0.087	0.130	−0.041	−0.038	−0.063
	(1.100)	(0.059)	(0.068)	(0.093)	(0.029)	(0.057)	(0.054)
other	−0.363	0.160°°°	0.044	−0.089	−0.058°°°	0.012	0.050
	(0.769)	(0.050)	(0.045)	(0.064)	(0.021)	(0.040)	(0.060)
education:							
high school	−0.041	−0.053	−0.040	0.018	0.025	−0.020	−0.050
	(0.846)	(0.040)	(0.047)	(0.072)	(0.016)	(0.040)	(0.041)
some college	0.908	0.045	−0.036	−0.132°	0.001	−0.017	0.037
	(0.850)	(0.040)	(0.046)	(0.071)	(0.017)	(0.039)	(0.041)
associate degree	−0.695	0.086°°	−0.050	−0.208°°°	−0.032	−0.035	0.043
	(0.883)	(0.043)	(0.049)	(0.075)	(0.021)	(0.042)	(0.044)
college	−1.384	0.119°°°	−0.072	−0.234°°°	−0.037°	−0.043	0.134°°°
	(0.861)	(0.041)	(0.047)	(0.072)	(0.019)	(0.040)	(0.043)
graduate school	−2.223°°	0.140°°°	−0.089°	−0.238°°°	−0.060°°°	−0.038	0.158°°°
	(0.910)	(0.043)	(0.049)	(0.075)	(0.022)	(0.041)	(0.048)
occupation:							
administrative	−1.603°°°	−0.154°°°	0.280°°°	0.283°°°	0.046°°°	0.322°°°	−0.008
	(0.553)	(0.030)	(0.030)	(0.048)	(0.011)	(0.027)	(0.024)
prof. and tech.	−0.593°	−0.145°°°	0.210°°°	0.249°°°	0.041°°°	0.283°°°	0.076°°°
	(0.338)	(0.019)	(0.020)	(0.029)	(0.008)	(0.018)	(0.020)

Continued

TABLE 6
Effect of HIGHMATCH1 and LOWMATCH1 (Against Omitted Base Group
NOMATCH1) on Worker Outcomes (Using Compensation Risk Variable
COMPRISK1) (*Continued*)

	daysabs (1)	lookhard (2)	motivation (3)	jobsatisfac (4)	longtime (5)	loyal (6)	suggestions (7)
sales	−3.420°°°	−0.256°°°	0.272°°°	0.435°°°	0.071°°°	0.437°°°	−0.080°°°
	(0.530)	(0.026)	(0.027)	(0.040)	(0.009)	(0.022)	(0.028)
customer service	−0.932	−0.136°°°	0.312°°°	0.033	0.028°	0.303°°°	0.065°°
	(0.620)	(0.037)	(0.040)	(0.062)	(0.015)	(0.035)	(0.032)
management	−1.969°°°	−0.210°°°	0.351°°°	0.421°°°	0.069°°°	0.429°°°	0.432°°°
	(0.407)	(0.022)	(0.024)	(0.035)	(0.008)	(0.020)	(0.028)
Constant	6.536°°°	2.170°°°	3.286°°°	4.107°°°	—	2.414°°°	1.962°°°
	(1.221)	(0.062)	(0.067)	(0.100)		(0.058)	(0.068)
Observations	18974	19318	19346	19371	19324	19065	13732
Pseudo R2	0.013	—	—	—	0.053	—	—
Adj. R2	—	0.075	0.083	0.066	—	0.115	0.127

Note: Equations are estimated using OLS, except for the DAYSABS equation, which is estimated using Tobit, and the LONGTIME equation, which is estimated using Probit (with Probit marginal effects presented in table entries). Robust standards are in parentheses. °, °°, °°° indicate significance at the 10%, 5%, and 1% levels, respectively. The omitted category for the ethnicity dummy variable group is WHITE, the omitted category for the education dummy variable group is NO HIGH SCHOOL, and the omitted category for the occupation dummy variable group is PRODUCTION.

TABLE 7
In the Subsample of Workers with NOMATCH1 = 1 (i.e., MATCH1 = 0), Effect of
NOMATCH10 (Against Omitted Base Group NOMATCH011) on Worker Outcomes
(Using Compensation Risk Variable COMPRISK1)

	daysabs (1)	lookhard (2)	motivation (3)	jobsatisfac (4)	longtime (5)	loyal (6)	suggestions (7)
nomatch101	−0.036	0.130°°°	0.013	−0.075°°	−0.039°°°	−0.084°°°	0.068°°°
	(0.404)	(0.020)	(0.021)	(0.032)	(0.010)	(0.019)	(0.019)
age	−0.093°°°	−0.009°°°	0.005°°°	0.008°°°	0.001°	0.009°°°	−0.003°°°
	(0.022)	(0.001)	(0.001)	(0.002)	(0.000)	(0.001)	(0.001)
female	3.190°°°	−0.107°°°	0.129°°°	0.156°°°	0.035°°°	0.150°°°	−0.121°°°
	(0.517)	(0.021)	(0.021)	(0.032)	(0.009)	(0.019)	(0.020)
union	0.812	0.161°°°	−0.105°°	−0.158°°	−0.055°°°	−0.108°°°	0.010
	(0.928)	(0.042)	(0.043)	(0.064)	(0.019)	(0.040)	(0.037)
tenure	−0.021	−0.003°°°	−0.007°°°	−0.008°°°	0.000	−0.002°	0.004°°°
	(0.028)	(0.001)	(0.001)	(0.002)	(0.001)	(0.001)	(0.001)
basepay	0.000	0.000	0.000°°°	0.000	0.000°°°	−0.000	0.000
	(0.000)	(0.000)	(0.000)	(0.000)	(0.000)	(0.000)	(0.000)
hours	−0.142°°°	0.003°°	0.006°°°	0.002	0.001	0.004°°°	0.007°°°
	(0.037)	(0.001)	(0.001)	(0.002)	(0.001)	(0.001)	(0.001)
atmkt	−0.574	−0.298°°°	0.181°°°	0.471°°°	0.101°°°	0.269°°°	−0.048°°°
	(0.392	(0.020)	(0.020)	(0.029)	(0.009)	(0.018)	(0.018)

Continued

TABLE 7
In the Subsample of Workers with NOMATCH1 = 1 (i.e., MATCH1 = 0), Effect of
NOMATCH10 (Against Omitted Base Group NOMATCH011) on Worker Outcomes
(Using Compensation Risk Variable COMPRISK1) (*Continued*)

	daysabs	lookhard	motivation	jobsatisfac	longtime	loyal	suggestions
	(1)	(2)	(3)	(4)	(5)	(6)	(7)
ethnicity:							
hispanic	−1.678°°	0.021	0.202°°°	0.276°°°	−0.009	0.144°°°	0.092°
	(0.792)	(0.043)	(0.045)	(0.070)	(0.020)	(0.041)	(0.047)
black	−0.166	0.200°°°	0.153°°°	0.063	−0.042°°	−0.129°°°	−0.152°°°
	(0.914)	(0.048)	(0.048)	(0.071)	(0.021)	(0.044)	(0.039)
asian	−6.368°°°	0.057	0.316°°°	−0.021	−0.046°°	0.039	−0.004
	(0.912)	(0.038)	(0.038)	(0.060)	(0.019)	(0.035)	(0.051)
native american	−1.539	−0.007	0.143°	0.137	−0.043	−0.037	−0.043
	(1.494)	(0.081)	(0.083)	(0.121)	(0.041)	(0.075)	(0.071)
other	0.621	0.121	0.070	−0.000	−0.038	0.095	0.056
	(1.527)	(0.088)	(0.072)	(0.108)	(0.035)	(0.071)	(0.077)
education:							
high school	−0.588	−0.068	0.011	0.041	0.034	0.059	−0.078
	(1.435)	(0.056)	(0.065)	(0.102)	(0.024)	(0.059)	(0.057)
some college	0.828	0.026	0.025	−0.121	0.013	0.072	0.030
	(1.447)	(0.056)	(0.065)	(0.102)	(0.025)	(0.059)	(0.057)
associate degree	−1.252	0.104°	0.011	−0.165	−0.034	0.046	0.032
	(1.517)	(0.062)	(0.069)	(0.109	(0.031)	(0.064)	(0.061)
college	−1.742	0.115°	−0.067	−0.231°°	−0.047	0.030	0.117°
	(1.494)	(0.060)	(0.068)	(0.106)	(0.030)	(0.062)	(0.061)
graduate school	−2.574	0.093	−0.091	−0.197°	−0.054	0.027	0.099
	(1.653)	(0.065)	(0.072)	(0.112)	(0.034)	(0.066)	(0.068)
occupation:							
administrative	−1.407	−0.119°°°	0.219°°°	0.190°°°	0.040°°	0.249°°°	0.015
	(0.897)	(0.042)	(0.042)	(0.067)	(0.018)	(0.037)	(0.034)
prof. and tech.	−0.817	−0.111°°°	0.207°°°	0.243°°°	0.031°°	0.264°°°	0.066°°
	(0.579)	(0.029)	(0.030)	(0.044)	(0.013)	(0.027)	(0.028)
sales	−4.253°°°	−0.205°°°	0.291°°°	0.373°°°	0.069°°°	0.486°°°	−0.074°
	(0.939)	(0.047)	(0.050)	(0.075)	(0.018)	(0.039)	(0.043)
customer service	−1.430°	−0.156°°°	0.322°°°	0.066	0.055°°°	0.310°°°	0.045
	(0.800)	(0.048)	(0.050)	(0.080)	(0.020)	(0.046)	(0.043)
management	−2.643°°°	−0.222°°°	0.387°°°	0.473°°°	0.091°°°	0.450°°°	0.429°°°
	(0.708)	(0.035)	(0.036)	(0.054)	(0.013)	(0.032)	(0.041)
Constant	5.813°°°	2.040°°	3.256°°°	4.256°°°	—	2.390°°°	1.891°°°
	(2.093)	(0.096)	(0.102)	(0.153)	(0.093)	(0.097)	
Observations	8137	8287	8287	8309	8281	8160	7131
Pseudo R2	0.009	—	—	—	0.051	—	—
Adj. R2	—	0.083	0.05	0.056	—	0.102	0.081

Note: Equations are estimated using OLS, except for the DAYSABS equation, which is estimated using Tobit, and the LONGTIME equation, which is estimated using Probit (with Probit marginal effects presented in table entries). Robust standards are in parentheses. °, °°, °°° indicate significance at the 10%, 5%, and 1% levels, respectively. The omitted category for the ethnicity dummy variable group is WHITE, the omitted category for the education dummy variable group is NO HIGH SCHOOL, and the omitted category for the occupation dummy variable group is PRODUCTION.

Conclusion

Past studies on risk preferences, compensation risk, and employee outcomes have either focused on the role of risk aversion in shaping attitudes toward variable pay or on the relationship between variable pay and worker outcomes. Our study is the first to link these two branches of the literature by examining how a preference–compensation risk match influences worker outcomes. Our primary finding is that a match between the worker's risk preferences and the extent of risk in his or her compensation increases motivation, job satisfaction, company attachment, and loyalty, though the risk averse are generally less responsive than the risk loving to a preference–compensation match. We also find that the risk averse are generally less negatively affected by a preference–compensation mismatch than the risk loving, and that shared capitalism is linked to improving numerous worker outcomes, even among the risk averse. These results suggest that even risk-averse workers do not react badly and, in many cases, may respond positively, to having at least a portion of their pay consist of variable pay despite the fact that it introduces risk into their compensation.

Thus, our findings shed a favorable light upon variable pay and employee ownership. One of the common criticisms made against employee ownership is that it has the downside of imposing compensation risk onto workers, but our results suggest that this may not reduce worker utility as standard theories would predict. We therefore view our results as a valuable contribution to the employee ownership literature, enabling us to update our beliefs on how workers react to employee ownership.

The General Social Survey of 2006 shows that 46.7% of workers in the private sector workforce have some combination of profit or gain sharing, employee stock ownership, or employee stock options. Indeed, almost half, 48.6%, of for-profit companies have one or more of these shared capitalist practices that provide workers with income based on the performance of the underlying capital of firms, and 62.6% of workers in corporations with stock have one or more of these practices. These levels of incidence demonstrate that the NBER Shared Capitalism Database, which our analysis is based on, does not merely reflect information about a small niche but about a meaningful sector within the economy. Furthermore, while inflation-adjusted wages have been relatively flat since the 1980s, capital income has been shown to play an important role in increasing inflation-adjusted family wealth (Mishel, Bernstein, and Shierholz 2009). We therefore view the subject of shared capitalist practices as one that merits continued research.

Endnotes

[1] The wording of the survey question is "Some people like to take risks and others dislike taking risks. Where would you place yourself on a scale of how much you like or dislike taking risks, where 0 is hating to take any kind of risk and 10 is loving to take risks?"

[2] This variable is constructed as the ratio of two variables—BONVAL, which indicates the total dollar value of performance-based payments in the previous year, including profit sharing; individual-based, workgroup-based, or department-based performance bonuses; and BASEPAY, which indicates the worker's annual base pay the previous year, excluding overtime, bonuses, and commissions.

[3] Later in the paper as a robustness check we also investigate an alternative compensation risk variable that includes further measures of employee ownership, such as stock and option holdings. However, we prefer COMPRISK and treat it as our main compensation risk variable because it is a sharper measure of the share of salary that comprises variable pay in a given year (in contrast, the alternative measure includes cumulative forms of employee equity participation that have been amassed over multiple years) and because workers have no choice over the portion of salary that comprises profit sharing and bonuses captured in COMPRISK (in contrast, some components of the alternative measure are subject to employee choice in a number of firms in the NBER survey, which creates potential endogeneity bias in the regression estimates). Our key regression results are robust to using the alternative compensation risk measure.

[4] We also tried dividing the distribution of COMPRISK into three (at the 33rd and 66th percentiles), and LOVERISK into three (at 4 and 7), defining MATCH, HIGHMATCH, and LOWMATCH similarly, but also defining MIDMATCH to indicate match in the center of the two distributions. The regression results were qualitatively very similar.

[5] This variable is constructed from the NBER Shared Capitalism Survey's variables as (BONVAL + EOVAL2 + SOVAL)/BASEPAY.

[6] COMPRISK1 equals 5% at the 25th percentile, 35% at the 50th percentile, and 123% at the 75th percentile of its distribution. Thirty-nine percent of workers have a high preference for risk and a high level of compensation risk (HIGHMATCH1 = 1), 14% have a low preference for risk and a low compensation risk (LOWMATCH1 = 1), 36% have a high preference for risk but a low compensation risk (NOMATCH101 = 1), and the remaining 11% of workers have a low preference for risk but a high compensation risk (NOMATCH011 = 1).

[7] We re-estimated the regressions in Tables 5 through 7 using the subset of seven firms in the NBER survey where the workers had no choice over their variable pay, to get around the endogeneity of COMPRISK1, but the regression sample sizes were much smaller than the sample sizes shown in Tables 5 through 7, resulting in low precision in the estimates (these were some of the smaller firms in the NBER survey). The coefficient estimates that were statistically significant, however, were larger in magnitude than both the estimates using COMPRISK1 in Tables 5 through 7 and the estimates using COMPRISK in Tables 2 through 4, suggesting that workers who have choice over the portion of pay that is variable are more responsive to a preference–compensation match, which is consistent with our earlier finding that the estimates of interest in the COMPRISK regressions in Tables 2 through 4 were

found to be larger in magnitude than the COMPRISK1 results in Tables 5 through 7, also suggesting that choice leads to greater responsiveness to a match. These auxiliary regression results are available from the authors.

Appendix

TABLE A

In the Subsample of Workers with Low LOVERISK, Effect of NOMATCH01 (Against Omitted Base Group MATCH) on Worker Outcomes (Using Compensation Risk Variable COMPRISK)

	daysabs (1)	lookhard (2)	motivation (3)	jobsatisfac (4)	longtime (5)	loyal (6)	suggestions (7)
nomatch 01	0.345	−0.043	0.047	0.031	0.023°	0.067°°	0.052°°
	(0.404)	(0.026)	(0.030)	(0.043)	(0.012)	(0.026)	(0.025)
age	−0.089°°°	−0.009°°°	0.004°°°	0.007°°°	−0.000	0.007°°°	−0.004°°°
	(0.024)	(0.001)	(0.001)	(0.002)	(0.001)	(0.001)	(0.001)
female	2.383°°°	−0.077°°°	0.156°°°	0.112°°°	0.021°	0.116°°°	−0.119°°°
	(0.435)	(0.024)	(0.028)	(0.039)	(0.011)	(0.024)	(0.023)
union	−0.248	0.426°°°	−0.214°°°	−0.182°	−0.134°°°	−0.202°°°	−0.076
	(0.819)	(0.075)	(0.079)	(0.107)	(0.033)	(0.068)	(0.055)
tenure	0.003	−0.004°°°	−0.006°°°	−0.009°°°	0.001°	0.000	0.004°°°
	(0.023)	(0.001)	(0.002)	(0.002)	(0.001)	(0.001)	(0.001)
basepay	0.000	−0.000	0.000°°	0.000	0.000°	−0.000	0.000
	(0.000)	(0.000)	(0.000)	(0.000)	(0.000)	(0.000)	(0.000)
hours	−0.161°°°	0.001	0.008°°°	0.005°	0.001	0.010°°°	0.006°°°
	(0.041)	(0.002)	(0.002)	(0.003)	(0.001)	(0.002)	(0.002)
atmkt	−0.641	−0.262°°°	0.192°°°	0.447°°°	0.091°°°	0.267°°°	0.003
	(0.399)	(0.021)	(0.027)	(0.038)	(0.011)	(0.024)	(0.022)
ethnicity:							
hispanic	−0.758	−0.030	0.178°°°	0.190°	−0.079°°	0.132°°	−0.013
	(0.740)	(0.059)	(0.063)	(0.102)	(0.032)	(0.056)	(0.065)
black	−0.858	0.127°	0.237°°°	−0.01	−0.035	−0.122°	−0.158°°°
	(0.788)	(0.067)	(0.073)	(0.110)	(0.029)	(0.064)	(0.055)
asian	−3.080°°°	0.094°	0.292°°°	0.157°	−0.054°°	0.124°°°	0.153
	(0.846)	(0.051)	(0.056)	(0.081)	(0.026)	(0.044)	(0.099)
native american	2.698	−0.047	0.177	0.243	−0.045	0.067	0.059
	(2.391)	(0.089)	(0.121)	(0.178)	(0.051)	(0.097)	(0.102)
other	−0.775	0.149	0.126	0.063	−0.026	−0.075	0.098
	(1.064)	(0.119)	(0.109)	(0.163)	(0.048)	(0.104)	(0.112)
education:							
high school	0.113	−0.039	−0.07	−0.055	0.006	−0.085	−0.022
	(0.964)	(0.071)	(0.081)	(0.123)	(0.029)	(0.069)	(0.063)
some college	0.509	0.058	−0.005	−0.160	−0.019	−0.056	0.047
	(0.961)	(0.074)	(0.082)	(0.125)	(0.031)	(0.071)	(0.064)
associate degree	−0.820	0.055	−0.034	−0.222°	−0.017	−0.062	0.062
	(1.016)	(0.079)	(0.088)	(0.134)	(0.036)	(0.077)	(0.070)
college	−1.112	0.081	−0.169°°	−0.238°	−0.049	−0.096	0.067
	(1.007)	(0.078)	(0.086)	(0.131)	(0.036)	(0.074)	(0.071)
graduate school	−1.933°	0.067	−0.137	−0.208	−0.056	−0.095	0.076
	(1.149)	(0.084)	(0.093)	(0.138)	(0.042)	(0.078)	(0.085)

Continued

TABLE A

In the Subsample of Workers with Low LOVERISK, Effect of NOMATCH01
(Against Omitted Base Group MATCH) on Worker Outcomes (Using Compensation
Risk Variable COMPRISK) (*Continued*)

	daysabs (1)	lookhard (2)	motivation (3)	jobsatisfac (4)	longtime (5)	loyal (6)	suggestions (7)
occupation:							
administrative	−2.599°°°	−0.160°°°	0.304°°°	0.394°°°	0.079°°°	0.391°°°	0.039
	(0.630)	(0.044)	(0.049)	(0.076)	(0.015)	(0.041)	(0.038)
prof. and tech.	−0.478	−0.088°°	0.227°°°	0.201°°°	0.048°°°	0.277°°°	0.111°°°
	(0.572)	(0.035)	(0.040)	(0.056)	(0.015)	(0.035)	(0.035)
sales	−1.175	−0.158°°	0.255°°°	0.310°°°	0.055°°	0.417°°°	−0.084°°
	(1.319)	(0.067)	(0.076)	(0.113)	(0.023)	(0.056)	(0.036)
customer	−0.525	−0.077	0.212°°°	−0.183	0.023	0.219°°°	0.116°°
service	(0.951)	(0.062)	(0.075)	(0.118)	(0.028)	(0.065)	(0.053)
management	−1.095	−0.113°°	0.316°°°	0.294°°°	0.066°°°	0.369°°°	0.383°°°
	(0.738)	(0.048)	(0.057)	(0.084)	(0.017)	(0.047)	(0.060)
Constant	7.362°°°	2.055°°°	3.158°°°	4.248°°°	°	2.306°°°	1.879°°°
	(2.127)	(0.119)	(0.136)	(0.191)		(0.113)	(0.122)
Observations	4573	4639	4635	4649	4632	4573	3652
Pseudo R2	0.009	°	°	°	0.054	°	°
Adj. R2	°	0.079	0.069	0.050	°	0.106	0.082

Note: Equations are estimated using OLS, except for the DAYSABS equation, which is
estimated using Tobit, and the LONGTIME equation, which is estimated using Probit
(with Probit marginal effects presented in table entries). Robust standards are in parentheses. °, °°, °°° indicate significance at the 10%, 5%, and 1% levels, respectively. The omitted category for the ethnicity dummy variable group is WHITE, the omitted category for
the education dummy variable group is NO HIGH SCHOOL, and the omitted category
for the occupation dummy variable group is PRODUCTION.

References

Becker, Brian E., and Mark A. Huselid. 1998. "High-Performance Work Systems and
Firm Performance: A Synthesis of Research and Managerial Implications." In G.
Ferris, ed., *Research in Personnel and Human Resources*, Vol. 16. Greenwich,
CT: JAI Press.

Blasi, Joseph R., Richard B. Freeman, Christopher Mackin, and Douglas L. Kruse.
2010. "Creating a Bigger Pie? The Effects of Employee Ownership, Profit
Sharing, and Stock Options on Workplace Performance." In Douglas L. Kruse,
Richard B. Freeman, and Joseph R. Blasi, eds., *Shared Capitalism at Work:
Employee Ownership, Profit and Gain Sharing, and Broad-Based Stock Options*.
Chicago: University of Chicago Press.

Brown, Sarah, Fathi Fakhfakh, and John G. Sessions. 1999. "Absenteeism and
Employee Sharing: An Empirical Analysis Based on French Panel Data, 1981–
1991." *Industrial and Labor Relations Review*, Vol. 52, no. 2, pp. 234–51.

Bryson, Alex, and Richard B. Freeman. 2010. "How Does Shared Capitalism Affect
Economic Performance in the United Kingdom?" In Douglas L. Kruse, Richard
B. Freeman, and Joseph R. Blasi, eds., *Shared Capitalism at Work: Employee
Ownership, Profit and Gain Sharing, and Broad-Based Stock Options*. Chicago:
University of Chicago Press.

Cadsby, C. Bram, Fei Song, and Francis Tapon. 2007. "Sorting and Incentive Effects of Pay-for-Performance: An Experimental Investigation." *Academy of Management Journal*, Vol. 50, no. 2, pp. 387–405.

Cornelissen, Thomas, John S. Heywood, and Uwe Jirjahn. 2008. "Performance Pay, Risk Attitudes, and Job Satisfaction." DIW Berlin Working Paper. Berlin: German Socio-Economic Panel.

Del Boca, Alessandra, Douglas Kruse, and Andrew Pendleton. 1999. "Decentralisation of Bargaining Systems and Financial Participation: A Comparative Analysis of Italy, U.K. and the U.S." *Lavoro e Relazioni Industriali*, Summer 1999.

Dohmen, Thomas, and Armin Falk. Forthcoming. "Performance Pay and Multidimensional Sorting: Productivity, Preferences and Gender." *American Economic Review*.

Dohmen, Thomas, Armin Falk, David Huffmann, Uwe Sunde, Jürgen Schupp, and Gert Wagner. Forthcoming. "Individual Risk Attitudes: Measurement, Determinants and Behavioral Consequences." *Journal of the European Economic Association*.

Green, Colin, and John S. Heywood. 2008. "Does Performance Pay Increase Job Satisfaction?" *Economica*, Vol. 75, pp. 710–28.

Holmstrom, Bengt. 1979. "Moral Hazard and Observability." *Bell Journal of Economics*, Vol. 10, no. 1, pp. 74–91.

Ichniowski, Casey, Thomas Kochan, David Levine, Craig Olson, and George Strauss. 1996. "What Works at Work: Overview and Assessment." *Industrial Relations*, Vol. 35, no. 3, pp. 299–333.

Ichniowski, Casey, Kathryn Shaw, and Giovanna Prennushi. 1997. "The Effects of Human Resource Management Practices on Productivity: A Study of Steel Finishing Lines." *American Economic Review*, Vol. 87, no. 3, pp. 291–313.

Jones, Derek C., and Takao Kato. 1995. "The Productivity Effects of Employee Stock-Ownership Plans and Bonuses: Evidence from Japanese Panel Data." *American Economic Review*, Vol. 85, no. 3, pp. 391–414.

Kruse, Douglas, Joseph Blasi, and Rhokeun Park. 2010. "Shared Capitalism in the U.S. Economy: Prevalence, Characteristics, and Employee Views of Financial Participation in Enterprises." In Douglas L. Kruse, Richard B. Freeman, and Joseph R. Blasi, eds., *Shared Capitalism at Work: Employee Ownership, Profit and Gain Sharing, and Broad-Based Stock Options*. Chicago: University of Chicago Press.

Kruse, Douglas, Richard Freeman, and Joseph Blasi. 2010. "Do Workers Gain by Sharing? Employee Outcomes Under Employee Ownership, Profit Sharing, and Broad-Based Stock Options." In Douglas L. Kruse, Richard B. Freeman, and Joseph R. Blasi, eds., *Shared Capitalism at Work: Employee Ownership, Profit and Gain Sharing, and Broad-Based Stock Options*. Chicago: University of Chicago Press.

Kurtulus, Fidan Ana, Douglas L. Kruse, and Joseph R. Blasi. 2011. "Worker Attitudes Towards Employee Ownership, Profit Sharing and Variable Pay." *Advances in the Economics of Participatory and Labor Managed Firms*, Vol. 12.

Milgrom, Paul, and John Roberts. 1992. *Economics, Organization and Management*. Englewood Cliffs, NJ: Prentice Hall.

Mishel, Lawrence, Jared Bernstein, and Heidi Shierholz. 2009. *The State of Working America, 2008–2009*. Ithaca, NY: Cornell University Press.

Niederle, Muriel, and Lise Vesterlund. 2007. "Do Women Shy Away From Competition? Do Men Compete Too Much?" *Quarterly Journal of Economics*, Vol. 122, no. 3, pp. 1067–1101.

Shavell, Steven. 1979. "Risk Sharing and Incentives in the Principal and Agent Relationship." *Bell Journal of Economics*, Vol. 10, no. 1, pp. 55–73.

Wilson, Nicholas, and Michael J. Peel. 1991. "The Impact of Absenteeism and Quits of Profit-Sharing and Other Forms of Employee Participation." *Industrial and Labor Relations Review*, Vol. 44, no. 3, pp. 454–68.

CHAPTER 7

Employee Ownership and Corporate Performance: Toward Unlocking the Black Box

MARCO CARAMELLI
INSEEC Business School

The practice of encouraging employees to become stockholders of their employing company has become more and more popular in various countries and particularly in such world-leading economies as the United States (NCEO 2009), Europe (Poutsma et al. 2006), and China (Chiu, Hui, and Lai 2007). Governments and companies can encourage the development of employee stock ownership, respectively, through tax incentives and by setting up schemes allowing employees to purchase stock at a discounted price. These favorable conditions are costly for governments and companies, and the main reason for their adoption is the widespread belief that linking employee compensation to company performance gives employees an incentive to work better and harder, thereby enhancing their productivity and ultimately improving corporate performance (Iqbal and Hamid 2000; Jones and Kato 1993). Nevertheless, economic theory typically yields conflicting predictions about the effects of employee ownership (Jones and Pliskin 1988). In fact, some authors argue that employee ownership (EO) leads to free-rider problems, reduces management power, and is costly in terms of implementation (Doucouliagos 1995; Jones and Kato 1993; Trébucq 2004).

A large number of empirical studies have been performed in the last 30 years to investigate the net effect of EO on several indicators of corporate performance. Kaarsemaker (2006) reviewed this empirical research and found that, among the 70 reviewed studies, 48 gave evidence of a positive effect, while only 6 studies found negative effects. The general conclusion of other literature reviews on this topic has been summarized by Kruse and Blasi: "There is no automatic connection between employee ownership and firm productivity or profitability. While several studies indicate better or unchanged performance under employee ownership, almost no studies find worse performance" (1997:143).

A second main conclusion is that there is a lack of theoretical development about the mechanisms connecting EO to corporate performance. Even after 30 years of research, we still do not know much about the mechanisms through which EO and other financial participation arrangements function "inside the black box" (Kruse, Freeman, and Blasi 2010) to influence corporate performance. In fact, many empirical articles that examine the connection between EO and firm performance do not even have a section about theory (e.g., Davidson and Worrell 1994; Frye 2004), or they mention only elements of theory in the introduction or conclusion (e.g., Park and Song 1995).

In this chapter, I argue that the empirical research on the effects of EO on corporate performance lacks a precise theory and has failed to make incremental progress over the last 30 years. The aim of the present research is to bring new insights into the understanding of the mechanisms relating EO and corporate performance. To achieve this, I reviewed and integrated past research, and performed a qualitative study. Forty semistructured interviews were carried out with different key players involved in EO in the context of French multinationals. I address particularly the case of large public companies because EO is more prevalent in these firms (Kruse and Blasi 1997; Kruse, Freeman, and Blasi 2010).

This chapter offers several theoretical contributions. First, it provides a more complex picture of the relationships between EO and corporate performance that goes beyond much of the existing work, which has tended to focus only on employee attitudes and behaviors. Second, it suggests that EO does not affect such performance indicators as productivity, economic performance, and market performance through the same mechanisms. Third, it offers explanations for *both* causal directions of the EO–performance relationship.

This chapter is divided into four parts. I begin by reviewing the theory used in the empirical literature addressing the relationship between EO and corporate performance. Then I describe the practice of EO in the context of large French corporations. In the third section, I present my methodology followed by the empirical analysis. Finally, I consider the implications of the conclusions for research and for practitioners.

Employee Ownership and Corporate Performance

My goal in reviewing past literature was not to be exhaustive but to gain a representative idea of the existing theory on the EO–performance relationship that researchers have used as a basis for their empirical studies. To create a list of references, I examined three major electronic databases (ABI/INFORM Global, EBSCO, and JSTOR) and analyzed the references reported in the identified articles. I used the keywords "employee ownership," "financial participation," and "ESOP" and selected articles dealing with the EO–corporate performance relationship. I also found other articles by using Google Scholar and SSRN. I obtained approximately 40 references containing peer-reviewed articles, working papers, books, and reports covering the period 1986 through 2010.

Defining Employee Stock Ownership

Employee ownership refers to the fact that employees of a company are also stockholders of the company for which they work. Employee ownership is not a simple, unidimensional concept. There are a variety of ways by which employees may own stock in their company, and such practices may yield varying combinations of owner/manager/worker roles, rights, and responsibilities. Furthermore, workers can hold anything from a nominal stake to full collective ownership (Ben-Ner and Jones 1995; Rousseau and Shperling 2003; Toscano 1983). Employee ownership forms vary according to different dimensions. A first dimension is the cost of acquiring the stock. Employees can acquire stock by receiving it as grants, such as in the popular employee stock ownership plan (ESOP) arrangement in the United States. In an ESOP, employees do not pay for the stock with their wages or savings, but acquire it initially through a loan that is gradually paid back through company profits. At the other extreme, employees can acquire stock by purchasing shares with only their own savings. This happens when an employee buys company stock, for example, such as in the popular 401(k) plan arrangement in the United States. In these plans, some companies will also match employee purchase of investment assets with more company stock or cash, so this acquisition can take place at some discount. Another U.S. approach is an employee stock purchase plan (ESPP), where employees typically receive a 15% discount on the market price and purchase shares on a few predetermined days. Some companies have encouraged employees to fund the purchase of company stock with cash profit-sharing payments.

Another important dimension, therefore, is the origin of the funds to purchase stock: plans differ in their combination of employee contributions, employer matching contribution, profit-sharing bonus, and funds borrowed by a trust fund. Also, the percentage of employees who participate in ownership may vary, and employees may own different percentages of stock within the company. Finally, stock ownership may confer different rights and responsibilities to employees. In this chapter, I consider only the companies that implement a broad-based employee ownership plan (i.e., plans in which the majority of employees within the company are eligible to participate), and I do not address specific cases of worker cooperatives and labor-managed firms, or employee stock option programs.

The Effects of Employee Ownership Through Employee Attitudes and Behaviors

In existing empirical studies of the EO–corporate performance relationship, productivity is by far the most researched indicator. Other outcomes studied include sales, profitability, share price, wealth distribution, employment, investment, and income. These can basically be divided between indicators of economic and market performance. Economic performance concerns the effectiveness of a company in the use of its assets and is generally evaluated in terms of productivity and profitability. Market performance is the effectiveness of companies in enriching their shareholders and is generally assessed in terms of stock value and dividends.

The main argument found in the literature to explain how EO improves corporate performance relies upon changes in employee attitudes toward the company and work behaviors. In a very limited number of cases, authors also evoked tax advantages (Chang 1990) or the fact that the implementation of an EO plan is seen by the market as a signal that the firm is a likely takeover candidate, which is supposed to increase stock price (Park and Song 1995).

In most cases, changes in employee attitudes and behaviors under employee ownership are explained by the capacity of stock ownership to provide financial returns and participation in decision making. Concerning the effect of the financial value EO represents for employees, two main theories have been used: agency theory and justice theories. Agency theory suggests that in the presence of costly monitoring, financial participation is a way by which owners can ensure that employees will behave in a way that maximizes their welfare and interests (Kruse 1993; Welbourne and Gomez-Mejia 1995). Employee ownership is expected to provide employees with incentives to work more and better, and to cooperate with colleagues and management, since their income will increase if company performance improves (Pérotin and Robinson 2003). Because EO links individual well-being to the firm's well-being, it is also expected to enhance employee commitment to the firm and identification with its goals (Ben-Ner and Jones 1995). Employee ownership is also believed to enhance information sharing because of the alignment between individual and corporate interests, which is also likely to improve the decisions made within the company (Cin and Smith 2002; Robinson and Wilson 2006). The justice argument is based on the fact that most stock ownership arrangements are more an "add-on" than a substitute for wages (Kruse, Freeman, and Blasi 2010). Therefore, employees who are paid more than the "going wage" may develop feelings of fairness and equity leading to better attitudes toward their compensation, their work, and the company overall (Fitzroy and Kraft 1992; Frohlich, Godard, Oppenheimer, and Starke 1998).

In addition, a number of scholars have further hypothesized that EO has a negative effect on employee turnover and absenteeism through enhanced motivation, job satisfaction, commitment, and the feelings of being owners, or psychological ownership (Cohen and Quarrey 1986; Jones and Pliskin 1988). In turn, lower turnover is believed to lower training costs and to enhance the firm's specific human capital investments (Estrin and Jones 1992; Jones 1987; Smith, Cin, and Vodopivec 1997). In fact, long-term workers develop more detailed knowledge of the firm's operations, and, likewise, long associations among workers foster good communication and high-trust relationships in work groups that should help eliminate organizational inefficiencies (Jones 1987). According to Marsh and McAllister (1981), EO increases employee acceptance of company goals and understanding of management objectives. In addition, loyalty to traditionally antagonistic unions may decline, and campaigns to form unions in nonunion companies and strike in unionized companies may be abandoned.

Finally, as a profit-sharing tool, EO is believed to attract better workers in the long run (Fitzroy and Kraft 1992). The logic is that more productive employees would be attracted to performance-dependent compensation systems. However, others suggest that the best employees are likely to be more attracted to compensation systems based on individual performance and lower-quality workers by group-based performance schemes (Blasi, Conte, and Kruse 1996).

Researchers have also proposed that employee ownership influences corporate performance when it provides employees with some decision-making rights. Authors suggest that participation in decision making has positive effects both on the individual and corporate level. First, according to Jones (1987), participation is thought to lower turnover. In the specific context of worker co-ops, it has been suggested that workers in participatory firms might exhibit more cooperative behavior, which would reduce the costs of monitoring workers' effort (Jones and Pliskin 1988). Moreover, employees with representative participation rights are more likely to assign legitimacy to managerial authority, lessening the distrust and conflict that tends to arise in conventional authority relationships (Frohlich, Godard, Oppenheimer, and Starke 1998), thereby improving industrial relations overall (Cin and Smith 2002). Participation in decision making may also improve performance by leading to better decisions. In fact, decisions in which workers take part will be implemented more swiftly than unilateral management decisions, and thus will produce superior organizational performance (Craig and Pencavel 1995; Jones 1987; Lee 2003).

A Fallacy of Performance?

Virtually all the research in the field in the last 30 years has accepted the idea that the observed relationships between EO and several performance indicators are mainly due to enhanced employee work attitudes and behaviors. However, it is arguable these enhanced worker attitudes and behaviors have little impact on company performance. In fact, whatever the effect of EO on employee work attitudes and behaviors, it would be only one of a larger set of other determinants of employee work attitudes and behaviors. In addition, the performance of individual employees is only one of a plethora of determinants of corporate performance, regardless of the performance indicator. Therefore, even if EO improves outcomes such as employee commitment and motivation, the net effect on corporate performance is likely to be very weak at best. Blasi (1988:238) provides a rare example of serious recognition of this issue, which he described as a "fallacy of productivity," or the "belief that workers can make a financial difference in a company simply by working harder and smarter, thus speeding up the production." He also explains that "at the root of the poor research and the exaggerated stories about ESOPs performance is a refusal to recognize the complex interaction of forces in productivity."

Beyond productivity, authors have also relied upon agency theory or other behavior/alignment arguments to explain the relationship between EO and market performance (Iqbal and Hamid 2000; Pugh, Jahera, and Oswald 2005). Most researchers examining the EO performance link have used these same arguments to explain both the effects of financial participation and participation in decision making on individual, economic, and market performance. Note that the "work attitudes and behavior" explanation is even less plausible for market-based performance indicators than for individual productivity. In fact, the relationship between an employee's work attitudes and behaviors and his or her individual productivity is far closer and direct than the relationship between employee work attitudes and behaviors and the company's market performance, which is determined by a large set of internal and external forces.

Even worse, it has also been suggested that a number of EO plan characteristics are likely to reduce the incentive effects. Trébucq (2004), for example, observes that the percentage of capital held by employees in publicly traded companies is often not sufficient to provide any positive attitudinal or behavioral effects, and that ESOPs are often perceived as complex devices that remain too far removed from the daily concerns of employees to incite them to modify their behavior at work. In the same fashion, Blasi (1988) notes that the annual contribution to the EO plan represents a small percentage of an employee's compensation, and employees lack property rights and voting rights to affect crucial company decisions. Finally, Blasi (1988) considers that U.S. ESOPs are not likely to improve productivity because their goals and structure do not necessarily "lead to substantial, practical, ongoing labor/management cooperation about technology and the production process, and the use of physical and human capital" (p. 233). Put differently, there are reasons to believe that even the main (weak) argument explaining the EO–performance relationship is unlikely to hold in most cases.

A last issue concerns the direction of causality between EO and performance (Doucouliagos 1995). In fact, one may wonder whether performance affects the adoption and development of employee ownership instead of the opposite. Because the research methods used in most of the past studies can only establish an association and not a causal relationship between EO and performance, it is hard to clearly interpret the results of past studies.

The obvious outcome of such a picture is that the relationship of employee ownership with positive economic performance is far more complicated than proponents have anticipated. A tentative first step toward investigating the complexity of the EO–performance relationship has been made in addressing some preconditions or moderating factors. According to Kruse and Blasi (1997:114), for example, the EO–performance relationship depends "on the circumstances in which EO is implemented, the history of employee relations in the company, and other company policies that may support or work against positive effects of EO." More specifically, the authors suggest that, to improve performance, EO arrangements must provide a combination of sufficiently meaningful incentives to motivate sufficiently meaningful participation rights to make critical decisions, and a workplace environment that reduces free-rider problems (Kruse et al. 2004).

Another explanation is that the studies that found a positive relationship between employee ownership and performance failed to identify the real explanatory variable. It has been suggested that in order to increase their performance, companies need employees who work smarter, generate new ideas, and organize tasks in new ways. To make that possible, companies must create a specific structure through various kinds of workplace involvement. However, it is suggested that simple involvement without ownership leads people, over time, to back off and participate less. It is the culture that counts, and ownership is the reward system that holds the structure together (Corey Rosen, executive director and co-founder of the National Center for Employee Ownership, pers. comm.). According to the U.S.-based National Center for Employee Ownership (NCEO), this so-called ownership culture defines companies that (1) provide a financially meaningful ownership stake—enough to be an important part of employee financial security, (2) provide ownership education that teaches people how the company makes money and their role in making that happen, (3) share performance data about how the company is doing overall and how each work group contributes to that, (4) train people in business literacy so they understand the numbers the company shares, (5) share profits through bonuses, profit sharing, or other tools, (6) build employee involvement not just by allowing employees to contribute ideas and information but by making it part of their everyday work organization through teams, feedback opportunities, devolution of authority, and other structures (NCEO 2010). A company's ownership culture has also been defined as "a business community composed of people sharing the values of ownership, and working together in an organized way for their mutual benefit as co-workers" (Brohawn 1997:1).

Figure 1 summarizes the mechanisms found in the literature to explain how employee ownership relates to corporate performance. It first shows that EO is believed to operate through its financial value, the rights provided to employees to participate in decision making, and tax and market mechanisms. Financial value and participation in decision rights are both considered to affect individual and collective work attitudes and behaviors, but the indicators of corporate performance they are believed to affect are not specified. However, tax advantages are believed to increase economic performance, and market-based mechanisms are believed to increase market performance. It is important to note that the links shown in Figure 1 represent an aggregation of the different mechanisms found in the literature. However, such mechanisms vary highly in terms of frequency of citation. For example, 75% of the studies reviewed evoke changes in employee attitudes and behaviors to explain why EO is believed to affect corporate performance, 8% of the studies mention "better decision making," 8% the tax advantages, 4% the fact that EO is considered by the market as a signal that the company is a potential takeover candidate, 4% evoke a decrease of strikes and better industrial relations, and 8% of the studies do not provide any theory at all.

The review of the existing knowledge on how employee ownership relates to better corporate performance clearly suggests a need for further investigation. In fact, the incentive explanations that are usually set forth by researchers seem to be too weak to explain the observed relationships between EO and corporate performance. Moreover, the existing literature fails to explain how EO can affect different indicators of corporate performance. To this end, my study adopted an exploratory approach to qualitatively capture specific mechanisms that large-scale quantitative studies often cannot identify.

FIGURE 1
Employee Ownership and Performance: A Synthesis of the Literature

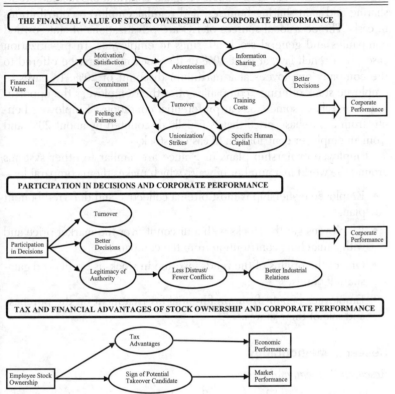

Employee Ownership in French Multinationals

French companies have implemented a large variety of forms of financial participation as a result of a tradition of support by the French policy makers. Consequently, France, along with the United Kingdom, is the European country that has developed the most extensive legal and fiscal frameworks for financial participation in general and EO in particular. Employee ownership is generally managed through a *Plan d'Epargne d'Entreprise* (PEE), which is a deferred collective employee benefit plan invested in stock. Stock ownership is generally indirect, meaning that a trust savings fund (*Fonds Communs de Placement d'Entreprise*, FCPE) is the legal owner, and employees actually own some fund shares. The corresponding voting rights are exercised by a supervision council (*Conseil de Surveillance*, CS). In the direct form of EO, employees directly own the shares and exercise the voting rights.

The employees' account in the PEE may receive different types of regular and occasional contributions. Regular contributions include profit-sharing and gain-sharing bonuses, and regular employee contributions in cash. The occasional sources of EO are privatizations of state-owned companies and general stock offerings to employees. In privatization cases, by French law, at least 10% of the stock must first be offered to the company employees at a maximum discount of 20%. In cases of employee stock offerings, companies offer their employees the opportunity to purchase some stock at preferential conditions. Employees benefit from a purchase price that is usually discounted by about 20% and from an employer contribution in cash or stock.

Employee ownership plans in France are similar to other systems around the world in a number of ways, which makes them comparable:

- Employee ownership is most often a collective and deferred benefit plan.
- Employees get the stocks with a discount over the market price and with a matching contribution from the company.
- One of the origins of the funds invested in stocks is profit- and gain-sharing bonuses.
- Employees benefit from preferential tax treatment on the purchase and sale of their shares.

Research Methodology

Research Strategy and Design

Data for this study were collected through face-to-face, semistructured interviews with different people involved in the practice of employee ownership in France. Qualitative data collection and analysis were well-suited for the purpose of this study because the aim was to determine the processes by which employee ownership relates to corporate performance: Theory building requires the rich knowledge that only qualitative methods can provide (Shah and Corley 2006).

Interview Participants and Processes

The interviewees consisted of 31 specialists and practitioners in employee stock ownership, and 9 employee stockholders working in French multinationals, 1 in an Italian multinational. In determining the sample, I did not look for representativeness. Rather, I adopted a snowball sampling methodology because professionals and specialists of employee ownership are not very numerous and quite difficult to approach. The primary objective was to obtain a sample representing a variety of professional functions and a diverse cross section of organizations in terms of industry. This diversity was a source of richness in the data, and it increased the likelihood that the observed patterns might be generalizable and that most of the processes implied in the EO–performance relationship might be addressed by the interviewees.

Professional interviewees were approached during conferences or contacted directly by telephone. All but two interviews (conducted by telephone) were conducted in a face-to-face setting, most of the time in the interviewee's office. All interviews lasted around an hour and a half and were tape recorded and later transcribed before analysis. Data collection took place in two waves: the first between March and August 2005, and the second between September and December 2010. The final sample of interviewees comprised individuals practicing six different functions; Table 1 provides more details about the interviewees, which are summarized here:

- Sixteen individuals were employee stock ownership managers.
- Three respondents were consultants in financial participation and employee stock ownership.
- Two interviewees were experts at asset management institutions.
- Four respondents were the executive directors of associations of employee stockholders.
- Two individuals were executives of two of the main French trade unions.
- Three of the respondents were executive directors of French and international institutions promoting employee ownership.
- Nine interviewees were employee shareholders working in large French companies, and one interviewee worked in a large Italian company.

TABLE 1
Profile of Interviewees.

Employee Ownership Managers		
	Industry	Type of Company
Interviewee 1	Banking	CAC 40 Stock Index
Interviewee 2	Telecommunications	CAC 40 Stock Index
Interviewee 3	Retail	CAC 40 Stock Index
Interviewee 4	Cement	CAC 40 Stock Index
Interviewee 5	Manufacturing	CAC 40 Stock Index
Interviewee 6	Oil and Gas	CAC 40 Stock Index
Interviewee 7	Energy	CAC 40 Stock Index
Interviewee 8	Chemical	CAC 40 Stock Index
Interviewee 9	Entertainment	CAC 40 Stock Index
Interviewee 10	Energy	CAC 40 Stock Index

Continued

TABLE 1
Profile of Interviewees. (*Continued*)

Employee Ownership Managers		
	Industry	Type of Company
Interviewee 11	Pharmaceuticals	CAC 40 Stock Index
Interviewee 12	Electronics	CAC 40 Stock Index
Interviewee 13	Consulting	Nonquoted
Interviewee 14	Automotive	CAC 40 Stock Index
Interviewee 15	Banking	CAC 40 Stock Index
Interviewee 16	Oil and Gas	CAC 40 Stock Index

Consultants		
	Type of Consultant	Type of Consultancy
Interviewee 17	Junior	NYSE
Interviewee 18	Senior	SBF 250 Stock Index
Interviewee 19	Senior	SBF 250 Stock Index

Experts at Asset Management Institutions	
	Type of Company
Interviewee 20	Subsidiary of CAC 40 company
Interviewee 21	Subsidiary of CAC 40 company

Presidents of Associations of Employee Stockholders		
	Industry	Type of Company
Interviewee 22	Banking	CAC 40 Stock Index
Interviewee 23	Telecom	CAC 40 Stock Index
Interviewee 24	Oil and Gas	SBF 120 Stock Index
Interviewee 25	Banking	Mibtel (Italian Stock Index)

Trade Union Executives		
	Industry	Type of Company
Interviewee 26	Telecommunications	CAC 40 Stock Index
Interviewee 27	Oil and Gas	SBF 120 Stock Index

Executive Directors of International	
Institutions Promoting Employee Ownership	
Interviewee 28	Belgium
Interviewee 29	Belgium
Interviewee 30	France

Continued

TABLE 1
Profile of Interviewees. (*Continued*)

	Employee Shareholders	
	Industry	Type of Company
Interviewee 31	Retail	Nonquoted multinational
Interviewee 32	Banking	CAC 40
Interviewee 33	Banking	CAC 40
Interviewee 34	Telecom	CAC 40
Interviewee 35	Automotive	Mibtel (Italian Stock Index)
Interviewee 36	Cement	CAC 40
Interviewee 37	Cement	CAC 40
Interviewee 38	Cement	CAC 40
Interviewee 39	Cement	CAC 40
Interviewee 40	Cement	CAC 40

The Interview Guide

After a brief introduction highlighting the aims of the research and initial questioning to elicit background information from each interviewee, the interviews were organized around two main themes through which I tried to gather information about how the respondents conceived the relationship between employee ownership and corporate performance. The first theme concerned the reasons companies implement employee ownership plans. The second theme dealt more directly with the relationship between EO and performance. Responses were then followed up with more-probing inquiries to gain a deeper understanding of underlying perceptions and beliefs.

In order to discover individuals' real beliefs and to avoid stereotypes and politically correct responses, I wanted the interviews to be as undirected as possible. Interviews were open ended and did not follow a standard list of questions. As an example, instead of mentioning the possibility that EO could affect corporate performance, I asked the interviewees, "Why do you think companies implement stock ownership plans?" Only when they mentioned performance did I ask for more details.

Data Analysis

Qualitative content analysis and thematic coding techniques were used to analyze the interviews. Themes were derived from reading the interview transcriptions on a post hoc basis. In the initial analysis, I created a large number of themes coded into categories and subcategories. However, when these themes were seen as dealing with the same underlying concept or meaning, they were combined to form one theme/

category. I implemented this recoding process after the analysis of each interview. The analysis of the next interview implied the addition of new themes and subthemes, thereby leading to combining themes when necessary. The logic and interconnections between themes were presented by structuring the suggested themes in an iterative process.

I considered that the frequency of appearance of each theme was not relevant in this research. In fact, the aim was not to determine whether a specific theme was more or less popular among interviewees but rather to determine a set of mechanisms relating employee ownership and corporate performance. Put differently, I considered that the fact that a specific mechanism (e.g., employee ownership is good for employee motivation) is frequently evoked does not mean that the mechanism is particularly relevant. On the contrary, I considered that a mechanism that was presented by a limited number of individuals could be very relevant because of the position and/or experience of these interviewees.

Limitations

The findings of this study must be interpreted in the light of a number of limitations. First, a sample size of 40 is relatively small, even for a qualitative study. Moreover, this study focuses on the French context, which is different from the common Anglo-Saxon systems, which raises some questions about the generalizability of the findings. One may also wonder about the extent to which practitioners and employee shareholders have enough hindsight to clearly perceive the mechanisms relating EO and corporate performance. However, since the aim of this study was to generate ideas in order to complete existing knowledge rather than to test the validity of specific mechanisms, the research design used and the data collected can be considered effective in reaching this goal.

Summary of the Findings

The following section of this chapter presents the results of the qualitative study. The analysis suggests a reciprocal relationship between employee ownership and corporate performance (i.e., there are several processes by which employee ownership may enhance company performance), but, at the same time, different elements of performance may positively impact the likelihood of the implementation and the scope of employee ownership.

Figure 2 presents an overview of the findings of this study and suggests that there are three main ways in which EO can positively affect corporate performance: improvement of individuals' work attitudes and behaviors, tax benefits, and financial/market benefits. At the same time, the results suggest that there are three ways by which corporate performance can positively affect the development of employee ownership in companies:

FIGURE 2
The Reciprocal Relationship Between Employee Ownership and Corporate
Performance

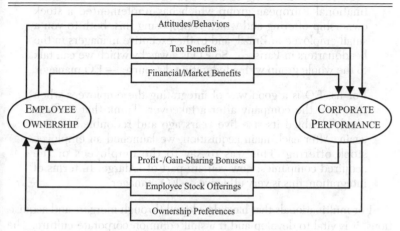

the distribution of profit- and gain-sharing bonuses, the decisions to set up
employee stock offerings, and employee ownership preferences.

In what follows, these mechanisms will be developed and illustrated
with representative examples from the interview data.

The Effects of Employee Ownership on Corporate Performance: Workforce Attitudes, Tax Advantages, and Financial Benefits

Employee Ownership and Workforce Attitudes and Behaviors

Many interviewees discussed the possibility that EO could have positive effects on employee attitudes and behaviors. However, beyond what
has been suggested in past research, the evidence suggests that EO may
also affect top management's attitudes and behaviors.

Commitment and Transmission of Corporate Culture. Many respondents described the relationship between employee ownership and
performance as related to affective organizational commitment by using
such concepts as a feeling of belonging and attachment to the company
(Meyer and Allen 1997). In the large majority of cases, EO is considered
a way to develop a feeling of belonging to the same group for employees
working in different subsidiaries of the same corporation. Two typical
situations were mentioned by the interviewees. The first concerned the
cases of mergers, while the second concerned conglomerates with a
large number of divisions of different sizes, situated all over the world
and often in unrelated businesses. As two respondents noted:

> Imagine a guy who lives in a favela, who has five children, and doesn't make a lot of money. . . . Through EO you tell him, "You see? You belong to this. You are an actor of this multinational European group which has implemented a stock ownership offering and which is proposing this, both to you a small employee in Brazil, and to the executive managers in the headquarters in Paris. . . . So EO is a way by which we can talk to the whole group with a federating discourse. —EO manager

> For us, EO is a good way of integrating the employees when they join the company after a takeover. Think that Lafarge nearly doubled its size five years ago and redoubled its size again. After each main acquisition, we launched an employee stock offering. This was to say to the employees of the acquired companies: now you are part of Lafarge. In terms of integration, this is very effective. —EO manager

For multinationals that have developed through mergers and acquisitions, it is vital to develop and transmit common corporate culture. The implementation of global stock ownership offerings is considered by many experts as unique opportunities for communicating on the same basis, in the same way, and on the same topic to all the employees all over the world. In conglomerates, equity stock is often one of the only things that all employees have in common. Employee ownership was also considered by some respondents as a way of creating relationships among people working in different subsidiaries, countries, or industries. For example, implementing a global stock offering plan is a project that involves many people from different departments in different countries. Two of the interviewees explained that EO helps the headquarters in developing an international network, which then becomes a key element in successfully implementing other practices and policies:

> When you want to implement a global human resources policy, it is important to have a network at your disposal. Otherwise, some subsidiaries may refuse to implement practices imposed by the headquarters. EO is a good way by which we can start working with the people within the subsidiaries and, after that, they will pay more attention and will be more willing to listen to discussions about other topics like staffing, training and development, or compensation. —EO manager

Motivation. Interviewees also often associated employee ownership with increased motivation.

> When you work for a company that works well, and you are a stockholder of this company, it's normal that you would be

more motivated. On the other side, if you own stock in a company that does not perform well, this can decrease your motivation. —Employee stockholder

However, my impression is that, in most cases, interviewees mentioned motivation simply because they had been previously exposed to this connection. In fact, it is popular in France to say that stock ownership motivates employees.

Some respondents were skeptical about the motivational properties of stock ownership because, in their view, employees do not perceive a relationship between their own work and the financial parameters related to EO. As an example, an EO manager explained:

The goal of EO is not motivating. EO is more a matter of fairness. What motivates is gain sharing because the employee can directly impact his/her bonus with his/her own effort at work.

Turnover Intention. Many professionals suggested, both directly and implicitly, that EO had a positive effect on employee loyalty, thereby lowering their intent to leave. Two reasons have been presented to explain this effect. The first reason is essentially financial: EO lowers turnover intention by linking employees to the financial development of the company. Employees would be less willing to leave the company to avoid losing the benefits of future stock ownership offerings, dividends, stock market value growth, and performance-related bonuses. In this first case, the effect of EO on turnover intention could be explained by Meyer and Allen's (1991) continuance commitment, or the need to maintain employment in an organization because of the awareness of the costs associated with leaving the organization. The second suggested reason is related to affective commitment:

Employee loyalty is to some extent the reward of the attachment of the employee to the company. The employee will feel more committed to his/her company because it is a bit his/her company to some extent. —President of an employee stockholder association

Absenteeism and Organizational Citizenship Behavior. There was some disagreement among respondents concerning the effects of EO on absenteeism and organizational citizenship behavior. Some believed that EO affects such variables by developing a sense of ownership for the company and because they believe that EO enhances organizational commitment. However, a majority of respondents were very skeptical and thought that such beliefs were "simplistic and childish":

I do not think, as some consultancies say, that because they have become stockholders, the employees will switch the lights off when they leave their office to lower the company costs. I find this simplistic and childish. I think that whether employees try to lower costs or not, it's more a matter of corporate culture. —President of an employee stockholder association

Developing a Stockholder Culture. Some of the respondents explained that EO has the potential for developing a stockholder culture among employees by introducing them to the company's main business issues and by associating them with the company's creation of wealth. Respondents defined a "stockholder culture" as employees feeling that they are—and act like—true stockholders. This basically means that they are interested in the company's strategy and economic performance. An EO manager explained:

Concerning AXA, EO is seen as a way to associate the employees in an educational and collective way to discover and develop their stockholder culture. That is, knowledge of the stock markets, knowledge of the AXA equity share, discovering the determinants of our stock price fluctuations, etc.

Overall, the respondents agreed that EO can improve employee organizational commitment and decrease turnover, but the beliefs concerning other work attitudes and behaviors were more variable between individuals. Also, some respondents suggested preconditions and success factors relating to the EO–performance link.

The Philosophical Commitment of Management to Employee Ownership. The meaning that companies give to EO has been considered by the respondents as fundamental in the capacity of such a practice to affect employee attitudes. Is EO aimed at empowering employees or is it just a tax and financial tool? Two indicators of such a philosophy have been suggested: the primary reason for EO implementation and the department within the company that manages EO. Employee ownership can be implemented for several reasons along a continuum from tax and financial reasons to reasons more related to human resource strategies. Even if companies implement EO for a mix of different reasons, there is often a dominant philosophy. For instance, as one of the EO managers explained:

We are a group which makes an employee stock offering every year; few groups do so every year. We do so because from a cultural point of view, from a development strategy point of view, we believe in employee ownership.

Another EO manager also pointed out:

> You may not believe it, but Lafarge is a bit philanthropic in
> its human resources policy, and we consider that it is fair for
> our employees to participate in our profits, even if it is very
> expensive.

Far from cultural and philosophical considerations, some interviewees
suggested that EO was implemented by some companies primarily
because of legal reasons. In fact, the French law stipulates that when
state-owned companies are privatized, at least 10% of the stock must
first be offered to employees. Many interviewees explained that EO
in France started with the different waves of privatizing large, state-
owned companies. Some interviewees admitted that some companies
implemented EO "just to do as the others do" or "without a specific
reason."

The company department responsible for EO also reflects how
management views EO, and respondents highlighted two important
distinctions. The first is whether EO is managed by the human resource
management (HRM) department or by the department in charge of the
individual stockholder relationships:

> We consider that employee stockholders must benefit from the
> same rights as other individual stockholders. I am convinced
> that in companies where EO is managed in the HRM depart-
> ment, employee stockholders do not receive the same informa-
> tion about the company's activity and strategy. —EO manager

One of the EO consultants highlighted the importance of the distinction between the "compensation and benefits" department and the
"social policies" department:

> We often give the case of Lafarge as a best practice. They have
> decided not to tie up EO to the compensation division of the
> HR department but to the "social policies" division, and this
> is a strong and very meaningful message. This gives evidence
> that they do not consider EO merely as an element of the com-
> pensation package but more as an important element of the
> human resources and social policy as a whole.

Overall, the interviewees confirmed existing research on the relevance of how management conceives of employee ownership and the
large variance among companies regarding their management's philosophical commitment to EO. However, the information I gathered from
interviews goes beyond past knowledge by suggesting a new indicator of

management's commitment to EO: the company's department in charge of employee ownership. Some interviewees mentioned elements of the EO plan's design as success factors in terms of attitudinal effects. However, there was little agreement among respondents on these topics.

Sources of EO. I previously suggested that, in the French context, EO has different sources. According to some respondents, employee stock offerings are more likely to generate positive attitudinal effects compared with other sources:

> An employee stock offering is an important event with a lot of communication and strong HR support; so this is more likely to have a deeper psychological effect on employees than when they just have to choose to invest their profit-sharing bonus in one of the available funds. —Asset manager

The respondents' comments about the recurrence of the EO plan were remarkably divergent. According to some interviewees, "rolling plans" must be avoided because employees end up considering them a mere element of the compensation package. Also, the subscription rate of rolling plans is usually low. On the other hand, many experts explained that in order to develop an ownership culture, the EO stimuli must be sent to employees on a regular basis. Also, because EO mechanisms can be difficult to understand and because stock offerings are the moments when the company communicates the most with its employees, recurrent plans are more likely to develop in employees a feeling that they are stockholders.

Risk Level. Employee ownership is generally considered to be a risky investment for employees (Kuvaas 2003; Sparrow 2002). However, the level of risk actually depends on several factors, such as the percentage of discount over the stock price, the level of the company's contribution, or the risk of the company stock itself. Some companies offer systems in which employee investments are completely secured from losses. The interviewees explained that companies have different philosophies concerning this issue. Some companies believe that EO must be risk free because it would be unfair for low-level or poor employees in some countries to take financial risks with EO. Other companies consider risk to be an essential part of EO: the actual risk of losing money with EO is what will develop employees' interest in the company's activities and strategy, and promote a feeling that "the company's problems are also theirs."

Direct Versus Indirect Ownership. The views also diverged remarkably on whether direct or indirect ownership is preferable in terms of attitudinal effects. The advocates of direct ownership believe that it is the only system able to affect employees psychologically. Under direct ownership, employees own stock directly, receive information about the company's activity and strategy like all other stockholders, vote their stock, and receive dividends. In the indirect system, the stock is actually owned by a trust fund, the dividends are integrated in the fund automatically, and voting rights are exercised by the president of the supervision council. Some experts think that, in the direct system, employees cannot exert any power in the decision-making process. However, in the indirect ownership system, the stock owned by employees is voted collectively and thereby represents real power in the decision-making process. Overall, it seems that direct ownership is preferable in terms of psychological impact, while indirect ownership is more effective in terms of corporate governance.

Impact on Management Attitudes and Behaviors. Some interviewees mentioned the idea that EO could have an impact on management's work attitudes and behaviors. First, respondents noted that when EO is substantial in a company, top management tends to behave in a more ethical way and to take employees' interests more into consideration. Employee ownership, when combined with employee stockholders having representation at the governance level, represents a power that prevents management from making decisions that are contrary to the company's general interest:

> EO can represent a power which can be a safeguard for the management to protect a minimum of values and ethical standards. I think that the CEO of a company with relevant EO thinks often about it, as he/she thinks every day about the stockholders, the public administration, and the environmental associations who will annoy him/her on this or that matter.
> —President of an employee stockholder association

The second way in which EO can influence management behavior is that it encourages the gathering of information from employees. Since employees typically have more complete knowledge of their work than management does, they can provide management with better pools of information.

> The day before the annual general meeting, we were received by the CEO as representatives of an association of employee stockholders. The next day of the general meeting, nearly all our questions as well as his responses were included in his speech. We have a different vision of the bottom line employee and we can bring him a message that can be useful for the good functioning of the company. Some CEOs don't like that. But I think that it's a way by which companies can be better run if it's done in an intelligent way. —President of an employee stockholder association

Finally, some respondents noted that EO limits short term–oriented decision making by managers. In fact, employee stockholders tend to be more interested in the long-term continuity of the company than in short-term profits—and are likely, therefore, to support corporate governance decisions that are more likely to affect long-term performance.

In this section, I presented the interviewees' beliefs about how employee ownership can affect individuals' work attitudes and behaviors. Some of the comments by the respondents confirmed past research, while others went beyond it. Virtually all respondents believed that EO can lead to enhanced organizational commitment, and specific mechanisms were suggested, such as in the case of multinational groups that are the result of mergers and acquisitions. There was also broad agreement that EO decreases turnover through enhanced commitment. However, there was substantial disagreement about the capacity of EO to lower absenteeism and to enhance employee motivation and citizenship behavior.

Some success factors were also suggested by the respondents: management's philosophical commitment to EO, consistent with past research (Gamble, Culpepper, and Blubaugh 2002; Logue and Yates 2001; Rosen, Klein, and Young 1986), as well as some elements of EO design, such as the sources of EO, the level of risk, and the difference between the direct and indirect systems of stock ownership. The latter elements are quite specific to the French context, which explains why they have not been discussed extensively in past research.

Finally, this section emphasized that EO can also affect management's work attitudes and behaviors, a topic that has not been significantly discussed in past research.

The Tax and Financial Benefits of Employee Ownership

As shown in Figure 2, beyond changes in individuals' attitudes and behaviors, interviewees explained that EO can affect corporate performance through tax benefits and different financial mechanisms.

Tax Benefits of EO. In countries such as the United States, France, and the United Kingdom, EO and its sources (i.e., profit sharing and other performance-related bonuses) qualify for preferential tax treatment for employees and the employers alike. Most interviewees discussed tax advantages as one of the reasons why companies implemented EO plans. As the president of an association of employee stockholders explained, "Employee ownership is, from a fiscal point of view, the most efficient way of giving money to the employees."

An Attractive Source of Self-Funding. Many of the interviewees believed that stock issues restricted to employees are a "simple, controllable, and advantageous" source of funding for companies:

With five offerings in the last five years, we gathered some 630 million euros from employees. The cost of raising 630 million euros through public share issues is much larger because the bank fees are considerable. —EO manager

Beyond the cost, raising money from employees seems to have many advantages over issuing new stock to the public. First, the failure of a new stock issue to the public would have a serious negative impact on the company's image. In fact, it would be perceived as a signal of a lack of trust in the company. Second, when issuing new stock to the public, it is difficult to control the scope of the operation. In the case of a highly successful public issue, there can be a significant dilution of stock value.

EO as a Stabilizer of Stock Value. Employee ownership is considered by many professionals as a way of forming a stable and loyal stockholder base. In fact, employee stockholders are usually "captive" for a period of five years and tend to keep their stock even after the vesting period. It has also been suggested that, *ceteris paribus*, EO enhances stock value by creating an additional demand for stock that would not exist if the company did not have a stock ownership plan.

EO as a Positive Signal to the Stock Market. Even if there was some disagreement among interviewees, the dominant view was that EO is considered a positive signal to the stock market:

> Dexia is a group which was originally French. The *Crédit Local de France* and the *Crédit Communal de Belgique* first merged. Then, the *Crédit Communal de Belgique* acquired the *Banque Internationale* in Luxembourg. We then became a group in 1996, composed of three main entities from three different countries. The message given to the stock market was, "We form a homogeneous group." The market can ask itself what is homogeneous in that group. . . . That is why we decided to create an employee ownership plan. It's important to show to the market that Dexia is something homogeneous. —Asset manager

As previously suggested, EO is generally believed to be a way of aligning the employees' interest with those of stockholders:

> When I was an EO manager, I used to receive surveys from Anglo-Saxon pension funds. They asked us the extent to which the employees had the same interests as the stockholders in our company. You know, those people are more interested in finance than in human resources. . . . But when we explained that we had a global stock ownership plan for all our employees worldwide, they were completely astonished. Because

the Anglo-Saxons are more familiar with stock options or restricted share plans offered to the top management only.
—Asset manager

Finally, EO is considered as being viewed positively by stock market investors for the following reasons, as explained by an EO consultant:

Financial analysts see EO as an indicator of the employees trust in their company. . . . A company without any EO is not attractive to either employees or investors. . . . Some financial analysts believe that companies with EO perform better.

In the previous two sections, I presented several explanations of how EO can lead to better corporate performance, as suggested by the interviewed professionals. Some of the presented mechanisms confirm what is generally found in the existing literature, while others are new, such as the suggested effects on management's attitudes and behaviors, the financial advantages of employee ownership, the attitudes of investors toward employee ownership, and the specific case of multinational groups.

The possibility that performance affects the development of EO has rarely been a finding in past research. In the next section, I present the mechanisms discussed by the interviewees that suggest a reversal of the EO–performance causality.

The Effects of Corporate Performance on Employee Ownership

The empirical evidence in my study suggests three main processes by which corporate performance may positively affect EO. First, companies that perform well are more likely to implement EO and to develop it more extensively. Second, in companies that perform well, profit- and gain-sharing bonuses are higher. Since most of such bonuses are invested in the company's stock (because of the tax advantages), we clearly see that more performance leads to more EO. Finally, the evidence suggests that employees tend to invest more in their company's stock when the stock price performs well. The empirical evidence also suggests an interesting reversal in employee attitudes and behavior link—that employees who are more committed and motivated might be more likely to invest in company stock. I address the evidence for each of these processes in this section.

Corporate Performance, Implementing and Developing Employee Ownership, and Employee Investment Choices

Performance and the Implementation and Development of EO. Much of the evidence I collected suggests that companies that perform well are more likely to implement EO and develop it more extensively, as explained by an asset manager:

> Nobody implements EO in a company with no projects for the future and that is losing money, because the aim is to send a message to the market of stock value increase, a message of hope. . . . So I think that EO is implemented from the beginning in companies that have a good potential for stock market growth.

When asked whether his company was thinking about implementing a new employee stock offering, an employee ownership manager replied:

> Not for the moment. To implement such an offering, our stock price would have had to follow the growth that we expected after the merger, and this has not happened. So I think that this is not a good period for an employee stock offering.

Corporate Performance and Employee Investment Behavior. There is a worldwide trend toward EO plans in which investment decisions are made by the plan participants themselves (Benartzi and Thaler 2002). In France, employees have the choice between investing bonuses or cash in their company stock or in some diversified or monetary funds. The interviews revealed different cases in which a company's performance can determine employee investment choice. First, past stock value trends and future outlook seem to play a determining role in participation rates and in the amounts invested during stock offerings. In fact, most respondents explained that participation rates in employee stock offerings were higher when the stock had performed well in the past. The explanation is that dramatic drops in the stock price create a negative attitude toward investing in the company's stock, as suggested by some interviewed employees:

> For our first stock offering, the stock price was 14 euros, and we reached a participation rate of around 45%. At the moment of the second offering, the stock price was at 40 euros and, as it was growing fast, the employees subscribed massively and we got an amazing subscription rate. —EO manager

Also, after a five-year period of unavailability, employees can choose between selling their stock and keeping it. Again, the interviewed employees explained that they tend to keep stock when past performance has been good. Finally, employees can invest their profit-sharing bonuses in their company's stock or in diversified funds. Again, it was suggested that this choice largely depends on past performance of the company stock. This evidence provides support for the "excessive extrapolation hypothesis" suggested by Benartzi (2001), who shows that employees believe that past returns are likely to persist, even if they are largely unpredictable.

Concerning profit-sharing bonuses, it is important to note that many blue-collar workers have limited financial resources to invest in stock. Therefore, they usually limit their investment in the company stock to the amount of the bonuses they receive and do not invest money from their personal funds. Companies often schedule the offerings just after payment of such bonuses to help employees participate in the offering. As a consequence, the greater the bonus amount, the more money the employees invest in the company's stock. Again, the better the performance, the larger the bonuses, and, consequently, the higher the subscription of stock.

Work Attitudes and Employee Ownership

In this section, I present evidence that suggests a reversal in the direction of causality between employee ownership and work attitudes. In fact, I suggest that EO is more likely to be implemented and developed in companies with good top managers and that committed and motivated employees are more likely to invest in their company stock.

Good Managers and EO. Some interviewees suggested that EO is more developed in companies where the top management "is of quality," meaning that it has a long-term view, a participative philosophy, and places importance on human resources. One EO manager said, "I think that Lafarge has developed EO because it had a very humanistic, very participative, very philanthropic human resource policy." Another EO manager agreed: "In my view, if EO is relevant in a company it's because the social policy behind it was already dynamic."

The president of an association of employee stockholders added:

> Maybe, in companies with EO, the top management is better than in other companies. A top management that is not afraid of questioning itself with its employees that are also stockholders is a top management which has an ethical and behavioral framing which is different from the others.

Employee Attitudes Toward the Company and EO. Discussions with professionals and employee stockholders all suggested that employee attachment and the feeling of belonging to the company were strong determinants of the decision to invest in company stock.

> We have seen many stock offerings that were not that interesting from a financial point of view, and which have been massively

subscribed to by the employees. This gives proof of a particular link with the company, an attachment to the company. —EO consultant

An employee stockholder also explained why he invested in stock of his company:

> If I purchase stock in my company it's because I love my company. It's affective. If I take some stock it's because I want to participate in my company; it's not the monetary value that I am interested in. Let's say it's 75% affective and 25% financial.

On the other hand, another employee explained why he didn't want to participate in the stock offerings:

> I refused to participate in the offering because I thought that the company owners didn't want to invest in the automobiles, and when you don't put passion into an activity you pay a high price for it. It's not because I feared losing my money, but because of the company. I think that both aspects are important. If I believe in this business, I will be willing to invest money in it. In this case, the people who asked me for the money were not motivated themselves. —Employee of Fiat

An interesting case concerned participation rates in employee stock offerings among different subsidiaries and/or sites of the same corporation. Again, the employees' feeling of "belonging to the company" seemed to matter. For example, an EO manager explained that the participation rate in his group was the highest at the headquarters level and declined in the subsidiaries where the "personalities" were the most independent from the group's personality. A consultant explained that the participation rate in a stock offering is an indicator of the general attitude of the workforce toward the company:

> The participation rate to a stock offering is very indicative of the social climate. . . . From the subscription data, I always advised my clients to try to make sense of the figures by thinking about possible conclusions to draw in terms of social dynamics and human resources policies in the different countries.

Discussion and Conclusion

The empirical literature on employee ownership over the past 30 years has generally found that EO is positively related to corporate performance. However, little theory has been developed to explain this relationship. The aim of this study was to reach a better understanding of the mechanisms relating EO and corporate performance. To accomplish this, I integrated past research and conducted a qualitative study of a group of key actors in the world of EO in France.

Figure 2 shows that EO and corporate performance are likely to have a reciprocal relationship, meaning that each affects the other, while past research essentially suggests a unidirectional relationship of EO affecting performance. The findings of this study support claims that EO can affect performance through enhanced work attitudes and behaviors, tax benefits, and other financial and stock market benefits. In fact, EO is an efficient source of self-funding for companies and, according to many professionals, it is something positively valued by investors and analysts. However, the findings also suggest that the causal direction may be reversed (i.e., corporate performance positively affects the development of EO through employee ownership preferences, profit- and gain-sharing bonuses, and employee stock offerings).

Figure 3 is a more detailed presentation of the upper part of Figure 2. It integrates the findings of past research, augmented by the findings of the empirical study (shaded rectangles). The whole model provides a more complex picture of the mechanisms relating EO to three indicators of corporate performance.

FIGURE 3
A Theoretical Framework of the Effects of Employee Ownership on Three Indicators
of Corporate Performance

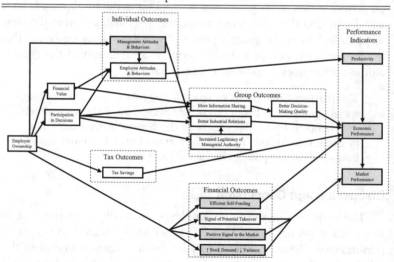

It shows that EO may affect different indicators of performance through different mechanisms, while past empirical research has often failed to make such a distinction. The upper half of Figure 3 concerns what could be called the management mechanisms because they deal with people's attitudes and behaviors. It shows that EO directly affects management work attitudes and behavior (e.g., fewer short term–oriented decisions and more-ethical behavior) and affects employee attitudes and behaviors through its financial value and the rights to participate in decision making (when such rights are available to employees). Employee ownership can also affect such group outcomes as information sharing, industrial relations, and the perceived legitimacy of managerial authority. These, in turn, distinctively affect individual productivity in particular or economic performance in general.

The lower half of Figure 3 describes the tax and financial mechanisms by which EO can affect corporate performance. Three of the so-called financial mechanisms are believed to directly affect market performance, while efficient self-funding affects economic performance. The first mechanism applies only when a new EO plan is set up: seeing it as a signal of a potential takeover, the market would react positively. More generally, EO would be viewed by investors as an indicator of corporate wealth because they believe that EO leads to better performance and that only well-performing companies can afford to develop EO. Finally, EO increases stock value by creating an artificial demand that would not otherwise exist, and because employees generally do not engage in speculative behavior stock price variance is lowered.

The last main group of findings of the qualitative study concerns the preconditions of the relationship between EO and employee attitudes and behaviors. This is another area where past research is limited. Management's philosophical commitment to employee ownership is a well-known and important variable in the EO human resources literature (Gamble, Culpepper, and Blubaugh 2002; Klein 1987; Pierce, Rubenfeld, and Morgan 1991). The qualitative data analyzed in this chapter provide a more detailed and real-world view of this concept as manifested in large companies. Other preconditions concern the design of the EO plan itself. The results here do not lead to clear guidelines or best practices, but they do highlight the need for managers to carefully consider the meaning they wish to give to EO in their company and the outcomes they wish to achieve. These options include the sources of the plan, the risk level, and direct versus indirect forms of ownership.

The findings of this study have several implications for theory, managers, and policy makers. The results clearly give future researchers better theoretical tools to set up empirical research. For example, researchers will be able to use different theoretical reasoning, depending on the indicator of performance analyzed in their studies. When individual productivity is the outcome under study, incentive theories will likely be the most applicable, because they deal with people's attitudes and behaviors at work. However, when the main outcome is an indicator of market performance, other market-based arguments should be more relevant.

One of the limits of past research was that the main argument of the EO–performance relationship—the incentive explanation—had not been shown to hold in most cases. The model presented in this chapter shows that EO can still affect companies' economic and market performances in the absence of an incentive effect. Finally, past research concluded that the effect of EO on performance was not automatic and that a set of preconditions was necessary. The evidence presented in this chapter suggests that this is true only for the managerial part of the model, for which the attitudinal and behavioral effects are difficult to obtain. However, the tax and financial mechanisms of EO seem to be pervasive, which means that EO likely has some potential for positively affecting economic and market performance in most cases.

The reciprocal nature of the EO–performance relationship, even if it holds particularly true in the French context, suggests that the existing empirical evidence should be interpreted with caution. More research using longitudinal data is needed to ensure the direction of causality between EO and performance. However, this is especially relevant for market performance because productivity likely affects the development of EO less than the economic and market indicators of performance do.

As previously suggested, the findings of this study must be interpreted in light of a number of limitations. The inherent limitations of qualitative research techniques (e.g., limited sample size) in general and of manual thematic content analysis with a single coder in particular are well known. Moreover, the models presented in Figure 2 and Figure 3 and the overall results are exploratory in nature: refinements and further elaboration require additional empirical investigation and tests of specific elements of the presented models.

I consider the fact that the findings are based on French multinationals to only slightly detract from the generalizability of the results. More specifically, only the lower part of Figure 2 may lack generalizability because of the specific structural characteristics of the French system, in which profit- and gain-sharing bonuses are used to purchase stock for employees. However, these causal connections may exist in other contexts, albeit through other mechanisms. For example, in the United States, profit-sharing bonuses can be invested in stock, employees are free to participate or not in ESPPs, and, in their 401(k) plans, employees can decide between EO funds and diversified funds.

This chapter has attempted to open the black box within the existing EO–performance literature that likely contains better insight into the mechanisms linking EO and corporate performance. The hope is that future research can shine more light onto these mechanisms and expand our understanding of what is necessary for managers, employees, and policy makers to promote the implementation of EO that improves firm performance.

References

Ben-Ner, A., and D.C. Jones. 1995. "Employee Participation, Ownership, and Productivity: A Theoretical Framework." *Industrial Relations*, Vol. 34, no. 4, pp. 532–54.

Benartzi, S. 2001. "Excessive Extrapolation and the Allocation of 401(k) Accounts to Company Stock." *Journal of Finance*, Vol. 56, no. 5, pp. 1747–64.

Benartzi, S., and R.H. Thaler. 2002. "How Much Is Investor Autonomy Worth?" *Journal of Finance*, Vol. 57, no. 4, pp. 1593–1616.

Blasi, J.R. 1988. *Employee Ownership: Revolution or Ripoff?* Cambridge, MA: Ballinger Publishing Company.

Blasi, J.R., M. Conte, and D.L. Kruse. 1996. "Employee Stock Ownership and Corporate Performance among Public Companies." *Industrial and Labor Relations Review*, Vol. 50, no. 1, pp. 60–79.

Brohawn, D. 1997. *Journey to an Ownership Culture: Insights from the ESOP Community*. Washington, DC: Scarecrow Press and the ESOP Association.

Chang, S. 1990. "Employee Stock Ownership Plans and Shareholder Wealth: An Empirical Investigation." *Financial Management*, Vol. 19, no. 1, pp. 48–58.

Chiu, W.C.K., C.H. Hui, and G.W.F. Lai. 2007. "Psychological Ownership and Organizational Optimism amid China's Corporate Transformation: Effects of an Employee Ownership Scheme and a Management Dominated Board." *International Journal of Human Resource Management*, Vol. 18, no. 2, pp. 303–20.

Cin, B.-C., and S.C. Smith. 2002. "Employee Stock Ownership and Participation in South Korea: Incidence, Productivity Effects and Prospects." *Review of Development Economics*, Vol. 6, no. 2, pp. 263–83.

Cohen, A., and M. Quarrey. 1986. "Performance of Employee-Owned Small Companies: A Preliminary Study." *Journal of Small Business Management*, April, pp. 58–63.

Craig, B., and J. Pencavel. 1995. "Participation and Productivity: A Comparison of Worker Cooperatives and Conventional Firms in the Plywood Industry." *Brookings Papers on Economic Activity, Special Issue on Microeconomics*, pp. 121–74.

Davidson, W.N.I., and D.L. Worrell. 1994. "ESOP's Fables: The Influence of Employee Stock Ownership Plans on Corporate Stock Prices and Subsequent Operating Performance." *Human Resource Planning*, Vol. 17, no. 4, pp. 69–87.

Doucouliagos, C. 1995. "Worker Participation and Productivity in Labor-Managed and Participatory Capitalist Firms: A Meta-Analysis." *Industrial and Labor Relations Review*, Vol. 49, no. 1, pp. 58–77.

Estrin, S., and D.C. Jones. 1992. "The Viability of Employee-Owned Firms: Evidence from France." *Industrial and Labor Relations Review*, Vol. 45, no. 2, pp. 323–37.

Fitzroy, F.R., and K. Kraft. 1992. "Forms of Profit Sharing and Firm Performance." *Kyklos*, Vol. 45, no. 2, pp. 209–26.

Frohlich, N., J. Godard, J.A. Oppenheimer, and F.A. Starke. 1998. "Employee Versus Conventionally-Owned and Controlled Firms: An Experimental Analysis." *Managerial and Decision Economics*, Vol. 19, pp. 311–26.

Frye, M.B. 2004. "Equity-Based Compensation for Employees: Firm Performance and Determinants." *Journal of Financial Research*, Vol. 27, no. 1, pp. 31–54.

Gamble, J.E., R.A. Culpepper, and M. Blubaugh. 2002. "ESOPs and Employee Attitudes: The Importance of Empowerment and Financial Value." *Personnel Review*, Vol. 31, no. 1, pp. 9–26.

Iqbal, Z., and S.A. Hamid. 2000. "Stock Price and Operating Performance of ESOP Firms: A Time-Series Analysis." *Quarterly Journal of Business and Economics*, Vol. 39, no. 3, pp. 25–47.

Jones, D.C. 1987. "The Productivity Effects of Worker Directors and Financial Participation by Employees in the Firm: The Case of British Retail Cooperatives." *Industrial and Labor Relations Review*, Vol. 41, no. 1, pp. 79–92.

Jones, D.C., and T. Kato. 1993. "The Scope, Nature and Effects of Employee Stock Ownership Plans in Japan." *Industrial and Labor Relations Review*, Vol. 46, no. 2, pp. 352–67.

Jones, D.C., and J. Pliskin. 1988. *The Effects of Worker Participation, Employee Ownership and Profit Sharing on Economic Performance: A Partial Review.* Unpublished paper, Bard College, NY.

Kaarsemaker, E. 2006. *Employee Ownership and Human Resource Management: A Theoretical and Empirical Treatise with a Digression on the Dutch Context.* PhD Diss., Radboud University, Nijmegen, the Netherlands.

Klein, K. 1987. "Employee Stock Ownership and Employee Attitudes: A Test of Three Models." *Journal of Applied Psychology Monographs*, Vol. 72, no. 2, pp. 319–32.

Kruse, D., R. Freeman, J.R. Blasi, A. Buchele, L. Scharf, L. Rodgers, and C. Mackin. 2004. "Motivating Employee-Owners in ESOP Firms: Human Resource Policies and Company Performance." In V. Pérotin, and A.M. Robinson, eds., *Employee Participation, Firm Performance and Survival*, Vol. 8, pp. 101–27.

Kruse, D.L. 1993. *Profit-Sharing: Does It Make a Difference? The Productivity and Stability Effects of Employee Profit-Sharing Plans.* Kalamazoo, MI: Upjohn Institute Press.

Kruse, D.L., and Blasi, J.R. 1997. "Employee Ownership, Employee Attitudes and Firm Performance: A Review of the Evidence." In D. Lewin, D.J.B. Mitchell, and M. Zaidi, eds., *The Human Resource Management Handbook*. Greenwich: JAI Press, pp. 113–52.

Kruse, D.L., R.B., Freeman, and J.R. Blasi, eds. 2010. *Shared Capitalism at Work: Employee Ownership, Profit and Gain Sharing, and Broad-Based Stock Options.* Chicago: University of Chicago Press.

Kuvaas, B. 2003. "Employee Ownership and Affective Organizational Commitment: Employees' Perceptions of Fairness and Their Preference for Company Shares over Cash." *Scandinavian Journal of Management*, Vol. 19, no. 2, pp. 193–212.

Lee, Y.-T. 2003. "The Productivity Effects of Employee Stock-Ownership Plans: Evidence From Panel Data of Taiwan Electronic Companies." *International Journal of Management*, Vol. 20, no. 4, pp. 479–89.

Marsh, T.R., and D.E. McAllister. 1981. "ESOPs Tables: A Survey of Companies with Employee Stock Ownership Plans." *Journal of Corporation Law*, Vol. 6, no. 3, pp. 551–623.

Meyer, J.P., and N.J. Allen. 1991. "A Three-Component Conceptualization of Organizational Commitment." *Human Resource Management Review*, Vol. 1, no. 1,
pp. 61–89.

Meyer, J.P., and N.J. Allen. 1997. *Commitment in the Workplace*. Thousand Oaks,
CA: Sage.

National Center for Employee Ownership (NCEO). 2009. *A Statistical Profile of
Employee Ownership*. <http://www.nceo.org/library/eo_stat.html>. [May 4,
2009].

National Center for Employee Ownership (NCEO). 2010. *Creating the Ownership
Edge at Your ESOP Company*. <http://www.nceo.org/main/article.php/id/27>.
[January 8, 2011].

Park, S., and M.H. Song. 1995. "Employee Stock Ownership Plans, Firm Performance and Monitoring by Outside Blockholders." *Financial Management*, Vol.
24, no. 4, pp. 52–65.

Pérotin, V., and A.M. Robinson. 2003. "Employee Participation in Profit and Ownership: A Review of the Issues and Evidence." *Working Paper, SOCI 109 EN,
European Parliament*.

Pierce, J.L., S.A. Rubenfeld, and S. Morgan. 1991. "Employee Ownership: A Conceptual Model of Process and Effects." *Academy of Management Review*, Vol.
26, no. 2, pp. 121–44.

Poutsma, E., D. Albaraccin, P. Kalmi, A. Pendleton, C. Trébucq, and E. Voss. 2006.
Changing Patterns of Employee Financial Participation in Europe. Unpublished
paper, Nijmegen School of Management, the Netherlands.

Pugh, W.N., J.S. Jahera Jr., and S.L. Oswald. 2005. "ESOP Adoption and Corporate
Performance: Does Motive Really Matter?" *Journal of Business and Economic
Studies*, Vol. 11, no. 1, pp. 76–92.

Robinson, A.M., and N. Wilson. 2006. "Employee Financial Participation and Productivity: An Empirical Reappraisal." *British Journal of Industrial Relations*, Vol.
44, no. 1, pp. 31–50.

Rousseau, D.M., and Z. Shperling. 2003. "Pieces of the Action: Ownership and the
Changing Employment Relationship." *Academy of Management Review*, Vol. 28,
no. 4, pp. 553–70.

Shah, S.K., and K.G. Corley. 2006. "Building Better Theory by Bridging the Quantitative–Qualitative Divide." *Journal of Management Studies*, Vol. 43, no. 8,
pp. 1822–35.

Smith, S.C., B.-C. Cin, and M. Vodopivec. 1997. "Privatization Incidence, Ownership
Forms, and Firm Performance: Evidence from Slovenia." *Journal of Comparative Economics*, Vol. 25, pp. 158–79.

Sparrow, P. 2002. "The Psychological Consequences of Employee Ownership: On the
Role of Risk, Reward, Identity and Personality." In C. Cooper and D. Rousseau,
eds., *Trends in Organisational Behaviour*, Vol. 6. London: Wiley.

Toscano, D.J. 1983. "Toward a Typology of Employee Ownership." *Human Relations*,
Vol. 36, no. 7, pp. 581–602.

Trébucq, S. 2004. "The Effects of ESOPs on Performance and Risk: Evidence from
France." *Corporate Ownership and Control*, Vol. 1, no. 4, pp. 81–93.

Welbourne, T.M., and L.R. Gomez-Mejia. 1995. "Gainsharing: A Critical Review and
a Future Research Agenda." *Journal of Management*, Vol. 21, no. 3, pp. 559–609.

CHAPTER 8

The Determinants and Consequences of Broad-Based Stock Option Plans: The View from Economics and Finance

SERDAR ALDATMAZ
PAIGE OUIMET
University of North Carolina

A rich literature in finance and economics has explored the costs and benefits of providing equity-based incentives to top management. Jensen and Meckling (1976) were among the first to argue that firm value can increase when the incentives of top management are aligned with those of shareholders. They suggest that management should retain a significant fraction of the firm's equity because any actions by management that reduce shareholder value, such as the consumption of excess perks, will also adversely affect management by reducing the value of their share holdings. Following Jensen and Meckling (1976), a number of empirical papers have sought to document the relation between managerial ownership and firm value, with results both supporting and contesting the earlier theory—leaving the question open for debate.

In contrast, a smaller literature in finance and economics has explored the costs and benefits of providing incentives to all employees at a firm. The importance of understanding how managerial ownership affects firm value is clear. Top managers typically have the greatest impact on firm value compared with any other employee. However, it is also important to understand how granting stock-based incentives to all employees affects firm value. For example, the total effect on firm productivity from nonmanagerial employees is likely to dominate the total effect from top management. Furthermore, lower-level employees are less likely to be subjected to direct monitoring by shareholders and, thus, the potential for such employees to act in a manner inconsistent with shareholder preferences is greater.

In this chapter, we survey the relevant studies covering broad-based stock option plans (BBSOPs), a form of employee ownership. Through BBSOPs, firms provide employees with the right to purchase company stock, at a fixed price, for a fixed period of time. Since these plans receive no special tax privileges, they tend to be loosely defined, and managers have a great deal of flexibility in deciding who participates and how much stock employees receive. The convention is to define a broad-based stock option plan as any plan that awards options to more than 50% of the firm's employees (Oyer and Schaefer 2005; Hochberg and Lindsey 2010).

Employee ownership via stock options has been increasing in the United States over the last decade. The 1993–1994 Employee Benefits Survey by the Bureau of Labor Statistics found that less than 0.5% of U.S. private sector employees received stock options at that time. More recently, the General Social Survey found that 10% of the surveyed American public sector workers reported owning stock options of their employer in 2006. Furthermore, the 2000 National Compensation Survey (NCS) program by the Bureau of Labor Statistics found that 1.7% of U.S. private sector employees (after excluding owners) had received new stock option grants in 1999. According to the 2000 NCS, stock option grants are more common at public firms, where 5.3% of workers received grants. See Crimmel and Schildkraut (2001) for a detailed summary of the coverage of stock options in the 2000 NCS.

The 2004 NCS continued to show the importance of stock options as a form of compensation for U.S. workers, although the findings in the 2004 NCS are not directly comparable to those in the 2000 NCS because the 2000 NCS measured actual stock grants while the 2004 survey measured access to stock option plans. However, both surveys tell a similar story. The 2004 survey found that 8% of U.S. workers in the private sector had access to stock options in 2003. As reported in the earlier survey, workers with higher wages were more likely to benefit from stock options. In 2003, 13% of workers who earned at least $15 per hour had access to stock option plans as opposed to only 6% of workers who earned less than $15 per hour. The 2004 survey also found that workers at larger establishments were more likely to have access to stock options.

While a large fraction of these options are allocated to senior executives, there is also strong evidence of broad-based participation. The 2000 NCS found that 12% of establishments owned by U.S. public firms gave options to at least 20% of their employees in 1999. Among nonexecutive employees, the incidence of granting options increases with increasing base pay. While only 0.7% of nonexecutive employees earning less than $35,000 per year received option grants, 12.9% of nonexecutives earning $75,000 or more per year received option grants. Furthermore, since top executives represent a small fraction of the total workforce at a given firm, the total dollar value of options granted to other employees dominated. Hall and Murphy (2003) find that only 9.5% of the value of options granted to employees in S&P 500 companies is allocated to the CEO and other top five executives in 2002. The remaining 90.5% of the value of the options is granted to other managers and employees at the firm.

Unfortunately, data limitations prevent Hall and Murphy (2003) from identifying how the remaining options, which are not allocated to top executives, are dispersed within a firm across job titles. While these summary statistics are consistent with broad-based participation, it is possible that the allocation of options that are not allocated to top-five executives at these firms is concentrated in the next tier of junior executives. Thus, the firms may have large employee stock option plans but concentrated participation. While it is not always possible to identify the extent of participation in an employee stock option plan from all data sources, studies that do have sufficient data indicate that a high fraction of firms with large stock option plans do indeed have broad-based participation. For example, a survey by William M. Mercer found that 39% of large firms in 1999 granted stock options to at least one half of their employees. This is an increase from 17% in 1993. (The survey results are described in an article, "Stock Options Trickle Down" in USA Today, October 6, 1999, page 1B.)

In this review, we compare results across studies on BBSOPs in the finance and economics literature, and we relate these findings to theories suggesting which types of firms are most likely to benefit from greater shared capitalism through BBSOPs. We also review studies that document the effects of these plans on firm performance, including shareholder returns and accounting profits. We focus exclusively on BBSOPs at public firms since limited data availability on BBSOPs at private firms has hampered research at these firms. However, the use and effects of BBSOPs at private firms remain a significant gap in the literature. Finally, it is also important to note that we have not incorporated the larger set of studies on BBSOPs that have been conducted within neighboring disciplines, such as psychology, sociology, industrial relations, human resource management, and accounting. Our focus is specifically on work within finance and economics.

Defining Broad-Based Stock Option Plans

A stock option gives an employee the right to buy a specific number of company shares at a fixed price over a fixed period of time. The price at which employees can buy the company stock in the future is called the strike price (or sometimes the grant price). The typical employee stock option is granted with the strike price set equal to the current stock price

(Hall and Murphy 2003). If the company's stock appreciates in the future, employees will be able to exercise their options and purchase company shares with higher valuations at the lower strike price. Because employees profit from the difference in the stock price and the strike price, the more the stock appreciates, the greater the profit for employees.

Employee options are typically associated with a vesting period, following which employees receive the right to exercise their options. Vesting schedules can be either time or performance based. Options may vest all at once, or the process can be gradual, with a fraction of granted options vesting each year. According to the 2000 NCS, the average stock option grant vested in three years (Crimmel and Schildkraut 2001). Alternatively, the National Center on Employee Ownership finds a slightly longer mean vesting period of four years (Oyer and Schaefer 2005). Once vested, employees have the right to exercise their options; however, employees do not typically need to immediately exercise this right. The 2000 NCS found that, on average, employees had 8.9 years to exercise their option before the option expired. If an employee leaves the company before an option has vested, he or she typically forfeits his or her unvested options.

We define broad-based stock option plans as those that grant stock options to at least 50% of a firm's employees. However, few of the studies covered in our review have sufficient data to directly confirm that over 50% of the firm's employees are participating in the stock option plan. Instead, it is common to assume broad participation when the number or percentage of stock option grants awarded to nonexecutives at a firm is large. The definition of "nonexecutive" varies by study. Core and Guay (2001), in their study of 756 large U.S. public firms, define nonexecutives by excluding the top five officers in a firm. After excluding those top executives, they found that the remaining employees hold option portfolios valued at over $17,000, on average.

Oyer and Schaefer (2005) modify this measure to also exclude options assumed to have been granted to other senior executives, such as the sixth, seventh, etc., highest-paid executives. While they do not have data on the actual option allocations to these other senior executives, they proxy for their awards by assuming that these other senior executives receive options following a similar pattern, albeit at a smaller magnitude, to the options awarded to top executives. Specifically, they assume that these other senior executives comprise ten percent of the employees at a public firm, on average. The authors estimate that each employee in this group of other senior executives receives a stock option grant equal to one tenth of the average option grant awarded to the second through fifth most compensated executives. The authors assume that workers not in this group of senior executives are rank-

and-file workers. Thus, to estimate whether rank-and-file workers are also receiving options, they take the total options allocated at the firm and subtract (1) options allocated to the top five officers and (2) options assumed to be allocated to other senior executives. If this difference is positive, they identify a firm as having a BBSOP. In a random sample of 1,000 publicly traded firms, they find that 48.9% of firms had broad-based option plans in 1999. Alternatively, other studies, such as that by Ittner, Lambert, and Larcker (2003), use proprietary data sets for which they have a smaller sample of firms but more information on the job titles of employees receiving option grants.

BBSOPs were relatively uncommon prior to the early 1990s; however, in the last decade, they have become an increasingly common type of employee compensation in the United States. As the number of companies that use these plans and, hence, the number of employees participating in these plans, increase, we need to better understand both the determinants and implications of these plans. In the next section, we review the research on why companies are adopting these plans, and the consequences of these plans for corporate performance and employee outcomes. Due to limited data availability on BBSOPs at private firms, the research to date in this area has been on public firms. Thus, our review also focuses only on BBSOPs at public firms. In reviewing the literature on BBSOPs, we do not rely on one common definition of these plans. Instead, we include studies from the finance and economics literature in which the researchers have identified BBSOPs according to their individual definitions.

Why Do Companies Adopt BBSOPs?

The growing prevalence of BBSOPs among American companies has led to increasing attention to these plans in the finance and economics literature. In this section, we discuss various motivations suggested in the academic literature that may drive the establishment of these plans. While some of these motivations have received more attention than the others, it is still an ongoing debate as to what motivates the adoption of these plans and what explains their success or failure in terms of improving company performance. In what follows, we review several studies that look at broad-based stock option granting behavior at public firms.

Incentive Creation and Productivity Enhancement

The adoption of a BBSOP by a firm is hypothesized to increase worker productivity. Jensen and Meckling (1976) theorize that greater stock ownership can help to align the incentives of managers with shareholders, thereby increasing the probability that managers will make decisions that will increase firm value. However, the benefit from granting shares to top management does not necessarily apply to equity-based incentives granted broadly to all employees. In Jensen and Meckling (1976), the manager is motivated because his or her actions will directly impact the value of the firm and, thus, his or her ownership stake. However, in the context of a BBSOP, the actions of any one worker are unlikely to have a significant impact on the overall value of the firm. With a BBSOP, workers are not compensated directly on their actions. Instead, workers gain when the stock price of the firm increases. This introduces a potential free-rider problem. For example, suppose upon being granted stock options, a worker increases his or her effort, thereby increasing the value of the firm by x dollars. This hard-working employee will not capture the full benefit of his or her additional labor and will instead share these gains with all share and stock option holders. This equal sharing of gains, commonly referred to as the free-rider problem, will dilute the incentives for employees to put forth greater effort.

Demsetz and Lehn (1985) argue that this free-rider problem will be most acute when the number of owners in the firm increases. Applying this argument to a BBSOP, we should expect free riding to be minimized at firms with a small number of employees. Firm size will alter the incentive effects of a BBSOP not only because employees will have to share any gains derived from their personal effort with a larger group but also because workers will be less able to co-monitor within large employee groups (Knez and Simester 2001).

Kandel and Lazear (1992) posit that this free-rider problem can be overcome by peer pressure: workers covered by a BBSOP may profit as a whole if everyone agrees to work harder. However, in the absence of peer pressure, incentives to cooperate are likely to be weak due to the free-rider problem. However, if employees as a group can (1) observe one another's work and (2) effect behavior through peer pressure, cooperation resulting in a high-work regime becomes more likely. These theories suggest that a BBSOP alone may be insufficient to increase worker productivity. However, a BBSOP implemented in a corporate culture that promotes group cooperation and co-monitoring is likely to have a much stronger effect on firm productivity (Hochberg and Lindsey 2010).

Survey evidence supports the arguments that peer monitoring can reduce the free-rider effect. Freeman, Kruse, and Blasi (2010) surveyed over 40,000 employees from 14 companies with employee ownership plans as part of the National Bureau of Economic Research (NBER) Shared Capitalism research project. This survey, conducted between 2001 and 2006, asked employees how they would respond if they observed a co-worker underperforming. In response to this question, surveyed employees were given the choice to (1) talk directly to the employee, (2) speak to a supervisor, or (3) do nothing. For each question, employees were asked to respond on a four-point scale as to how likely they were to take any of the actions. Using these answers, the authors constructed an anti-shirking index. Consistent with the expected co-monitoring benefits of BBSOPs, they find that employees who received a stock option grant in the previous year are more likely to actively respond to shirking by a co-worker.

However, the empirical literature offers a more mixed assessment as to the ability of BBSOPs to enhance productivity based on the types of firms that adopt these plans. Core and Guay (2001), in their study of 756 public U.S. firms, conclude that companies adopt BBSOPs to improve employee incentives and enhance productivity. The authors argue that a BBSOP will increase employee productivity if it reduces the need for costly monitoring. They identify firms with high monitoring costs as those that are larger or have greater growth opportunities (as proxied by investments in research and development). The authors contend that monitoring is more costly at larger firms and at firms with more growth opportunities due to fewer measures of individual employee performance at these firms. As predicted, they find that larger firms and firms with greater R&D investments provide more stock options to their rank-and-file workers. The authors acknowledge that the free-rider problem may offset some of the incentive effects of BBSOPs, thereby making it more costly to minimize monitoring needs through such plans. However, they also note that monitoring can be an especially costly process, especially for companies whose production process makes it difficult to observe the efforts of employees. When monitoring costs are sufficiently large, companies may prefer to use broad-based stock option plans as an alternative to more expensive direct monitoring.

Likewise, in their study of new economy firms, such as software, semiconductors, Internet, computers, and other high-technology manufacturing firms, Ittner, Lambert, and Larcker (2003) argue that such firms use BBSOPs as a substitute for other, more expensive, means of monitoring. BBSOPs can serve as a substitute for monitoring since these plans will induce employees to put forth higher levels of effort by tying the employees' wealth to company value. In line with this hypothesis, they find that companies that are subject to more outside monitoring from either debt-holders or an active outside shareholder are less likely to adopt BBSOPs, relative to firms that do not have any of these other monitoring mechanisms.

Kedia and Mozumdar (2002) argue that aligning incentives between employees and shareholders is most important at firms with valuable growth opportunities. Direct monitoring may be less effective at these firms because information related to growth opportunities may be released slowly over time. Consistent with the incentive motivation, they find that firms that grant more stock options to nonexecutives have higher growth opportunities, as proxied by higher Tobin's Q and R&D intensity. This result is consistent with the earlier findings of Core and Guay (2001) and has been repeated in later studies as well. Kedia and Rajgopal (2009) and Kroumova and Sesil (2005b) also confirm a positive association between the presence of BBSOPs and R&D expenditures.

While the earlier studies all report evidence indicating that BBSOPs appear to be implemented as a means to reduce the need for monitoring by improving employee incentives, Oyer and Schaefer (2005) disagree with these conclusions. For example, they argue that Core and Guay (2001), given their identification approach, may be incorrectly classifying firms as having BBSOPs. Core and Guay (2001) identify broad-based employee stock options as those options granted to employees but not granted to top executives. Oyer and Schaefer (2005) construct a new measure of BBSOP that they feel is more reflective of true broad-based participation. They modify the BBSOP identification approach used in Core and Guay (2001) by subtracting options assumed to be granted to other senior executives and classify a firm as having a BBSOP only if the total number of options granted is positive after excluding options granted to top executives and assumed to have been granted to other senior executives. With this new identification strategy, they reverse one of the findings in Core and Guay (2001). Oyer and Schaefer (2005) now find that smaller firms are more likely to implement BBSOPs.

Oyer and Schaefer (2005) also argue that cross-sectional tests cannot provide definitive proof in support of or against the incentive motivation. To identify cross-sectional variation in the gains from increased incentives, the authors adapt a theoretical model used in Holmstrom and Milgrom (1987, 1991). Using this framework, they find that employees should receive more equity-based compensation when such compensation does not impose too much costly risk on employees. (A more detailed discussion of the costs associated with compensating employees with equity is covered in the following section on cash conservation.) Furthermore, employees should receive more equity-based compensation when the marginal return on additional employee effort is high and when employees are unlikely to exert this effort themselves without additional incentives. While their model offers clear predictions of where equity-based incentives should be most valuable, the difficulty lies in identifying proxies in the data that can be used to test these predictions. This leads to concerns regarding omitted variables and, as a result, unreliable tests.

Instead, Oyer and Schaefer (2005) suggest an alternative approach. They calibrate their model using data on option grants, compensation risk, and typical levels of individual risk aversion. With these inputs, they are able to backout the employee's cost of effort (how much additional compensation an employee must receive to be willing to exert an additional unit of effort) and risk premium (how much additional compensation the firm must give the risk-averse employee when substituting risky options for cash). They find no support for the incentive motivation for establishing a BBSOP. Their derived estimates suggest that much of the gains from increased effort provision associated with the granting of broad-based stock options are dissipated due to the high-risk premiums that must be given to employees to compensate them for bearing additional compensation risk.

However, it is important to emphasize that these studies all reach their conclusions by exploring the characteristics of firms that chose to implement BBSOPs. These studies do not directly explore ex-post changes in estimated employee monitoring costs or even ex-post changes in firm performance. One exception to this approach is taken by Babenko (2009b), who provides novel support that BBSOPs are implemented to improve employee incentives to increase shareholder value by exploring share repurchases. When a firm repurchases its shares, employees are typically restricted from participating. Thus, following a share repurchase, the fraction of the firm owned by employees increases. This, in turn, increases the pay-for-performance sensitivity of the wage contracts given to the firm's employees. As such, a share repurchase at a firm with a BBSOP can have the same effect on worker incentives as allocating new stock options to employees. Using this insight, Babenko (2009b) then explores several cross-sectional predictions. First, she documents that firms with more unvested broad-based stock options are more likely to implement a share repurchase as a means to distribute cash to shareholders. Furthermore, she finds that the market reacts most positively to share repurchases announced at firms with large BBSOPs. While this is not direct evidence that BBSOPs lead to higher future firm performance, this evidence indicates that the market believes increasing rank-and-file employee pay-for-performance sensitivity through a BBSOP will lead to higher future firm performance.

In sum, several papers, such as Core and Guay (2001), identify cross-sectional evidence that firms that would benefit the most from greater employee incentive alignment are more likely to adopt BBSOPs. However, Oyer and Schaefer (2005) argue such cross-sectional tests are insufficient to provide indisputable evidence that BBSOPs are adopted to achieve incentive benefits due to the difficulty in identifying all the key variables that will predict the costs and benefits of providing increased employee incentives via BBSOPs. One exception to the Oyer and Schaefer (2005) critique is found in Babenko (2009b), who finds that stock repurchases will increase the incentive benefits of a pre-existing BBSOP. Consistent with an employee incentive motivation for adopting BBSOPs, Babenko (2009a) also finds that the stock market reacts more positively to share repurchases at firms with pre-existing BBSOPs.

Cash Conservation

Since stock options require no cash investment on behalf of the firm at the time of grant, a second motivation for publicly traded firms to adopt a BBSOP is to use options as a substitute for cash compensation. In doing so, the firm can preserve cash for other purposes, such as making investments or paying off debts. If cash conservation is a motivation for the adoption of BBSOPs, we would expect companies subject to cash constraints to use these plans more. Indeed, that is what Core and Guay (2001), Kedia and Mozumdar (2002), and Kedia and Rajgopal (2009) argue in their studies of the determinants of BBSOPs. Core and Guay (2001) find that BBSOPs are more common at firms that have high capital needs and high costs of accessing capital markets. Kedia and Mozumdar (2002) find that firms that grant more BBSOPs pay fewer dividends (have less excess cash to distribute to shareholders) and have higher net operating losses carried forward (indicating that these firms have been unprofitable in past years). Kedia and Rajgopal (2009) find that firms with BBSOPs are more likely to have had recent operating losses.

However, not all studies agree. Ittner, Lambert, and Larcker (2003) find no evidence that cash-constrained firms provide more equity-based compensation. In fact, they find that firms that appear less cash constrained are associated with greater equity-based compensation. Likewise, Bergman and Jenter (2007) find that BBSOPs are positively associated with high cash balances and cash flows at the firm. Oyer and Schaefer (2005) find mixed evidence in support of the cash conservation motivation. In support, they find that firms with a positive cash flow are less likely to grant more stock options to nonexecutives. However, they also find that firms making large investments relative to their equity are less likely to grant broad-based stock options. Given the large cash needs of these firms, the cash-constrained motivation would have predicted that these firms would be more likely to grant broad-based stock options.

Differences in the results found in the previous studies could be driven by differences in (1) the sample of firms used, (2) the measurement of equity-based compensation, or (3) the use of controls. Core and Guay (2001) use a sample of 756 of the largest U.S. public firms.

Oyer and Schaefer (2005) examine a random sample of 1,000 public firms. Kedia and Mozumdar (2002) use a sample of 200 NASDAQ firms. Alternatively, Ittner, Lambert, and Larcker (2003) explore a sample of 217 firms operating exclusively in high-tech sectors, such as computers, software, semiconductors, and Internet. Core and Guay (2001) and Kedia and Mozumdar (2002) estimate the importance of broad-based stock option grants as a form of compensation at a given firm as the ratio of the log of the change in employee wealth to a 1% change in the stock price, for the average rank-and-file employee. Stock options granted to rank-and-file workers are identified as total stock options granted to all employees at a firm minus option grants to the top five executives. Oyer and Schaefer (2005) modify this identification by also excluding options assumed to be granted to other senior executives. Ittner, Lambert, and Larcker (2003) combine both stock options and restricted stock into one measure of equity-based compensation. While Ittner, Lambert, and Larcker (2003) do not report separate statistics for stock options relative to restricted stock, they do note that the presence of a stock option plan is over three and a half times more common in their sample, compared with restricted stock grants. Finally, Core and Guay (2001) use a simultaneous estimation model to control for the contemporaneous effect of stock option exercise on new grant allocations. The authors argue that this is a key control because firms may manage new option grants to achieve a target level of total options outstanding. Other papers reviewed do not include this control.

Putting aside the debate in the empirical literature, a natural question follows from the theoretical argument: Are employees the best and cheapest source of financing for cash-constrained firms? First, individual employees are likely to be more cash constrained relative to cash-constrained firms. Second, by granting stock options to employees through BBSOPs, employers expose their employees to more company-specific risk. One of the key tenets of finance is that individuals prefer less risk to more risk and therefore require higher compensation when exposed to higher risk. This argument is particularly acute when considering that, in the case of BBSOPs, an employee is exposed to even more company-specific risk given that the employee also depends on the firm for employment. When the company does well, the employee does well. However, when the company fares poorly, the consequences for the employee can be significant. The value of an employee's stock options (and, hence, his or her wealth) will decline at the same time that the employee risks losing his or her job.

Consequently, a risk-averse employee will undervalue stock options, relative to cash, and require more than one dollar of stock options to replace a dollar of cash compensation. For example, Brennan and

Torous (1999) find that a typical investor would be indifferent if given a choice between investing $1 in a single stock over a ten-year period and receiving a guaranteed $0.36. Thus, a risk-averse employee will require a risk premium, which can be paid in the form of more stock options or more cash, to be compensated for the risk of being underdiversified if holding shares in a BBSOP. This required risk premium makes it more expensive for the firm to compensate employees with stock options. Following a similar reasoning, Oyer and Schaefer (2005) argue that motivations based on cash conservation are hard to justify. They suggest that BBSOPs might help to conserve cash only when employees are optimistic about company prospects, which would make the employees overvalue the stock options.

Babenko, Lemmon, and Tserlukevich (2010) suggest another cash-related motivation for the adoption of BBSOPs. They argue that stock options provide a cash inflow to the company when the employees exercise their options. To exercise an option, an employee must pay the firm the strike price in order to receive one share of stock. The company could purchase a share of stock from an outside investor in order to then sell this share to the employee. In doing so, the firm would suffer a net cash loss since, by definition, options are exercised only when the strike price is less than the current stock price. Alternatively, the firm could issue the employee a new share of stock. In this case, the firm would receive a net inflow of cash equal to the strike price.

Using a sample of over 1,400 large public firms, Babenko, Lemmon, and Tserlukevich (2010) find that cash inflows when employees exercise stock options averages 1.3% of beginning-of-period assets, or approximately 20% of total capital expenditure spending. They further note that these cash inflows are most likely to occur when the firm's stock price—and, thus, its demand for investment—is high. As such, cash inflows when employees exercise stock options may represent an important source of investment financing. The study shows that the level of investment at firms with BBSOPs increases with these cash inflows: a $1 increase in option exercise cash inflows leads to an increase in investment spending of $0.34. The authors predict and find consistent evidence that the relation between these cash inflows and investments is strongest at firms with (1) greater need for external cash and (2) higher costs of external finance.

Tax Savings

Accounting considerations are yet another possible motivation for companies to adopt BBSOPs. Nonqualified stock options, which constitute a high fraction of employee stock options (Hanlon and Shevlin 2002), give the firm a tax deduction equal to the difference between the stock price and the exercise price of the option at the time of the exercise.

These tax deductions can be substantial. Graham, Lang, and Shackelford (2004) estimate that, in the year 2000, aggregate tax deductions associated with employee stock options reduced corporate taxes by approximately one hundred billion dollars for the set of S&P 100 and NASDAQ 100 firms. To get a sense of the scale of these deductions at such large firms, consider that for the set of NASDAQ firms, the aggregate tax deduction exceeds aggregate pre-tax income.

Babenko and Tserlukevich (2009) extend the arguments in Graham, Lang, and Shackelford (2004) by noting that tax deductions associated with employee stock options are uniquely well timed. Timing differences can result in a greater tax deduction from a dollar of compensation granted via a stock option compared with the deduction associated with a dollar of cash compensation. The justification for the timing difference is as follows: employees are more likely to exercise their options when stock prices are high. A firm tends to realize high stock prices when also reporting high profits. Furthermore, years when firms post high profits are associated with higher marginal taxes. As a result, stock option compensation tends to shift tax deductions from years in which marginal tax rates are low to years in which marginal tax rates are higher.

To identify the magnitude of this benefit, Babenko and Tserlukevich (2010) directly estimate the tax benefits of employee stock options for S&P 500 firms by calculating the counterfactual tax bill for each firm. The counterfactual tax bill is calculated as if the firm had replaced all stock option grants to their employees with an equivalent value of cash compensation. For the average firm, they find this would result in an increase of $12.6 million in taxes per year, a 9.8% increase in the total tax bill. The authors also note that while stock options allow companies to take larger tax deductions during years of high marginal tax rates, they also cause employees to have a higher tax bill during years of high personal marginal tax rates, since employees must pay taxes on the difference between the strike price and the current stock price when the option is exercised. As such, higher personal taxes for the employees receiving the stock option grants mitigate some of the benefits of lower corporate taxes. However, the convexity in the tax structure for individuals is typically modest compared with that for corporations; therefore, the magnitude of the corporate tax advantage surpasses the personal tax disadvantage. Consistent with the results from their tax simulations, Babenko and Tserlukevich (2010) find that firms that would benefit more from shifting tax deductions to years with higher marginal tax rates (i.e., firms with more convex tax schedules) tend to grant more stock options to employees.

Earnings Management

Under Generally Accepted Accounting Principles (GAAP), firms must expense the value of stock option grants awarded to employees. However, until 2005, firms were granted flexibility in how they accounted for these options. Options are typically valued using the Black-Scholes model or a similar formula. However, prior to 2005, in reporting the impact of new stock option grants in an income statement, firms had the option to report the "intrinsic value" of an option, defined as the difference between the strike price and the current stock price as of the grant date (Hall and Murphy 2003). As most options are granted with a strike price set to the current stock price, this flexibility allowed firms to avoid reporting any costs associated with new stock option grants on their income statement.

It is important to note that firms were still required to report the Black-Scholes value of employee stock options in footnotes to their accounting statements. Thus, it is possible to re-estimate net income using the Black-Scholes value of granted options (Aboody, Barth, and Kasznik 2004). However, managers may still have an incentive to shift employee compensation from cash wages to stock options due to the differential accounting treatment. For example, managerial bonuses may be tied to measures of profit based on the income statement, such as net income. In such cases, a manager may be able to increase net income and his or her bonus by replacing cash compensation with new option grants. Also, managers may naïvely believe the market will not fully incorporate this information (Hall and Murphy 2003).

Oyer and Schaefer (2005) estimate the costs of BBSOPs under the assumption that stock options are offered solely as a result of favorable accounting treatment. They find that by replacing $1 of cash compensation with an option grant, the firm will increase reported income by $1. However, this comes at a substantial cost. Given that workers are risk averse and will value a dollar of risky stock option compensation less than they value a dollar of risk-free cash compensation, firms will have to increase total compensation to maintain an equivalent level of risk-adjusted pay. The authors estimate that the median firm will have to increase total compensation by $0.64 to achieve this $1 increase in accounting profits. Based on their estimates, they conclude that option granting to employees cannot be entirely driven by the accounting treatment of the options. Furthermore, more recent changes to accounting rules have reduced this accounting flexibility. In 2004, the Financial Accounting Standards Board (FASB) revised the rules governing stock option accounting and, as of 2005, all stock options must be expensed at their Black-Scholes valuations. This revision has eliminated any difference in the accounting treatment of employee stock options relative to cash compensation on the income statement.

Sorting Employees Based on Sentiment

Looking from a behavioral perspective, BBSOPs could also serve as a device to identify and hire employees based on their sentiment, or outlook, about the company's prospects, as Bergman and Jenter (2007) find. As previously mentioned, employees typically require higher compensation if they are exposed to higher levels of firm-specific risk from stock option compensation. However, employees who are optimistic about the company's prospects may overvalue the firm's stock options, thereby making stock options a relatively cheap form of employee compensation. The authors note that overvaluation alone is insufficient to justify BBSOPs since employees can purchase the firm's stock on the open market. However, firms can benefit from employee overvaluation if they can offer equity-based contracts that are unavailable on the open market and preferred by employees. Employee stock options are likely to meet these criteria since employee options tend to have significantly longer maturities compared with options available on the open market. Under these circumstances, firms can hire employees who are optimistic and, thus, cheaper to compensate. Furthermore, by compensating new employees with stock options, firms may also be able to identify potential employees based on their optimism about future company performance. Optimistic employees may be more productive workers if they are more willing to invest in attaining firm-specific human capital, as Oyer and Schaefer (2005) suggest.

The empirical evidence in Bergman and Jenter (2007) supports the employee sentiment argument. They find that BBSOPs are most common among firms with superior prior stock performance. Past stock performance may predict employee optimism if employees assume past returns are a strong predictor of future returns. Evidence in Benartzi (2001) that higher past returns lead employees to purchase more company stock supports this assertion. Furthermore, employees should be less optimistic about the firm's future prospects if they believe the firm is in financial distress. Consistent with this second prediction, Bergman and Jenter (2007) find that option granting is negatively associated with interest burden and leverage, and positively associated with higher cash balances and cash flows.

The sorting motivation is also supported in Oyer and Schaefer (2005). The authors calibrate an agency model based on Holmstrom and Milgrom (1987, 1991) and find that if employees are somewhat risk tolerant and have optimistic views about the future stock price performance of the firm, then they will prefer a compensation package that includes options over one with cash alone. The authors find that this sorting motivation can only be justified at firms with high stock volatility—in other words, at firms where a large price appreciation is most likely. In further support of this motivation, they find that firms that adopt BBSOPs tend to have very high stock volatility.

Employee Retention and Optimal Wage Indexation

Employee turnover can be very costly to a firm. Estimates of the cost of turnover, which include costs associated with the hiring and training of a replacement employee and any associated lost productivity, range from 150% to 175% of the lost employee's annual salary (Hansen 1997). Thus, if a BBSOP can reduce turnover, it can be a strong motivation for adopting such a plan. BBSOPs are assumed to enhance employee retention due, in part, to the fact that these options typically have to vest before they can be exercised. The typical vesting period is estimated to be between three and four years (Crimmel and Schildkraut 2001; Oyer and Schaefer 2005). If the employee quits during this vesting period, he or she has to forgo his or her options, which makes it costly to leave the firm. Hence, by deferring compensation payments, BBSOPs can help companies to retain employees.

An employee retention motivation has been argued to be one of the drivers of BBSOPs by many studies in the literature, including Core and Guay (2001), Kedia and Mozumdar (2002), Oyer (2004), and Oyer and Schaefer (2005). Oyer (2004) presents a theoretical model showing that BBSOPs can reduce employee turnover. He finds that stock-based compensation is an optimal form of deferred compensation since the value of the stock-based compensation will reflect outside employment opportunities. Assuming that the stock price of the company is positively correlated with industry conditions, the value of any stock option will be highest when industry conditions are favorable, which is also when an employee is likely to have the best outside employment opportunities. Hence, the increased willingness of the employee to quit the company due to better outside opportunities will be countered by increased unvested option compensation values. On the other hand, if market conditions are unfavorable, the decreased value of the option compensation would provide companies an automatic wage reduction mechanism without having to deal with the difficult process of wage renegotiations. Thus, BBSOPs can potentially enhance employee retention more effectively relative to deferred cash compensation, which will not automatically adjust with outside job opportunities. This theoretical model is supported by survey evidence. Blasi, Freeman, Mackin, and Kruse (2010) find that workers report that they are less likely to search for another job when their company offers them stock options. Likewise, in a survey of high-technology firms, Ittner, Lambert, and Larcker (2003) find that employers rank the retention of existing employees as the most important motivation for adopting a broad-based employee stock option plan.

Support for the prediction that BBSOPs are implemented to increase employee retention has also been found by examining the types of firms that elect to establish BBSOPs. Core and Guay (2001) argue that retaining employees is most important in firms where human capital is a relatively more important factor of production. They identify such firms in a cross section of the 756 largest U.S. public firms as those with higher growth potential per employee, where growth potential per employee is defined as the residual market value of the firm above and beyond the value of existing assets in place. As predicted, they find that firms with higher growth options per employee are associated with more BBSOPs. The employee retention motivation is also supported in Oyer and Schaefer (2005). The authors calibrate an agency model based on Holmstrom and Milgrom (1987, 1991) and find that if employees are somewhat risk tolerant and there exists significant variance in local wages, then BBSOPs can be justified as a means to reduce employee turnover.

In a more direct test of the employee retention motivation, Carter and Lynch (2004) also find consistent evidence that BBSOPs can reduce turnover. The empirical evidence in Carter and Lynch (2004) is found by exploring option repricing events. Following a decline in the firm's stock price, options can become "underwater" when the firm's current stock price falls below the strike price. These underwater options may be essentially worthless. Employees will realize gains from an option only when the firm's stock price exceeds the strike price. Depending on how low the current stock price is relative to the strike price, employees may have little expectation that an underwater option may ever be sufficiently valuable to exercise. Firms may choose to reprice these options by resetting the strike price equal to the current stock price. In doing so, they will increase the value of these options. A significant repricing will have an effect similar to granting new employee stock options, where new options are assumed to be issued with the strike price set equal to the current price of the stock. Thus, if broad-based employee stock options decrease employee turnover, then employee turnover should decrease following a repricing event. As predicted, the authors find that repricing options allocated to nonexecutives lead to lower overall employee turnover.

Mitigation of Negative Stock Market Reactions to Equity Offerings

Myers and Majluf (1984) argue that if managers have information about the value of a firm's assets, and investors do not share this information, then issuing stock to outside investors can reveal negative information about firm value. They hypothesize that a manager will sell stock to less-informed outsiders only when the manager can secure a good price; otherwise, the manager will cancel the deal. As such, outside investors will interpret the announcement of a stock issuance as a signal that the stock price is currently overvalued in the market. As investors update their beliefs about the value of the firm, the firm's stock price will drop.

Following this argument, Babenko (2009a) argues that granting stock options to employees might give a positive signal to the market about the quality of the firm. She argues that the firm would not offer overvalued equity to employees due to the fear of being deprived of fairly priced financing by the employees in the future. So, the manager will issue shares to employees whenever he or she has positive information. Hence, the model predicts that the price reaction of the market to a seasonal equity offering will be less negative when the company has previously granted stock options to employees. Thus, another motivation for the adoption of BBSOPs might be mitigation of problems associated with symmetric information. Consistent with the predictions of the model, Babenko (2009a) finds that firms granting stock options to employees do larger equity issuances, and these equity issuances are associated with higher announcement returns.

Peer Effects

Kedia and Rajgopal (2009) argue that a firm may be motivated to adopt a BBSOP given the actions of neighboring firms. Peer effects may be picking up employee retention motivations. Rank-and-file workers are unlikely to move outside of their metropolitan statistical area (MSA), resulting in geographically segmented labor markets. As such, local labor market conditions will affect employees' decisions to remain at their firm or pursue outside opportunities. In tight labor markets, firms may be more likely to adopt BBSOPs, as found in Mehran and Tracy (2001). Alternatively, peer effects may be picking up differences in state laws. For example, noncompete agreements are difficult to enforce in California, making employee turnover more likely and more costly to firms (Kedia and Rajgopal 2009). As such, firms in California may rely more heavily on BBSOPs to minimize employee turnover. Finally, peer effects may be picking up social pressures created after neighboring firms adopt BBSOPs.

Kedia and Rajgopal (2009) find that firms headquartered in a metropolitan area where a higher fraction of other firms are using BBSOPs are more likely to adopt stock option plans. This result holds even after controlling for those factors associated with greater BBSOP adoption found in earlier papers. The authors also find evidence indicating that labor market conditions can, at least partially, explain the peer effects. For example, firms whose stock is more likely to co-move with the stocks of their peer local firms are more likely to adopt BBSOPs. This result follows the intuition in Oyer (2004). Stock options are particularly effective tools to minimize employee turnover when the firm's stock price is correlated with employees' outside job opportunities. This scenario will be achieved when the firm's stock price is correlated with those of local firms, given the assumption that workers are unlikely to search for job opportunities outside of their MSA. As such, this result is consistent with the argument that BBSOPs are motivated to retain employees in light of local labor market conditions. Kedia and Rajgopal (2009) also find that firms located in states where noncompete agreements are harder to enforce are more likely to adopt BBSOPs. The authors find more modest support for the social interaction explanation of the peer effects. They observe that peer effects are more pronounced in areas where the population is more educated. Interactions among a more educated population may lead to a more pronounced collective behavior.

Summary of Reasons and Evidence for Offering BBSOPs

Multiple motivations are suggested in the finance and economics literature for why firms may choose to adopt a BBSOP. Incentive alignment and productivity enhancement, cash conservation, and employee retention are the most common explanations for the use of these plans, but tax considerations, earnings management, mitigation of negative stock market reaction to equity offerings, and peer effects are also among the motivations found in studies.

Many public U.S. firms have adopted BBSOPs in the last two decades. These firms share several common characteristics. For example, new economy firms, such as pharmaceuticals, software, computer equipment, and other high-technology manufacturing firms, make up a large portion of the firms with BBSOPs (Sesil, Kroumova, Blasi, and Kruse 2002). In line with this observation, firms using BBSOPs typically have higher growth potential per employee, where the growth potential of the company is proxied by the ratio of market value of the company to its book value and is then divided by the number of employees. Additionally, firms with BBSOPs are usually smaller in size, as measured by total assets and total employment. BBSOP firms also have more volatile stock returns, lower profitability, and lower levels of cash.

The common characteristics of companies that adopt BBSOPs are consistent with a number of different explanations as to the motivations for adopting these plans. The finding that firms with BBSOPs have higher growth options per employee is consistent with an employee retention explanation since higher growth options per employee would mean that these types of companies would value their employees more and want them to stay with the company. The finding that BBSOP firms have fewer employees is consistent with a productivity enhancement motivation based on mutual monitoring and coordination. Furthermore, evidence of lower cash levels and higher stock return volatilities at BBSOP firms is consistent with cash conservation and employee sorting explanations, respectively.

Consequences of BBSOPs

In this section, we discuss the existing empirical evidence about the consequences of BBSOPs. We first look at how these plans affect firm performance and employee welfare. We then discuss the drivers behind these performance and welfare changes.

How Do BBSOPs Affect Firm Performance?

Kedia and Mozumdar (2002), in one of the first papers looking at the performance impact of BBSOPs, examine a sample of NASDAQ firms. The authors find that these plans are associated with positive one-year abnormal stock market returns, as estimated by the difference in returns of the BBSOP firm and a set of comparable firms. They also find that firms that grant more stock options to nonexecutive employees are associated with larger growth rates in sales, employees, net income, and operating income. While they argue that options granted to retain employees and conserve cash are associated with positive abnormal returns, they do not find evidence for the presence of this effect for options granted to create incentives. Overall, they conclude that the positive abnormal returns might be a spurious result (i.e., these returns may be due to the market's incorrect estimate of the costs of option plans rather than expected performance enhancement).

Ittner, Lambert, and Larcker (2003) also study the performance impacts of BBSOPs in a sample of new economy firms. They find that lower than expected levels of grants to executives and directors have negative performance effects; however, they do not find any evidence for performance impacts of broad-based plans. These results are inconsistent with Kedia and Mozumdar (2002), possibly due to sample differences. Ittner, Lambert, and Larcker (2003) use a sample of 217 firms operating exclusively in high-tech sectors, such as computers, software, semiconductors, and Internet, whereas Kedia and Mozumdar (2002) use a sample of the 200 largest NASDAQ firms.

Sesil, Kroumova, Blasi, and Kruse (2002) also examine how BBSOPs impact firm performance at new economy firms. They identify BBSOPs using survey data from the National Center on Employee Ownership (NCEO) and end up with a sample of 229 public firms with BBSOPs.

When comparing mean summary statistics of a new economy BBSOP firm to a matched control firm (which operates in the same industry and is of comparable firm size), the authors note that BBSOPs are associated with higher levels of value added (defined as sales minus cost of materials) per employee, higher levels of Tobin's Q, and more new knowledge generation, as proxied by patent applications and grants. The authors also find that total shareholder return is higher at these new economy BBSOP firms compared with the matched control firms. In another study, Kroumova and Sesil (2005a) again find that BBSOPs have positive performance impacts. They look at three different performance measures— labor productivity, return on assets, and profit margin. They find that for both small and large firms, all of the three performance measures increase following the adoption of BBSOPs. Furthermore, they find that the effect on labor productivity is higher for smaller firms, whereas the other two performance measures show similar effects regardless of firm size.

With the exclusion of Ittner, Lambert, and Larcker (2003), these studies all report positive firm performance following the adoption of a BBSOP. Ittner, Lambert, and Larcker (2003) report no significant correlation between the adoption of a BBSOP and firm performance, indicating at least no negative post-BBSOP performance. As such, these results may indicate a causal relationship between BBSOPs and performance. The BBSOP may drive the performance improvement through greater employee incentives, lower employee turnover, or other direct benefits. However, this is not the only interpretation of these findings. Alternatively, the relationship may instead be driven by an omitted variable. For example, firms may adopt BBSOPs when they anticipate better times ahead. A manager expecting positive future performance may feel that this provides him or her with the opportunity to be especially generous to his employees. This manager may choose to share some of these future gains with employees by granting them stock options through a BBSOP. Hence, a spurious positive correlation between company performance and adoption of BBSOPs might appear as a result.

Hochberg and Lindsey (2010) attempt to distinguish between the causal and noncausal interpretations of improved post-BBSOP performance. The authors use an instrumental variable approach, which is a way for researchers to try to mitigate the effect of omitted variables. They instrument for a firm's endogenous decision to adopt a BBSOP with the adoption of BBSOPs at other firms that are located in the same geographic area (i.e., they construct a geography-based measure of broad-based option plans derived from the granting behavior of local peer firms). A successful instrumental variable must meet two conditions. First, it must be significantly correlated with the potentially endogenous variable—in this case, the choice by the manager to adopt a BBSOP. Second, except for indirect effects through the endogenous variable, the instrumental variable must not directly affect the dependent variable—in this case, firm performance. The first condition is met given the findings in Kedia and Rajgopal (2009) that firms are more likely to adopt BBSOPs when they are located in an area where other firms have more BBSOPs. The second condition is subject to a natural concern because the granting behavior at peer firms might be correlated with firm performance through local industry shocks to firm performance. Indeed, if an industry-wide shock affects both the option granting of the other firms and the firm's own performance, the instrument may be invalid. To address this concern, Hochberg and Lindsey (2010) use the option-granting behavior of local firms (i.e., located in the firm's two-digit ZIP code) that are not within the same industry as the firm itself to construct the instrument. Excluding same-industry firms provides a stronger instrument because the BBSOPs at neighboring other-industry firms will not likely have a significant effect on the firm's performance.

For each firm, Hochberg and Lindsey (2010) estimate the average intensity of BBSOPs in the local area, after excluding firms in the same industry. BBSOP intensity is measured as the average nonexecutive option portfolio delta per employee, where delta measures the change in employee wealth for a 1% change in stock price. Since delta directly measures how much an employee is affected by changes in his or her firm's stock price, it is often the method preferred to quantify stock options when considering incentive effects (Core and Guay 2001). In sum, they instrument for a firm's BBSOP as the average sensitivity of rank-and-file workers at local firms that do not operate in the same industry to changes in their firm's stock price.

While Hochberg and Lindsey (2010) use the local geographic density of BBSOPs as their main instrument, they also use two other instrumental variables to predict BBSOPs at their firm of interest. As a second instrument, the authors use firm size, as measured by employees. They argue that broad-based incentives are likely to be more effective at smaller firms because the free-rider effect is less likely to be an issue. As a third instrument, they use the number of shares outstanding for the firm. Firms with large BBSOPs tend to repurchase shares in order to redistribute these shares to their employees as employee options are exercised (Babenko 2009b). As a result, firms with large BBSOPs will have fewer shares outstanding.

Using this instrumental variable approach, Hochberg and Lindsey (2010) conclude that the positive association between BBSOPs and firm operating performance is indeed a causal relation. They find that the presence of a BBSOP is associated with a 2.59% increase in firm operating performance. The authors also estimate the relative effect of larger BBSOPs. They find that firm operating performance increases by 0.4% for every $1,000 increase in the option portfolio delta per employee.

What Drives the Performance Gains?

Potential benefits associated with BBSOPs include enhanced productivity, cash conservation, and increased employee retention, which results in lower turnover costs. Kedia and Mozumdar (2002) argue that the performance gains are driven by the retention of employees and relaxing of cash constraints. Retention of employees might enhance firm performance by reducing turnover costs and increasing human capital. Their results also show that stock-option grants by companies with larger financial constraints are associated with higher positive returns, compared with grants by firms with lower financial constraints. By preserving cash through option plans, firms may participate in positive net present value investment projects, which they otherwise would have to forgo, and these investments might increase firm performance.

Kroumova and Sesil (2005a) show that the increase in labor productivity associated with the adoption of BBSOPs is higher for smaller firms. This evidence provides support for the productivity enhancement motivation, given that the free-rider problem is more likely to be overcome in small firms. However, not all the evidence is consistent with this argument. The authors also report that increased return on assets and profit margins for firms with BBSOPs, but neither of these measures of firm performance varies by firm size. Additionally, the evidence for increased value-added reported by Sesil, Kroumova, Blasi, and Kruse (2002) provides further support for the argument that the performance gains result from increased worker productivity since value-added per employee is arguably closely associated with employee effort and motivation. Furthermore, the increased worker productivity evidence might also be associated with benefits from lower turnover since retained employees will have higher firm-specific human capital and thus be more productive.

Hochberg and Lindsey (2010) find that their evidence of increased performance among firms that adopt BBSOPs is limited to firms that are small and have higher growth rates per employee. As we have discussed before, mutual monitoring and enhanced coordination as a result of BBSOPs are more likely to happen at smaller firms. Therefore, this evidence further suggests that incentive effects are the cause of performance gains.

How Do Employees Fare?

BBSOPs expose workers to greater compensation risk. The final value of any stock option is unknown at the time of the grant. Furthermore, this final value is correlated with employment risk. Option values are likely to be high when the firm and its industry are performing well—a time when the employee likely has the greatest employment opportunities. On the other hand, when the firm and its industry are underperforming, layoffs become more likely and alternative employment opportunities more scarce. At this point, granted options may be worthless. This is costly to a risk-averse employee.

Empirical evidence confirms the theory that employees dislike compensation risk. Huddart and Lang (1996) find that workers, on average, exercise stock options once vested. By exercising early, workers receive the difference in the current stock price and the exercise price, a fixed payment. However, in doing so, workers are giving up the "time value" of the option. An option is typically worth more than the current difference between the stock price and exercise price. For risk-neutral investors, exercising an option at expiration is typically optimal. Huddart and Lang (1996) quantify this lost value associated with early exercise and find that employees are giving up significant value by exercising early. According to the Black-Scholes model, by exercising early, employees give up almost one half of the value of their options.

An alternative approach to documenting evidence that workers dislike compensation risk is to explore cross-sectional patterns in exercise rates. If compensation risk is costly to employees, then we should observe that employees are more likely to exercise their options when compensation risk is high, such as when stock return volatility is high. Consistent with costly compensation risk, Huddart and Lang (1996) find that employees are more likely to exercise their options early at firms with high volatility. Likewise, Babenko (2009b) finds that employees are more likely to exercise their options after the firm has announced a share repurchase. This evidence is consistent with risk-averse employees attempting to minimize compensation risk, because a share repurchase will increase the volatility of employee stock options. However, Carpenter, Stanton, and Wallace (2009) find no relation between early exercise rates and stock price volatility. The authors argue that this result is not inconsistent with the theory that workers dislike compensation risk because higher volatility also increases the rewards for waiting to exercise the option.

However, while BBSOPs will increase compensation risk for employees, it is impossible to argue whether BBSOPs are good for employees or not unless we know what alternatives management considered before granting the options. If management did not give employees options, would they have given employees an equivalent cash bonus? If so, rational and risk-averse employees would prefer the cash bonus over stock options since stock options expose employees to high levels of company-specific risk. However, if management anticipates that the options will effectively pay for themselves through better incentive alignment, lower turnover, or other benefits, then it would be unlikely for management to consider a cash bonus as an alternative to an option grant. Therefore, if employees are given the choice between options or nothing, then, clearly, employees will prefer the options over nothing regardless of the associated risk.

Furthermore, empirical evidence indicates that employees gain from BBSOPs. In their study of the option exercise behavior of employees, Carpenter, Stanton, and Wallace (2009) find that voluntary option exercise is positively related to the level of stock price, providing evidence that employees are profiting from option exercises. It is interesting to note that they also find that the ratio of stock price to exercise price at the time of the exercise significantly differs across and within industries, suggesting different profit levels for employees from these options. The mean ratio of stock price to exercise price at the time of the exercise is highest in health services (11.48), building construction (10.08), and business services (7.03) sectors, and lowest in electronic and other electrical (1.57), rubber and plastics products (1.64), and eating and drinking places (1.69) sectors.

Summary of Consequences of BBSOPs

We find that the adoption of BBSOPs is typically associated with better firm performance, most commonly measured as higher stock market and operating performance. However, most of the papers reviewed lack sufficient evidence to conclude that the relationship between BBSOPs and firm performance is causal. Furthermore, the various studies have not yet come to a conclusion about the specific mechanisms driving the performance gains. Retention of employees, relaxation of cash constraints, and enhancement of productivity through incentives are potential mechanisms through which BBSOPs may increase company performance.

Conclusion

Just as BBSOPs have become more popular at U.S. firms in the last two decades, we find that these plans are also attracting increased attention from academic researchers, such as those in the disciplines of finance and economics. Recent studies in this area have shown that improved employee incentives, cash conservation, tax savings, and employee retention are among the possible motivations for the adoption of BBSOPs. In spite of these potential benefits, these plans come at a clear cost: when stock options are given to employees, the shares of existing shareholders will be diluted if new shares are issued to give to employees upon exercise. Similarly, there are direct costs when a firm buys existing shares on the market to sell at a discount to employees. Thus, value-maximizing managers who choose to implement these plans must do so in anticipation of counterbalancing benefits, and, in summary, the literature appears to support this view. Most of the papers reviewed in this chapter report improvements in firm performance following the adoption of BBSOPs. At a minimum, no paper reports a statistically significant negative average effect associated with employee ownership.

We caution the reader to keep in mind three important caveats when interpreting these average effects: (1) the mean effect is estimated on a self-selected group, (2) while evidence is consistent with a causal interpretation, noncausal explanations are never fully excluded, and (3) a mean effect can disguise significant cross-sectional variation.

The positive average effect found in the literature should be interpreted as the average effect on a select group—the firms that endogenously chose to establish BBSOPs. This treatment group is self-selected. Firms that expect the greatest gains from encouraging employee ownership should be the first to adopt such plans. Thus, the treatment group should be dominated by firms at which employee ownership should be expected to have greatest positive effect. As such, existing evidence should not be interpreted as proof that all firms could see similar gains if they were to adopt broad-based employee stock option plans. Differences in firm characteristics may make BBSOPs either more or less effective in certain firms.

The second caveat in interpreting the mean effect relates to the question of whether the relation between value gains and BBSOPs is causal. If the relation is causal, then the adoption of the employee ownership plan leads to firm performance changes through better employee incentives, cash conservations, lower employee turnover, or other specific mechanisms. Alternatively, these studies could be picking up an omitted variable that is not observed but which is positively correlated with the adoption of a BBSOP. For example, firms that adopt a BBSOP may do so at times when they anticipate stronger profits in the future. During those times, the manager may feel that he or she has sufficient slack to be able to implement new employee incentives, or he or she may want to share some of these expected gains with labor. If true, we would observe a spurious positive relation between employee stock options and future firm value. This is a particularly difficult alternative interpretation to disprove since the researcher will never observe the future expectations of the manager at the time the

BBSOP was implemented. However, Hochberg and Lindsey (2010) offer evidence that is inconsistent with this interpretation. They use an instrumental variable approach that effectively controls for managerial choice and find that BBSOPs are associated with superior future performance.

While Hochberg and Lindsey (2010) report evidence consistent with a causal interpretation of the relationship between employee ownership and firm value, it is never possible to exclude all other noncausal interpretations. Additional evidence showing either a causal or noncausal relationship would assist in settling the debate. However, while we wait for this future evidence, it is worth comparing the conclusions of broad-based employee stock options with those of executive stock ownership. The literature on executive employee stock ownership has likewise shown a positive correlation between executive ownership and firm value, at least for low levels of executive ownership. However, the same question regarding interpretation applies to these results as well. Definitive evidence proving that this relation is causal has yet to be documented. Therefore, while doubts remain as to whether the relation between broad-based employee ownership and firm value is indeed causal, the same doubts remain about whether executive ownership causes an increase in firm value as well.

While the mean reported effect is positive, significant cross-sectional variation exists, indicating that BBSOPs are not associated with positive value gains at all firms. Understanding this cross-sectional variation is an important goal for future research because it will offer clues as to the specific mechanisms through which a BBSOP can create value. Theory suggests employee ownership should be more effective at small firms, firms with high growth options, and firms with high-performance workplaces. Cross-sectional empirical evidence about employee ownership has been inconsistent to date. Evidence from the BBSOP literature indicates that smaller firms are associated with the greatest firm performance gains—findings consistent with an employee incentive effect supported by mutual monitoring and peer pressure.

Finally, the interaction of firm culture and employee ownership has been generally overlooked by the research in finance and economics. This is a significant oversight given the results from Freeman, Kruse, and Blasi (2010), which suggest that the success of employee ownership is highly dependent on the presence of certain corporate culture characteristics, such as high employee participation.

To conclude, we would like to highlight two additional topics in the BBSOP literature that have been generally overlooked in the finance and economics literature: the use of broad-based employee stock option plans at private firms and at international firms. BBSOPs at private firms are likely to have very different interpretations. Private firms tend to be significantly smaller relative to public firms. Consequently, some of the concerns regarding a potential free-rider problem may not apply, resulting in greater employee-incentive effects. However, the absence of a publicly traded stock price may diminish this incentive benefit if employees view a private company stock price as less informative. Research on BBSOPs at private firms would help to answer these questions about these plans and incentive effects. Another interesting question is, are the effects of these plans different in other countries where labor relations and laws are likely to be very different from those in the United States? In particular, differences in job protection laws across countries may allow researchers to explore the interaction of job security and long-term, equity-based incentives. So, cross-country comparisons of the adoption of BBSOPs might be helpful in understanding the motivations behind these plans.

Despite the increased attention of finance and economics scholars to the topic of employee ownership, the net benefits of employee ownership have yet to be unambiguously documented. The studies looking at BBSOPs suggest positive performance gains through this type of employee ownership; however, which specific mechanisms lead to the reported gains is still an open question. Understanding the mechanisms through which BBSOPs increase firm value is key to identifying at which types of firms these plans will be most successful and in answering how best to implement them. We leave those questions for future research.

Acknowledgments

Ouimet acknowledges support from the Beyster Foundation.

References

Aboody, David, Mary Barth, and Ron Kasznik. 2004. "SFAS No. 123 Stock-Based Compensation Expense and Equity Market Values." *The Accounting Review*, Vol. 79, no. 2, pp. 251–75.

Babenko, Ilona. 2009a. *Adverse Selection and Stock-Based Grants to Non-Executive Employees*. Working Paper. Kowloon: Hong Kong University of Science and Technology Center.

Babenko, Ilona. 2009b. "Share Repurchases and Pay-Performance Sensitivity of Employee Compensation Contracts." *Journal of Finance*, Vol. 64, pp. 117–51.

Babenko, Ilona, Michael Lemmon, and Yuri Tserlukevich. 2010. "Employee Stock Options and Investment." *Journal of Finance*, forthcoming.

Babenko, Ilona, and Yuri Tserlukevich. 2009. "Analyzing the Tax Benefits from Employee Stock Options." *Journal of Finance*, Vol. 64, pp. 1797–825.

Benartzi, S. 2001. "Excessive Extrapolation and the Allocation of 401(k) Accounts to Company Stock." *Journal of Finance*, Vol. 56, pp. 1747–64.

Bergman, Nittai, and Dirk Jenter. 2007. "Employee Sentiment and Stock Option Compensation." *Journal of Financial Economics*, Vol. 84, pp. 667–712.

Blasi, Joseph, Richard Freeman, Christopher Mackin, and Douglas Kruse. 2010. "Creating a Bigger Pie? The Effects of Employee Ownership, Profit Sharing, and Stock Options on Workplace Performance." In Douglas Kruse, Richard Freeman, and Joseph Blasi, eds., *Shared Capitalism at Work: Employee Ownership, Profit and Gain Sharing, and Broad-Based Stock Options*. Chicago: University of Chicago Press.

Blasi, Joseph, Douglas Kruse, and Harry Markowitz. 2010. "Risk and Lack of Diversification Under Employee Ownership and Shared Capitalism." In Douglas Kruse, Richard Freeman, and Joseph Blasi, eds., *Shared Capitalism at Work: Employee Ownership, Profit and Gain Sharing, and Broad-Based Stock Options*. Chicago: University of Chicago Press.

Brennan, Michael, and Walter Torous. 1999. "Individual Decision-Making and Investor Welfare." *Economic Notes*, Vol. 28, no. 2, pp. 119–43.

Carpenter, Jennifer, Richard Stanton, and Nancy Wallace. 2009. *Estimation of Employee Stock Option Exercise Rates and Firm Cost*. NYU Working Paper No. FIN-06-043. New York: NYU Stern School of Business.

Carter, Mary, and Luann Lynch. 2004. "The Effect of Stock Option Repricing on Employee Turnover." *Journal of Accounting and Economics*, Vol. 37, pp. 91–112.

Core, John, and Wayne Guay. 2001. "Stock Option Plans for Non-Executive Employees." *Journal of Financial Economics*, Vol. 61, pp. 253–87.

Crimmel, Beth, and Jeffrey Schildkraut. 2001. "Stock Option Plans Surveyed by NCS." *Compensation and Working Conditions*, Spring, pp. 3–21.

Demsetz, Harold, and Kenneth Lehn. 1985. "The Structure of Corporate Ownership: Causes and Consequences." *Journal of Political Economy*, Vol. 93, no. 6, pp. 1155–77.

Freeman, Richard, Joseph Blasi, and Douglas Kruse. 2010. "Shared Capitalism at Work: Employee Ownership, Profit and Gain Sharing and Broad-Based Stock Options."In Douglas Kruse, Richard Freeman, and Joseph Blasi, eds., *Shared Capitalism at Work: Employee Ownership, Profit and Gain Sharing, and Broad-Based Stock Options*. Chicago: University of Chicago Press.

Freeman, Richard, Douglas Kruse, and Joseph Blasi. 2010. "Worker Responses to Shirking Under Shared Capitalism." In Douglas Kruse, Richard Freeman, and Joseph Blasi, eds., *Shared Capitalism at Work: Employee Ownership, Profit and Gain Sharing, and Broad-Based Stock Options*. Chicago: University of Chicago Press.

Graham, John, Mark Lang, and Douglas Shackelford. 2004. "Employee Stock Options, Corporate Taxes and Debt Policy." *Journal of Finance*, Vol. 59, no. 4, pp. 1585–1618.

Hall, Brian, and Kevin Murphy. 2003. "The Trouble with Stock Options." *Journal of Economic Perspectives*, Vol. 17, no. 3, pp. 49–70.

Hanlon, Michelle, and Terrence J. Shevlin. 2002. "Accounting for Tax Benefits of Employee Stock Options and Implications for Research." *Accounting Horizons*, Vol. 16, no. 1, pp. 1–16.

Hansen, Fay. 1997. "Currents in Compensation and Benefits." *Compensation & Benefits Review*, Vol. 29, no. 6, pp. 6–18.

Hochberg, Yael, and Laura Lindsey. 2010. "Incentives, Targeting, and Firm Performance: An Analysis of Non-Executive Stock Options." *Review of Financial Studies*, forthcoming.

Holmstrom, Bengt, and Paul Milgrom. 1987. "Aggregation and Linearity in the Provision of Intertemporal Incentives." *Econometrica*, Vol. 55, pp. 308–28.

Holmstrom, Bengt, and Paul Milgrom. 1991. "Multi-Task Principal-Agent Analyses: Incentive Contracts, Asset Ownership and Job Design." *Journal of Law, Economics and Organization*, Vol. 7, pp. 524–52.

Huddart, Steven, and Mark Lang. 1996. "Employee Stock Option Exercises: An Empirical Analysis." *Journal of Accounting and Economics*, Vol. 21, pp. 5–43.

Ittner, Christopher, Richard Lambert, and David Larcker. 2003. "The Structure and Performance Consequences of Equity Grants to Employees of New Economy Firms." *Journal of Accounting and Economics*, Vol. 34, pp. 89–127.

Jensen, Michael, and William Meckling. 1976. "Theory of the Firm: Managerial Behavior, Agency Cost and Ownership Structure." *Journal of Financial Economics*, Vol. 3, pp. 305–60.

Kandel, Eugene, and Edward Lazear. 1992. "Peer Pressure and Partnerships." *Journal of Political Economy*, Vol. 100, no. 4, pp. 801–17.

Kedia, Simi, and Abon Mozumdar. 2002. *Performance Impact of Employee Stock Options*. Working Paper. Boston: Harvard Business School.

Kedia, Simi, and Shiva Rajgopal. 2009. "Neighborhood Matters: The Impact of Location on Broad Based Stock Option Plans." *Journal of Financial Economics*, Vol. 92, pp. 109–27.

Knez, Marc, and Duncan Simester. 2001. "Firm-Wide Incentives and Mutual Monitoring at Continental Airlines." *Journal of Labor Economics*, Vol. 19, no. 4, pp. 743–72.

Kroumova, Maya, and James Sesil. 2005a. *The Impact of Broad-Based Stock Options on Firm Performance: Does Firm Size Matter?* Center for HR Strategy Working Paper. Piscataway, NJ: School of Management and Labor Relations, Rutgers University.

Kroumova, Maya, and James Sesil. 2005b. *Intellectual Capital, Monitoring and Risk: What Predicts the Adoption of Broad-Based Employee Stock Options?* Center for HR Strategy Working Paper. Piscataway, NJ: School of Management and Labor Relations, Rutgers University.

Mehran, Hamid, and Joseph Tracy. 2001. "The Effect of Employee Stock Options on the Evolution of Compensation in the 1990s." *Federal Reserve Bank of New York Economic Policy Review*, Vol. 7, pp. 17–34.

Myers, Stewart, and Nicholas Majluf. 1984. "Corporate Financing and Investment Decisions When Firms Have Information That Investors Do Not Have." *Journal of Financial Economics*, Vol. 13, pp. 187–221.

Oyer, Paul. 2004. "Why Do Firms Use Incentives That Have No Incentive Effects?" *Journal of Finance*, Vol. 59, no. 4, pp. 1619–49.

Oyer, Paul, and Scott Schaefer. 2005. "Why Do Some Firms Give Stock Options to All Employees? An Empirical Examination of Alternative Theories." *Journal of Financial Economics*, Vol. 76, pp. 99–133.

Sesil, James, Maya Kroumova, Joseph Blasi, and Douglas Kruse. 2002. "Broad-Based Employee Stock Options in US 'New Economy' Firms." *British Journal of Industrial Relations*, Vol. 40, no. 2, pp. 273–94.

CHAPTER 9

Assessing Mondragon: Stability and Managed Change in the Face of Globalization

SAIOA ARANDO
FRED FREUNDLICH
MÓNICA GAGO
Mondragon University

DEREK C. JONES
Hamilton College

TAKAO KATO
Colgate University

Introduction

The recent economic crisis has stimulated much interest among researchers and policy makers in the possibilities of alternative ways to structure economic organizations. One option is worker or producer cooperatives (hereafter, PCs).[1] The Mondragon group is one of the best-known examples of "real-world" PCs. Founded in 1956 with some 25 workers in the Basque Country of Spain, Mondragon was originally a group of mainly industrial cooperatives. Subsequently, the group has grown to include firms in other areas, notably retail and finance, and, by 2008, the Mondragon group is composed of about 250 cooperatives, subsidiaries, and affiliated organizations, including 73 manufacturing plants overseas, altogether employing almost 100,000. Membership has always been closely linked with employee ownership and, in the early decades, essentially only and all workers were members. Membership provides a guarantee of employment and relocation or 80% of salary during times of slack demand, as well as the right to participate in the firm's general assembly, vote for and serve on electoral bodies, and receive a share of profits. However, as we discuss in this chapter, membership is often a more complicated matter today, especially in the retail group, which includes Eroski, a hybrid consumer–worker cooperative. Other distinguishing features at Mondragon include provision for profit pooling and a rich set of institutions to support primary firms.

The Mondragon experience has long attracted interest by diverse scholars (e.g., Johnson and Whyte 1977; Bradley and Gelb 1982; Cheney 1999; Dow 2003) and sometimes has been presented as an exemplary model of feasible alternative enterprise structure in today's globalized economy (e.g., Sackrey, Schneider, and Knoedler 2008). At the same time, the nature and scope of work on Mondragon, especially recent work by economists, is quite limited. In part, this reflects restrictions on economic and financial data, which has meant that most studies are somewhat dated and often highly aggregative (e.g., Thomas and Logan 1982). Also, many studies do not take account of the astonishing changes in the Mondragon structure that have occurred during the last 20 years, while others tend to focus on a particular theme (e.g., Joshi and Smith 2008). Finally, while many accounts highlight specific features of the Mondragon system of co-ops such as, under certain conditions, the ability of member-workers to be transferred among co-ops, most accounts of these crucial mechanisms often lack substantive detail on the operation of these distinguishing institutions. In this chapter, which is one of a series of papers by the authors (see also Arando, Gago, Jones, and Kato 2010a, 2010b), we begin to redress some of the aforementioned shortcomings of the literature. We draw on evidence derived from more than 20 interviews with key actors at Mondragon conducted between 2007 and 2010, and also financial and economic data, including new data made available to us from Mondragon.

After briefly reviewing theoretical and empirical work on PCs, we attempt to improve on the available evidence concerning the importance and performance of the Mondragon co-ops. Our focus is on the overall *group* of co-ops as well as on the groups' two key sectors—industrial co-ops and retail chains. By using diverse kinds of data, we document a growing economic presence within and outside Spain, as well as a group record that suggests strong performance.

To better understand the reasons behind this strong group record, we argue that Mondragon's ability to be institutionally adaptive (e.g., Moye 1993) continues to play a major part in sustaining the success of the group. In facilitating that adaptability, we also argue that it is the essential democratic nature of the Mondragon set-up that enables measured and effective adjustments to be continually undertaken—and at a lower cost than competitors in conventional firms. To support this claim, we highlight key institutional developments in the Mondragon group during the last 20 years and provide more detailed information than heretofore on the scope and nature of some of the key distinguishing institutional mechanisms of the Mondragon group. These mechanisms include the extent of worker-member transfers, the patterns of profit pooling, and the type and volume of training. It is our contention that the aggressive use of these and other mechanisms helps account for key features of the strong Mondragon group record.

Theoretical and Empirical Evidence on Producer Cooperatives

In this section, our discussion is organized around some of the main themes that are evident in the economics literature on PCs (e.g., Bonin, Jones, and Putterman 1993; Dow 2003). One major area of interest to economic theorists is whether mechanisms within PCs,[2] such as employee ownership and/or participation in decision making, will lead to employees supplying efficient effort, thereby testing the proposition that democratic firms suffer from only modest shirking by employees and ultimately achieve high levels of output. A large literature has empirically examined these links in PCs, and a commonly favored approach to test this and similar hypotheses has been to use individual firm data and augment a standard production function by a vector of ownership and participation variables (e.g., Estrin, Jones, and Svejnar 1987). Typically, the null hypothesis that the various forms of ownership participation taken together do not affect productivity is rejected (e.g., Dow 2003).

Another key concern is employment. A vast body of theoretical work was triggered by a seminal paper by Ward (1958) in which a PC was believed to maximize per capita income of worker-members rather than total profits, as in a capitalist firm. A key finding emerging from this early model is that, relative to a capitalist twin, the PC tends to have fewer employees and that employment varies inversely with product price. Most subsequent theoretical work overturned the pessimistic conclusions that resulted from this simple model. Also, the more rigorous empirical inquiries, notably Craig and Pencavel (1992) for U.S. plywood firms; Pencavel, Pistaferri, and Schivardi (2006) for Italian PCs; and Burdin and Dean (2009) for co-ops in Uruguay, find that PCs have more stable employment and discover no evidence of short-run inefficiencies or perverse supply curves.

The way in which capital requirements are financed and the resulting structure of ownership of the firm's assets are matters that have attracted the interest of many researchers, especially students of PCs. The issues are particularly interesting since assets may be owned by members individually or collectively, and sometimes by nonmember financiers. The nontransferability of ownership rights in many PCs has led some theorists to argue that PCs will face persistent underinvestment. However, empirical support for such predictions is weak (e.g., Jones and Backus 1977), a conclusion that many find unsurprising since many real-world cooperatives have implemented specific institutional designs to ameliorate potential problems that theorists have identified.

In another line of inquiry, researchers have analyzed the tendency of PCs to transform themselves into organizations within which control rights are vested in a small number of worker-members (e.g., Ben-Ner 1984). As with other key issues, there is a disconnect between early theory and empirics, and most empirical work has *not* found strong evidence in support of this degeneration thesis (e.g., Estrin and Jones 1992, for France).

Based on this brief review, we make three observations. First, reflecting the dominant neoclassical approach in economics, the vast majority of empirical work has been structured to test hypotheses relating to the behavior of an average or representative cooperative compared with a similar capitalist firm. However, if PCs, through mechanisms such as profit pooling and member transfers, are closely integrated (as is the case for Mondragon) then, arguably, it is also important to investigate aspects of behavior for the overall group of closely integrated co-ops. Second, very little empirical work by economists has been informed by the Mondragon experience: the most influential empirical papers investigate other PCs. Third, most investigations of the Mondragon experience by economists (e.g., Bradley and Gelb 1985) were undertaken when the institutional set-up was different from what we observe today. In the following section, we examine more recent evidence on the importance and performance of the Mondragon co-ops. While we do not pursue a formal hypothesis-testing approach, we do provide evidence that relates to the broader themes evident in the theoretical and empirical literature on PCs.

The Mondragon Record

The conventional wisdom is that the Mondragon group is economically important—Mondragon itself reports that it is "the seventh largest consortium in Spain" (Mondragon Annual Report 2007). One indicator of performance is the oft-quoted remark that no members have ever been made redundant at Mondragon (e.g., Moye 1993:253). However, empirical support for claims that relate to comparative performance is often slim. Hence, in this section, to try to present a more detailed picture of these issues, we report economic data on basic indicators such as sales and employment.

Our evidence includes information derived from public sources such as Mondragon's annual reports and similar financial data on major enterprises within Mondragon, such as Eroski, the main firm in its retail group. We also draw on a proprietary data set that covers Mondragon's industrial co-ops during the period 1995 through 2005, which was supplied to us by Mondragon. In endeavoring to make comparisons of importance and performance with comparable capitalist firms, we draw on official data, including data from the Basque National Statistics Office (EUSTAT), as well as data that have been used in other contexts.[3] We are well aware of the statistical limits of these types of comparative exercises. Consequently, great caution must be exercised when drawing conclusions based on such comparisons.

Sales and Productivity

One source we draw on to document the record for the overall group of Mondragon co-ops concerning basic indicators such as output/sales is Mondragon's annual reports. Figure 1 shows sustained and rapid growth in sales for the Mondragon group, at least until late 2007, with the onset of the current global recession.

In trying to see how this growth record for the Mondragon co-op group compares with that for conventional firms in Spain, we note that Mondragon's 2007 annual report states that, since its inception, Mondragon has become the largest group in the Basque Country (as well as the seventh largest in Spain). When comparisons with other co-ops in Spain are made, the Mondragon group is the largest co-op from the perspective of sales and employment. Moreover, five of the ten largest individual cooperatives in Spain belong to the Mondragon group, including the two largest, Eroski and the Caja Laboral. A review of comparisons with co-ops elsewhere, including PCs, a list assembled by the Interna-

FIGURE 1

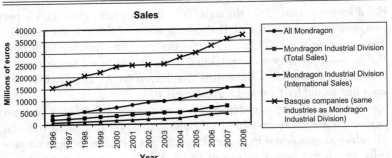

tional Co-operative Alliance (http://www.global300.coop) indicates that in 2008 the Mondragon group was the ninth largest group of co-ops in the world—and that ranking has moved up one place since the list was compiled in 2004.

Turning to the Mondragon industrial group and our internal data, Figure 1 shows a record of growing sales. In Figure 1, we also compare that record with the record for sales in all types of firms within the Basque economy (comparisons are restricted to sectors within which Mondragon firms operate).[4] These comparisons show a more rapid rate of sales growth in Mondragon firms compared with conventional firms in the same sectors. Mondragon co-ops' sales grew by more than 213%, whereas Basque company sales grew by about 140% during the period 1996 through 2008. This is reflected in growth in the comparative importance of Mondragon industrial sales relative to total Basque sales in the same industries—in 1996, that ratio was 13.3%; by 2007 it had grown to 20.8%.[5]

Looking at the data for the retail chain Eroski, its annual report states that sales were 8.42 billion euros in 2009, compared with 6.36 billion euros in 2006. That record compares favorably with similar conventional retail companies. Based on sales, Eroski is now the third largest retail chain in Spain (INDISA 2007–2008). Also, based on sales, if we break out Eroski from the Mondragon group, Eroski, a hybrid producer–consumer cooperative, is also the biggest Spanish cooperative (see http://www.cepes.es). A recent global ranking of retailing firms (Deloitte 2010) signals the growth in importance of Eroski: in 2009, it was ranked as the 76th largest retail chain in the world, a gain of 16 positions in one year.[6]

Finally, we can also make comparisons of the sales records for other well-known examples of employee ownership in the retail sector, such as the John Lewis Partnership (JLP) in the United Kingdom. Between 2006 and 2009, the sales figures reported in JLP's annual report indicate growth in nominal sales of about 21% compared with 32.4% for Eroski. For a longer period, 2003 through 2008, Eroski's sales grew 11.4% per year, compared with that of JLP, which was of 6.9% (Deloitte 2010). Also, whereas the 2008 International Co-operative Alliance data rank JLP as the 18th largest co-op/mutual in the world, if we break out the Eroski data from that of the entire Mondragon group, Eroski alone had sales that would have ranked it ahead of JLP.

In sum, while the available evidence on comparative sales is far from perfect, it seems reasonable to conclude that, by this indicator, the Mondragon group and its major divisions have become more economically significant actors in recent years. While assessing comparative performance is a trickier task (in part because of differing rates of acquisitions), it also appears that, on the basis of sales, the Mondragon group has performed well, especially compared with conventional firms and co-ops elsewhere. This record of strong growth in sales/output is consistent with those who argue that, in PCs—which combine high levels of participation and employee ownership—powerful incentive mechanisms exist that can be expected to lead to high levels of productivity. Moreover, in another study (Arando, Gago, Jones, and Kato 2010a), we use *microeconometric* data (store-level data for the population of stores within Eroski) to formally test this hypothesis. Our preliminary findings provide evidence in support of the proposition that firms with substantial employee ownership (Eroski's co-op stores) have higher productivity than do stores with significantly less employee ownership (Eroski's GESPA stores) and stores with conventional ownership structures (i.e., no employee ownership).[7]

Employment

Evidence on the employment record for Mondragon co-ops is limited and dated, although Luzarraga, Aranzadi, and Irizar (2008) is an exception.[8] To help fill this gap, we first look at total employment in Mondragon firms since 1983, as reported in the group's annual reports. The data show that the co-ops have registered almost a five fold growth in total employment during the period 1983 through 2007 and tripled in the last ten years of that period. There have, however, been some reversals since the current recession began, and overall employment has shrunk by about 9.3% since 2007. But this still compares favorably with developments in Spain and the Basque Country. As shown in Figure 2,

FIGURE 2

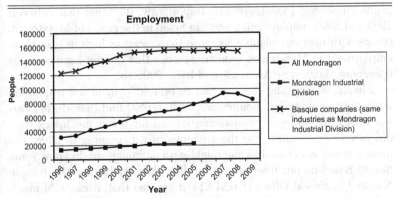

from 2003 through 2009, overall Mondragon employment in Spain increased by 17%, while total employment in Spain increased 13% and in the Basque Country only by about 1%.[9]

Compared with other cooperatives, the share of total employment in Mondragon co-ops in Spain as a percentage of employment in all cooperatives in Spain increased from 19% in 2003 to 24% in 2009.

We turn next to the industrial group at Mondragon, using the internal data and focusing on employment in the Basque region. Figure 2 shows that, from 1996 through 2005, total employment grew by about 64%. While this growth is substantial, it is still a less rosy picture than that of the overall group, as discussed previously. This group picture includes job growth overseas as well as in other sectors, notably retail, with employment in the Eroski chain growing from 29,192 employees in 2003 to 52,711 in 2009, a gain of more than 80% in six years. Figure 2 also shows evolution of employment in conventional firms in the Basque Country in sectors in which there are Mondragon co-ops. Comparative performance during the period 1996 through 2005 reflects a better performance for Mondragon industrial co-ops: overall job growth for conventional firms was 29%, about half the rate experienced by Mondragon industrial co-ops. Consequently, whereas in 1996, employment in Mondragon industrial co-ops in the Basque Country accounted for 8.1% of total employment, by 2005 this total had increased to 10.3%.

The next issue we consider for industrial co-ops is the relationship between employment in Mondragon industrial co-ops in Spain and how it is potentially influenced by employment in co-op plants overseas. The best available study on this matter to date is Luzarraga, Aranzadi, and Irizar (2008), which provides interesting detail concerning the history of this internationalization process. They note that the first Mondragon industrial co-op to establish an overseas plant was COPRECI in 1989 and that, by 2006, 25 co-ops had overseas operations in 65 productive plants employing 14,601 workers. Importantly, they find that between 1999 and 2006, employment growth in Spain in the group of Mondragon co-ops with overseas plants was more than twice as high as growth in employment in Mondragon industrial co-ops that did *not* have overseas operations (Luzarraga, Aranzadi, and Irizar 2008:18).

Finally, we consider the way that co-op employment has responded during economic crises. Bradley and Gelb (1987) find that, during earlier crises, Mondragon co-ops experienced far fewer job losses than did private companies. For the current crisis, beginning in 2008, the picture is not as detailed as one might wish, although we do know some things. Based on our interviews, as well as data available at the Basque National Statistical Office (EUSTAT), it appears that, because of insufficient demand for members' labor, by 2009, fewer than 200 of more than 20,000 members in industrial co-ops were temporarily not at their workplaces, although they still received 80% of their regular wages. This evidence of a modest amount of furloughs for members is reinforced by Basterretxea and Albizu (2010b), who report that, for the whole Mondragon group in 2008, only 12 members were dismissed with compensation, 96 worker-members took early retirement, and about 350 of them worked fewer hours (averaging about 160 hours fewer per worker-member per year, or approximately 10% of a full-time position). At most, two firms faced a threat of closure or temporarily shut down. As such, this reinforces evidence from previous periods that has documented the rarity of Mondragon co-op closures and established a lower failure rate in Mondragon enterprises than in private firms (e.g., Ellerman 1984).

When employment in co-ops has contracted—in Figure 2, we see that, since 2007, total employment in the Mondragon group has fallen by about 9.3%—it is clear that the brunt of such adjustments fell on the shoulders of temporary and nonmember workers. But even this volume of layoffs probably compares favorably with the record of conventional firms in Spain, including the Basque region, where there has been substantial growth in layoffs and unemployment rates in 2010 of more than 20% and about 12%, respectively. It seems safe to conclude that, compared with other firms, there has been less shrinkage of employment in Mondragon co-ops during the current crisis. When comparisons are restricted to employment of co-op members, then the differences are dramatic, with virtually no shrinkage of the co-op membership labor force. In tandem with higher employment stability in Mondragon co-ops, there is also evidence of greater wage flexibility during crises. Several interviewees reported examples of wage flexibility during the current crisis—for example, members at the FAGOR group agreed to an 8% cut in wages for the period April 2009 through March 2010.

In sum, the employment data show a Mondragon group that is far bigger today than in the 1990s. The data also suggest a record that is quite strong in terms of employment growth and job retention, even during times of economic crisis. While Ward (1958) predicts employment restriction to be the norm in PCs, in the main, the Mondragon data point to sustained employment expansion of the group and a tendency for the average PC to increase its labor force.

Investment

Moye (1993) finds that gross capital formation in Mondragon co-ops occurred at an annual rate of about 9% between 1971 and 1989, which is more than twice the overall rate for Spain. Since then, however, little systematic data are available. In providing evidence on investment, it is important to note that different sources often define "investment" differently. That said, Figure 3 shows a moderate upward trend in investment (defined as expenditures on both new and existing fixed assets) through 2007, when such spending surged dramatically, in part following the acquisition of the Caprabo chain by Eroski. Unsurprisingly, the global financial and economic crisis then took a massive toll, and investment declined significantly in 2009.

Within Mondragon's industrial group, the internal data indicate that overall investment more than quadrupled in the ten-year period from 1996 to 2006, and that gains have been steady even during business downturns (Figure 3), except for the current recession. Figure 3 indicates a different picture for conventional firms in similar industries during the years 1996 through 2005: total investment essentially has doubled, and a significant contraction in total investment began as early as 2001.

However, these data do not take into account *differences in average size* among firms. When we normalize with respect to the workforce, the rate of investment per employee in Mondragon industrial co-ops is higher than in conventional firms (Figure 4). Also, investment in the Mondragon co-ops was much less sensitive to the business cycle. Whereas in conventional firms, investment per worker dropped off dramatically during the business cycle beginning in 2001, the opposite pattern typically prevailed in the industrial co-ops.

FIGURE 3

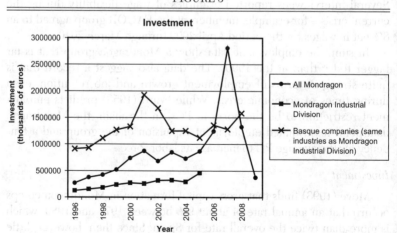

FIGURE 4

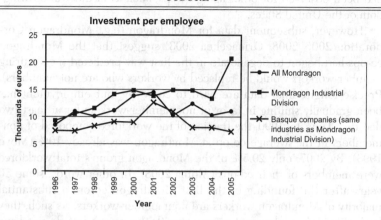

For the Eroski retail chains, during the period 2001 through 2005, investment oscillated between 274 and 618 million euros, although these represented substantial sums for a firm with 5 to 6 billion euros in sales. Investment increased dramatically in 2007 to more than 2.2 billion euros with the acquisition of a large supermarket chain, Caprabo, centered in Catalonia. Subsequently, investment declined in 2008 and, reflecting the sharp downturn in consumer spending in Spain, undoubtedly has fallen further since then.

In sum, the available evidence on investment also suggests a group record that is strong and indicates growing economic importance for the Mondragon group and its main divisions. It would appear that the Mondragon group investment policy serves to guard against under-investment, which continues to be suggested by some theorists as an Achilles heel that will undermine PC performance.

Instability and Degeneration?

A number of theorists hypothesized that PCs will necessarily "degen-erate" (e.g., Ben-Ner 1984). One key prediction is that, over time, the incentive grows for worker-members to replace retiring members with employees who remain nonmembers and that, consequently, the frac-tion of the workforce that is composed of members will inexorably decline. Another "degeneration" prediction is that successful co-ops will end up being sold to private corporations. In the eyes of many (e.g., Jones 1980), the apparent tendency of Mondragon co-ops not to suc-cumb to such phenomena was an important strength of the Mondragon PC structure, and it contrasted with collapsing membership rates that had been observed for other aging co-ops, such as in the United Kingdom or the United States.

However, subsequent data for Mondragon (e.g., Mondragon Corporation 2006–2008; Ormaechea 2003) suggest that the Mondragon co-ops had begun to degenerate in the first way predicted (i.e., retiring member-workers would be replaced by workers who are not members). Precise longitudinal data are hard to come by, but employment has been gradually shifting in favor of nonmember-workers for at least two decades. Thus, by 1990, the fraction of the workforce composed of non-members in the average co-op at Mondragon was already 10% (Moye 1993). By 2007, only 29.5% of the Mondragon group's total workforce were members of their co-ops (Altuna 2008). In other words, some 50 years after the founding of the first Mondragon co-op, a substantial majority of Mondragon workers are nonmember-workers. As such, they have standard employment contracts with the co-ops but do not have the rights and responsibilities associated with membership, nor do they have voting rights with respect to choosing members of elected bodies, employment guarantees, or an obligation to be employee-owners. On the other hand, nonmember-workers do receive an annual profit share, which, at a minimum, is 25% of the share a worker-member at the same pay grade receives. However, it is important to note that, in more recent years, the group has developed strategies to reverse this situation. In the following paragraphs, we explore these strategies.

The bulk of these nonmember-workers are employed in conventionally owned subsidiaries and joint ventures that the co-ops have established outside the Basque Country, particularly in the Eroski retail chains in Spain (approximately 30,000 nonmember-workers) and in overseas manufacturing plants (approximately 12,000 nonmember-workers). Still, several thousand others are "temporary workers" inside the cooperatives themselves. These various situations involving nonmember-workers have been controversial in the group for many years and have led to numerous major debates that, in turn, have produced changes in policy and practice. Developing and implementing these changes, however, has been complex to some degree, depending on the situation.

The least complex of these changes has been the use of temporary nonmember-workers, mainly inside industrial cooperatives, because of the seasonal and/or cyclical nature of production (and hence demand for labor) and the prohibitive cost of providing all workers with membership. During the 1990s, the group began to emphasize the importance of minimizing the use of temporary workers and set a goal that a minimum of 85% of the co-ops' internal workforce should be made up of

TABLE 1
Membership Ratios in Mondragón Industrial Co-ops.°

1995	1996	1997	1998	1999	2000	2001	2002	2003	2004	2005	2006	2007	2008	2009
82.4%	78.0%	73.0%	71.6%	71.5%	71.2%	73.3%	74.7%	76.7%	81.1%	81%	81.7%	80.9%	83%	88.1%

Sources: Internal Mondragón data set (1995–2003) and annual reports (2003–2009).
°Refers to employment internal to the cooperative firms only, not to subsidiaries.

worker-members. In Table 1, we present the evolution of the ratio of members to total employees in Mondragon's industrial group and see steady if modest improvement in the membership ratio beginning early in this decade and continuing through 2008, when the group approached its 85% membership goal.[10]

A more complex situation involving nonmember-workers can be found primarily within the Eroski retail chains. The main driver of Eroski's use of nonmember-workers was a growth strategy initiated in 1989 characterized by massive and rapid expansion outside its traditional base in the Basque Country. This expansion occurred mostly in response to competitive pressures, especially from large French chains. The majority of this growth has involved the start up and acquisition of noncooperative supermarkets and other stores as subsidiaries of the Eroski cooperative. The need to expand quickly and substantially in the 1000s was pressing. Eroski felt it was potentially too slow, risky, and complicated to expand by using cooperative legal structures, especially outside the Basque Country in what was largely uncharted territory, both in terms of business practice and workers' responses to cooperative ideas and structures.

Eroski's expansion strategy was successful in business terms, but the balance between cooperative and noncooperative employment gradually became very lopsided. To address the issue, Eroski established in the late 1990s a voluntary, partial employee-ownership structure (called GESPA) that eventually involved about 5,000 employees in several of its Spanish subsidiaries. It was very popular among employee participants. Eroski concluded that it was not only capable of doing business successfully around the country, but that it was also capable of using cooperative principles and related organizational/ownership structures in many different places and under different circumstances.

As Eroski continued to grow apace through the 1990s and 2000s, GESPA, as it was initially structured and implemented, could not keep up with the speed of expansion. Hence, an increasing percentage of the Eroski workforce came to consist of nonmember-workers in conventionally owned subsidiaries. By 2008, only about 9,000 (18%) of Eroski's roughly 50,000 workers were co-op members and another 5,000 or so (10%) participated as partial employee-owners in GEPSA (Altuna 2008). As a result, and based on the accumulated success of the GESPA process, Eroski has approved a multi-year initiative to "cooperativize" its operations that will begin to be implemented in 2011. When this initiative is completed (somewhere between 2014 and 2016), the great majority of Eroski workers, who today are nonmember-workers working in conventional subsidiaries or partial worker-owners in GESPA, will become worker-members of cooperative firms. Thus, in a short period, this transformation will increase the ratio of members to total workforce to about 70% to 75% in the Mondragon group as a whole.

The most complex of the situations involving nonmember-workers is that of the overseas manufacturing subsidiaries of co-ops in the industrial group, which employ approximately 12,000 people. This foreign expansion was driven by a complex series of factors involving the imperative to grow in order to protect employment at home, competitors' own location of plants in countries with low labor costs, and the need to be "close to market" in a variety of industries. In general, the co-ops have felt that opening up membership to workers in these plants is legally, financially, and culturally problematic. Hence, in the short term, employee ownership overseas has been viewed as nonviable or excessively risky. This perspective has begun to change, however. During the last several years, the Mondragon headquarters organization, led by its president, has developed a policy for overseas operations to promote employee participation in three areas: decision making, profits, and ownership. A number of co-ops had concrete plans to experiment with partial employee ownership in their foreign plants, but those plans have largely been put on hold by the financial and general economic crisis. Others are debating different financial, legal, and related strategies for achieving this three-pronged approach to participation in different countries where legislation, workers' economic circumstances, and cultural norms vary widely. The jury is still out on whether Mondragon can put in place substantial cooperative or similar employee ownership arrangements in its overseas activities. Since overseas employment can only grow in coming years, this issue bears close monitoring by researchers, policy makers, and others. It is one of the key strategic issues that the Mondragon cooperatives face in the medium to long term.[11]

In sum, when we consider how the evidence we have presented squares with theories of cooperative degeneration, certainly some degeneration has taken place. Things are different than in the 1970s, when virtually 100% of Mondragon workers were members. However, overall, it turns out that a simple story of sustained degeneration both for Eroski and the industrial co-ops is inadequate. Upon closer inspection, the story is more nuanced and not as simple as some would suggest (e.g., Kasmir 1996). In particular, the case of Eroski suggests that institutional changes can be introduced to inhibit the theorized inevitable process of declining membership rates. The challenging situation with subsidiaries overseas remains to be addressed and evaluated in future research.

In drawing overall conclusions for the record described in this section of our chapter, we are mindful of the need to be cautious when making such assessments, given the limits of the data. However, taken together, the evidence presented strongly indicates that the Mondragon group and the main industrial and retail divisions have grown in relative economic importance within and outside Spain and that this may also be the case compared with other co-ops and other well-known employee-owned firms. Furthermore, when using basic indicators of group performance such as sales, employment, and investment, the Mondragon record appears to at least compare favorably with (and may even substantially outstrip) that of other firms, including conventionally owned private firms.[12] As such, the record does not appear to support predictions that, compared with conventional firms, PCs will be less productive, have declining employment, and be prone to underinvestment. There is also evidence suggesting that the group is especially resilient during crises. Finally, while the picture is complex, the overall evidence does not support the standard degeneration hypothesis.

Accounting for the Record: Mechanisms That Facilitate Managed Change

The key question we examine in this section is how has Mondragon, when facing a fast-changing environment, been able to sustain a strong record without sacrificing essential cooperative features? While analysts covering earlier periods were largely optimistic about Mondragon's capacity to adapt (e.g., Moye 1993; Whyte 1999), other accounts often have been more pessimistic as to whether and how co-ops located in northern Spain would be able to respond to the numerous challenges confronting them in Spain and around the world (e.g., Cheney 1999). Some of these challenges, such as more rapid globalization and a faster pace of technological change, were common to most businesses in advanced economies. Other challenges, such as the disappearance of an initial advantage based on low labor costs in Spain, were more specific to Spanish employers. The emergence of the "Basque miracle" (Porter, Ketels, and Delgado 2004), which was characterized by rapidly declining rates of unemployment and rapid growth, presented new challenges. To facilitate change and adaptation in such a taxing environment, we argue that the fundamental democratic feature of the Mondragon set-up enables Mondragon to undertake measured and effective adjustments and to do so at a lower cost than competitors in conventional firms.

Some of the institutional arrangements that distinguish Mondragon from both conventional firms and other PCs—and that facilitate the high degree of adaptability and flexibility in the Mondragon group and its member cooperatives—are reasonably well known and ably described elsewhere. These arrangements include the ability of members to transfer among Mondragon firms during times of depressed demand and the use of profit pooling (e.g., Mathews 1999; Thomas and Logan 1982). However, specific details on the operation of these mechanisms in Mondragon are scarce, and other practices, such as the focus on continual training, do not appear to have received the attention they deserve in the literature. Also, during the last 20 years, there have been important developments that need to be taken into account in order to understand the mechanisms that underpin group performance. In our discussion, we aim to provide a fuller and more current documentation of the scope and nature of several of these mechanisms than is contained in other studies. We concentrate on how these arrangements, within a framework that provides for sustained democratic deliberations, help to nurture and reinvigorate integration within the group and, in turn, help to sustain strong group performance. Together these features provide for a degree of integration among Mondragon member firms that is very high and distinguishes Mondragon from most other less-integrated groups of PCs.[13]

Autonomy, Flexibility, and Change Within the Group and Individual Firms

Important changes have occurred at the organizational level. These changes reflect continuing attempts to solve the dilemma of how best to provide for a high degree of democracy and autonomy in individual firms, yet also allow central bodies to promote changes, economies of scale, and sustained efficiency in the whole group. During the first generation of the group, Mondragon companies worked out common policy and governance arrangements through joint membership in their own banking cooperative, the Caja Laboral, which is a second-degree cooperative—that is, a cooperative whose members are other cooperatives (Thomas and Logan 1982). As years passed, the potential advantages of joint action for investment and employment planning, training, new product development, exporting, and other activities became clearer.

Starting in 1964 with the establishment of ULARCO, a grouping of three of the largest and oldest cooperatives, but mainly in the 1970s and 1980s, the cooperative firms decided to form subgroups based on geographic proximity. One of the implications of this decision was that the well-known arrangements for surplus/profit redistribution would take place within such regional groups.

The growth of newer sectors such as auto parts manufacturing and retailing, as well as the general sense of a need for more economically rational organizing criteria, continued to create momentum for change. Hence, after substantial discussion and debate in the late 1980s, the group decided to reorganize itself again, this time with two other features principally in mind: (1) the establishment of central structures for overall governance, strategic coordination, and the provision of management services, and (2) the creation of subgroups of firms and the groups/divisions by industrial sector instead of by region. In the main, it simply seemed to make more economic sense to the co-ops to join in subgroups according to product/market affinity and not geographic proximity. In 1991, the Mondragon Cooperative Corporation (MCC) was born to put these ideas into practice. At first, three different sectoral groups were created: financial, manufacturing (called industrial), and retail. Later, a knowledge group was added. As part of this restructuring process, the manufacturing group was divided into a number of divisions. However, while the push was to move away from regional groups, it is also true that, within this new manufacturing group, some regional groups have remained active to some degree (e.g., at FAGOR and ULMA). Other structural modifications have taken place since 1991 and, in 2008, the name changed from MCC to Mondragon. Nevertheless, the basic organizing principles at Mondragon remain largely intact, seeking, again, to balance autonomy for individual co-ops with strategic coordination and common governance.

These structural changes might be seen as reflecting shifting views in the ongoing debate about the optimal degree of decentralization/centralization for individual firms. While the changes mean that management practices and governance structures at the highest levels are not as "close to the shop floor" or as participatory today as during earlier periods, a consistent theme in our interviews was that these organizational changes did not really affect day-to-day operational fundamentals. While individual firms willingly surrendered some autonomy to the groups/divisions, the balance of power continued to reside with individual firms rather than the center. The existence of individual firm autonomy is perhaps best illustrated in two areas: (1) those rare cases of co-op closures, and (2) firms' decisions to enter or leave the Mondragon group.

In the first area, when an individual company is under serious threat, Mondragon will provide consultative and even financial help so long as it seems possible to sustain the business. But the decision to close—and to protect any remaining individually owned stakes—is taken by the particular cooperative.[14] By contrast, in anticipation of shifting market opportunities, the center might take the initiative in suggesting concrete ways in which individual co-ops could shift their product mixes and even give advice on new plant locations. But final decisions rest with the individual co-op: those at the center do have substantial authority, formal and informal, but when there is disagreement, they tend to negotiate decisions with individual co-ops and make recommendations. They do not have traditional executive authority.

In the second area, the preeminence of co-op autonomy is also clear. The decision to enter or remain a part of the Mondragon sectoral network depends on a decision by each co-op's general assembly of worker-members. A small number of co-ops did, in fact, decide not to join the MCC structure when it was first proposed (e.g., ULMA) or to leave the structure in later years (e.g., AMPO). Several of these co-ops have since voted to return to the Mondragon network, but the key point here is that the authority for these decisions rests in the individual cooperative firm, not in a centralized, corporate body.

Most people interviewed as part of our research reported that strategic decisions typically reflected standard business criteria with a focus on generating sustained sales and profits. This is clearly the case, especially during good economic times such as the second half of the 1990s and early in the 21st century, when it appeared as if members were content with what many might view as "satisfying behavior." However, during economic crises, as several interviewees stressed, the paramount concern of managers shifts to maintaining employment for members. Arguably, the focus on job security is triggered by the experiences of the generation that came of age between 1980 and 1995. They had lived during times characterized by long periods of persistent high unemployment in the Basque Country[15] and in Spain generally, though not nearly as severe as in the greater Mondragon area. Joblessness during that period was constantly reported in the mass media, deeply affected the general economic environment, and may have significantly influenced the mentality of that generation.

Mondragon has also shown itself to be very flexible in another key area: the legal structure of joint ventures and subsidiaries. During the early years at Mondragon, all enterprises in the group were cooperatives located in the Basque region, and new firms entered the group as start-up co-ops or through immediate conversions or mergers of existing firms into co-ops before or upon entry. Over the years, however, the group has purposefully evolved to include enterprises that are not restricted to cooperatives. We have already discussed the now-extensive use of conventionally owned subsidiaries outside the Basque Country, particularly in the Eroski retail chain and in the industrial co-ops' internationalization process. In addition, since the late 1980s, the Mondragon group has expanded by acquiring existing firms both outside and inside the Basque Country. While some of these later acquisitions soon became cooperatives (e.g., MAPSA), as in the early years, the acquired companies—initially, at least—often continued to be structured as conventional firms.

One example was the 1989 acquisition of FABRELEC, a local domestic appliance manufacturer. During the acquisition process, a plan to provide the opportunity for cooperativization was drawn up. All parties felt that it would take time for the Mondragon co-op buyer to provide information and training about the cooperative option, to shift ingrained management policy and practice toward the cooperative model, and for the workforce to assimilate and debate the advantages and disadvantages of the new circumstances. It was agreed, as a consequence, that approximately five years after the acquisition, workers would be given the opportunity to vote on whether to join the FAGOR Home Appliances manufacturing co-op as worker-members. The five-year period passed, and, after substantial discussion, a vote was taken and an overwhelming majority became members. More or less similar processes have been undertaken in other conventional firms acquired by Mondragon co-ops.

Another new organizational form that has been created is the so-called mixed cooperative. These emerged because of rising capital requirements in start-up situations, especially in capital-intensive manufacturing sectors, and the inability to obtain sufficient capital either from the traditional core source (i.e., worker-members' initial investments), or, given the high debt-to-equity ratios involved, through standard debt from the Caja Laboral or other banks. These mixed cooperatives allow for "investor" members, generally other cooperative firms in the Mondragon group, and are structured to provide explicitly limited control rights for the investor members supplying new capital. An example is Eko3r, a firm that designs, manufactures, installs, and telematically monitors cooking oil collection/recycling equipment for cities and towns. Eko3r started in May 2009 with nine worker-members and has as investor members the FAGOR group and two venture capital funds—Mondragon Investments and Mondragon Innovation.

The other key organizational change since the initial decades of the 1950s, 1960s, and early 1970s is that much more of the group's resources are devoted to strengthening existing co-ops and much less to nurturing new ones. Rapidly growing globalization of many of the co-ops' markets led them to internationalize production (e.g., Errasti, Heras, Bakaikoa, and Elgoibar 2003). To help this process along and manage change, a Department of Internationalization was established at Mondragon headquarters. These actions are clear indicators of the group's focus on consolidating existing co-ops rather than opening new ones. Further, large amounts of money have been invested in new technology in existing co-ops in order to reinforce their position in existing markets and to open up markets for allied products and services. Both dimensions of this trend continue to a significant degree today but are not as dominant as earlier. Since such a large proportion of Mondragon's companies are in traditional sectors, the group has also established as a strategic priority the development of new businesses in sectors that are seen to have significant future potential, regardless of the amount of experience Mondragon has in those sectors. They include medical and energy technology businesses, as well as home care and health services.

Compensation Policies

Other major changes that have affected the operations of individual cooperatives include shifts in compensation policy (i.e., in the permissible differences in salaries between the highest and lowest paid). When the first cooperative was created in 1956, a key aim was to diminish social and economic inequalities among co-op workers. Consequently, salary differences were restricted, and initially it was decided to adopt maximum differentials of 1:3. However, over time, pressure for widening these differentials emerged as the Spanish economy began to catch up with wealthier European countries, the group itself grew, its workforce and management ranks became more representative of the broader society in their attitudes toward pay, and demand for skilled managers and engineers increased. After ten years, the range was increased to 1:4.5 and in 1987, during the first Mondragon Cooperative Congress, the range was increased again, this time to 1:6. This change, however, did not automatically mean that senior managers would be paid six times more than shop floor workers, but rather it was a permissible ratio for a co-op to use and continue to belong to the group. A co-op could then internally debate changes in its salary ratio, taking into account all its particular circumstances. Any change would ultimately have to be approved by its general assembly of member-workers. A number of the larger co-ops held these debates and widened pay ratios, but most cooperatives maintained ratios very close to the earlier ones. By 2002, in response to market pressures, the range was widened again, to 1:8.9. Indeed, it has been argued that if compensation took full account of all forms (including, for example, bonuses) the range was, in fact, 1:11 (Ormaechea 2003:420). Still, it is important to qualify this point.

Clearly, Mondragon co-ops responded to social, cultural, and market pressures and widened the salary differential, a move which, for many, was at odds with cooperative principles. At the same time, it is important to realize that decisions about how to apply the maximum allowable differential are made in accordance with cooperative principles (i.e., in individual co-ops after extensive discussion and debate and, finally, a vote by a firm's general assembly). Ultimately, very few workers are affected by these maximum differentials. Also, not all co-ops make use of them; in fact, most do not. In several interviews, top managers reported policies whereby by-laws of the co-op stipulated that its maximum permissible differentials were only 1:5. It also remains true, even taking into account changes in the salary differential over the years, that senior managers in Mondragon typically earn less than their counterparts in conventional companies; in larger cooperatives, the differences are dramatic.

Hence, as far as bonuses are concerned, several managers reported that they primarily make use of low-powered financial incentives and that only modest use has been made of performance-related pay, even for top executives. Thus, an executive contract in which as much as 20% of rewards consisted potentially of a performance bonus was viewed as being exceptional. Also, bonuses have been nearly always based on sales and productivity rather than job retention or employment growth.

Changes Concerning Membership and the Practice of Member Relocation

The crisis of the 1980s demonstrated to the co-ops that they needed more-flexible labor forces. As already discussed, one consequence is that major changes have taken place concerning the nature of membership. One central change was the creation of the temporary member category. A new type of contract was created in 1993 for temporary members, and it was adopted by cooperatives in the following years. This new contract was seen as an instrument of guarantee both for cooperatives and employees. Temporary members have most of the same rights as full members do (e.g., they share in surpluses based on the individual's salary and may vote for and can serve on elected bodies). The main difference is that they do not have job security. Temporary members, however, also have most of the same obligations as full members do (e.g., for ownership stakes to be written down during crises and related financial sacrifices, or to serve on the local work-area body, if elected). The difference in this case is that their membership fee is only 10% of the full membership fee.

Importantly, their situation is transitory: workers can be temporary members for a maximum of five years and, at any given time, no more than 20% of a co-op's full membership can consist of temporary members.

The relative importance of the initial membership fee has also declined over the years. However, this has not been the result of a specific change in membership fee policy but rather of changes in compensation policy. The initial membership fee is equivalent to one year's salary at the lowest potential compensation level in the group. Since the gap between lowest and highest paid in the group has increased on a number of occasions as a result of policy changes over the last 25 years, the relative weight of the membership fee has declined.

One of the key adjustment mechanisms used among the group of co-ops is the requirement that a firm experiencing relatively strong demand must be ready to hire member-workers from a firm that is experiencing soft demand. This worker relocation policy reflects the Mondragon commitment to essentially guarantee a member job security—but not in a particular position or a particular firm. However, the implementation of the policy can lead to various tensions. Individuals may not embrace the need to commute over a much longer distance than they are used to or to work in an unfamiliar position, although they are compensated for the difference in commuting distance. For firms, sometimes this worker relocation policy has been viewed as requiring them to make sacrifices that were too costly. Nevertheless, the policy seems to be a stable fixture at Mondragon, ready to be widely and extensively used during economic crises, and is a key component of worker satisfaction with being a cooperative member (Freundlich and Pisano 2010).

Thus, an interviewee reported that in the ULMA group alone during the crisis of 1984, about 18% of worker-members (66 workers) moved among different firms in the group on a temporary basis. In the subsequent crises of 1992–1993 and 2008–2009, the corresponding numbers for temporary transfers were about 5% and 3%, respectively (with the last figure representing about 110 workers, compared with fewer than 100 in the previous crisis, and 66 in 1984). Another interviewee at Mondragon estimated that, in the depths of the recent global recession of late 2009, about 500 members were temporarily working in other co-ops. Unlike the Japanese case of lifetime employment, whereby a significant proportion of workers on temporary transfer will never return and become permanently transferred (Kato 2001), at Mondragon there appear to be far fewer permanent transfers. Thus, Basterretxea and Albizu (2010b), drawing on internal sources from Mondragon, report that, during the period 2000 through 2008, the greatest number of permanent transfers for all of Mondragon in one year was 29 in 2007. Interestingly, however, even during good years, some permanent reallocations did take place—two in 2001, nine in 2003, and two in 2005.

Profit Pooling

Sharing a portion of profits at the division level—profit pooling—continues to have a central place in Mondragon. When individual co-ops pool parts of their surpluses, they establish "solidarity funds" that are available to assist co-ops in difficulties. Since 1991, the practice has operated both at the regional/sectoral level as well as for the overall group. As additional funds have been developed, it appears that the importance of this practice has increased in recent years.[16]

At the decentralized levels, one interviewee reported that, within the ULMA group of co-ops, up to 50% of profits (surplus) recorded at individual entities within ULMA (such as construction and manufacture of greenhouses) were pooled. In other regional or sectoral groups in Mondragon, the norm for profit pooling was in the range of 15% to 40% of surplus.

At the overall group level, individual co-ops contribute to or invest in two kinds of funds. First, Mondragon policy requires that member co-ops invest in a venture capital fund called Mondragon Investments. Co-ops make an initial investment in this fund and also make an annual investment, both based on formulae that take into account various factors related to size and performance. Second, Mondragon firms make post-tax donations to a central foundation that amounts to 5% of profits for industrial and retail firms, and substantially more for the bank, Caja Laboral. The foundation funds are used to finance education and training activities, to diminish losses in weaker co-ops (if they are taking concrete measures to improve performance), and for other not-for-profit initiatives. While the role of the Caja in risking its own assets by making loans to co-ops facing economic problems has diminished over time, it has continued during the crisis to try to retain lending to individual co-ops in difficulties.

Training

The scope and nature of training within Mondragon is a very distinctive feature of the group and arguably an important source of its strong record (Meek and Woodworth 1990). In an enlightening paper, Basterretxea and Albizu (2010a) provide a fresh perspective on actual practices surrounding training for managers in the Mondragon group. They note that the ability to attract and retain highly qualified managers is of paramount concern for Mondragon. At the same time, it is especially challenging in view of both the policy of compressed wage differences and the fact that many co-op managers are hired as young adults and, based on their work history, do not necessarily have any pre-existing commitment to co-op values. Indeed, Mondragon firms say it is exceedingly difficult to apply a "cooperative values filter" in the selection process. Still, one incentive to stimulate management retention follows from the fact that the managerial labor market at Mondragon is an internal labor market—essentially all professional positions within the group are filled from within the group—hence, young managers are likely to have a career ladder.

Another critical policy has been the development of an extensive set of training centers geared to the special needs of managers (including a facility at Otalora). One of the key managerial training programs results in what is equivalent to an MBA in co-op management, and about 20 of those degrees are awarded each year, reflecting steady growth over time. Several of our interviewees reported that the majority of top executives at Mondragon have gone through this training program. In view of the high degree of mobility of managers within the group, one would expect that there would be a high degree of knowledge transfer, as information learned in these courses on best practices is efficiently and cheaply disseminated within the group.

In another informative paper, Basterretxea and Albizu (2010b) discuss policies and practices at Mondragon concerning training for nonmanagerial employees. An important point of departure is the recognition that worker-members have the right to a job, though not to a particular position. To meet the challenges presented by this job security guarantee, in addition to the worker relocation policy previously discussed, the Mondragon group has emphasized a policy of continual and general training. The aim is to have a well-trained and flexible workforce. To this end, the authors report several indicators that underscore the importance attached to general training at Mondragon. Investment in continual training in Mondragon represents 2.7% of the wage bill (compared with averages of 1.2% for Spanish firms and 1.6% in EU companies). Hours of training average 23.7 for Mondragon workers, almost double the EU-27 average of 12 hours. In the EU-27, about one of four employees is reported as benefiting from training. In Mondragon, the proportion is closer to one of two. So far as the type of training is concerned, Basterretxea and Albizu (2010b) discuss several examples of innovative training practices—training that was often quite generic and long-lasting. For example, "The whole workforce at Orkli [an important cooperative] . . . has already gone through retraining courses."[17]

In sum, while there have been major changes in the structure and functioning of the Mondragon co-ops during the last 20 years or so, it is our sense that the essential nature of the Mondragon co-ops has not fundamentally changed. At root, the co-ops are still responding to the wishes of the core membership, although certain decisions (e.g., creating non-cooperative subsidiaries), have been highly controversial inside and outside the group. These decisions, in turn, have led to substantial structural and policy responses by the group and by individual co-ops—in particular, the cooperativization of the Eroski group, an initiative that will be closely examined for its applicability to overseas operations. At the same time, we also note that the process of integrating the co-ops has deepened and that mechanisms such as continual training appear to have become more important.

Conclusion

Commenting on the literature on worker cooperatives up to the early 1990s, Bonin, Jones, and Putterman (1993) note that the literature had been theory led and that empirical literature had lagged significantly behind. At the same time, it was apparent that theory building had often ignored many well-known stylized facts. Early empirical studies often contained results that contradicted the most basic propositions of early theory. Since then, empirical research on cooperatives has continued to make great strides. However, it is clear that much remains to be done, especially concerning the famous Mondragon co-ops. In this chapter, we have made a modest start by analyzing new empirical data about the Mondragon group.

More specifically, by drawing on several types of data, including new interview evidence derived from many field trips to Mondragon, and new financial and economic data, including internal data, this chapter has documented and assessed the changing importance and performance of the Mondragon group and its two largest sectors. Compared with conventional firms in the Basque area and in Spain (and co-ops and employee-owned firms elsewhere) in general, we find evidence of Mondragon's importance to the larger economy and strong performance for the group as a whole and for the industrial and retail divisions. Most of the stylized facts concerning the record of the group, such as growing investment and employment, do not sit well with predictions based on the early theory of the labor-managed firm, including predictions that co-ops restrict employment and become progressively comparatively undercapitalized (as reviewed in Bonin, Jones, and Putterman 1993).

In accounting for this record, we highlight key institutional features and developments in the Mondragon group during the last 20 to 25 years. At root, individual Mondragon firms continue to be worker owned and governed, while various mechanisms point to sustained solidarity within, and integration of, the group. While some of these changes (e.g., new types of firms and new categories of membership) may be viewed as representing movements away from the founders' ideals, we argue that it is too early to determine whether they represent fundamental changes.

Moreover, to deal with emerging challenges, the capacity of the group to innovate and make institutional adjustments continues. There is evidence that many of these developments, which appear to represent departures from the founders' ideals, are not likely to be sustained but rather may turn out to be temporary phenomena. This is most clearly the case with Eroski and its ongoing strategy of cooperativization. There is also evidence that firms that begin as mixed cooperatives soon assume a traditional cooperative organizational form.

We provide more detailed information than what has been previously available regarding some of the key distinguishing institutional mechanisms of the Mondragon group, such as the extent of worker-member transfers, the patterns of profit pooling, new organizational forms, and the type and volume of training. It is our contention that extensive use of these and other mechanisms—themselves formulated and refined only after a deliberative democratic process—help to underpin the strong Mondragon group record and enable the group to manage change that, while not perfect, occurs at a more measured pace and lower cost than that of its competitors. For example, Mondragon's extraordinary levels of training may reflect the fact that Mondragon firms do not face similar degrees of pressure as do privately owned firms to distribute profits to shareholders. Mondragon firms can take a longer-term view on investment in human capital which, in turn, is expected to pay off in enhanced organizational efficiencies in the long run. By contrast, as Bassi, Ludwig, McMurrer, and von Buren (2002), among others, have argued, pressure from financial markets may cause underinvestment in training for conventional firms. Moreover, we expect that job security (together with the worker relocation policy), along with various mechanisms for employee involvement and strong financial participation through worker ownership, will foster powerful motivations for enhanced worker productivity.

In highlighting these particular strategic mechanisms, we emphasize a more complex interplay of factors than past accounts do, and we highlight some factors that were not previously identified as factors for the success of the Mondragon group. Thus, early analytical work by economists tends to stress the roles of incentives stemming from the interplay of employee involvement and employee ownership alone. While we do not by any means dismiss the potential impact of these features, our sense is that the unusual attention given to lifetime training is probably at least as important in accounting for group success. In addition, these findings suggest that there is a Mondragon cooperative difference. Compared with other PC experiences past and present, the degree of integration among the Mondragon co-ops, as exemplified in practices such as worker-member transfers and profit pooling, is extraordinary.

At the same time, we are keenly aware that Mondragon continues to face enormous challenges. Many of its core businesses, especially those in manufacturing, are threatened by the intensification of competition in today's globalized economy. The process of institutional adaptation will need to continue and probably accelerate, likely with a growing role for institutions whose central mission is knowledge creation, such as technology parks and the University of Mondragon.

We are also keenly aware that some of the findings reported in this paper are preliminary and that more rigorous analysis is needed. This is especially the case for issues surrounding the links between domestic and overseas employment growth. In ongoing work (e.g., Arando, Gago, Jones, and Kato 2010a, 2010b), we address key unanswered questions such as the comparative performance of PCs and conventional firms, as well as the comparative performance of firms with majority and minority employee ownership. In one paper (Arando, Gago, Jones, and Kato 2010a), we also find evidence that some of the institutional mechanisms that we highlight for the group, such as training, help to underpin the superior performance of the co-op stores.

One broader implication of our findings concerns the range of organizational forms that are feasible in today's advanced economies. Many have argued (e.g., Stiglitz 2003) that, besides privately and publicly owned firms, cooperatives represent a third, highly viable organizational form. Our account of the Mondragon co-ops provides further evidence in support of the feasibility and sustainability of the cooperative alternative. In a world of declining labor power (Gordon 2010), in which CEOs of for-profit firms quickly shed labor during crises and slowly rehire during upswings, the sophisticated institutional arrangements that characterize the Mondragon co-ops are worthy of deeper study by policy makers and others.

Acknowledgment

Co-authors Saioa Arando, Fred Freundlich, and Monica Gago are affiliated with Mondragon Innovation and Knowledge (MIK) and the Faculty of Business, Mondragon University.

Endnotes

[1] See, for example, http://economix.blogs.nytimes.com/2009/11/23/the-case-for-worker-co-ops.

[2] In PCs, as in other cooperatives, principles such as "one-member, one-vote" and limited interest on capital apply. However, unlike in other cooperatives, worker management in PCs exists alongside employee ownership. There is a large body of economic theory that examines the behavior of the "pure" PC—the theory of the labor-managed firm.

[3] These include attempts to compare the growth in importance of Mondragon co-ops with co-ops elsewhere, including PCs. In that process, we make limited use of other sources, such as the list of the biggest co-ops and mutual societies in the world (http://www.global300.coop) and Spanish co-op sources (such as http://www.cepes.es).

[4] Regrettably, the available data do not permit decomposing total sales into those in domestic and foreign markets.

[5] Comparisons using the theoretically preferred value-added criterion are more difficult, in part because Mondragon measures "value added" differently than conventional firms do. However, preliminary attempts to adjust measures to make comparisons on a consistent value-added basis also suggest that co-ops have long enjoyed a substantial edge. Nevertheless, during the first decade of this century, by this measure, it appears that the comparative advantage of industrial co-ops is being eroded.

[6] However, this movement was probably heavily influenced by the largest acquisition that Eroski has ever made—that of Caprabo.

[7] Conversely, an unpublished study of a small sample of industrial co-ops does not yield such a favorable picture (see Martin 2000).

[8] For earlier evidence see, for example, the various exercises reported by Moye (1993).

[9] We have used the Encuesta de Población Activa (Labor Force Survey) from the Spanish National Statistical Office (http://www.ine.es).

[10] Data for the financial group are not readily available (although that group represents fewer than 5% of total employment in Mondragon).

[11] See Vanek (2008) for a discussion of a plant in the Czech Republic.

[12] Other, more qualitative, evidence exists that speaks to the performance of the Mondragon group and its main divisions. This evidence includes winning a considerable number of Basque, Spanish, and European awards for quality and being a finalist for the European Environmental Award.

[13] For example, arrangements that provide for members to transfer to other PCs or for profit pooling appear to be either absent or of very limited importance in other PCs (for French PCs, see, e.g., Estrin and Jones 1992; for Uruguay, Burdin and Dean 2009; and for the United States, Craig and Pencavel 1995). For earlier discussions and comparisons that draw attention to the distinctive nature of the Mondragon setup, including its extensive supporting structures, see Jones 1980 and Bonin, Jones, and Putterman 1993.

[14] An interviewee provided details of the steps surrounding the closure of two co-ops, COVIMAR and VICON, during earlier crises. The process of managing this change involved many stages, including pay cuts (that increased over time) and technical and financial assistance from the Caja Laboral (on behalf of the group). While sustaining jobs was a key concern, repayment of creditors was also of central importance. Ultimately both co-ops decided to close.

[15] As recently as 1994, the unemployment rate hit 24% in the Basque Country.

[16] Intriguingly, Japanese keiretsu play a similar role in monitoring and rescuing (when appropriate) its affiliate firms (Aoki 1988).

[17] One reason Mondragon can support such high levels of training is that their extremely low unemployment rates produce favorable "experience ratings" and very low contributions for unemployment insurance (UI). Basterretxea and Albizu (2010b) estimated that during the years 2000 through 2008, UI in Mondragon firms averaged 1%, whereas UI for firms affiliated with the Spanish Social Security system averaged 7.05% in 2009.

REFERENCES

Altuna, L. ed. 2008. *La Experiencia Cooperativa de Mondragon: Una Séntesis General*. Eskoriatza, Spain: Lanki.

Aoki, Masahiko. 1988. *Information, Incentives, and Bargaining in the Japanese Economy*. Cambridge, UK: Cambridge University Press.

Arando, Saioa, Monica Gago, Derek C. Jones, and Takao Kato. 2010a. *Productive Efficiency in the Mondragon Cooperatives: Evidence from an Econometric Case Study* (mimeo). Hamilton College, Clinton, NY; and paper presented at the Allied Social Sciences Association Annual Conference, Atlanta, GA, January 3–5, 2010.

Arando, Saioa, Monica Gago, Derek C. Jones, and Takao Kato. 2010b. *The Effects of Self-Managed Teams in Worker Cooperatives: Evidence from Mondragon*. Working Paper. Clinton, NY: Department of Economics, Hamilton College.

Bassi, Laurie J., Jens Ludwig, Daniel P. McMurrer, and Mark von Buren. 2002. "Profiting from Learning: Firm-Level Effects of Training Investments and Market Implications." *Singapore Management Review*, Vol. 24, no. 3, pp. 61 76.

Basterretxea, Imanol, and Eneka Albizu. 2010a. "Management Training as a Source of Perceived Competitive Advantage: The Mondragon Cooperative Group Case." *Economic and Industrial Democracy*, Vol. 20, no. 10, pp. 1–24.

Basterretxea, Imanol, and Eneka Albizu. 2010b. "®Es posible resistir a la crisis?: Un análisis desde la gestión de las políticas de formación y empleo en Mondragon." *CIRIEC-España, Revista de Economía Pública, Social y Cooperativa*, No. 67 (April), pp. 75–96.

Ben-Ner, Avner. 1984. "On the Stability of the Cooperative Type of Organization." *Journal of Comparative Economics*, Vol. 8, September, pp. 247–60.

Bonin, J., D. Jones, and L. Putterman. 1993. "Theoretical and Empirical Studies of Producer Cooperatives: Will the Twain Ever Meet?" *Journal of Economic Literature*, Vol. 31, pp. 1290–320.

Bradley, Keith, and Alan Gelb. 1982. "The Replication and Sustainability of the Mondragon Experiment." *British Journal of Industrial Relations*, Vol. 20, no. 1, pp. 20–33.

Bradley, Keith, and Alan Gelb. 1985. *Cooperation at Work: The Mondragon Experience*. London: Heinemann.

Bradley, Keith, and Alan Gelb. 1987. "Cooperative Labour Relations: Mondragon's Response to Recession." *British Journal of Industrial Relations*, Vol. 25, no. 1, pp. 77–97.

Burdin, Gabriel, and Andres Dean. 2009. "New Evidence on Wages and Employment in Worker Cooperatives Compared with Capitalist Firms." *Journal of Comparative Economics*, Vol. 37, no. 5, pp. 517–33.

Cheney, G. 1999. *Values at Work: Employee Participation Meets Market Pressure at Mondragon*. Ithaca, NY: Cornell University Press.

Craig, B., and J. Pencavel. 1992. "The Behavior of Worker Cooperatives: The Plywood Cooperatives of the Pacific Northwest." *American Economic Review*, Vol. 82, pp. 1083–105.

Craig, B., and J. Pencavel. 1995. "Participation and Productivity: A Comparison of Worker Cooperatives and Conventional Firms in the Plywood Industry." In *Brookings Papers on Economic Activity: Microeconomics*. Vol. 1995, pp. 121–74. Washington, DC: Brookings Institution.

Deloitte. 2010. *Emerging from the Downturn: Global Powers of Retailing 2010*. n.p.: Deloitte.

Dow, Greg. 2003. *Governing the Firm: Workers' Control in Theory and Practice*. Cambridge, UK: Cambridge University Press.

Ellerman, David. 1984. "Entrepreneurship in the Mondragon Cooperatives." *Review of Social Economy*, Vol. 42, pp. 272–94.

Errasti, A.M., I. Heras, B. Bakaikoa, and P. Elgoibar. 2003. "The Internationalization of Cooperatives: The Case of the Mondragon Cooperative Corporation." *Annals of Public and Cooperative Economics*, Vol. 75, no. 4, pp. 553–84.

Estrin, S., and D.C. Jones. 1992. "The Viability of Employee-Owned Firms: Evidence from France." *Industrial and Labor Relations Review*, Vol. 45, No. 2, pp. 323–38.

Estrin, S., D.C. Jones, and J. Svejnar. 1987. "Productivity Effects of Worker Participation: Producer Cooperatives in Western Economies." *Journal of Comparative Economics*, Vol. 11, pp. 40–61.

Freundlich, Fred, and Franco Pisano. 2010. *The Relationship Between Level of Employee Ownership and Psychosocial Perceptions in the Firm: A Preliminary Analysis of the Eroski Group*. Paper presented at the International Association for the Economics of Participation 15th Annual Conference, Paris, July 2010.

Gordon, Robert J. 2010. *The Demise of Okun's Law and of Procyclical Fluctuations in Conventional and Unconventional Measures of Productivity*. <http://faculty-web.at.northwestern.edu/economics/gordon/The%20Demise%20of%20Okun's%20Law_NBER.pdf>. [February 7, 2011].

INDISA. 2007–2008. *Anuario de la Distribución*. <http://www. indisa.es>. [September 2010].

Johnson, Ana Gutierrez, and William Foote Whyte. 1977. "The Mondragon System of Worker Production Cooperatives." *Industrial and Labor Relations Review*, Vol. 31, no. 1, pp. 18–30.

Jones, D., and D. Backus. 1977. "British Producer Cooperatives in the Footwear Industry: An Empirical Evaluation of the Theory of Financing." *Economic Journal*, Vol. 87, pp. 488–510.

Jones, Derek C. 1980. "Producer Cooperatives in Industrialized Western Economies." *British Journal of Industrial Relations*, Vol. 18, July, pp. 141–54.

Joshi, Sumit, and Stephen C. Smith. 2008. "Endogenous Formation of Coops and Cooperative Leagues." *Journal of Economic Behavior and Organization*, Vol. 68, no. 1, pp. 217–33.

Kasmir, S. 1996. *The Myth of Mondragon*. Albany, NY: SUNY Press.

Kato, T. 2001. "The End of Lifetime Employment in Japan? Evidence from National Surveys and Field Research." *Journal of the Japanese and International Economies*, 2001, Vol. 15, no. 4, pp. 489–514.

Luzarraga, J.M., D. Aranzadi, and I. Irizar. 2008. *Understanding Mondragon Globalization Process: Local Job Creation through Multi-Localization* (mimeo). Oñati, Spain: Mondragon University.

Martin, T.H. 2000. *The Impact of Worker Ownership on Firm-Level Performance: A Comparative Study*. Unpublished doctoral dissertation, Department of Economics, Yale University, New Haven, CT.

Mathews, R. 1999. *Jobs of Our Own: Building a Stakeholder Society*. Sydney: Pluto Press.

Meek, C.B., and W.P. Woodworth. 1990. "Technical Training and Enterprise: Mondragon's Educational System and Its Implications for Other Cooperatives." *Economic and Industrial Democracy*, Vol. 11, pp. 508–28.

Mondragon Corporation. 2007. *Mondragon Annual Report, 2006*. <http://www.mcc.es/CAS/Magnitudes-Econ%C3%B3micas/Informe-anual.aspx>. [June 5, 2010].

Mondragon Corporation. 2008. *Mondragon Annual Report, 2007*. <http://www.mcc.es/CAS/Magnitudes-Econ%C3%B3micas/Informe-anual.aspx>. [June 5, 2010].

Mondragon Corporation. 2009. *Mondragon Annual Report, 2008*. <http://www.mcc.es/CAS/Magnitudes-Econ%C3%B3micas/Informe-anual.aspx>. [June 5, 2010].

Moye, A. Melissa. 1993. "Mondragon: Adapting Cooperative Structures to Meet the Demands of a Changing Environment." *Economic and Industrial Democracy*, Vol. 14, pp. 251–76.

Ormaechea, Jose Maria. 2003. *Didactica de una Experiencia Empresarial: El Cooperativismo de Mondragon*. Arrasate-Mondragon: Caja Laboral.

Pencavel, John, Luigi Pistaferri, and Fabiano Schivardi. 2006. "Wages, Employment, and Capital in Capitalist and Worker-Owned Firms." *Industrial and Labor Relations Review*, Vol. 60, no. 1, pp. 23–44.

Porter, Michael, Christian Ketels, and Mercedes Delgado. 2004. *Basque Country: The Strategy for Economic Development*. Harvard Business School Case 705-432. Cambridge, MA: Harvard University.

Sackrey, Charles, Geoffrey Schneider, Janet Knoedler. 2008. "The Mondragon Cooperative." In *Introduction to Political Economy Dollars and Sense* (5th ed.). Boston: Dollars & Sense, pp. 245–72.

Stiglitz, Joseph. 2003. "Towards a New Paradigm of Development." In John H. Dunning, ed., *Making Globalization Good: The Moral Challenges of Global Capitalism*. Oxford: Oxford University Press, pp. 76–107.

Thomas, H., and C. Logan. 1982. *Mondragon: An Economic Analysis*. London: Allen and Unwin.

Vanek, Jaroslav. 2008. *Mondragon Cooperative Offspring Firms in Moravia*. Paper presented at the International Association for the Economics of Participation 14th Annual Conference, Clinton, NY, July 15–17, 2008.

Ward, Benjamin. 1958. "The Firm in Illyria: Market Syndicalism." *American Economic Review*, Vol. 48, September, pp. 566–89.

Whyte, W.F. 1999. "The Mondragon Cooperatives in 1976 and 1998." *Industrial and Labor Relations Review*, Vol. 52, no. 3, pp. 478–81.

CHAPTER 10

Ohio's ESOP Companies Through Two Decades: Growing Up or Growing Old?

JOHN LOGUE
JACQUELYN YATES
Ohio Employee Ownership Center, Kent State University

In the last 30 years, employee stock ownership plans (ESOPs), which were very uncommon in the United States prior to legal changes recognizing them as qualified pension plans in 1974, have become the most common form of employee ownership and a significant factor in the American economy (Blasi, Freeman, Mackin, and Kruse 2008). According to the National Center for Employee Ownership (NCEO), as of early 2010 there were about 10,500 partially or wholly employee-owned companies through ESOPs, stock bonus plans, and profit sharing plans, investing primarily in employer securities, with 12.7 million employee-owners who held about $901 billion in equity in the companies they work for (NCEO 2010). We estimate that 90% to 95% of the 10,500 ownership plans were ESOPs, based on the latest information available from IRS Form 5500 reports filed mostly in 2007 (Larkspur Data Resources, version 12.1).

The intent of Congress in establishing ESOPs was to create financial assets for company employees, not to promote employee involvement or participation in corporate governance. United States Senator Russell Long, the author of every major piece of ESOP legislation from 1973 until he retired in 1987, put it succinctly, "Our capitalistic system should have a great many more capitalists. From where are they to come? Logically, from the ranks of employees" (Long 1989:vii). ESOPs were designed to achieve this end.

The number of ESOPs grew rapidly in the years immediately after 1974 through the 1980s. This growth was aided by public policy. Friendly laws that existed between 1976 and 1986 created two special types of ESOP plans, TRASOPs (Tax Reduction Act Stock Ownership

Plans) and PAYSOPs (Payroll Stock Ownership Plans), which provided dollar-for-dollar tax credits for corporate contributions of very limited amounts of equity to employees and encouraged many large corporations to set up plans. Tax-deductible contributions of corporate stock to 401(k) SOPs (a combination of a 401(k) plan and an ESOP) also encouraged broad-based but shallow employee stock ownership while slashing cash outlays for corporate matching funds. Employees received only a tiny share of the company's stock and had no greater voice in management than before the 401(k) SOP. The "1042 rollover," enacted in 1984, enabled owners of closely held companies to sell at least 30% of the stock in their companies to employees through an ESOP and defer taxes on the capital gains by "rolling" them "over" into a stock account, making employee ownership a retirement planning strategy. A Delaware court decision permitted ESOPs to be used as a takeover defense [*Shamrock Holdings, Inc.* v. *Polaroid Corp.*, 559 A.2d 257 (Del. Ch. 1989)]. From 1989–1996, banks were allowed to deduct part of the interest on loans to ESOPs from their taxable income, which encouraged lending to leveraged ESOPs. Since 1998, ESOP companies can be S corporations under federal tax law, allowing the portion of the company owned by the ESOP to be exempt from corporate income tax. In addition, several state ESOP centers were established to educate business owners and managers and to facilitate the sale of companies and company stock—largely in closely held companies—to the employees.

Despite the legislative intent of asset creation, initial studies of the performance of employee-owned companies, vis-à-vis their conventionally owned competitors, suggested that ESOPs also seemed to enhance corporate performance in terms of productivity, sales, and profitability. Initially, in the 1970s and early 1980s, the causal relationship was held to be between employee ownership per se and company performance. We know in retrospect that these studies were flawed by low response rates. Their respondents were atypical of ESOP firms (i.e., they were those companies that were most enthusiastic about their ESOPs and appeared to have had the greatest employee participation in decision making). The 1986 General Accounting Office (GAO) study, which remains the most comprehensive national study of ESOP companies ever done, found no impact of ownership on performance except in companies that combined employee involvement with employee ownership (GAO 1987). This finding has since been replicated in several dozen studies that compare participatory employee-owned firms to nonparticipatory or less participatory employee-owned companies (for summaries of this literature, see Freeman 2007; Logue and Yates 2005:7–34; and Kruse and Blasi 1997:134–6).

After an initial surge of ESOP creation between 1974 and 1990, the growth rate of ESOP company numbers slowed in the decade between 1990 and 2000, and the size of the ESOP sector has been roughly stable in the last ten years. Yet clearly the continued existence of an employee-owned sector, with a core of firms that have been employee owned for 30 years or more, permits us to test the very old, but persistent, claim that employee-owned firms cannot endure because employee-owners lack the self-discipline to defer immediate consumption in favor of long-term gain. The specifics of the charges include the following points: greed drives employee-owners to hoard their profits by hiring new workers as ordinary employees, not as co-owners, thus converting shared ownership to conventional ownership; employee-owners will undercapitalize their firm by preferring consumption to investment in new and replacement capital; employee-owners are reluctant to hire more employees who can become owners because they do not want to share the benefits of ownership; employee-owners hire too many employees in order to help their friends and family; and employee-owners simply cannot cooperate well enough to run their own firm.

Webb and Webb (1914) wrote the first criticism based on empirical data, documenting the failures of many worker cooperatives, and no doubt there was some truth in their criticisms. Nobel laureate Herbert Simon (1083:37–8) argued that democratic control of firms by employees would lead to undesirable consequences for the firm and for society at large, bluntly stating, "An employee's view of what is a good day's work is not always the same as his employer's." He argued for "market control" of firms (as though worker-managed firms are not subject to the market). Scholarly literature revealing a similarly dark view of the possibilities of agricultural and other cooperatives is reviewed in Logue and Yates (2005: 41–3).

Not all ESOPs flourish or endure. Indeed, judging from the results reported in this chapter, only a minority do. Why should this matter? It matters in part because ESOPs can help to maintain small businesses in local communities, contributing to the creativity, diversity, and resilience of capitalism. By preserving small firms, ESOPs help to buffer harm done at the extremes of business cycles. It also matters because ESOPs are a means of redistributing wealth by creating more owners and also more wealth within the framework of capitalism. Finally, employee ownership bypasses the welfare state by enabling citizens of little wealth to build it through their own efforts, with minimal involvement by government. All this arises from a slight change in a legal system that already supports private ownership of enterprise.

What are the structures and behaviors that enable some ESOP companies to survive and prosper while others fall by the wayside? While we know a great deal about the salutary effects of employee participation in employee-owned companies through cross-sectional data (snapshots at single points in time), we do not know very much about how ESOP companies develop over time. There are no longitudinal studies of groups of ESOPs in the literature. Indeed, there are not even cross-sectional studies over time of the same ESOP populations. This chapter seeks to provide some insight into the longitudinal development of ESOP companies (i.e., change in the same companies over time) in a single ESOP population—that of Ohio—over 20 years. We believe that Ohio's experience with ESOPs is fairly reflective of U.S. ESOPs as a whole. While not a perfect mirror of the nation, Ohio is a state that is close to the national averages on many statistics. Its economy is diversified enough to stand in for the national economy, and, as in the rest of the United States, most ESOPs were established by small business owners who found selling to their employees a more attractive choice than the alternatives, even while a small number of buyouts of distressed companies grabbed most of the headlines. Ohio is a little more unionized than the United States as a whole, and companies in our 2005 study are probably a little more unionized than the state generally. When 12.5% of the national workforce was unionized in 2005, Ohio reported 16% unionized, which can be roughly compared with the 20% of firms with unions in the 2005 study (BLS 2010b). In one respect, however, Ohio is different. Drawing on IRS Form 5500 data, we found that Ohio's ESOPs resemble the nation's in terms of median numbers of employees in the company and median ESOP plan value per participant, but the median Ohio plan had about twice as many participants as the national median.

To provide insight into the longitudinal development of ESOPs, this chapter draws on a unique data set: three total population surveys of Ohio ESOPs conducted by the Ohio Employee Ownership Center (OEOC) in 1985–1986, 1992–1993, and 2004–2006.[1] We will refer to the surveys, respectively, as the 1986 survey, the 1993 survey, and the 2005 survey, as these were the years when the majority of the reports were made.

The estimated population of ESOPs in Ohio was 168 when the 1986 survey was conducted, 275 at the time of the 1993 survey, and 330 at the time of the 2005 survey. The longitudinal data collected in the three surveys provide the opportunity to investigate the key question of the long-term viability of participatory employee-owned firms. It also offers the opportunity to explore what drives changes in employee-owned companies. How does public policy affect them? Is there a "natural" development process among ESOP companies apart from changes driven by law? Over time, do they tend to communicate more extensively, to train more actively, to become more participative on the shop floor or in the work unit and more democratic in firm governance? Or do they backslide? We wonder if they tend to include more of their employees in the ESOP and about the fate of union-organized firms. We are also interested in changes in levels of payroll contribution as ESOP firms finish paying off their acquisition debt: Do they continue to make significant contributions to build accounts for new employees? Or do they restrict ownership primarily to the original employee-owners? And, in the end, what is their fate: to continue as ESOP companies, to be sold for a one-time cash benefit for employee-owners, to terminate employee ownership before it can build significant wealth, or to fail at business?

To track the developmental process inside individual companies, we profile the general characteristics of companies for which we have multiple survey records, looking at both stability and change, and we compare them to other companies that appeared in just one survey. Next, we document their remarkable success in creating wealth for the employee-owners. Then, we try to explain that achievement in terms of what the companies may have done to bring about their success. Finally, we look at their fate—what has happened to ESOP companies over the years.

Methodology and Data

We combined the survey data with IRS Form 5500 filing data from 1993–1994 and 2004–2006, matching plans to survey data and each other by Employer Identification Number and plan number. We will refer to these as the IRS 1993 and 2005 data, as the majority were filed in those years. To conduct each survey, we first sought to create a list of all ESOP companies in Ohio. The exact number of such companies at the time of each survey is something of a guess. Business dynamism is the norm for American capitalism, and reporting—even to the IRS—is incomplete. The development of usable data sets generates additional errors. In the first two surveys, it was often difficult to determine which companies even had ESOPs.

We created an initial list for the 2005 survey from all companies that had ever responded to an OEOC survey, along with all companies listed in recent prior IRS Form 5500 reports (Larkspur Data Resources, versions 8.2, issued in 2001, and 9.1, issued in 2003). Dates of reports for Ohio ESOPs and stock bonus plans ranged from December 1996–November 2001. Once we had the initial list, we called each firm to determine if it had an ESOP and to identify the most appropriate respondent, and then mailed an extensive survey instrument. Those who did not respond received a second survey by mail, followed up with one or several telephone calls. The methodologies of our 1986 and 1993 surveys are discussed at some length in Logue and Rogers (1989:9–12) and in Appendix 1 of Logue and Yates (2001:181–89), respectively. We observe that over time, the effectiveness of telephone follow-up has declined with the spread of voice mail systems, which have become the 21st-century equivalent of the dead letter office.

For the 2005 study, surveys went out in two waves. The first, to 403 companies in late July 2004, included all companies with ESOPs, leveraged ESOPs, and stock bonus plans with more than three participants, as well as to companies that responded to previous studies in 1986 and 1993. Companies with initial plan filings were excluded, but those with recently terminated plans were included, in the hope that they would reflect on the recent experience of their ESOPs. A second wave of mailings followed, directed to additional ESOP and stock bonus plan filings identified in later Form 5500 reports through November 2004 (Larkspur Data Resources, version 10.2), and to companies known by OEOC staff to have been exploring employee ownership or to have said they established an ESOP but were not included in the Larkspur databases. In all, 567 companies were contacted.

Later, using the most recent Form 5500 data (Larkspur Data Resources, version 12.1) available to us, we were able to update the source of some nonresponses (principally ESOP terminations). Since we had cast our net to include all respondents to our two previous surveys (whether they had continued to provide Form 5500 filings or not), we had a higher rate of firms that could not be located, were now headquartered out of state, had terminated the ESOP because they had been sold, or had failed as businesses than we otherwise would have anticipated had we limited ourselves to more recent 5500 filings. (Twenty-nine percent of the 567 fell in these categories versus 7% in 1986 and 16% in 1993.) The number that denied having an ESOP currently or ever, or had terminated the ESOP for reasons other than having been sold or gone out of business, was comparable to other surveys (22% in 2005 versus 20% in 1986 and 30% in 1993). Ultimately, the list was culled to 264 firms believed to have ESOPs. Table 1 offers details about the development of the respondent lists for all three surveys. Judging by the percentage of 2010 Ohio's Employee-Owned Network ("Network") member firms that have been ESOPs since 2003 or earlier but did not appear on the list of 264, we believe that at least 10% more ESOPs in fact exist than we were able to locate at the time of the survey.

TABLE 1
Responses to Survey Mailings and Calls, 1983–2006.

Status	1986	1993	2005
Total companies thought to have ESOPs	168	518	567
Duplicate listings	0	28	0
Could not be located	11	51	105
Now headquartered outside Ohio	0	0	14
"Possible ESOP companies" located	157	439	448
Those that responded or were found through Form 5500			
"No longer or never an ESOP"	33	77	80
Have 401(k) or converted to 401(k)	—	—	7
Sold	—	—	27
ESOP terminated or dissolved	—	76	47
Closed/bankrupt	—	6	16
Those remaining believed to have ESOP	124	280	271
Had direct share ownership/co-op	—	—	3
Merged with another ESOP	0	—	4
Could not confirm existence of plan	—	10	—
Those still believed to have ESOP	124	270	264
Have/had ESOP but did not respond	54	42	94
Refused to respond	6	22	51
Stated "plan inactive"	—	7	1
Provided baseline data by phone	—	32	—
Answered survey questionnaire	64	167	118
Survey respondents as % of "those still believed to have ESOP"	52%	62%	45%

The response rate from this overall group of 264 was 45%, and we are concerned about the rate of return. There is clear evidence that surveys of ESOP companies with low rates of return include more companies that are enthusiastic about their ESOPs. Those tend to be companies with relatively high levels of employee participation in decision making and governance as well as relatively high levels of employee ownership. As in 1993, firms responding later in the survey period were slightly less favorable on the impact of the ESOP. For the 2005 survey, the Pearson correlation coefficient between the order of survey return and impact of the ESOP (assuming those who are more enthusiastic return their surveys earlier) was a statistically significant –0.333.

As in 1993, respondents were more likely to be members of Ohio's Employee-Owned Network. Of the 2005 respondents, 40% were or had been in the network, compared with total network membership over the years of roughly 20% of all ESOPs surveyed. By definition, network companies tend to be more interested in participative management, because the main benefit of membership is low-cost training for employees. In addition, the respondents were more likely to be small companies and less likely to be publicly traded companies listed on the large exchanges.

The data were self-reported by company executives who had some role in ESOP administration. The disadvantages of such self-reporting are well known, but there is no other way to investigate the internal organizational structure of employee-owned companies. Comparisons between self-reporting on our survey and public record information in the Form 5500 filings suggest that the survey reporting is accurate. Of course, Form 5500 also reflects self-reporting. Presumably, self-reporting to the IRS, however, is more reliable than reporting in a survey.

Profile of Cohorts and Comparison Groups

With the data from the 2005 study, longitudinal data for as many as 20 years became available for 37 Ohio ESOP companies, which were about 20% of all of Ohio's still-viable ESOP plans in 2005 that were established earlier than 1992. With these data, we could trace developments in the practices and organizational structures of companies where the ESOP had "matured," in the sense that any initial acquisition debt had been paid, a substantial fraction of the workforce were likely to be "founding participants" nearing retirement age, and the company had weathered at least one economic cycle, meaning that it had survived at least one downturn of economic activity, one peak, and the transitions in between.

We did not have detailed expectations of what we would find, but from interaction with network companies and other companies the OEOC has assisted, we did expect that the companies would grow in employment and wealth, that more companies would become majority owned by their employees, and, as a consequence, they would become more participatory in decision making and more democratic in governance over the years. Nine companies had data for both 1986 and 2005, and seven of them provided data for all three surveys. These nine are the older cohort. Twenty-eight companies provided data for 1993 and 2005. These are the younger cohort. Companies in the two cohorts resemble each other in many ways, being almost entirely closely held, established by a retiring owner, mostly in manufacturing or construction, with a small labor force, and a little more likely than companies not in the cohorts to embrace the philosophy that "employees deserve to be owners, and we would have a plan even if there were no tax incentives to share ownership." However, with respect to other characteristics, they seem to be at different points in development, especially in terms of the percentage of the company owned by the ESOP and S corporation status.

Older and Younger Cohorts Compared. All of the older cohort were closely held, as were 96% of the younger cohort. The median year for establishing the ESOP in the older cohort was 1980; for the younger cohort, it was 1986.

For both cohorts reporting in 2005, a retiring owner was the most common reason for establishing the ESOP—89% of the older cohort, and 77% of the younger cohort. The next most common reason given was a philosophical commitment to employee ownership, mentioned by 22% of older cohort and 46% of the younger. Other reasons mentioned by two to ten cohort companies as a major or minor reason for establishing the ESOP included establishing another benefit plan (10), a desire for participative management (7), reducing borrowing costs (6), corporate divestiture (3), company expansion (2), averting a takeover bid (2), or bargained in union contract (2). The public often associates employee ownership with failed efforts to rescue floundering firms, but just one of the older cohort and one of the younger cohort reported in 2005 that the ESOP was established to avert shutdown or job loss. A little more than half of the older cohort (56%) and about a third (32%) of the younger cohort gave up wages or benefits, or converted another retirement plan to establish the ESOP.

About half of each cohort was in manufacturing: 55% of the older and 46% of the younger. About a quarter of the older cohort (22%) was in wholesaling, compared with 7% of the younger, and about a tenth of the older cohort (11%) and a sixth (18%) of the younger were in construction. Other cohort companies were distributed over a variety of industries, including arboriculture, banking, business or professional services, insurance, retail, and transportation.

The older cohort reported a median of 125 employees in 1986; the younger, a median of 140 in 1993. By 2005, the older cohort median increased to 220 employees, while the younger cohort rose to 210. In all, the older cohort employed 2,564 in 1986 and 2,717 in 2005. The younger cohort employed 10,112 in 1993 and 12,176 in 2005. A third of the older cohort was unionized, compared with 29% of the younger, but just 11% of each cohort included union members in the ESOP.

The cohort companies saw steady growth in the percentage of their company that was owned by the ESOP (Table 2). There is some evidence of such growth, but it is much more modest.

TABLE 2

Percentage of Ownership by Cohort and Comparison Group (Number of Companies Is Indicated in Parentheses).

	Survey year		
	1985–86	1992–93	2004–06
Median percentage of ownership			
1986–2005 cohort (9)	37.5% (8)	56% (7)	100% (9)
1992–2005 cohort (28)		52% (27)	80% (28)
Others, surveyed in 1986, 1993, or 2005	15% (51)	28% (125)	35% (80)
	20% (33)*	—	—
Percentage 100% owned by the ESOP			
1986–2005 cohort (9)	25% (8)	29% (7)	56% (9)
1993–2005 cohort (28)	—	4% (27)	29% (28)
Others, surveyed in 1986, 1993, or 2005	2% (51)	6% (125)	17% (80)

*Excluding 5 anonymous PAYSOPs and 11 that had PAYSOPs and terminated employee ownership after tax policy benefits expired.

In 1986, two in the older cohort had established PAYSOPs, but in contrast to most PAYSOPs, these continued as ordinary ESOPs after the tax credits expired. In 2005, 89% of the older cohort were S corporations, compared with 39% of the younger cohort and 42% of others surveyed.

Philosophically, firms in the older cohort had moved from near universal skepticism about the ESOP, with just one stating that the "best reason for setting up the ESOP" was "we believe employees deserved to be owners, and we would have set up a plan even if there were no tax incentives to share ownership," to more acceptance, with a third agreeing by 2004–2006 that "employees deserve to be owners, etc. . . ." (Questions on philosophy were first used by Rosen, Klein, and Young 1986:73–84.) In the younger cohort, about a third reported that "employees deserve to be owners." in both 1993 (37%) and 2005 (36%).

Cohort Companies Compared with Others Surveyed. Were the cohort companies fundamentally different from other companies surveyed? The most obvious way in which they were different is that all companies in the cohorts still had ESOPs and were still in business at the time of the 2005 survey, compared with 24% of other companies surveyed in 1986 and 29% of other companies surveyed in 1993. (We will examine the fate of ESOP companies in more detail at the end of this chapter.) Despite their exceptionally long survival, in the early years of their ESOPs, the companies in each cohort looked very much like other companies surveyed at the same time, with some interesting exceptions. In terms of number of employees, median annual sales, rate of unionization, economic sector, and vesting schedules, they resembled other ESOP companies. However, from our earliest picture of them, the cohort companies were more likely to be majority owned than other companies in each survey, and this becomes more so as time passes. They were also more debt averse. Although their rate of leveraging was about the same as other companies in the 1986 (older cohort) and 1993 (younger cohort) surveys, by 2005, just 13% of the older cohort were leveraged, compared with about a quarter of the younger cohort and nearly three quarters of other companies surveyed. The companies in the cohorts were also somewhat more likely to report that the reason for establishing the ESOP was a retiring owner, while others leaned toward reasons such as participative management, a philosophical commitment to employee ownership, or reducing borrowing costs. In the older cohort, the median percentage of employees who were in the ESOP was consistently slightly higher than the younger cohort or the other companies surveyed. The older cohort were more likely to report that replacement of another plan was a reason for establishing the ESOP and, in the first two surveys, they were less likely to mention a philosophical commitment to employee ownership. They were also more likely to have given up future wages or benefits in order to establish the ESOP.

Growth of Wealth. One of the most remarkable developments revealed by the longitudinal survey was the growth of account values (Table 3). Within each cohort, the value per participant of ESOP accounts grew more rapidly than inflation, stock market investments, or the value per participant in other ESOP companies. Per-participant values should be read mindfully: the benefits of shared capitalism are often not equally distributed (Carberry 2010). For 1985–1986 in Table 3, we used information the companies reported directly to us. Otherwise, we used IRS Form 5500 data because they were more complete. The older cohort's total wealth in the ESOP was $266 million by 2005. Wealth of the younger cohort, which had their ESOPs for a shorter time, was $272 million.

The growth of employee wealth in fact understates the total wealth created through the ESOPs, since almost every firm that existed over time would have made distributions from the ESOP trust to retirees, survivors, and employees who separated from the firm prior to retirement age.

How did the cohort companies achieve such success as mostly "Rust Belt," "old economy," or "sunset" manufacturing and construction

TABLE 3
ESOP Value per Participant and Net Assets, Comparing Survey Data and IRS Form
5500, by Cohort and Comparison Group.

	Survey year		
		1993	2005
	1986	IRS Form 5500	IRS Form 5500
	Self-reported	(circa 1993)	(circa 2005)
1986–2005 cohort (9 in all)			
Median	$12,039	$42,277	$64,837
Range	$2,500 to	$10,651 to	$11,102 to
	$200,000	$217,067	$224,322
(n)	(8)	(9)	(9)
1993–2005 cohort (28 in all)			
Median			
Range	n.a.	$18,147	$53,362
(n)		–$430 to	–$1,574 to
		$114,705	$219,417
		(24)	(27)
Others, surveyed in 1986,° 1993, or 2005			
Median	$3,897	$14,539	$26,336
Range	$0 to	–$10,685 to	–$4,123 to
	$100,000	$170,243	$316,679
(n)	(33)	(91)	(67)

°PAYSOPs excluded.

companies, with many blue-collar workers with little or no college education? We now turn to possible explanations of this record of success.

How They Survived and Prospered: Participative Management and Fiscal Prudence

In most cases, ESOPs are a "get rich slow" plan where employees build value in retirement accounts by building their companies. We have witnessed some companies in Ohio's Employee-Owned Network doing just exactly that and providing substantial sums at retirement for long-serving employees. If the ESOP does not remain in place for a long period of time, employees have much less opportunity to benefit, even if they make exceptional sacrifices and efforts to improve their companies. Considering this, the rapidity with which some ESOPs are established and vanish is astonishing. One wonders if the only beneficiary may have been the seller, the financial professional who set up the ESOP in the first place, or a management buyout group that "flipped" the company. An inquiry into four tranches of Form 5500 reports from

Ohio's ESOP and stock bonus companies from 1993–2001 revealed that 205 ESOPs had endured for a decade and were still viable in 2001. In the same period, 37 terminated the ESOP, 123 ESOPs were started and continued through the end of the period, and 99 were established and terminated within an interval of just eight years (Yates 2004). Some of the 205 were members of the Network, allowing us to inquire informally, as the opportunity arose, about what they thought helped them to survive and prosper. Along with many specifics, their replies pointed in two general directions: the first, participative management; the second, business caution and fiscal prudence, particularly in borrowing, acquisition, and expansion.

Participative Management: Training, Communication, Work-Unit Involvement, and Governance Participation

From the mid-1980s to the present, the fruitful combination of participative management and employee ownership has been documented and studied (GAO 1987; Blasi, Freeman, Mackin, and Kruse 2008). There are three essential elements that a participative management strategy must include if it is to improve ESOP firm operations and financial returns. These elements are training, communication, and participation. Training helps employees develop the skills and knowledge to understand their jobs, the company, and the business context in which it operates. Communication provides specific information about the company's performance and passes timely information to the employees so they can react promptly and effectively. Participation gives employees practices and structures through which to act on their knowledge in their work units and in the governance of their company.

Benefits can be gained from introducing limited aspects of communication, training, or participation, but the benefit is maximized when many specific techniques are used together (Logue and Yates 2001:138–42). At OEOC annual conferences, managers often remark that finding the right mix of techniques requires some experimentation. There seems to be no particular technique or focused approach that always works to maximize the potential of employee ownership. Effective management tailors training, communication, and participation to the specific conditions of the firm. Those who succeed often say that they "just kept trying things" until they found out what worked. When participative management succeeds, the members of the enterprise develop a sense of ownership and a shared culture, and they contribute to success in hundreds of small and large actions. For example, from staff experience, we have heard about one-time events that are difficult to capture in surveys, such as a department that reorganized its warehouse to reduce labor costs and speed up deliveries, or an employee-owner committee that pointed the way to a profitable new product line. In addition, our research indicates a beneficial impact of the ESOP in areas where only changes in employee behavior could account for the improvement, such as lower turnover or better labor–management relations (Logue and Yates 2001:37).

Simecek (2001, 2008, 2010) offered a brief practical and philosophical road map to developing a healthy culture of ownership by discovering and rewarding employee behavior that builds trust and cooperation. Some companies build culture with a surprisingly large number of committees that somehow do not seem to reduce productivity even though people must take time away from their direct job responsibilities. We suspect that work time lost to committee work is recovered for the bottom line through some combination of keeping the focus on creating wealth, maintaining interest in work, generating new ideas, and coordinating activity by sharing knowledge.

Because it is not entirely clear that some techniques reliably work better than others, we measured training, communication, and participation with simple indices that count how many different techniques a company has used over time. At a minimum, this measure suggests how actively a company is trying to develop its culture of ownership, since the introduction of any new practice is an investment of employees' paid time and may also entail capital costs for the firm.

Communication. Expectations for more and better communication are almost universal in this digital age. In 1993, five choices of methods of communication a company might have used were offered in the survey; by 2005, eleven choices were listed. An increased number of choices was necessary because of changes in business practices and communications technology. We report the median number of communication methods used by the cohorts and the comparison groups in Table 4. It is not surprising to find that most ESOP companies surveyed in 2005 were using four or more methods of communication. Two companies even reported using all eleven methods in 2005. It appears that the number of methods used grew gradually. By 2005, the medians of the cohort companies resembled those of other companies surveyed that year. Where the cohorts stood out was in being more likely to provide financial communication about the performance of the company (86% of the older cohort and 58% of the younger cohort in 2005, compared with 36% of others surveyed in 2005); to hold annual, quarterly, or monthly meetings with employees (89% of the older cohort and 68% of the younger cohort reported holding annual meetings in 2005, compared with 53% of others surveyed; 78% of the older cohort and 68%

TABLE 4

Median Communication Techniques by Cohorts and Comparison Groups (Number Responding to the Item Is Indicated in Parentheses).

| | 1993 survey original 5 techniques | | 2005 survey 11 possible techniques | |
	Before ESOP	Since ESOP	Before ESOP	Since ESOP
1986–2005 cohort	3 (5)	3 (7)	2 (9)	4 (9)
1993–2005 cohort	1 (27)	2 (27)	2 (28)	5 (28)
Others, surveyed in 1993	1 (106)	2 (109)	—	—
Others, surveyed in 2005	—	—	2 (81)	4 (81)

N.b.: Missing data on the following questions was counted as "no use" of a technique if the respondent checked other techniques in the battery of choices. If the respondent skipped all of the questions in the battery, the answers were coded as "missing."

1993, Question 40: How does the company keep employee-owners informed about the business?

Before ESOP established? (Y/N)
Payroll envelope stuffer
Newsletter
Annual meeting for all employees
Monthly or quarterly meetings
Through local union

Since ESOP established? (Y/N)
Payroll envelope stuffer
Newsletter
Annual meeting for all employees
Monthly or quarterly meetings
Through local union

2005, Question 57: Check all that apply: How does the company keep employee-owners informed about the business?

Before establishing the ESOP, or 10 years ago? (Y/N)
Payroll envelope stuffer
Newsletter
Annual meeting for all employees
Monthly or quarterly meetings
Through local union
Company website
E-mail
Handouts
Bulletin boards
Team or unit meetings
Informal communication network

Since establishing the ESOP, or Now? (Y/N)
Payroll envelope stuffer
Newsletter
Annual meeting for all employees
Monthly or quarterly meetings
Through local union
Company website
E-mail
Handouts
Bulletin boards
Team or unit meetings
Informal communication network

of the younger cohort reported holding monthly or quarterly meetings, compared with 51% of the others surveyed); and to sponsor ESOP communication committees to educate employees about the ESOP (three quarters of each cohort, compared with about half of others surveyed in 2005).

Training. Ever since Japanese companies began to claim a noticeable share of American automobile and consumer electronics markets, consultants have commanded lucrative fees by promising to train U.S. workers to be more like Japanese workers. For a while, books and consultants were flooding into the market, promising to enhance profits through greater productivity, higher-quality products, and improved cooperation within work units and between rank-and-file workers and management. All that activity left behind some improvements in productivity, but at root it seems to have been more of a fad (Miller, Hartwick, and Le Breton-Miller 2004). This is largely, we believe, because it was not tied to compensation. Interestingly, many Japanese companies had ESOPs, so workplace training and participation there occurred within a context of long-term ownership (Kato 2003).

Training employees to perform their jobs effectively, to see how their efforts fit into the work of others in the enterprise, and to exercise effective cooperation and supervisory skills is essential to the success of any firm. Also helpful in employee-owned companies are two kinds of training not usually found in conventional firms: financial training that helps employee-owners to read the company's financial reports, and ownership training to understand the basics of business—what kind of decisions must be made to help a company succeed, what each employee's role is in contributing to the success of the company, and how the company's success is connected to the value of ESOP accounts (Thomas and Maxwell 2001:62–3). With financial and ownership training, employees are better able to see their firm through the eyes of management and to think like owners.

Companies in the two cohorts used training a little more than did other companies surveyed. Median numbers of training techniques used are shown in Table 5. In 1993, companies could check a maximum of six techniques; in 2005, a maximum of ten (the original six, plus four others suggested by the OEOC training staff). Perhaps what is most telling is that none of the companies in the cohorts reported that they were doing *no* training or communication, compared with other surveyed companies, where 12% to 15% reported no training at all in 1993 or 2005, even after their ESOP was in place. The cohort companies were considerably more likely to provide financial and ownership training. In 2005, two thirds of the older cohort and 54% of the younger offered financial training, compared with 42% of other companies surveyed; and three quarters of the older cohort and 64% of the younger offered ownership training, compared with 45% of the other ESOP companies.

Participation. Analysis of the 1993 data made it clear that employees regarded participation in everyday decisions in the work unit in a different light from participation in governance. Although participation in work-unit decisions had a statistically significant association

TABLE 5
Median Score on Training Methods Used, by Cohorts and Comparison Group (Number Responding to the Item Is Indicated in Parentheses).

	Six training techniques, 1993–2005			Ten training techniques, 2005 only	
	Median before ESOP was established 1993	Median since ESOP was established 1993	Median since ESOP was established 2005	Median before ESOP was established (or 10 years ago, for older ESOPs) 2005	Median since ESOP was established 2005
1986–2005 cohort	1 (6)	3 (6)	4 (8)	3 (9)	7 (9)
1993–2005 cohort	2 (28)	2 (28)	4 (28)	5 (28)	6 (28)
Others, 1993	2 (110)	2 (113)	n.a.	—	—
Others, 2005	n.a.	n.a.	3 (78)	4 (78)	5 (78)

1993, Question 35: Has your company provided any of the following forms of training for nonmanagerial employees? (Job-related training, apprenticeship program, ownership education, problem-solving training, group process training, and/or financial training)
2005, Question 50: Same as 1993, with same six options, plus informal training, basic skills training, online training, and/or coaching/mentoring.

with improved operations, it was governance, specifically nonmanagerial employees on the board of directors, that had the strongest tie to operational performance (Logue and Yates 2001:150–1). The typical employee probably can make more meaningful and informed contributions, more often, in work-unit committees, department meetings, and cross-functional teams, but nonmanagement representation on the board was more strongly correlated with greater employee interest in participation in decision making, which can be an important intervening variable linking participative management with improved operations (Yates 2000).

Shop-Floor or Work-Unit Participation. Employee involvement covers a set of techniques designed to engage the knowledge of the shop floor or work unit in improving the production process. To simplify the idea, employee involvement techniques promote information sharing, consultation, and consensus building among employees and supervisory management to reduce waste and improve efficiency. Employees acting through their work units are empowered to make some decisions without seeking approval from higher authority. In the 1993 survey, we queried respondents about some of these techniques, including quality circles, quality of work life program, problem-solving groups, labor–management participation teams, self-managing work groups, and total quality management. The programs, along with certain training, enjoyed a flowering of interest during the 1980s and 1990s as a means to compete with Japanese manufacturers.

By 2005, respondents' choices of employee involvement techniques were expanded after suggestions from OEOC staff trainers and from Network companies. The eleven choices included the original six techniques and five new techniques. Table 6 sets forth the median number of techniques used by each cohort and the other companies surveyed. Just a handful of companies in our surveys used any of the involvement techniques before establishing the ESOP. After the ESOP was established, the cohorts' use of the original six techniques increased sharply in 1993 but then declined (Table 6).

By 2005, a median of just one of the original six shop-floor involvement techniques seemed surprisingly low for cohorts that were more active than others in communication and training. The decline in use was consistent with the argument that the techniques listed in the six-variable index were fads rather than lasting methods. However, scores on the eleven-variable index in the 2005 survey suggested that the cohorts were using work-unit/shop-floor participation as much or more than before, but they were using different techniques. For example,

TABLE 6
Median Techniques Used for Employee Participation in Work-Unit/Shop-Floor Decision Making, by Cohorts and Comparison Groups (Number Responding to the Item Is Indicated in Parentheses).

	Six-variable indicator of employee involvement included in both 1993 and 2005 surveys				Eleven-variable indicator
	1993 survey, before ESOP	1993 survey, after ESOP	2005 survey, before ESOP (or 10 years ago, for older ESOPs)	2005 survey, after ESOP	2005 survey, after ESOP
1986–2005 cohort	0 (6)	2 (5)	0 (9)	1 (9)	4 (9)
1993–2005 cohort	0 (27)	2 (26)	0 (28)	1 (28)	3 (27)
Others, 1993	0 (104)	1 (93)	—	—	—
Others, 2005	n.a.	—	0 (77)	0.5 (78)	1 (75)

1993, Question 38: Does your company have any of the following involvement programs? (Quality circles, quality of worklife program, problem-solving groups, labor–management participation teams, self-managing work groups, and/or total quality management)

2005, Question 56: Same as 1993 with same six options, plus suggestion system, employee attitude survey, coaching/mentoring, joint steering committee, and/or joint management committee.

the use of a suggestion system had been included in the 1993 survey, but we did not consider it to be an "employee involvement" technique at the time. Between 1993 and 2005, its use had increased substantially in the older cohort and a little in the younger cohort. Other techniques for employee involvement included an employee attitude survey, coaching or mentoring, and the use of a joint management or joint steering committee. Respondents reported an increase in all except for the joint steering committee. The bottom line was that, in terms of overall work-unit participation, cohorts had increased their use of employee involvement, while other firms surveyed in 2005 reported low use of employee involvement before the ESOP (a median of zero), and after the ESOP, their median was just one technique, notably less than companies in the two cohorts (Table 6).

Participation in Governance. We count as participation in governance the pass-through of stock voting rights to the employees, representation of nonmanagerial employees on the board of directors, and the use of employee elections to select representatives of nonmanagerial employees. We expected that participation in governance might have spread extensively among the older companies in our latest survey. And yet, for all the power of governance participation to improve operations, most ESOP firms do not routinely establish structures that allow it. Some specific practices and structures used by companies to enable nonmanagerial employees to participate in governance are set forth in Table 7.

Pass-through voting gives full rights to vote shares to ESOP participants in closely held companies (rather than curtailing those rights as the law specifically permits). One might logically expect all 100%-employee-owned firms to pass through full stock voting rights to their employee-owners, but only about 40% do so. What is more, the longitudinal data do not suggest a tendency for the practice to spread over the years (Table 7). In the older cohort, none used pass-through voting in 1986. Since 1993, the same three companies have been using it. Eleven companies in the younger cohort passed through voting rights in both 1993 and 2005. Two firms added pass-through rights between 1993 and 2005, but one took them away in the same interval, and now its plan allows only the legally required minimum.

Three companies in the older cohort reported having nonmanagerial directors on the board in the five years prior to the 1993 and 2005 surveys, even though all but one were at or close to being 100% employee-owned. The younger cohort was a little more likely to have nonmanagerial board members in 2005 compared to 1993 (Table 7). Overall among the cohort companies with majority ownership in 2005, just half of them

TABLE 7
Governance Participation in Closely Held Companies, by Cohort and Comparison Group (Number Responding to the Item Is Indicated in Parentheses).

	1986	1993	2005
Full pass-through of voting rights°			
1986–2005 cohort	0% (9)	43% (7)	33% (9)
1993–2005 cohort	—	48% (27)	52% (25)
Others, surveyed in 1986, 1993, 2005	17% (35)	40% (97)	21% (56)
Nonmanagerial representatives on board of directors currently and last five years			
1986–2005 cohort	—	43% (7)	43% (7)
1993–2005 cohort	—	25% (28)	39% (28)
Others, surveyed in 1993, 2005	—	16% (103)	12% (66)
Number of nonmanagerial representatives on board currently and last five years			
1986–2005 cohort	—	3 (7)	9 (9)
1993–2005 cohort	—	14 (28)	20 (27)
Others surveyed in 1993, 2005	—	35 (87)	19 (59)
Nonmanagerial representatives on board of directors elected			
1986–2005 cohort	—	29% (2 of 7)	22% (2 of 9)
1993–2005 cohort	—	18% (28)	41% (27)
Others surveyed in 1993, 2005	—	11% (87)	9% (59)

°1986, Question 33 (closely held companies only): Does your ESOP voting pass through on all issues, not just the major issues required by law for closely held companies? (Yes/No)
1993, Question 34 (closely held companies only): On which issues do your ESOP participants have the right to vote their shares? Major issues (super majority issues) required by law only, major issues required by law and election of board of directors, and/or all shareholder issues?
2005, Question 49: Same as 1993.

had nonmanagerial employees on the board. Less than a quarter of other majority-owned companies did so. In addition, there has been a modest trend toward greater use of employee elections for nonmanagerial board members among the younger cohort. Companies that already had such directors were more frequently selecting them through election or other means of employee participation, an increase in use from less than 20% to about 40% of companies (Table 7). In addition, the total number of nonmanagerial employees serving on the board increased between 1993 and 2005 (Table 7). Growth in nonmanagerial board seats among the older cohort is due to increasing numbers of nonmanagerial board members among the same firms. In the younger cohort, it arose from increasing numbers of companies using the practice.

Fiscal Prudence: Debt Aversion, Investment, Wages and Benefits, Willingness to Sacrifice

Debt Aversion. In all, the cohorts seem averse to debt. In IRS Form 5500 reports from 1993, the total liabilities of the older cohort's ESOP plans were $2.7 million, and the median liability was zero. In 2005, the total liabilities of the older cohort were $28 million, but median liability was still at zero. In the younger cohort in 1993, 19 companies reported plan liabilities totaling $11.1 million with median liability of $150,000. By 2005, 14 companies reported plan liabilities totaling $4.4 million, but none had debt over $1 million, and the median was $1,200.

A way to see fiscal prudence in action in the cohort companies is to visit their facilities, as most OEOC staff members have done over nearly 25 years of the center's existence. There are no grand corporate headquarters. Facilities tend to be clean, functional, and plain, often with signs of wear. Employees care for their equipment meticulously and make do with existing tools and machines if they can. When new equipment is needed, employees often build it themselves. One Ohio company is legendary for operating machines that are beyond ancient—a few are a century old. They have been maintained, had worn parts replaced, and some have been refitted to run in a more or less automated fashion. The ancient machines have a Dickensian feel, but the shop floor is not crowded. Instead of Dickens's ragged children and maimed adults tending these hard-working relics, each booted and hardhatted minder tends a flock of rattling, clacking artifacts from the great age of industry. Fiscal prudence, however, is more than resourceful maintenance of capital goods.

Only our latest Ohio survey examined investment, wage, and benefit strategies compared with the companies' industries. We summarize our findings below.

Investment. A third to half of the cohort companies reported higher investment than their industry, compared with about a quarter of others surveyed in 2005.

Pay. About two fifths (43%) of the older cohort and a quarter (29%) of the younger cohort reported that they paid wages better than industry. About a quarter (26%) of the other companies in 2005 did the same. Blasi, Freeman, Mackin, and Kruse (2008:18) found that paying wages at or above market levels complemented the positive impact of high-performance human resource policies and shared capitalism.

TABLE 8
Contributions to the ESOP as Percentage of Payroll, by Cohort and Comparison
Group (Number Responding to the Item Is Indicated in Parentheses).

	1986	1993	2005
Median contribution to ESOP "last year"			
1986–2005 cohort	15.0% (9)	10.0% (7)	12.25% (8)
1993–2005 cohort		10.0% (25)	4.4% (20)
Others, 1986 (PAYSOPs and TRASOPs excluded)	0.75% (31)	—	—
Others, 1993 and 2005 (most reported for 2002)	—	6.05% (104)	1.1% (60)
Median contribution to ESOP "this year"			
1986–2005 cohort	15.0% (9)	10.0% (7)	12.25% (8)
1993–2005 cohort		9.0% (25)	5.0% (20)
Others, 1986 (PAYSOPs and TRASOPs excluded)	2.8% (31)	—	—
Others, 1993 and 2005	—	6.0% (107)	4.0% (61)

Benefits. Almost all of the companies reported offering better benefits than the industry. Part of this is a simple ESOP effect: ESOPs were generally added to other existing benefit plans, thereby increasing benefits. Fully 89% of Ohio ESOP companies responding to the 2005 survey maintained another retirement plan in addition to the ESOP. The younger cohort was the most likely to say that benefits were better than the industry average (69% compared with 43% of the older cohort).

Contributions to the ESOP. Long-lived ESOP companies have had more than usual experience with financial sacrifice. Older cohort companies consistently contributed a higher percentage of payroll than the younger cohorts, and considerably more than the other surveyed companies, even with PAYSOPs and TRASOPs excluded in 1986 (Table 8).

Other Sacrifices and Concessions. In addition, many in the two cohorts began life as employee-owned firms with weaker pension plans, arising from sacrifices made to initiate the ESOP. In 1986, five of the nine (56%) in the older cohort gave up a pension or profit-sharing plan or made other concessions to establish the ESOP. In 1993, 13 of 28 in the younger cohort (46%) did the same. Less than a third (29%) of other companies surveyed in 2005 reported making a sacrifice to acquire their company.

Impact of the ESOP on Employees' Interest in Participation, Company Operations, and Financial Performance

Participatory management and fiscal prudence cannot make a substantial impression if the employees do not become interested in implementing them. In analysis of the 1993 data, interest in participating in decision making emerged as an important intervening variable between efforts to improve the company and the impact of those efforts on operations and profits (Logue and Yates 2001:150–1; Yates 2000). The variable may be a surrogate for what Pierce, Kostova, and Dirks (2003:86) called psychological ownership "that state[s] where an individual feels as though the target of ownership or a piece of that target is 'theirs.'" We recognize that there are more powerful factors, especially economic factors, that influence performance and profits, but many of them are beyond the control of anyone in the company. The question for employee-owners must be "What can *we* do?" The will to ask that question and act on the answer begins with a change in interest.

Interest in Participation in Decision Making

In 1986, employees at the companies in the older cohort were already expressing greater interest in decision making than other companies (Table 9).

ESOP managers speak of an arc of interest among employee-owners—little interest at first because of little knowledge, then inflated expectations, followed by disillusion with low account balances. Then, as employees' account values grow, enthusiasm and interest revives (Seymour 2010). In the cohort companies, however, reports of increased interest did not fall back to pre-ESOP numbers or even as low as the other companies in each survey. What made the difference? We suspect that it was earlier efforts made toward developing the company with participative management. Our 1993 study showed strong correlations between participative management and interest in participating in decision making (Logue and Yates 2001:151).

TABLE 9

Employee Interest in Playing a Greater Role in Decision Making, by Cohort and Comparison Group (Number Responding to the Item Is Indicated in Parentheses).

	Greater interest	Much greater or mild increase	
	1986	1993	2005
1986–2005 cohort	37% (8)	71% (7)	63% (8)
1993–2005 cohort	—	82% (28)	64% (28)
Others, surveyed in 1986, 1993, 2005	26% (51)	54% (128)	54% (81)

1986, Question 31: Since the establishment of your ESOP, have employees expressed interest in playing a greater role in decision making? (Yes/No)

1993, Question 33: Since the establishment of your ESOP, have employees expressed an interest in playing a greater role in decision making? (Much greater interest, mild increase in interest, no change in interest, mild decrease in interest, much less interest)

2005, Question 48: Since the establishment of your ESOP or in the last ten years, have employees expressed an interest in playing a greater role in decision making? (Same choices as 1993)

Company Operations

Respondents were queried on the impact of the ESOP in 15 specific areas: absenteeism, manager–worker communication, job performance, worker job satisfaction, product quality, turnover, motivation, productivity, working conditions, customer service, employee participation, profitability, labor–management relations, production costs, and employee attitudes in general. Between the 1986 survey and the 1993 survey, judgments about the impact of the ESOP became more positive and remained so into the 2005 survey. Particularly improved was the impact on absenteeism and turnover, as well as on-the-job performance and product quality. Favorable impacts did not march forward in unison across all variables, but there were increases over time in both cohorts. Overall, the cohorts reported a more favorable impact of the ESOP than did the other companies in the two surveys.

Employment

As noted above, employment in the cohorts grew overall in a general context of decline in manufacturing jobs. Employment roughly matched Ohio's employment growth in the older cohort and was roughly twice the rate of the state's growth among the younger cohort. Among the manufacturers in the cohorts, employment grew slightly among the older cohort and declined slightly among the younger cohort so that, overall, between 1993 and 2005, there was a net loss of 3.5% of manufacturing jobs in the cohort companies, while in Ohio as a whole during the same period, manufacturing employment declined by 17% (BLS 2010a).

Number of Participants

One of the more remarkable findings of our analysis is growth in the number of ESOP participants. Participants in the older cohort grew by 90%, almost doubling between 1986 and 2005, while the younger cohorts' participants increased by 58% between 1993 and 2005. The growth was not in just one or two companies but generally spread across the board and appears to be the result of increasing employment, acquisitions that brought more participants into the ESOP, increases in retirees or their beneficiaries with active accounts in the ESOP, and, perhaps in the case of one company, a surge of retirements paralleling declining employment. Regardless of the causes, the increase in participants made more people eligible to receive wealth. What is more, the increase in participants took place while the median company's per-participant account value was growing. The pattern of growth in participants was mirrored in IRS Form 5500 data for all Ohio ESOPs, although much of the increase there can be attributed to six large firms.

Profits

In our three surveys, 63% to 72% of the cohort companies reported a favorable impact of the ESOP on profitability, compared with less than half of the other companies surveyed. In both the 1993 and 2005 surveys, a subtler measure of profit was taken by asking the companies how they were doing compared with their industries before the ESOP and since (or in the last ten years for older ESOPs in the 2005 survey). Furthermore, a measure of change in the company's profitability versus that of the industry was calculated by subtracting the "before" position from the "after" position, measuring whether companies improved their profit position within their industry after adopting the ESOP, or in the previous ten years for older ESOPs. This measured change over time and also provided a control for the reality that some industries are more profitable than others. The change measure usefully identifies companies that are upwardly and downwardly mobile within their industries. Each measure has its merits and uses. Considering their different wording and conceptual context, returns from the different measures of profitability were fairly consistent (Table 10).

All companies in the older cohort were at or above their industry in profitability, and none were below it. The younger cohort was approaching that pattern in 2005.

Stock Value

Since most of Ohio's ESOP companies are closely held, their stock value is set by professional valuators rather than by stock market trades. The valuators take into consideration a number of variables, including profits, the value of comparable companies, the health of the industry, debt and asset levels, and the value of likely future earnings. The annual valuation is reflected in the dollar value of participants' ESOP accounts at diversification, retirement, or other events that enable them to convert part or all of their holdings to cash. For employee-owners in publicly traded companies, the stock market sets the value of their shares. The median growth in share value in the cohort companies was not notably better than the comparison companies, but the cohorts were less likely to report large losses (Table 11).

Most companies were upbeat about the performance of their stock value in the 2005 study. Of companies in the 1986–2004 cohort, 78% ($n = 9$) said stock value had increased somewhat or substantially, as did

TABLE 10
Profits and Change in Profit Position vs. Industry, by Cohort and Comparison Group
(Number Responding to the Item Is Indicated in Parentheses).

	1986	1993	2005
Profits better than industry since			
ESOP was adopted/In last 10 years			
1986–2005 cohort	43% (7)	29% (7)	43% (7)
1993–2005 cohort	—	48% (28)	52% (27)
Others, surveyed in 1986, 1993, or 2005	35% (49)	40% (118)	41% (71)
Profits same or better than industry			
since ESOP was adopted/In last 10 years			
1986–2005 cohort	100% (7)	100% (7)	100% (7)
1993–2005 cohort	—	81% (27)	96% (27)
Others, surveyed in 1986, 1993, or 2005	84% (49)	86% (118)	83% (71)
Improved profit position relative			
to the industry			
1986–2005 cohort	n.a.	29% (7)	14% (7)
1993–2005 cohort	—	41% (27)	37% (27)
Others, surveyed in 1986, 1993, or 2005	n.a.	20% (113)	26% (65)

1986, Question 26: Since the establishment of your ESOP, how has your firm's rate of profit compared to that of your industry? (Considerably higher, somewhat higher, about the same, somewhat lower, considerably lower)

1993, Question 30: How has your firm's rate of profit compared to that of your industry before establishing the ESOP and since establishing the ESOP? (Choices same as 1986)

2005, Question 41: Same question as 1993 (Choices same as 1986)

82% (*n* = 28) of the 1993–2005 cohort. Of others from 2005, 58% (*n* = 79) said their stock increased somewhat or substantially.

Wealth Creation

We return to the growth of employee account values because they are the touchstone of the ESOP concept. "Father of the ESOP" Louis Kelso's view was that account values were the main benefit of ESOPs, not "acting like an owner" or participating in the management and governance of the business. It was Senator Russell Long who saw that employee stock ownership would turn employees into owners in terms of their attitudes as well as their wallets (McIntyre 2003). The record of wealth generation by the cohorts presented in Table 3 is quite impressive. To check that record more carefully, we examined only those firms with IRS data on account value in both 1993 and 2005. The medians are very close to the median for each cohort as a whole, suggesting that missing data have not substantially distorted the results.

TABLE 11
Median° and Range of Mean Stock Change, by Cohort and Comparison Group
(Number Responding to the Item Is Indicated in Parentheses).

	Two-year average 1983–1984	Three-year average 1989–1991	Three-year average 2001–2003
	1986	1993	2005
1986–2005 cohort			
Median	16.5% (9)	5.0% (7)	6.0% (6)
Range	–6.0 to 45.5%	–13.1 to 17.7%	0.31 to 32.3%
1993–2005 cohort			
Median	n.a.	7.0% (21)	4.8% (23)
Range		–20.0 to 16.3%	–12.7 to 75.7%
Others, surveyed in 1986, 1993, or 2005			
Median	7.0% (41)	7.5% (103)	5.5% (53)
Range	–30.0 to 37.5%	–29.5 to 400.0%	–71.7 to 232.7%

°Average stock change was calculated to create a single summary measure for each company. The medians of those averages are shown in Table 10.
1986, Question 19: What has been the annual change in the stock price value over the last two years?
1993, Question 21: What has been the percentage of change in the annual stock value over the last three years? (As of 12/31/91, as of 12/31/90, as of 12/31/89)
2005, Question 26: What has been the annual percentage of change in your company's stock value? (2001, 2002, 2003)

Dividend Income

Another way to assess the performance of a company is by the dividends it pays. Kelso envisioned an income stream of corporate dividends for workers with stock ownership. About 40% of companies in the older cohort paid dividends in 1993 and about 20% did so in 2005. About a quarter of the younger cohort paid dividends in 1993, and about 40% did so in the 2005 survey. Among other companies surveyed, about a quarter in each survey reported dividends.

Impact of ESOPs: Summing Up

What, then, is the overall impact of the ESOP in the judgment of our respondents? It is quite favorable, and more favorable among those companies that have had it in place for more than 15 years. It is important to emphasize that the ESOP companies that participated in the survey were probably among the more satisfied and successful. However, evidence discussed in the next section raises questions about that likelihood. It reveals that many surveyed companies terminated their ESOPs, even though their companies continued in business, showing that, while ESOPs do not cause business failures, many ESOPs fail to "take" for a variety of reasons, and perhaps the surveyed companies were not as satisfied with their ESOPs as we had imagined.

The Fate of ESOP Companies

In examining what works and what does not in ESOP companies, and how they change over time, one question always hovers in the background: What happened to the companies that did not respond to our surveys and to those that did respond once but never reappeared? Were there systematic differences in their outcomes that set them apart from the regular survey participants? To understand more completely what shapes the fate of ESOP companies that succeed and those that fail, we researched the fate of the ESOP in every company that had participated in any of the three surveys, along with every other company that indicated on the 1993 IRS Form 5500 that it had an ESOP or stock bonus plan.

A variety of means—telephone calls, Internet searches, and queries to OEOC staff—were employed to ascertain what had happened to each company that had ever been surveyed and those that appeared to be viable in 1993. "Viability" was approximated by a report of some number of employees, even zero, in the 1993 IRS Form 5500 data. By that criterion, we eliminated 217 companies, leaving 224 companies that said they had ESOPs but responded in writing to neither the 1986 nor the 1993 survey, or were among the anonymous survey respondents from 1986 (10) or 1993 (8).

At a minimum, the companies not surveyed provided a background for the survey results. At best, their data would complete some parts of our picture (which, by this point, was becoming a family album) of Ohio ESOPs. Outcomes for ESOPs established prior to 1985 were compared with companies surveyed in 1986, including the older cohort. Outcomes for ESOPs established prior to 1992 (including those prior to 1985) were compared with those surveyed in 1993 and 1986, including both cohorts (Table 12).

We researched several data sources to discover the fates of ESOPs, sometimes resorting to "preponderance of evidence" criteria to draw our conclusions. The most credible source was IRS Form 5500 reports. By the time research on the fate of ESOPs was done, we had data through 2007 for most companies (Larkspur Data Resources, version 12.1). Companies that were filing as ESOPs and had not terminated their plans were easily categorized. If a company did not report an ESOP or 401(k) holding employer securities, but had the same name and employer identification number as when it was surveyed or listed by the IRS in

TABLE 12

Fate (circa 2007 or later) of Companies from the 1986 and 1993 Survey Compared to Those of Similar Age That Did Not Respond in 1993 (Number of Companies in the Group Is Indicated in Parentheses).

	1986 survey (54)	Nonsurveyed companies established 1974–1984° (91)	1993 survey (159)	Nonsurveyed companies established 1974–1991° (203)
Still employee owned, through ESOP or 401(k)	35%	37%	44%	40%
Still in business, but ESOP terminated or no evidence of employee ownership	43%	52%	43%	46%
Distressed/bankrupt/closed	19%	11%	12%	12%
No information	4%	0%	1%	1%

°From IRS Form 5500.

1993, and if it had a website or numerous hits on a search engine, it was categorized as still being in business. If there was a website, the site was searched for further information about the company's history, including any sales or mergers that might have taken place. If the company appeared to be currently owned by another company, as indicated by the website, a business newsletter, or a different name or employer identification number on Form 5500, further Internet research was used to clarify the situation. Especially helpful were various websites with company histories (http://www.highbeam.com, http://www.alacrastore.com, and http://www.fundinguniverse.com) and, occasionally, local newspapers. We also used the website http://www.freeerisa.com to check for the presence of an ESOP or holdings of employer securities when questions remained about individual companies. In some cases, it was not possible to draw a solid conclusion, but if there was at least some evidence, a tentative conclusion was based on the preponderance of the evidence. We failed to find any information about a few companies in any of the researched sources, so they were listed as unknown.

The surveyed companies were about as likely to remain employee owned by 2007 as unsurveyed companies of comparable age, about as likely to be in business but no longer have an ESOP (whether the company was sold or simply terminated its ESOP), and about as likely to be closed in conditions of distress. It is likely that the survival rate of surveyed ESOPs compared with those not surveyed is at least a little better than what is suggested by Table 12, since we were not able to go back to 1985 in the IRS data and check on the fate of ESOPs not surveyed in that year.

But differences in the details matter. For example, among many ESOP terminations, only some plans distributed or rolled over substantial amounts. These distributions are partially captured in the IRS filings in our database, but the data we have are incomplete. From staff experience with the OEOC's succession planning program, we knew that some ESOP companies were acquired just for the customer list and then swiftly closed, but the data show two to five times that many are still in business years later, meaning that most of the employee-owners kept their jobs and may have received some benefit from the ESOP distribution as well.

We can capture part of the picture for distributions by examining the payouts to participants made in years close to the time of the surveys. These are not per-capita payments because the Form 5500 data does not report the number of recipients.

Since so many of the surveyed ESOPs are small, we expected that their median payouts would be smaller than those of companies not in our surveys. However, our expectations were in error. The payouts were roughly twice that of the nonsurveyed companies (Table 13).

What is more, companies in the cohorts made comparable or larger median payments in the selected years (Table 14). Comparing the fates of the companies that responded to the surveys to those that did not, we find strong evidence that companies that responded were not fundamentally different from those that did not, but evidence (from our partial record of payouts) points us back to the idea of the surveyed companies being generally more successful with their ESOPs, even if the ESOP was terminated.

TABLE 13
Median Amounts Paid to Participants, by Surveyed and Nonsurveyed Companies
(Number of Companies with Data Is Indicated in Parentheses).

	Nonsurveyed companies established 1974–1984° (72 companies in group)	1993 survey (159 companies in group)	Nonsurveyed companies established 1974–1991° (203 companies in group)
	1986 survey		
IRS Form 5500, circa 1993	$123,367 (28)	$57,831 (72)	$44,247 (123)	$22,893 (178)
IRS Form 5500, circa 2005	$632,915 (21)	$305,214 (27)	$219,651 (81)	$211,580 (73)

°From IRS Form 5500, circa 1993.

TABLE 14
Median Amounts Paid to Participants, by Cohort Companies (Number of Companies with Data Is Indicated in Parentheses).

	IRS Form 5500 (circa 1993)	IRS Form 5500 (circa 2005)
Older cohort 1986–2005	$256,906 (7)	$1,016,432 (7)
Younger cohort 1993–2005	$81,003 (24)	$216,744 (27)

Conclusion

In general, what we can say from the longitudinal study is limited by the restricted number of cases. Only 37% of the 1986 and 45% of the 1993 known and findable Ohio ESOP survey respondents were still in business and still had their ESOP in 2007. What this suggests is an unusual degree of instability in ESOPs relative to other pension plans, which squares with the GAO (1991) findings. While one hesitates to draw definitive conclusions from the data we have on the ESOPs that have survived and continued to report, the findings are at least indicative and worthy of follow-up research. The most obvious choice for follow-up would be the GAO respondents of 1986.

The cohorts with continuous data are small, but comparisons between the cohorts and other companies show a consistent pattern. Companies in the older and younger cohorts are repeatedly shown to have made more and greater efforts to develop their organizations into effective businesses, and appear more willing to make more and greater sacrifices. We conclude that they did grow up, not just become older, and this benefited their employee-owners. We also conclude that the problems with employee ownership documented in the Webbs' (1914) study of cooperatives are not axioms for employee ownership. Certainly, the context is more favorable now. There is stronger rule of law, better protection for property rights, specific law that recognizes ESOPs and regulates the disbursement of assets, fiduciary responsibility, and more literate and numerate employees. But our best evidence against the Webbs' dire views is the long-term existence of ESOP companies and the wealth they have distributed to their participants. Indeed, what stands out most of all in what we have found is the striking wealth that the long-term surviving ESOP companies produce when they persist over 20 years—just half the span of an employee's working life. This is wealth beyond what employees would otherwise own, since they are already working at jobs paying as well or better than other companies in the industry and receiving as good or better benefits. When the average American worker retires, his or her wealth is typically little more than the value of a home (Mishel, Bernstein, and Allegretto 2007:265–6).

ESOP retirees will have ESOP wealth, along with traditional pension plans or 401(k)s, as well as the value of their homes.

In retrospect, considering the wealth created in the ESOPs in our study, it seems unfortunate that few unions were included in their companies' ESOPs, as ESOPs seem to be creating surprising amounts of wealth over time as well as keeping union jobs with good pay and benefits in the domestic economy. By law, if unionized employees have another pension plan, the union can decline to join the ESOP, or management can choose to exclude them. In the 2005 survey, six of ten companies excluding the union(s) from the ESOP reported that it was the decision of management to do that, while three said it was the decision of the union. One respondent checked both.

More surprising was the growth in the number of plan participants. Companies that reported to the IRS in 1993 and 2005 created a great deal of wealth and allocated it broadly, extending the benefits of ownership to more people while building the average value of their accounts. Growth in the number of plan participants is also an indicator of the number of retirees and their beneficiaries who received payouts from ESOP accounts. At present, we do not have data to determine how many participants are current employees and how many are retired or beneficiaries. When data sources improve, the picture will be clarified. Another notable finding is the report of increasing employment in well-paying jobs with good benefits among the long-lived companies, especially among the younger cohort, where there was substantial employment growth. In the older cohort, employment increased a little in the context of declining employment in manufacturing. Both groups did better than Ohio overall, where many good jobs were moving offshore, and growth was mostly in low-wage jobs in the service sector (BLS 2010a).

What is also quite interesting in the Ohio results is that the ESOPs that survive moved along a maturation curve toward majority or 100% ownership and, more slowly, toward greater acceptance of participatory employee ownership over time, with better understanding of how to activate its potential. The findings suggest that, over the years, some employee-owned firms do take gradual measures toward implementing participative management. As we picture the adoption of new practices, the company tries an idea; if it succeeds, the way is smoothed for another, related practice. The use of such practices spreads, and skill at using them improves until their utility and benefit is exhausted, or even a little beyond that point, as may have happened with companies that reduced the number of older shop-floor participation programs. In general, however, there is not much evidence of "backsliding" among the cohort firms, but there are many successful businesses that terminate their ESOPs. Perhaps there is a tipping point that consists of some combination of participative management and percentage of ownership. If firms do not reach it, they are unlikely to benefit from the ownership advantage, and that increases the likelihood of early termination of the ESOP. There is a suggestive contrast between the cohort companies that slowly but steadily progress in development of their business organizations and the other companies in each survey that lag behind the cohorts.

Particular management practices mark the long-surviving ESOPs in our surveys. From our 1993 research and others' findings, we suspect that the effect size is small, but it appears consistently. The measures that seem to help are modest and doable—providing a credible and accessible stream of information, including regular meetings between management and nonmanagement, and offering appropriate training, including ownership and financial training. Companies seem to be continuing to work out effective routines for employee involvement.

There is evidence of some positive impact from particular practices of economic democracy within the firm. Pass-through voting, nonmanagement representation on the board of directors, and selection of those directors with significant employee involvement (usually elections but occasionally other forms such as an employee nominating committee or union selection) are usually positively related to improved operations, but, if basic participation in governance is not established early in the life of the ESOP, it is unlikely, but not impossible, that it will develop later. If nonmanagerial governance participation was in place early in the ESOP's life, companies seemed to find it easier to go a little further and replace management-appointed nonmanagerial board members with elected ones and to increase their numbers on the board. Nonetheless, only a minority of ESOP companies used the three practices of economic democracy that we investigated. This is despite reliable findings that without employee participation there is no ESOP advantage.

In companies where ESOPs survive, it is clear that something happens to increase employees' interest and enthusiasm for participating in the decisions of the company. That something may be the powerful symbolism of nonmanagement representation on the board. Interest in participation (and other attitudes that accompany it) is the bridge between efforts at organizational development and effects on the company's operations. The primary reward employee-owners collected for learning how to work together in new and constructive ways was that their companies were still in business and still had ESOPs. Many similar companies in manufacturing had closed their doors or outsourced, and more than 40%

of companies surveyed in 1986 or 1993 had terminated their ESOPs. In addition, the employee-owners had good jobs that paid as well or better than the competition, offered benefits better than the competition, and some paid the dividends that Kelso predicted. In addition to these traditional benefits from well-paying work, their ESOPs created substantial wealth, above and beyond what they would otherwise possess.

At the same time, it is clear that most ESOPs do not survive as pension plans. Only a little more than a third of those surveyed in the mid-1980s (established at the median year of 1978) remained ESOPs in 2004–2006, and only two fifths of those surveyed in the early 1990s (established at the median year of 1986) were still in existence in 2007. Their outcomes do not differ materially from ESOP companies not surveyed in 1993. That suggests that slightly more than one third survive more than 25 years and about two fifths survive more than 20 years.

ESOPs can vanish for a number of reasons (e.g., due to acquisitions of healthy ESOP companies by conventionally owned companies or management disillusionment with the ESOP—with its cost, burden of reporting, or failure of desired improvements in performance). Outright business failures are a rare cause. When ESOPs are established as a last-ditch measure to save an enterprise from closing, the decision typically occurs almost at the last hour of a company's life, and they usually do not succeed, but they contribute to ESOP mortality statistics. Some ESOPs that disappear may nonetheless create significant financial benefits for their participants.

For those who see employee ownership as a fundamentally different way of doing business, these results are disappointing. On the average, employee ownership lacks permanence, and it is not because they fail as enterprises. Three out of four of the companies terminating their ESOPs appear to be successful businesses. Yet unlike "demutualization" of cooperatives where the savings of previous generations are expropriated by the current owners, terminated ESOPs reward the generation that established them, though largely at the cost of the public purse.

Yet, in a minority of cases, ESOPs have great staying power. They do indeed reshape the way companies are structured and perform, and they lead to long-term broadened ownership. How can we go about encouraging such long-term ownership plans? As with all businesses, public policy has had an enormous impact on the ebb and flow of companies that are employee owned and the shape of those companies. Tax credit plans (TRASOPs and PAYSOPs) encouraged the formation of paper ESOPs that never had any element of employee involvement or participation and that generated little wealth for employees. The 1989–1996 tax credit for bank loans encouraged formation of ESOPs by providing a source of credit for employee buyouts. Finding the funds to finance a buyout is still a challenge for would-be employee-buyers and willing sellers. A proposed employee ownership bank could stretch taxpayer dollars with loan guarantees, reassuring lenders and loosening access to capital to create more ESOPs, and proposed state employee ownership centers could provide education and support.

Because employee ownership is still an unfamiliar concept in the U.S. business community, education and information are needed to extend the approach and to teach modifications of business practices that maximize the economic performance that employee ownership can inspire. A center recognized by attorneys, economic development professionals, and accountants can help owners who want to sell get started by providing basic information, a road map to the process, and referrals to competent professionals who will guide the sellers and buyers through the deal. Additionally, state centers would help to preserve small businesses in a variety of forms, not all employee owned, by educating owners on succession planning. The politics of state governments have operated to the detriment of employee ownership centers. A modest federal investment in state employee ownership centers could provide the outreach, support, and service tailored to local values and needs. Education of potential sellers and financial professionals would spread awareness of the evidence that employee participation enhances ESOP company performance. The existing evidence is, in fact, so strong that one could make an argument that ESOP fiduciaries who do not encourage it are failing the fiduciary obligation to plan participants because they are failing to enhance stock value in obvious and known ways.

As early tax breaks to encourage ESOPs ended, the rate of ESOP formation slowed substantially. The 1042 rollover offered the ESOP as an exit strategy for owners of closely held companies and has produced a steady stream of ESOP formations since it was enacted in 1984. That stream of new ESOPs has roughly balanced out the numbers of terminated ESOPs. Since 1997, tax relief for ESOP-owned S corporations has encouraged the formation of more such firms, more 100% ESOPs, and the conversion of C corporation ESOPs into S corporations. In stark contrast to earlier tax credit plans, S corporation ESOPs are decidedly not paper ESOPs. Of 26 100% employee-owned firms in the 2005 study, 24 were S corporations, and their median scores for communication and training were well above medians of the older and younger cohort. S corporation ESOPs were also more likely than others to use pass-through voting and more likely to have nonmanagerial employees on the board. The combination of employee interest and involvement, along with the tax advantages has helped these firms to succeed against their conventionally owned competitors.

What is quite surprising is that many ESOP companies, even about half of 100% ESOP-owned S corporations, do not incorporate more economic democracy into the structure and practice of the firm. The economic performance benefits of employee participation combined with employee ownership was established by the GAO (1987) more than 20 years ago. A tax incentive to encourage more employee involvement, even at the cost of tax expenditures that are now going to ESOP firms that are managed like conventional firms with no better performance than conventional firms, would accelerate the movement toward employee involvement and economic democracy. Why not require financial transparency for the employee-owners? Why not raise the threshold for the tax benefits S corporations enjoy by requiring that a company can qualify for the S corporation tax benefits only if they have pass-through voting for the company's CEO and their employee-owners can elect at least one representative to the board of directors, even if the votes only direct the ESOP trustee? This makes sense on the grounds that ESOPs combined with participative management are likely to provide better returns to the beneficiaries of the ESOP trust. We recognize that these proposals would profoundly change the nature of management in many ESOP companies, but we know companies that are successfully using variations of these practices, in Ohio, right now. Employee-owners and taxpayers alike would benefit from the improved economic performance that would almost certainly ensue.

Acknowledgments

We would like to thank current and previous administrations in the state of Ohio, which have supported employee ownership research, outreach education, and Ohio's Employee Owned Network. Thanks also to Kent State University's Division of Research and Graduate Studies for supporting data gathering and initial analysis. We are also grateful to the staff of the Ohio Employee Ownership Center at Kent State, who were a well of expert information and experience. The authors, of course, are responsible for all errors and omissions herein.

Endnote

[1] The Ohio Employee Ownership Center was established at Kent State University in 1987 to support the establishment of employee-owned companies in Ohio and contribute to their success with information, technical assistance, and employee training. The OEOC also offers succession planning information for retiring owners, with the goal of retaining more small businesses in the state, whether they become employee owned or not. For more information, see http://www.oeockent.org.

References

Blasi, Joseph, Richard B. Freeman, Chris Mackin, and Douglas Kruse. 2008. *Creating a Bigger Pie? The Effects of Employee Ownership, Profit Sharing, and Stock Options on Workplace Performance.* NBER Working Paper 14230. <http://www.nber.org/papers/w14230>. [October 14, 2010].

Bureau of Labor Statistics (BLS). 2010a. *State and Area Employment, Hours and Earnings.* <http://data.bls.gov:8080/PDQ/outside.jsp?survey=sm>. [November 1, 2010].

Bureau of Labor Statistics (BLS). 2010b. *Union Membership in Ohio, 2009.* <http://www.bls.gov/ro5/unionoh.pdf>. [December 5, 2010].

Carberry, Edward J. 2010. "Who Benefits from Shared Capitalism? The Social Stratification of Wealth and Power in Companies with Employee Ownership." In Douglas L. Kruse, Richard B. Freeman, and Joseph R. Blasi, eds., *Shared Capitalism at Work: Employee Ownership, Profit and Gain Sharing, and Broad-Based Stock Options.* Chicago: University of Chicago Press, pp. 317–49.

Freeman, Steven F. 2007. *Effects of ESOP Adoption and Employee Ownership: Thirty Years of Research and Experience.* Organizational Dynamics Working Papers #07-01. Philadelphia: University of Pennsylvania.

General Accounting Office (GAO). 1987. *Employee Stock Ownership Plans: Little Evidence of Effects on Corporate Performance.* GAO/PEMD-88-1. Washington, DC: GAO.

General Accounting Office (GAO). 1991. *Employee Stock Ownership Plans: Participants' Benefits Generally Increased, but Many Plans Terminated.* GAO HRD-91-28. Washington, DC: GAO.

Kato, Takao. 2003. "Participatory Employment Practices in Japan." In Seiritsu Ogura, Toshiaki Tachibanaki, and David A. Wise, eds., *Labor Markets and Firm Benefit Policies in Japan and the United States.* Chicago: University of Chicago Press, pp. 39–80.

Kruse, Douglas, and Joseph Blasi. 1997. "Employee Ownership, Employee Attitudes, and Firm Performance: A Review of the Evidence." In Daniel J.B. Mitchell, David Lewin, and Mahmood Zaidi, eds., *Handbook of Human Resource Management.* Greenwich, CT: JAI Press, pp. 113–51.

Logue, John, and Cassandra Rogers. 1989. *Employee Stock Ownership Plans in Ohio: Impact on Company Performance and Employment.* Kent, OH: Northeast Ohio Employee Ownership Center.

Logue, John, and Jacquelyn Yates. 2001. *The Real World of Employee Ownership.* Ithaca, NY: Cornell University Press.

Logue, John, and Jacquelyn Yates. 2005. *Productivity in Cooperatives and Worker-Owned Enterprises: Ownership and Participation Make a Difference!* Geneva, Switzerland: International Labour Organization.

Long, Russell. 1989. Foreword to Robert W. Smiley and Ronald J. Gilbert, eds., *Employee Ownership Plans: Business Planning, Implementation, Law and Taxation.* New York: Prentice Hall.

McIntyre, Bill. 2003. "ESOPs: The Legacy of Russell Long." *Owners at Work,* Vol. 15, no. 1, pp. 1–2.

Miller, Danny, Jon Hartwick, and Isabelle Le Breton-Miller. 2004. "How to Detect a Management Fad—and Distinguish It from a Classic." *Business Horizon,* Vol. 47, no. 4, pp. 7–16.

Mishel, Lawrence, Jared Bernstein, and Sylvia Allegretto. 2007. *The State of Working America 2006/2007.* Ithaca, NY: ILR Press.

National Center for Employee Ownership (NCEO). 2010. "A Statistical Profile of Employee Ownership." <http://www.nceo.org/main/article.php/id/2/>. [October 14, 2010].

Pierce, J.L., T. Kostova, and K.T. Dirks. 2003. "The State of Psychological Ownership: Integrating and Extending a Century of Research." *Review of General Psychology*, Vol. 7, pp. 84–107.

Rosen, Corey, Katherine Klein, and Karen Young. 1986. *Employee Ownership in America.* Lexington, MA: Heath.

Seymour, Kyle. 2010. "Xtek: Our Rocky Road to Success." *Owners at Work*, Vol. 22, no. 1, pp. 7–9.

Simecek, Jay. 2001. "A Model for Developing Positive Ownership Attitudes and Behaviors." *ESOP Report*, February, pp. 3, 11.

Simecek, Jay. 2008. "Questions on the Way to Behaving Like an Owner." *ESOP Report*, September, pp. 3, 6.

Simecek, Jay. 2010. "Surviving the Recession . . . Did Your Culture Make a Difference?" *ESOP Report*, April, pp. 3, 6.

Simon, Herbert. 1983. "What Is Industrial Democracy?" *Challenge*, January–February, pp. 30–9.

Thomas, Karen, and Jennifer Maxwell. 2001. "Communication and Training: Building a Learning Environment." In John Logue and Jacquelyn Yates, eds., *The Real World of Employee Ownership.* Ithaca NY: Cornell University Press, pp. 46–71.

Webb, Sidney, and Beatrice Webb. 1914. "Special Supplement on Co-operative Production and Profit Sharing." *The New Statesman,* February 14, Vol. 2, no. 45.

Yates, Jacquelyn. 2000. "Modeling ESOP Company Management for Better Operations and Profits." *Journal of Employee Ownership Law and Finance*, Vol. 12, no. 2, pp. 107–26.

Yates, Jacquelyn. 2004. "The Changing Face of Employee Ownership in Ohio." <http://www.oeockent.org/index.php/library/category/49/reprints-preprints-a-occasional-papers-on-employ?start=40>. [November 15, 2010].

CHAPTER 11

Employee Ownership in Britain: Diverse Forms, Diverse Antecedents

ANDREW PENDLETON
University of York

I feel that real efficiency cannot be attained until every worker is given some direct interest, not only in the performance of his individual job, but in the success of the whole undertaking, and is completely secured against any exploitation by his employer. It seems quite possible that these ends might be achieved, without detriment to the interests of organised labor, by a judicious blend of payment by results, profit-sharing and control-sharing. . . . A satisfactory scheme, however, has yet to be worked out.

Seebohm Rowntree (1921)

Introduction

Employee ownership is currently attracting more attention in Britain than possibly ever before. While a long-standing policy objective on the part of governments of all political persuasions has been to encourage employee ownership of shares, the current coalition government also aims to encourage the formation of employee-owned organizations to operate many public services. In particular, it intends to include a sizeable employee stake in the ownership of the Royal Mail when it is privatized shortly. This chapter provides a profile of employee ownership in Britain today and evaluates the application of various theoretical perspectives to the adoption of employee ownership. What kinds of firms have employee ownership, and what type of employee ownership do they have? In what circumstances do they introduce employee ownership, who is involved in the transition to employee ownership, and how do these factors influence the nature of ownership and governance?

311

The starting point is that various forms of employee ownership have often been insufficiently differentiated in terms of key ownership and organizational characteristics, and, as a result, the application of theory has become imprecise. The determinants of various forms of employee ownership, therefore, have been unclear, with the result that many studies are either inconclusive or contradictory. A key finding in this chapter is that the various forms of employee ownership, or "shared capitalism," have substantial differences in their ownership and organizational characteristics. I argue that the nature of ownership and participative structures reflects the interests and objectives of those involved in the creation of employee ownership (Pendleton 2001) and that this is a key consideration when evaluating the application of various theoretical perspectives to the determinants of ownership. Differentiating the forms of employee ownership more precisely reveals that the determinants vary among these perspectives.

In this chapter, I first distinguish the main forms of employee ownership in Britain today and undertake systematic comparisons of their ownership characteristics and the contexts in which employee ownership is introduced. I find substantial differences among cooperatives, minority employee share plans, and majority employee ownership, as well as within the group of majority employee-owned companies. I then consider the relevance of various theoretical perspectives on the determinants of employee ownership and find that the applicability of these differs among the various forms of employee ownership. The chapter draws on data collected on employee ownership over a 20-year period. The focus of the chapter is employee ownership in Britain, but, as the main forms of employee ownership are broadly similar to other countries such as the United States, the analysis should have a wider resonance.

Forms of Employee Ownership

In the literature on employee ownership, it has become commonplace for various forms of employee ownership to be considered together and for the features that differentiate these forms to become fuzzy and occasionally obscured. In particular, minority share ownership plans in listed firms tend to be conflated with substantial, or even majority, worker ownership. Most of the recent theory on employee ownership is derived from a rich stream of work in the United States in the late 1970s and early 1980s on substantial employee ownership after the passage of the Employee Retirement Income Security Act (ERISA) stimulated the development of employee stock ownership plans (ESOPs). Examples include Richard Long's work on employee attitudes in vari-

ous employee-owned firms (1978, 1979, 1980), Blasi's evaluation of
the ESOP form of ownership (1988), and Hammer and Stern's (1980)
investigation of patterns of employee participation in employee-owned
firms. Since then, many of the insights generated by this research have
been extended to other forms of employee ownership, such as minority
employee share plans in large listed firms. This is perhaps understand-
able in so far as similar instruments (e.g., tax-advantaged plans) are used
in various contexts.

However, if the structure and characteristics of employee ownership are substantially different between these contexts, it is debatable
whether determinants and outcomes will be similar (cf. Ben-Ner and
Jones 1995). One example of this is the finding from the early literature
on ESOPs that participation in decision making can be necessary for
employee ownership to generate positive performance outcomes (GAO
1987). This has developed into the "conventional wisdom" for all forms
of employee ownership despite the evidence from minority share plans
in large firms being unsupportive in many instances (Pendleton and
Robinson 2010). In contrast to this tendency to merge minority and
majority employee stock ownership, another rich stream of theory-based
work—that on worker cooperatives—has occurred more or less separately. There has been little interplay between the literature on cooperatives and other forms of worker ownership despite potentially similar
theoretical concerns.

Some of the literature sought to differentiate various forms of
employee ownership. Doucouliagos (1995), for instance, in his meta-
analysis of the productivity effects of employee ownership, distinguished
labor-managed from "participatory capitalist" firms (i.e., those with
low levels of worker ownership and profit sharing). Although employee
ownership has positive productivity effects in both types of firms, these
effects are stronger in the firms with more extensive worker ownership
and control. Ben-Ner and Jones (1995) outlined a matrix of 16 con-
figurations of ownership and control rights, based on the extent of each.
They showed that each combination of ownership and control can have
a distinct effect on productivity. Kruse and Blasi (1997) suggested that
employee ownership can be differentiated along four dimensions: the
amount/proportion of stock owned by employees, the proportion of
employees owning stock, the distribution of stock ownership among
employees, and the prerogatives and rights that ownership confers. These
distinctions are useful because they help us to pinpoint more precisely
the extent and characteristics of ownership. Although there is in principle a large number of possible combinations of ownership dimensions
and governance rights, in practice there tends to be a small number of

"constellations" of employee ownership. An important distinction, as will be shown shortly, is among firms with a low proportion of stock owned by employees, a minority of employees participating in the plan, and an unequal distribution of stock within firms that have substantial, majority, or full ownership by all or most employees, with either equal ownership rights between employees or ownership structured according to some other principle such as tenure.

Many quantitative studies of the determinants and effects of employee ownership, however, tend to be silent on these dimensions, using instead a simple dummy for the presence of a stock plan. A recent example is the study conducted on the productivity effects of stock ownership for the British Government (HMRC 2007). The problem is that it can conflate levels and forms of ownership that may be substantively different in terms of their determinants, organizational characteristics, and outcomes. For instance, Pendleton and Robinson (2010) found, using a measure of the proportion of employees participating in a stock plan, that the combination of ownership and employee voice has different effects on productivity when a minority of employees participates compared with majority participation.

It is clear, then, that we need greater awareness of variations in the dimensions of ownership. We also need to take the study of employee ownership a step back. The extent of ownership is likely to be a function of the objectives and interests of those involved in the creation of employee ownership, and the circumstances in which this takes place (Pendleton 2001). It seems probable that an employee-owned firm created by workers will have a high level of worker ownership, will have all or most employees involved in ownership, and will at least aim for more or less equal ownership stakes. For instance, Tower Colliery in South Wales was a worker-led 100% buyout in which nearly all workers contributed equal sums to become shareholders.[1] By contrast, managers or owners introducing employee ownership may be unwilling to provide employees with a large stake for fear that it would diminish their own return and control rights. A corollary for studies of determinants is that not only may there be differences among firms according to the extent of ownership, but there may also be substantial differences among firms in terms of the actors involved, the reasons for conversion, and the context of the conversion process. A majority employee-owned firm created by workers to protect jobs and employment seems likely to have characteristics different from those of a firm with a similar ownership structure created by an owner seeking to exit (see Pendleton 2001).

To illustrate these observations, I outline key characteristics of three types of employee ownership in Britain: worker cooperatives, firms with minority share plans, and firms that are substantially or wholly worker owned. I then go on to describe differences among groups of firms within the majority ownership category.

Worker Cooperatives

Worker cooperatives have a long tradition in the United Kingdom, as in other advanced industrialized countries. Worker co-ops can be seen as one strain among various organizational types that are based on member ownership and control, such as building societies, friendly societies, and clubs. They choose to abide by the International Statement of Cooperative Principles, which include equality of participation in ownership and control, voluntary and open membership, and active participation in management. Personal development of cooperative members and contribution to the local economy and community are also commonly seen as desirable objectives.

In terms of the Kruse and Blasi (1997) dimensions, worker cooperatives are distinctive. In their "pure" form, they are wholly employee owned, with ownership usually spread equally among participating employees. However, not all employees necessarily are members: many cooperatives open membership to employees once they have passed a probationary period. Even then, not all employees choose to join, given that a key principle is that membership is voluntary. Triangle Wholefoods—one of the largest worker cooperatives in Britain—has 143 members out of 150 employees. It is not customary for there to be a market for membership in British co-ops (see Dow 2003) beyond a typical requirement that members purchase a £ 1 share.

Most cooperatives in Britain are small—the average size was eight employees in 2008. Previous theoretical and empirical work on cooperatives has suggested that they tend to be labor rather than capital intensive (Bonin, Jones, and Putterman 1993) and, because of both ideological and practical difficulties in securing external finance, are often undercapitalized. The British evidence certainly fits with the claim about labor intensity. Worker cooperatives tend to cluster in certain subsectors such as organic food wholesale and retail, and bicycle retail. Recently, a variant of the worker cooperative form can be observed in sports centers that have been privatized from local authority control and that have a significant role in the provision of leisure services in some parts of the United Kingdom, including London. They are membership organizations, with membership shared between consumers and employees. Most members are employees (though often only a minority of employees are members). The coalition government elected in 2010 has advocated worker cooperatives and mutuals as a way of privatizing public services and elements of central government administration. These are, in effect, "labor supply" co-ops tendering for government contracts to run services. A number of pilot projects (Pathfinder Mutuals) were instigated in summer 2010, and, in November, the government announced that most public sector employees would be given the right to establish employee-owned organizations to bid to take over the running of the services provided by their employer.

Most cooperatives are established by the employees within them, though some are conversions by paternalist owners. Some are start-ups, but some are rescues in which workers have taken over failing conventional firms (see Paton 1989). There has been a rich debate within the cooperatives' literature on the formation of worker cooperatives, with a significant vein of theory and evidence suggesting that the formation of cooperatives is countercyclical. Workers create cooperatives out of failing firms to save their jobs when alternative job opportunities are in decline due to economic downturn (see Perotin 2006). It is also possible that the failure rate of rescue conversions is higher than that of new start-ups either because risk-averse workers prefer to return to conventional employment when the economy recovers or because the probability of turning around failing firms is fairly low. Unfortunately, flows into and out of cooperative organizations in Britain are too small to test these propositions.

Minority Employee Share Ownership

Nearly all of the recent research on employee ownership and equity-based remuneration in Britain has been on minority employee share ownership. In part, this is because the main quantitative data source for workplace industrial relations—the Workplace Employment Relations Survey—primarily captures this form of share ownership (see Bryson and Freeman 2007; Pendleton and Robinson 2010; Sengupta, Whitfield, and McNabb 2008). It is also because it is by far the most widespread form of employee ownership in Britain today. Official statistics show that 1,370 firms operated tax-advantaged, all-employee schemes in 2008 (HMRC 2010). The Workplace Employment Relations Survey indicates that 30% of private sector workplaces with ten or more employees are covered by a share ownership plan (Pendleton, Whitfield, and Bryson 2009:264–5). The amount of the firm that is owned by employees is usually less than 5%, with the remainder primarily owned by institutional investors (Pendleton 1997).

Two tax-approved, all-employee plans predominate in Britain. The long-standing Save As You Earn (SAYE) plan is an options-based plan coupled with a savings scheme. Employees are granted options—that is, the right to purchase shares, typically with a discount of 20% on the market price at the time of grant, to be exercised in three or five years (extendable to seven). At the same time, they take out a monthly savings contract to accumulate the funds necessary to exercise the options. Of course, this plan does not necessarily lead to ownership, as participants may exercise and sell their shares in a simultaneous exercise or may simply choose not to exercise (and take the accumulated savings instead). The evidence suggests that around 50% of participants exercise and hold at least some of their shares (Pendleton 2005a).

The other main scheme is the more recent Share Incentive Plan (SIP), introduced in 2000. The SIP has two main components: an employee share purchase plan and a free shares facility, supplemented by matching shares for share purchases. In the share purchase element (partnership shares), employees can acquire shares out of pre-tax income and receive very favorable tax treatment on the sale of these shares if they are retained for five years or more. The firm can award matching shares to participating employees on up to a 2-for-1 basis. A company can also award free shares, which can be awarded equally, on similar terms, or according to group or individual performance, and thus can deliver shares to all (eligible) employees. About one third of SIP plans award free shares (HMRC 2008a). Finally, dividends paid on employee shares may be reinvested in so-called dividend shares.

There are two other tax-approved plans that may be open to all employees, though they typically are targeted at top executives. The Company Share Options Plan, first introduced in 1984, allows for the award of options to be exercised in three to ten years, although without the savings plan mechanism found in SAYE. This has been used as an all-employee plan by ASDA, now a subsidiary of Walmart. The other plan is Enterprise Management Incentives (introduced in 2000). This is an option plan aimed at smaller firms. Although initially aimed at "key employees," about 30% of companies award options to all employees (HRMC 2008b).

Participation in share ownership is voluntary: SAYE and most cases of the SIP require employees to opt in to purchase options or shares. The typical participation rate in SAYE plans is between 10% and 49%. Only 16% of firms with a SAYE have a participation rate higher than 50% (HRMC 2008a). Participants tend to be higher-paid employees, with income levels being the strongest determinant of both the decision to participate and the level of contribution (see Pendleton 2010). Ownership is therefore typically partial and unequal, except when the primary form of share distribution is the award of free shares. In 2008–2009, 670 firms operated SAYE and 870 offered SIPs. Approximately

170 firms do both (HMRC 2010). In 2008, 500,000 employees enrolled in SAYE, while 700,000 received free shares through SIPs. All recent research has strongly shown that employee share ownership is concentrated in large, listed firms, which reflects the concentration of these schemes (SAYE especially) in larger, listed firms (see Pendleton, Whitfield, and Bryson 2009). The use of share ownership plans is found in all sectors, though to a much greater extent in the finance sector.

Minority share plans usually are instigated by top managers in the firm and typically are managed by external administrators, savings carriers, and the secretariat function within the firm. The evidence suggests that workers or unions rarely have a role in the decision to introduce these plans or the design and subsequent administration of them (Pendleton 2005b). This finding reflects several factors. One is that these plans are not usually aimed at enhancing employees' role in governance; instead, they are primarily aimed at encouraging employees to identify with the firm and/or providing a benefit to employees. A more cynical explanation is that top managers use these plans to secure legitimacy for their own share-based rewards, though there is currently no empirical evidence to support this claim. On the union side, there is little demand to be involved in the design and operation of these plans in most instances. How much of this lack of union demand is due to resource constraints, disinterest, or opposition to share plans is difficult to say.[2]

Since most firms operating these share plans are listed companies, company owners typically are institutional investors. These investors have little, if any, role in the initial decision to introduce these plans in most cases, although the main institutional investor trade associations are supportive of them. The remuneration guidelines operated by the main trade association, the Association of British Insurers, stipulate that new issues or reissued treasury shares to resource share plans should not exceed 10% and that the decision to introduce a plan should be ratified at the company's annual general meeting. The guidelines also state that employee share ownership trusts should not be used as an anti-takeover device and that prior shareholder approval should be secured before more than 5% of company equity is held within such a trust (Association of British Insurers 2005). A key but unspoken assumption in these rules is that share plans should not normally be used to give employees a significant voice in governance as a result of share ownership.

Majority Employee Ownership

Majority and substantial employee ownership are much rarer in Britain. Although majority ownership is not new—there have been some firms that have taken this form for many years, such as the John Lewis

Partnership (67,000 employees)—this type of ownership has become more prominent since the late 1980s. To some extent, this form is very similar to employee stock ownership plans (ESOPs) in the United States, and these firms are often also referred to in Britain as ESOPs. Much of the impetus to the development of this form of employee ownership came from the Thatcher government's (1979–1991) drive to privatize public corporations and other state or local-authority–owned companies. Most notably, much of the state and local-authority–owned bus industry became substantially employee owned beginning in the late 1980s. In the 1990s, the number of employee-owned firms was 60 to 70 (see Pendleton 2001), but the balance of evidence suggests that there are probably around 150 to 200 today. Since the early 2000s, there has been an escalation in the number of firms introducing substantial employee ownership. One recent estimate suggested that the income of firms with substantial employee ownership is approximately £25 billion (All Party Parliamentary Group on Employee Ownership 2008).

The typical mechanism for facilitating conversion to employee ownership is an employee benefits trust (EBT), which is similar to a U.S. ESOP. In most cases, an EBT provides a vehicle for acquiring equity from the former owner, avoiding the coordination costs and risk exposure of direct employee purchases. Unless stock is donated by the exiting owner to the EBT, it typically purchases stock using a loan from an external financial provider or, more rarely, directly from the owner. These loans typically are repaid from company profits paid to the trust. Equity may be either retained in trust or distributed to employees. In the case of the latter, stock may be passed free of charge or sold to employees (or a combination of the two).

The key dimensions of ownership tend to be different from those in firms with minority employee share plans. In these firms, employee ownership is at least 25% of equity—and is often higher. When employees as a group do not own all of the firm, either directly or indirectly, top managers typically own the rest (usually acquiring their stock separately from the employee ownership plan). In these instances, the distribution of ownership is obviously unequal. In cases where employees do own all or most of the firm, ownership tends to be structured more equally. If employees are permitted to acquire equity from the trust, it may be distributed freely or by subscription. Ownership is likely to be more equal with free distributions, but even those distributions are not necessarily done equally—they are often linked to seniority or salary. If share acquisition takes place via employee purchases, much will depend on employee preferences (coupled with any measures by the company to support acquisitions, such as cheap loans). However, some employee-owned firms retain all or most of the equity in trust rather than passing stock to employees. In those cases, all or most employees are likely to benefit from profit shares, though the shares may be unequal (linked to tenure or salary for instance). Some employee-owned firms, however, adopt cooperative principles of equality of ownership, even though they do not register as fully fledged worker cooperatives. Overall, it is apparent that there is considerable variety in ownership structures among firms with substantial employee ownership.

The choice of these key dimensions of ownership, as well as those of governance, depends on the actors involved in the conversion process and their objectives for ownership conversion. Substantial employee ownership occurs in several different contexts, with different actors involved in each case, with different objectives, and typically with different ownership characteristics.

On the basis of these criteria, I identify three main groups of employee-owned firms in Britain today: human capital firms, business succession firms, and management–employee buyouts. The three types identified cover nearly all firms with substantial employee ownership. The distinctions among them are not clear cut at the margin because, for instance, some human capital firms become employee owned when owners want to retire (i.e., business succession). They also do not cover every employee-owned firm in Britain, as the employee ownership sector is heterogeneous. Other forms of employee-owned firms that might be identified include companies that use stock ownership to provide incentives in management buyouts (often backed by private equity) and employee-owned start-ups. However, there do not seem to be many such ownership arrangements, possibly because of restrictions on the use of tax-advantaged schemes in private-equity–backed management buyouts, and the problem of raising capital for employee-owned start-ups. Overall, the three forms identified cover most firms, and there clearly are discernible differences among them in terms of ownership structure, governance arrangements, reasons and contexts for conversion, and the actors leading the conversion.

Human Capital Firms

One important group of employee-owned firms that has recently become prominent is composed of firms that are dependent on highly skilled and knowledgeable human capital. These firms include architecture, transportation, information technology, marketing, business consultancy, and firms offering other professional services. In such firms, employee ownership essentially widens the traditional professional partnership structure to include all employees, often without the financial contribution by employee-partners typically associated with partnership structures. The most famous firm of this type in Britain is Arup, the consulting engineering, design, and planning organization.[3] The firm's founder, Ove Arup, led a long-term transition from professional partnership to employee ownership whereby partners' ownership stakes were acquired by an EBT on retirement. The equity is retained in a trust for the benefit of employees and their dependents, thereby insulating the firm from takeover and providing the basis for annual profit shares to staff.

Firms in this category tend to fall into two size groups. On one hand are the large firms with their own bureaucracies and a support workforce for the experts. Arup, for instance, has just under 9,000 employees, while PA Consulting has around 2,700. On the other hand are micro-consultancies, composed of a handful of consulting specialists. It is also common for employee ownership to be created in both types of businesses by managers who are owners or partners and who continue to work in the firm.

In terms of the dimensions of ownership identified by Kruse and Blasi (1997), the following ownership characteristics have been observed among these companies:

- They tend to be entirely employee owned, either directly or indirectly by an EBT. If ownership is held in trust, usually all employees satisfying a tenure-based eligibility criterion (e.g., one year's employment) are the beneficiaries. Qualifying employees typically receive an annual profit share, but the profit shares may be unequal. If ownership is directly held by employees, the tendency is for stock to be owned equally among employees in very small firms and unequally in larger firms. This is because some of the distribution mechanisms take a subscription form as a way of transferring cash into the trust initially holding the shares.

- Employee participation in governance tends to be limited in such companies. Board representation of rank-and-file employees or elected board representation is rare. If employee ownership is secured via trust ownership, trustees typically are appointed rather than elected. Employee involvement is focused primarily on immediate work tasks, and employees often enjoy considerable autonomy in how work tasks are organized and executed. Company culture is often fluid and informal.

The relevance of employee ownership to this type of company has been clearly demonstrated in the literature. Margaret Blair (1995) in particular argued that employee ownership has the potential to provide an effective governance structure when it is important that highly skilled and knowledgeable employees commit their human capital to the company. It provides a clear signal that employees will be protected from managerial opportunism. In a related vein, it has been argued that when human capital investments are important, it is logical to provide rewards to that investment in a method commensurate to the way that finance capital is rewarded for supporting investments in the physical plant. Because human capital is so important to the production process, often exclusively so, employees could easily take their human capital elsewhere or start up their own businesses. Ownership helps tie employees to the particular company. Companies organizing conversions to employee ownership usually also aim to provide protection against takeovers and support cooperative and team-based modes of working.

Business Succession

Employee ownership in this group comes about from owners who want to find a way of divesting their business as an alternative to inheritance by family or a trade sale. The danger of the former is that family members may be ill qualified or uninterested in taking over the business, while the dangers of a trade sale are acquisition by a competitor and possible subsequent dismemberment or rationalization of the business. The motives of owners typically are twofold: to protect the firm they have built up and a paternalist desire to protect the interests of their workforce. In an earlier analysis, I termed these instances of employee ownership as "paternalist divestment" (Pendleton 2001). Although cases of business succession were a minority of employee ownership conversions in the 1990s, they have become a steadily more important element of the employee ownership sector and appear to account for at least half of the current stock of known employee-owned firms. Similarly, Logue and Yates (2001) found that most ESOP firms in Ohio come about in order to acquire stock from a retiring owner.

The driving force for employee ownership in these companies is nearly always the departing owner, and the design of ownership and governance structures usually is the owner's brainchild, at least in the first instance. Employees tend to have little involvement in the creation of these structures. A good illustration is the wholesale company Parfetts (in the north of England) in which the initial transfer of 55% of the company's ownership was made to an EBT without the involvement or knowledge of employees. Only after the ownership transfer did employees become involved in developing governance and participation structures.

The usual vehicle for employee ownership in such firms is an EBT, which may then hold the equity in perpetuity on employees' behalf, gradually distribute equity to employees, or offer some combination of the two. The EBT may acquire the firm in a number of ways. First, it may take on debt secured against the future income streams of the company. Second, the owner may, in effect, loan the purchase price of the company to the trust with loan notes. Over time, the trust repays the owner from the income stream accruing to it from profits. This arrangement was used in the case of Tullis Russell, one of Britain's most well-known employee-owned companies. The trust may also repay the loan by selling stock to employees. In other cases (e.g., switch manufacturer Herga), the departing owner gifted the stock to employees and the EBT (see Bibby 2009).

The use of an EBT to effect ownership transfer is a useful way of dealing with several key problems in implementing employee ownership. Employee risk aversion is surmounted by use of a trust vehicle. Furthermore, acquisition by an employee trust avoids the problems arising from worker wealth and credit constraints, at least at the point of ownership conversion. Lack of knowledge among workers about how to effect a buyout is not an obstacle because the owner often hires experts to bring about the ownership transfer. Finally, since subscriptions are not raised by employees, the coordination problem—getting all workers to make subscriptions at the same time—is side-stepped.

There is wide diversity in practice in terms of how equity is subsequently held in these companies, and this diversity reflects a continuing debate about the most effective forms of employee ownership. Some companies, of which the John Lewis Partnership is the most famous, hold all of the equity in trust in perpetuity. The advantage of this arrangement is that employee ownership is unlikely to be diluted. The downside is that this form of indirect ownership may lead to a weak sense of ownership among employees. An alternative is to distribute ownership from the trust to employees on the grounds that direct shareholdings are more likely to foster a sense of ownership responsibility among employees. When equity is distributed in whole or in part to employees, ownership tends to be unequal, usually because employees are given the opportunity to purchase shares in addition to any free allocations. The use of free allocations, however, means that nearly all employees have some stake in ownership. Some firms use a combination of direct and indirect ownership.

The primary role of the owner in ownership conversion colors the character of employees' role in governance and participation. Employee representation on the company board tends to be rare, though not unknown, in these firms: owners often take the view that employees should not be deeply involved in the management process itself. There usually is some employee representation on the EBT, but there rarely is a majority of elected employees. Instead, the main form of employee involvement in these firms tends to be elected employee councils, at either the company level, workplace level, or both. Company management provides information to these councils but is not likely to formally report to them. Generally, the structure of participation and governance in these firms leaves much of the managerial prerogative intact.

Management–Employee Buyouts

In the final group of firms with substantial employee ownership, managers and employees purchase the company from its owners in a management–employee or employee buyout. These cases usually occur in two particular kinds of circumstance: privatization and rescues. In the former, management, employees, and unions aim to prevent the company from becoming acquired by predators who may attempt to reduce wages and employment conditions, and replace the incumbent management. There was a wave of privatization buyouts in the early 1990s, especially among local transportation companies, in response to government privatization programs of the time. At one point in the early 1990s, most metropolitan bus transportation companies were employee owned, with the typical ownership conversion involving one or more EBTs (see Pendleton 2001). This form of employee ownership did not survive beyond the mid-1990s because highly leveraged employee-owned firms were vulnerable to takeover by a small number of acquisitive companies. Since employees did not receive dividends on their shares in most cases, the main financial benefit of ownership was secured via capital gains on sale of the shares, and the temptation for employees to sell when predators made offers to buy their companies was difficult to resist. Since then, there has been less privatization activity, and currently there are relatively few management–employee buyouts in operation. However, the coalition government elected in spring 2010 plans to rekindle substantial privatization as part of its program to "shrink the state."

The other main type of buyout is when employees attempt to rescue distressed companies or those that have been shut down due to insolvency. These cases are rare because mounting a buyout of a failing company is fraught with difficulty. A well-known example of a rescue buyout is Tower Colliery in South Wales, in which miners used some of their redundancy money to reopen the coal mine, which had closed down on economic grounds. Another is that of UBH International—a steel tank container manufacturer—in which employees rescued a liquidated business by contributing £5,000 each (Bibby 2009). Many rescue attempts, however, do not progress to completion or fail shortly afterward: a good case is Pendleton's Ices in Merseyside.[4] It had been a successful, family-owned ice cream firm but was shut down by new owners after a trade sale when the family owners retired. The workforce occupied the plant to prevent it being asset-stripped, then tried to resurrect ice cream manufacture. Although the workforce managed to secure financial support from government and local investors, the venture collapsed some six months later due to marketing difficulties. The company had been unable to break into the small shop market, where margins are greater than supermarkets, because the large manufacturers controlled supply through the provision of refrigeration equipment (Monopolies and Mergers Commission 1994).

The involvement of employees and their representatives in these ownership conversions influences the structures of ownership, participation, and governance. Since many such cases come about from privatization of public sector organizations or activities, trade unions tend to be involved to some degree in the ownership conversion, given high levels of unionization in the public sector. In most cases, union representatives have played a key role in organizing buyouts, even though trade unions tend to be wary of employee ownership. The level of employee ownership in these companies is high, with the average among the bus companies being 66% (see Pendleton 2001:85). Most employees participate in ownership, though the participation is not necessarily equal. Most companies link free share distributions to job tenure, though some provide for equal share allocations or subscriptions on a quasi-cooperative basis.

The extensive role of employees and unions in mounting buyouts of this type also means that employee involvement in governance structures is well developed. Typically, these firms have elected worker-directors on the main company board so that employee interests are directly integrated into top management decision making. In the case of UBH, mentioned previously, three members of the nine-person board are elected employee-directors. When employee benefit trusts are used to hold some or all of the equity, the majority of trustees tend to be elected employee representatives. However, the trusts usually do not have a strong directive role in governance, being conceptualized instead as "warehouses" for equity. Worker-directors typically are drawn from past or current union representatives, though they usually are required to withdraw from union office. However, the involvement of unions in these cases often has a contradictory effect on governance, representation, and participation structures. On one hand, unions seek to have a strong influence on the operation of governance. On the other, they do not want to become so closely connected with shareholder governance structures that it confuses or weakens the union's employee representation role (see Pendleton et al. 1995).

The Determinants of Employee Ownership

The previous section showed that there are several distinct groups of firms with employee ownership. These firms differ in their ownership and governance characteristics, the circumstances of their adoption of employee ownership, and the key actors involved in the transition. This diversity of forms has implications for the study of determinants of employee ownership—namely, whether companies have any particular characteristics that are correlated with employee ownership that may explain why employee ownership occurred in these firms. The premise of the preceding section is that there may be different determinants for different types of employee-owned firms. This premise contrasts with the prevailing approaches in the literature, which tend to look for universal determinants. In this section, I evaluate key theory-based perspectives on determinants and indeed find that the applicability of determinants varies among the types of employee-owned firms.

In the literature, there have been persistent attempts to explain the distribution and determinants of companies with employee ownership (e.g., Kruse 1996; Ben-Ner, Burns, Dow, and Putterman 2000). The typical approach has been to identify measures to proxy for phenomena such as monitoring costs and then to evaluate whether these features are more prevalent in firms or workplaces with employee ownership than others. Many studies of this type did not include the proportion of the company owned by employees, so it is not always easy to assess what kind of employee ownership firms were being analyzed. For the most part, this research appears to have focused on firms with minority employee share ownership, possibly because the population of such firms tends to be larger than those with substantial, majority, or full employee ownership (see Pendleton 1997; Jones and Pliskin 1997; Ben-Ner, Burns, Dow, and Putterman 2000). Usually based on a Probit- or Logit-based regression methodology, results have been inconclusive. Although some structural features, such as organizational size and stock market listing, are nearly always critical determinants in the case of minority employee ownership (see Pendleton, Poutsma, Brewster, and van Ommeren 2001; Pendleton, Whitfield, and Bryson 2009; Kruse 1996; Kruse, Blasi, and Park 2010), results for the measures that proxy for economic rationales for employee share ownership have been mixed, as will be shown shortly.

There are far fewer large-scale quantitative studies of the determinants of substantial and majority employee ownership, and they tend to be undertaken from a financial or economics point of view rather than a labor relations perspective (e.g., Chaplinsky, Niehaus, and Van de Gucht 1998). Data availability problems may explain the small number of studies. Many fully employee-owned firms are small and privately owned; hence, they may not produce publicly available reports and accounts. In countries such as Britain, the total population is fairly small, and securing sufficient sample sizes can therefore be problematic.

The logic of the preceding portrayal of the types of substantially employee-owned firms in Britain is that searching for a single or dominant factor to explain the presence of employee ownership is likely to be doomed to failure. As has been shown, there are clusters of employee ownership in a diverse set of circumstances, and different factors and actors may be important in different circumstances. As a result, the distribution of employee ownership may be a function of the interplay of circumstance, company features, economic imperatives, and actor objectives. The corollary is that the relevance of various theory-based explanations for the incidence of substantial employee ownership may vary between the employee ownership types and contexts identified earlier. In the remainder of the chapter, I evaluate the main theoretical perspectives in the literature in the light of agency theory, the protection of human capital investments, and the costs of collective decision making.

Agency Theory and the Costs of Monitoring Employees

The most widespread explanation for employee ownership is based on principal–agent theory and suggests, following Alchian and Demsetz (1972), that it will be more appropriate when the nature of employee work tasks generates high monitoring costs. If employee tasks are highly diffuse, complex, or interdependent, monitoring work effort and output can be costly (see Pendleton 2006). Various forms of contingent pay can provide either a potentially "high-powered" incentive to expend effort (as in the case of output-based pay) or align employee interests with those of the firm (as is the case of weaker incentives such as share ownership). Monitoring costs are rarely observed directly in empirical studies; instead, various proxies are used to capture them. For instance, the proportion of skilled or white-collar workers has been used on the grounds that workers in these categories are more likely to undertake work tasks that are costly to monitor (McNabb and Whitfield 1998). Other proxies include the ratio of managers or supervisors to workers (Drago and Heywood 1995) and capital intensity (Kruse 1996). Unfortunately, the literature does not provide clear evidence in support of this proposition. Nearly all studies have been of minority share plans, though that is not always clear, and results have been inconclusive, unsupportive, or contradictory (see Ben-Ner, Burns, Dow, and Putterman 2000; Pendleton 2006). For instance, in Jones and Pliskin (1997), the proxy for machine-paced work (i.e., where monitoring costs are presumably relatively low) was positively rather negatively associated with the use of stock plans. A more troubling limitation of the incentives perspective is that the concentration of stock plans in large firms runs up against the "free-rider" effect. As Prendergast (1999) observed, it seems highly unlikely that the typical stock ownership plan will have strong incentive effects, unless, as Freeman, Kruse, and Blasi (2010) showed, workers exert effective peer pressure against shirkers.

The small amount of evidence relating to majority employee-owned firms does not clearly support the agency explanation even though, as smaller firms (on average) than those typically operating minority stock plans, they are less prone to the free-rider problem. Some years ago, Raymond Russell (1985) suggested that monitoring difficulties (in conjunction with labor mobility) helped explain the presence of employee ownership among refuse collectors, taxi firms, and professional services firms such as lawyers. However, as Hansmann (1996) argued, the work processes and output of those occupations can usually be monitored effectively in routine ways. Similar observations can be made of many of the firms currently owned by their employees in Britain. In terms of core work tasks, the activities of employees in at least some human capital firms can be readily monitored insofar as engineering design, for instance, involves routinized applications of engineering principles and calculations, while many of the manufacturing firms in the business succession group make relatively discrete products and components. Most management–employee buyouts (bus companies, mining) also comprise occupations that are relatively straightforward to monitor. Meanwhile, as has been observed in the literature (Bonin, Jones, and Putterman 1993), most cooperatives tend to be engaged in relatively simple activities, for which monitoring should not be costly.

It is also instructive to refer to the objectives of those involved in ownership conversions. In the case of management–employee and employee buyouts, the primary aim behind conversion to employee ownership is to protect wages and employment. In that of business succession firms, retiring owners typically are concerned with finding an exit route that preserves the company and protects employees against predators. In human capital firms, the typical objectives are to lock in valuable human capital and to insulate against takeovers. In interviews conducted with key architects of employee ownership in all of these groups, provision of incentives to employees so as to align interests rarely features as a primary factor in conversion to employee ownership. The only setting in which incentives appear to be important is in management buyouts when there is a minority, though nevertheless substantial, employee share (say 15% to 20%). Here, provision of employee incentives typically is an explicit rationale for including employees in ownership. But whether this is because monitoring is especially costly in these firms is difficult to judge.

Protecting Investments in Human Capital

A second set of explanations for the incidence and distribution of employee ownership is located in contracting theory. Set in an incomplete contracts framework, the argument is that employees need to protect their investments in human capital against managerial opportunism. Deriving from Williamson's transaction costs approach, this perspective is especially associated with Margaret Blair (1995). She advocated employee ownership as a means of protecting firm-specific human capital from expropriation by managers and employers. Ownership provides a guarantee that workers will secure returns from their human capital investments when they are vulnerable to hold-up by monopsonistic employers. At the same time, the control rights emanating from ownership provide a governance structure to allocate risk and returns. Blair argued that employee ownership is an appropriate means for resolving this contracting problem, especially because other forms of protection of employee investments, such as job security guarantees, internal labor markets, and unions, are apparently in decline.

The evidence to date suggests that this perspective applies well to some employee ownership contexts but not others. It does not work well for the cooperative sector because, as earlier evidence has shown, cooperatives tend to be concentrated in labor-intensive, low-skilled sectors such as simple manufacturing, where skills appear to be readily transferable between firms (Bonin, Jones, and Putterman 1993). However, quantitative studies of minority employee ownership firms provide some support for the contracting perspective. Several studies found a clear association between employer-provided training and use of share ownership plans (see Pendleton and Robinson 2010; Robinson and Zhang 2005), while Ben-Ner and colleagues (2000) found that low transferability of skills is associated with the probability of having an ESOP. Turning to majority employee-owned firms, the heterogeneity of the sector means that this contracting perspective is unlikely to apply across the board. While some parts of the employee-owned sector clearly require high levels of employee skills and knowledge, as in the human capital group, the same is not true of many firms in the business succession and management–employee buyout groups.

Nevertheless, the contracting perspective provides illuminating insights into two contexts for employee ownership identified earlier. In human capital firms, it is undoubtedly the case that many employees have a high level of skills and knowledge and that those workers need to be nurtured and protected. Employees in professional occupations are also more likely than any other occupational group to receive employer-provided training (Kersley et al. 2006). However, while many of these skills may be firm specific (e.g., knowledge of proprietary or custom-ized software, relationships with key customers), many also appear to be general or industry specific.[5] As a result, employees have the capacity to be highly mobile among firms where labor markets are thick, and this counteracts employee vulnerability to the "hold-up" problem identified by Blair (1995). The centrality of human capital, combined with mobil-ity, can shift the balance of power between workers and firms in favor of the former (Rousseau and Shperling 2003). In those circumstances, employee ownership may function as a protection for employer invest-ments in human capital as much as those made by employees. Employee ownership can lock highly skilled, mobile employees to the firm by promising to share the benefits of corporate success and providing pro-tection against takeovers (Blasi, Kruse, and Bernstein 2003). It also helps to attract skilled employees in the first place, especially where there is competition for talent (Liebeskind 2000).

While Blair (1995) highlighted the role of employee ownership as providing a governance structure for protecting employee investments in human capital (insulation against takeovers, for instance), the evidence suggests that the design of governance structures in British human capital firms with employee ownership is weighted toward employer interests. Employee ownership is nearly always initiated by owners or owner/managers rather than employees, and post-conversion governance structures are therefore likely to be especially influenced by them. This is borne out by the limited role of employees in governance structures. In such firms, employee ownership often resides in an EBT functioning on behalf of employees. A key issue is the composition and selection of members of these trusts. In most cases, membership in EBTs is domi-nated by top managers of the companies, with new trustees selected by existing trustees (who initially were selected by top management). Although management boards may report to the EBT, formal lines of accountability to employees appear to be weakly developed in most cases.

The second context concerns management–employee buyouts dur-ing privatization. Here the transition to employee ownership can be interpreted as a means of protecting employee investments in firms experiencing uncertainty and market shocks (see also Gordon 1999 on the U.S. airline industry). During privatization and deregulation of the

British local transportation industry in the 1990s, employee ownership provided protection for wages and employment conditions. Other
contenders for ownership of these firms were known to undercut wage
rates, and employee ownership was an explicit attempt to insulate firms
from these pressures. Employees and unions aimed to protect wages and
conditions of employment that had been underpinned by regulation,
collective bargaining, and state support from the competitive shock to
product and labor markets arising from deregulation of transportation
markets. This is not to say that employee-owned firms were able to resist
changes to wages. Rather, employee ownership provided a governance
structure in which effective concession bargaining could take place,
in which both sides achieved many of their objectives. Workforce and
union agreement to productivity enhancements and changes to labor
utilization (including the limited introduction of two-tier employment
conditions) could be more readily achieved if there were guarantees that
labor (as shareholders) would benefit from new labor policies. Employee
ownership provided a guarantee that managers would not take all the
gains of workforce concessions. It is notable that, in these cases, employees and unions were deeply involved in the transition to employee ownership and played a key role in designing governance institutions. Unlike
other forms of employee ownership reviewed in this chapter, employee
board-level representation was the norm in these companies.

The Costs of Collective Decision Making

A final perspective on the factors influencing the incidence and
distribution of employee ownership is that which emphasizes the costs
of collective decision making (Hansmann 1996). The argument here is
that resolving divergences of interest among heterogeneous workforces
provides a high barrier to the formation, conversion, and continuing
existence of shared ownership among employees. By implication, firms
becoming substantially employee owned are likely to have relatively
homogeneous workforces. Coordinating diverse workforces to commit
their resources to acquire their firm is likely to be challenging, to say the
least. And allocating surpluses among very different occupational groups
in a way that is acceptable to all is likely to be time consuming and to
generate damaging conflict. Hansmann argued that the most striking
evidence of the importance of the costs of collective decision making is
"the scarcity of employee-owned firms in which there are substantial differences among the employees who participate in ownership" (1996:91).
Hansmann's analysis focused on firms that are wholly or majority owned
by employees. He noted that many recent examples of firms with minority employee ownership, such as many publicly owned ESOPs in the

United States, are governed by fiduciaries rather than employees and that employees have very limited control rights. This kind of ownership and governance, usually instigated by managers rather than employees or unions, is not likely to be substantially inhibited by the costs of collective decision making.

Workforce composition in majority or wholly employee-owned firms in Britain appears to be broadly consistent with Hansmann's propositions. Most worker cooperatives have highly homogeneous (and small) workforces, often with job rotation (as was also the case in the U.S. plywood cooperatives). Among the human capital firms, smaller companies are highly homogeneous, typically composed of a small number of consultants in the same specialization. Although the larger firms have a supporting bureaucracy (administrators, secretaries, etc.), the professionals or consultants are clearly a core and dominant group. It is less easy to generalize about the business succession firms: some appear to have a numerically dominant group (e.g., retail assistants in the John Lewis Partnership), but others do not. Management–employee buyouts in the erstwhile group of employee-owned bus companies were characterized by three distinct occupational groups: drivers, engineers, and office staff. However, drivers were the numerically dominant group by a good margin (approximately 75% of workforces on average) and had the strongest power resources within these firms. Similar observations may be made of employee-owned firms outside Britain. Employee-owned airlines have a number of major and distinct occupational groups, but pilots, though not the largest group, are generally dominant. These observations suggest that Hansmann's (1996) perspective needs to be modified somewhat: employee-owned firms tend to have relatively homogeneous workforces or else contain an occupation that is politically dominant within them.

Although there are obvious costs to collective decision making when there is more than one interest group, employee-owned firms in Britain appear to mitigate these costs in several ways. Thus, these costs may not be as obstructive of or damaging to employee ownership as the Hansmann (1996) thesis implied. The first thing to note is that most conversions to employee ownership are initiated and managed by owners rather than employees. Furthermore, ownership conversion is typically effected using an EBT rather than direct employee subscriptions. Thus, coordination costs during conversion may be relatively limited. Once firms are employee owned, employee involvement in governance is typically kept clearly distinct from day-to-day management. The most widespread forms of involvement are employee representation on the EBT, employee representation on an "employee shareholders council," and employee representation on the company board. Only in the latter do employees have a (potentially) strong and regular role in management and governance, and, in those cases, participating employees are required to relinquish allegiance to any particular constituency within the firm (directors' obligations are to the company). They also have minority representation in every case of which I am aware. Employee benefit trusts generally have a small involvement in management and governance, being primarily "warehouses" for shares and blocks against takeovers.

The costs of collective decision making seem likely to be higher when there are shareholder councils, which typically are elected on a constituency basis. Some firms have elaborate structures for employee participation and representation. For example, the John Lewis Partnership has an extensive participation structure, with partnership councils at company and store levels. Scottish papermaker Tullis Russell has a share council composed mainly of elected representatives with a remit to oversee the operation of the stock ownership scheme, to reflect the views of employee shareholders, and to discuss business performance with the board of directors. Operation of these structures is costly (they meet several times a year), though top managers at both John Lewis and Tullis Russell believe that there is a payoff in terms of staff engagement and commitment. It is also important to note that the constitutions of partnership arrangements at companies such as these place limits on the powers of shareholder councils to become involved in "management issues." For this reason, divergent employee interests (e.g., concerning wage differentials) tend not to find expression in these councils and are more likely to be articulated through other forms of employee representation, such as unions, when they are present.

To recap, the evidence suggests that many employee-owned firms in Britain have either fairly homogeneous workforces or else are dominated by one particular occupational grouping. This is broadly consistent with Hansmann's (1996) claim that workforce homogeneity is a necessary condition for employee ownership, but it is impossible to say how and to what extent heterogeneity obstructs conversion to employee ownership. A major problem for researchers, however, is how to operationalize workforce homogeneity in a way that is satisfactory for empirical research and testing. Hansmann is not a great deal of help on this question, as he merely noted that homogeneity is a relative concept. To some extent this is true—what is important is the perceived extent of divisions within a workforce, which may, of course, vary between organizational actors. In the absence of relevant large-scale employee survey data for both employee-owned and conventional firms, workforce homogeneity will therefore inevitably be impressionistic. Furthermore, it is not possible to assess with any reasonable degree of confidence, given current data availability, whether employee-owned firms are more homogeneous in workforce composition than most conventional firms.

Conclusions

One of the primary goals of this chapter was to illuminate the diversity of the employee ownership sector in terms of ownership structure, governance arrangement, contexts for ownership conversion, and involvement of key actors. The literature has not always distinguished among the various types of employee ownership. In particular, minority employee ownership in stock market–listed companies has often been conflated with majority employee ownership, and there has been a tendency to extend the application of theory that appears appropriate for one form of ownership to others where it may be less useful. Diversity within the majority employee ownership sector has also been emphasized, echoing earlier observations by Ben-Ner and Jones (1995), among others. Besides worker cooperatives, three major species of majority employee-owned firms have been identified: human capital–rich firms such as consultancies and professional services companies, business succession firms converted to employee ownership when owners retire, and management–employee buyouts. Drawing on Kruse and Blasi's (1997) dimensions of ownership, it has been shown how these groups of employee-owned firms differ in their structures of ownership and governance.

The chapter also considered various theoretical explanations of the incidence and distribution of employee stock ownership. As has been noted before (Pendleton 2006), agency theory–based explanations do not work very well, with evidence being mixed and inconclusive. This chapter emphasized the importance of the objectives of those involved in employee ownership conversions and showed how they do not appear to focus on the types of issues that agency perspectives would suggest. Contracting theory appears to work better, but not for all forms of employee ownership. In contrast to recent expositions of contracting perspectives on employee ownership, the evidence suggests that, in many instances, employee ownership may provide a governance structure to protect employer rather than employee investments in human capital. Finally, the applicability of Hansmann's (1996) argument about the costs of collective decision making was considered. Of course, this perspective, as presented by its author, is aimed at explaining the absence rather than presence of employee ownership and, as such, focused on necessary conditions for employee ownership rather than its causes. Nevertheless, Hansmann's work provided a useful analytical perspective, especially for considering the typical governance features of firms with employee ownership. However, in showing how the costs of collective decision making influence the design of governance structures, it is also demonstrated that these costs do not necessarily deter conversion when actors want it to take place.

The diversity of employee ownership has implications for research agendas and the design of policy instruments to encourage employee ownership. It is feasible that the outcomes of employee ownership on company performance and employee attitudes will differ systematically among the various groups of employee-owned firms. If this is so, it is possible that effects will cancel each other out if these groups are considered together without differentiation. For example, while business succession firms tend to have a track record of success, management–employee buyouts of distressed companies do not. Analyzing these firms together may obscure their performance differences. Similarly, variations in ownership and governance structure may be associated with differences in employee attitudes. Future research in these areas should pay more attention to these differences within the employee-owned sector. Similarly, policy instruments to encourage employee ownership may well benefit from more precise targeting of the various contexts in which employee ownership occurs. For instance, financing of conversions is likely to be more problematic in the case of management–employee buyouts, and there may well be more of a case for public financial support for conversions of this sort than there is for others. To conclude, theory, empirical analysis, and practical initiative all need to embrace the diversity of the employee-ownership sector.

Endnotes

[1] Tower Colliery was taken over by its workforce in 1995 after British Coal closed the mine on economic grounds. It ceased production in 2008 due to exhaustion of the coal seams.

[2] Finance-sector trade unions tend to be more involved in the operation of stock plans than unions in other sectors.

[3] Arup came to prominence for its work on the structural design of the Sydney Opera House, Australia, and the Pompidou Centre in Paris, France.

[4] The author is not related to the family that owned this company.

[5] Lazear (2009) argued that much employer-provided training is in general skills, but the combinations of these skills may be firm specific, depending on the thickness of labor markets. Of course, high labor mobility also suggests that hiring costs should be low, but there are verification costs and uncertainty ex ante that general skills will combine effectively into skill sets that are valuable for the hiring firm.

References

Alchian, Armen, and Harold Demsetz. 1972. "Production, Information Costs, and Economic Organization." *American Economic Review*, Vol. 62, pp. 777–95.

All-Party Parliamentary Group on Employee Ownership. 2008. *Share Value: How Employee Ownership Is Changing the Face of Business*. London: House of Commons.

Association of British Insurers. 2005. *Principles and Guidelines on Remuneration*. London: Association of British Insurers.

Ben-Ner, Avner, W. Allen Burns, Gregory Dow, and Louis Putterman. 2000. "Employee Ownership: An Empirical Exploration." In Margaret Blair and Thomas Kochan, eds., *The New Relationship: Human Capital in the American Corporation*. Washington, DC: Brookings Institution, pp. 194–232.

Ben-Ner, Avner, and Derek Jones. 1995. "Employee Participation, Ownership, and Productivity: A Theoretical Framework." *Industrial Relations*, Vol. 34, pp. 532–53.

Bibby, Andrew. 2009. *From Colleagues to Owners: Transferring Ownership to Employees*. London: Employee Ownership Association.

Blair, Margaret. 1995. *Ownership and Control: Rethinking Corporate Governance for the Twenty-First Century*. Washington DC: Brookings Institution.

Blasi, Joseph. 1988. *Employee Ownership: Revolution or Rip-Off?* New York: Harper Business.

Blasi, Joseph, Douglas Kruse, and Aaron Bernstein. 2003. *In the Company of Owners: The Truth About Stock Options*. New York: Basic Books.

Bonin, John, Derek Jones, and Louis Putterman. 1993. "Theoretical and Empirical Studies of Producer Cooperatives: Will Ever the Twain Meet?" *Journal of Economic Literature*, Vol. 31, pp. 1290–1320.

Bryson, Alex, and Richard Freeman. 2007. *Doing the Right Thing? Does Fair Share Capitalism Improve Workplace Performance?* London: Department of Trade and Industry, Employment Relations Research Series No. 81.

Chaplinksy, Susan, Greg Niehaus, and Linda Van de Gucht. 1998. "Employee Buy-outs: Causes, Structure, and Consequences." *Journal of Financial Economics*, Vol. 48, pp. 283–332.

Doucouliagos, Chris. 1995. "Worker Participation and Productivity in Labor-Managed and Participatory Capitalist Firms: A Meta-Analysis." *Industrial and Labor Relations Review*, Vol. 49, no.1, pp. 58–77.

Dow, Gregory. 2003. *Governing the Firm: Workers Control in Theory and Practice*. Cambridge: Cambridge University Press.

Drago, Robert, and John Heywood. 1995. "The Choice of Payment Schemes: Australian Establishment Data." *Industrial Relations*, Vol. 34, pp. 507–31.

Freeman, Richard, Douglas Kruse, and Joseph Blasi. 2010. "Worker Responses to Shirking under Shared Capitalism." In Douglas Kruse, Richard Freeman, and Joseph Blasi, eds. *Shared Capitalism at Work: Employee Ownership, Profit and Gain Sharing, and Broad-Based Stock Options*. Chicago: University of Chicago Press.

General Accounting Office (GAO). 1987. *Employee Stock Ownership Plans: Little Evidence of Effects on Corporate Performance*. Washington DC: Government Printing Office.

Gordon, Jeffrey. 1999. "Employee Stock Ownership in Economic Transitions: The Case of United and the Airline Industry." In Margaret Blair and Mark Roe, eds., *Employees and Corporate Governance*. Washington DC: Brookings Institution, pp. 317–54.

Hammer, Tove, and Robert Stern. 1980. "Employee Ownership: Implications for the Organisational Distribution of Power." *Academy of Management Journal*, Vol. 23, pp. 78–100.

Hansmann, Henry. 1996. *The Ownership of Enterprise*. Cambridge MA: Belknap Press.

Her Majesty's Revenue and Customs (HMRC). 2007. *Tax-Advantaged Employee Share Schemes: Analysis of Productivity Effects, Reports 1 and 2*. London: HMRC.

Her Majesty's Revenue and Customs (HMRC). 2008a. *Evaluation of Tax-Advantaged All-Employee Share Schemes*. London: HMRC.

Her Majesty's Revenue and Customs (HMRC). 2008b. *EMI Evaluation Survey: Use of EMI and Its Perceived Impact*. London: HMRC.

Her Majesty's Revenue and Customs (HMRC). 2010. *Share Schemes*. <http://www.hmrc.gov.uk/stats/emp_share_schemes/menu.htm>. [January 24, 2010].

Jones, Derek, and Jeffrey Pliskin. 1997. "Determinants of the Incidence of Group Incentives: Evidence from Canada." *Canadian Journal of Economics*, Vol. 30, pp. 1027–45.

Kersley, Barbara, Carmen Alpin, John Forth, Alex Bryson, Belen Bewley, Gill Dix, and Sarah Oxenbridge. 2006. *Inside the Workplace: Findings from the 2004 Workplace Employment Relations Survey*. London: Routledge.

Kruse, Douglas. 1996. "Why Do Firms Adopt Profit Sharing and Employee Ownership Plans?" *British Journal of Industrial Relations*, Vol. 34, pp. 515–38.

Kruse, Douglas, and Joseph Blasi. 1997. "Employee Ownership, Employee Attitudes, and Firm Performance: A Review of the Evidence." In David Lewin, Daniel Mitchell, and Mohammed Zaira, eds., *The Human Resource Management Handbook*. London: JAI Press, pp. 113–51.

Kruse, Douglas, Joseph Blasi, and Rhokeum Park. 2010. "Shared Capitalism in the U.S. Economy: Prevalence, Characteristics, and Employee Views of Financial Participation in Enterprises." In Douglas Kruse, Richard Freeman, and Joseph Blasi, eds., *Shared Capitalism at Work: Employee Ownership, Profit and Gain Sharing, and Broad-Based Stock Options*. Chicago: University of Chicago Press.

Lazear, Edward. 2009. "Firm-Specific Human Capital: A Skills-Weights Approach." *Journal of Political Economy*, Vol. 117, no. 5, pp. 914–40.

Liebeskind, Julia. 2000. "Ownership, Incentives, and Control in New Biotechnology Firms." In Margaret Blair and Thomas Kochan, eds., *The New Relationship: Human Capital in the American Corporation*. Washington DC: Brookings Institution, pp. 299–326.

Logue, John, and Jacquelyn Yates. 2001. *The Real World of Employee Ownership*. Ithaca, NY: Cornell University Press.

Long, Richard. 1978. "The Effects of Employee Ownership on Organizational Identification, Employee Job Attitudes, and Organizational Performance—A Tentative Framework and Empirical Findings." *Human Relations*, Vol. 31, pp. 29–48.

Long, Richard. 1979. "Desires for and Patterns of Worker Participation in Decision-Making After Conversion to Employee Ownership." *Academy of Management Journal*, Vol. 22, no. 3, pp. 611–7.

Long, Richard. 1980. "Job Attitudes and Organizational Performance Under Employee Ownership." *Academy of Management Journal*, Vol. 23, no. 4, pp. 726–37.

McNabb, Robert, and Keith Whitfield. 1998. "The Impact of Financial Participation and Employee Involvement on Financial Performance." *Scottish Journal of Political Economy*, Vol. 42, pp. 171–87.

Monopolies and Mergers Commission. 1994. *Ice Cream: A Report on the Supply in the UK of Ice Cream for Immediate Consumption*. London: Monopolies and Mergers Commission.

Paton, Rob. 1989. *Reluctant Entrepreneurs: Extent, Achievements and Significance of Worker Takeovers in Europe*. Milton Keynes, UK: Open University Press.

Pendleton, Andrew. 1997. "Characteristics of Workplaces with Financial Participation: Evidence from the Workplace Industrial Relations Survey." *Industrial Relations Journal*, Vol. 28, pp. 103–19.

Pendleton, Andrew. 2001. *Employee Ownership, Participation, and Governance*. London: Routledge.

Pendleton, Andrew. 2005a. "Sellers or Keepers? Employee Behaviour in Stock Option Plans." *Human Resource Management*, Vol. 44, no. 3, pp. 319–36.

Pendleton, Andrew. 2005b. "Employee Share Ownership, Employment Relationships, and Corporate Governance." In Bill Harley, Jeff Hyman, and Paul Thompson, eds., *Participation and Democracy at Work: Essays in Honour of Harvie Ramsay*. London: Palgrave.

Pendleton, Andrew. 2006. "Incentives, Monitoring, and Employee Stock Ownership Plans: New Evidence and Interpretations." *Industrial Relations*, Vol. 45, no. 4, pp. 753–77.

Pendleton, Andrew. 2010. "Employee Participation in Employee Share Ownership: An Evaluation of the Factors Associated with Participation and Contributions in Save As You Earn Plans." *British Journal of Management*, Vol. 21, no. 2, pp. 550–70.

Pendleton, Andrew, Erik Poutsma, Chris Brewster, and Jos van Ommeren. 2001. *Employee Share Ownership and Profit Sharing in the European Union*. Dublin: European Foundation for the Improvement of Living and Working Conditions.

Pendleton, Andrew, and Andrew Robinson. 2010. "Employee Stock Ownership, Involvement, and Productivity: An Interaction-Based Approach. *Industrial and Labor Relations Review*, Vol. 64, no. 1, pp. 746–72.

Pendleton, Andrew, Andrew Robinson, and Nicholas Wilson. 1995. "Does Economic Democracy Weaken Trade Unions? Recent Evidence from the UK Bus Industry." *Economic and Industrial Democracy*, Vol. 16, no. 4, pp. 577–604.

Pendleton, Andrew, Keith Whitfield, and Alex Bryson. 2009. "The Changing Use of Contingent Pay at the Modern British Workplace." In William Brown, Alex Bryson, John Forth, and Keith Whitfield, eds., *The Evolution of the Modern Workplace*. Cambridge: Cambridge University Press.

Perotin, Virginie. 2006. "Entry, Exit, and the Business Cycle: Are Cooperatives Different?" *Journal of Comparative Economics*, Vol. 34, no. 2, pp. 295–316.

Prendergast, Canice. 1999. "The Provision of Incentives in Firms." *Journal of Economic Literature*, Vol. 37, pp. 7–63.

Robinson, Andrew, and Hao Zhang. 2005. "Employee Share Ownership: Safeguarding Investments in Human Capital." *British Journal of Industrial Relations*, Vol. 43, no. 3, pp. 469–88.

Rousseau, Denise, and Zipi Shperling. 2003. "Pieces of the Action: Ownership and the Changing Employment Relationship." *Academy of Management Review*, Vol. 28, no. 4, pp. 553–70.

Rowntree, Seebohm. 1921. *The Human Factor in Business.* London: Longman and Green.

Russell, Raymond. 1985. "Employee Ownership and Internal Governance." *Journal of Economic Behavior and Organization*, Vol. 6, pp. 217–41.

Sengupta, Sukanya, Keith Whitfield, and Robert McNabb. 2008. "Employee Share Ownership and Performance: Golden Path or Golden Handcuffs?" *International Journal of Human Resource Management*, Vol. 18, no. 8, pp. 1507–38.

ABOUT THE CONTRIBUTORS

Serdar Aldatmaz is a Ph.D. candidate in finance at the Kenan-Flagler Business School at the University of North Carolina. He is currently working on a project examining the impact of BBSOs (broad-based stock options) on employee turnover. His other current research examines investment cash flow sensitivities of U.S. firms before major crises. His research interests also include executive compensation, corporate governance, capital structure, and mergers and acquisitions. Before entering the Ph.D. program, he received his B.A. from Koc University, Istanbul, with a double major in economics and business administration.

Saioa Arando is the scientific coordinator at Mondragon Innovation and Knowledge (MIK). She holds a Ph.D. in economics and business administration from Universidad de Deusto. Her research areas are entrepreneurship and the behavior of worker cooperatives. Her work has been published in various journals, and she has participated in several international conferences. In 2006, she was awarded the Horvat-Vanek Prize for the best young researcher, presented by the International Association for the Economics of Participation.

Daphne Perkins Berry is a Ph.D. candidate in management at the University of Massachusetts, Amherst, and a Rutgers research fellow at the School of Management and Labor Relations at Rutgers University. Her dissertation is an exploratory study of how productivity (quality of care) in home health aide agencies operating under different forms of governance is affected by participatory decision making and ownership. Her work background is in the telecommunications industry with U.S., British, and Japanese multinationals and start-up firms. Daphne has B.S. and M.E.E. degrees in electrical engineering from the University of Notre Dame and Rice University, respectively.

Joseph R. Blasi is a professor at the School of Management and Labor Relations at Rutgers University, a research associate at the National Bureau of Economic Research, and the J. Robert Beyster Professor of Employee Ownership at the School of Management and Labor Relations at Rutgers University. He has made seminal contributions to research on employee stock ownership, broad-based stock options, employee involvement, and corporate governance. He holds an Ed.D. from Harvard University and a B.A. in social psychology from the University of Pittsburgh.

Francesco Bova is an assistant professor of accounting at the University of Toronto's Joseph L. Rotman School of Management and a Rutgers research fellow at the School of Management and Labor Relations at Rutgers University. His broad research interests focus on uncovering the managerial decisions that not only maximize shareholder value but also maximize the utility of other nonshareholder stakeholders. These other stakeholders include the firm's employees, customers, and, more broadly, the communities that benefit from infrastructure investments made by a company. Francesco was a finalist for the 2009 Shared Capitalism Through Employee Ownership Dissertation Award.

Marco Caramelli is an associate professor at INSEEC Business School in Paris. He received a Ph.D. in management from the University of Montpellier II in France, and he teaches and conducts research on a variety of topics, including cross-cultural management, employee ownership, and corporate governance. Marco also serves on the board of the FAS, the French federation of the associations of employee stockholders, and is a frequent presenter at many domestic and international professional and academic conferences.

Edward J. Carberry is an assistant professor in the Department of Business-Society Management at the Rotterdam School of Management, Erasmus University, and the former J. Robert Beyster Visiting Professor and a Beyster fellow at the School of Management and Labor Relations at Rutgers University. His research uses organizational sociology to examine the adoption, design, and consequences of compensation systems, human resource practices, and workplace authority structures. He is currently conducting research on the effects of employee ownership and executive compensation on economic inequality. He holds a Ph.D. in sociology from Cornell University and formerly was research director at the National Center for Employee Ownership.

Adrienne E. Eaton is chair of the Labor Studies and Employment Relations Department at Rutgers University. She is the co-author, along with Tom Kochan, Paul Adler, and Robert McKersie, of the book *Healing Together: The Kaiser Permanente Labor–Management Partnership* (2009), editor with Jeff Keefe of *Employment Dispute Resolution in the Changing Workplace* (2000), and author of numerous articles published in journals such as *Industrial and Labor Relations Review, Industrial Relations, Labor Studies Journal,* and *Advances in Industrial and Labor Relations.*

Fred Freundlich has been working and carrying out research in the field of broad employee participation in enterprise ownership since 1985. Currently, he teaches at the Faculty of Business, Mondragon University, co-manages its master's program in Cooperative Enterprise Management and, through its research arm, Mondragon Innovation and Knowledge (MIK), coordinates the Mondragon Cooperative Academic Community, an international research initiative. Before shifting his focus to the academic world, he worked for 15 years for Ownership Associates, a consulting firm involved in developing employee ownership and participation.

Mónica Gago is a professor of economics at the Faculty of Business at Mondragon University. She holds a Ph.D. in economics from the University of the Basque Country. Her research focuses on nonparametric estimators in finance and econometric analysis of firms with employee participation in capital ownership. She has experience doing empirical research with large-scale data sets. Her work has been presented at several international conferences and has appeared in the *Spanish Economic Review* and *Investigaciones Económicas*. Her work has been funded by the European Social Fund, the Spanish government's José Castillejo Programme, and the Basque government.

Derek C. Jones is the Robert D. Morris Professor of Economics at Hamilton College; research director in economics at Mondragon Cooperative Academic Community, Mondragon University; a research fellow at the Davidson Institute, University of Michigan; and a research fellow at the Centre on Skills, Knowledge and Organisational Performance at Oxford University. He has published over 120 articles in refereed journals and chapters in edited volumes and has edited three books and several volumes in the series *Advances in the Economic Analysis of Participatory and Labor-Managed Firms*, for which he is a founding editor. He is a past president of the Association for Comparative Economic Systems and the International Association for the Economics of Participation.

Takao Kato is W.S. Schupf Professor of Economics and Far Eastern Studies at Colgate University. He is also a research fellow at IZA Bonn and a research associate at the Center on Japanese Economy and Business at Columbia University, at the Tokyo Center for Economic Research, and at the Center for Corporate Performance at Aarhus University. He is currently series editor of *Advances in the Economic Analysis of Participatory and Labor-Managed Firms* and co-editor of the *Journal of the Japanese and International Economies*. He has published widely on employee participation, corporate governance, and comparative industrial relations in eminent journals, including *American Economic Review*.

Douglas L. Kruse is a professor in the School of Management and Labor Relations at Rutgers University, a research associate at the National Bureau of Economic Research, and a Beyster fellow at the School of Management and Labor Relations at Rutgers University. His research includes econometric studies on profit sharing, employee ownership, pensions, and disability. He holds a Ph.D. in economics from Harvard University, an M.A. in economics from the University of Nebraska, Lincoln, and a B.A. in economics from Harvard University.

Fidan Ana Kurtulus is an assistant professor in the Department of Economics at the University of Massachusetts, Amherst, and a Beyster fellow at the School of Management and Labor Relations at Rutgers University. She has conducted research in a number of labor economics topics, including workplace diversity, affirmative action, and employee participation in firm financial performance and decision making. She holds a Ph.D. in economics from Cornell University and an A.B. in economics from the University of Chicago.

The late **John Logue**, a professor of political science at Kent State University and department chair from 2004 through 2008, was the founder and director of the Ohio Employee Ownership Center (OEOC) at Kent State from 1987 through 2009. Since 1987, the OEOC has worked with roughly 570 companies and employee groups with more than 100,000 workers; of those, 88 firms with more than 15,000 workers implemented partial or complete employee ownership. Logue was deeply involved in the conceptualization and development of the Evergreen Cooperatives, an ongoing project launched in 2009 to address poverty and neighborhood decline in Cleveland by developing a network of cooperatives. He had also served on the boards of several employee-owned companies. Logue wrote widely on employee ownership and workplace democracy in the United States and on the politics of Scandinavia including, most recently, co-editing *Transitions to Capitalism and Democracy in Russia and Central Europe: Achievements, Problems, Prospects* (2000) and co-authoring *Participatory Employee Ownership: How It Works* (1998), *The Real World of Employee Ownership* (2001), *Modern Welfare States: Scandinavian Politics and Policy in the Global Age* (2nd ed., 2003), and *Productivity in Cooperatives and Worker-Owned Enterprises: Ownership and Participation Make a Difference!* (2005). Logue held a Danforth Fellowship, a Danish Social Science Research Council Fellowship, the Swedish Bicentennial Fellowship, and a Fulbright Professorship at the University of Copenhagen. Kent State honored him as a Distinguished Scholar in 2002, and the Ford Foundation/Advocacy Institute gave him the prestigious Leadership for a Changing World Award in

2003. Born and reared in Texas, he received a B.A. from the University of Texas summa cum laude in 1970; an M.A. from Princeton University in 1973; and a Ph.D. from Princeton in 1976. He was a member of Phi Beta Kappa. He passed away in December 2009.

John E. McCarthy is a third-year doctoral student at Rutgers School of Management and Labor Relations. His research centers on the antecedents to successful knowledge transfer and combination within and between organizations. He is also interested in the differential interpretations that employees form regarding group-level network structures and how these interpretations help to frame a broader range of attitudes, including perceptions of climate.

Joan S.M. Meyers is a postdoctoral associate and Rutgers research fellow at the School of Management and Labor Relations at Rutgers University. Her work focuses on the intersections of gender with race/ethnicity and class in the workplace. Her current research uses both quantitative and qualitative methods to examine inequality in majority employee-owned companies. She holds a Ph.D. in sociology from the University of California, Davis, and an M.A. in women's studies from San Francisco State University.

Paige Ouimet is an assistant professor at the Kenan-Flagler School of Business at the University of North Carolina and is the current J. Robert Beyster Visiting Professor and a Beyster fellow at the School of Management and Labor Relations at Rutgers University. Her work has been published in the *Review of Financial Studies*. She has researched the role of hedge funds in the PIPEs (private investment in public equity) market and mergers and acquisitions of emerging-market firms. She is currently working on several projects related to ESOPs and their impact on labor productivity and wages. She received her Ph.D. and M.B.A. from the Ross School of Business at the University of Michigan and her B.A. from Dartmouth College.

Andrew Pendleton is professor of human resource management at the University of York Management School, York, UK. He has also taught industrial relations and human resource management at Bath, Bradford, Kent, and Manchester Metropolitan universities. His main research interests are employee ownership, employee share plans, workplace financial education, and corporate ownership and governance.

Stu Schneider serves as the business development manager of Cooperative Home Care Associates (CHCA) and is a member of its Labor/Management Committee with 1199 SEIU. In this position, he secures funding from private foundations and government programs for CHCA's workforce development and asset-building work. In 2009, he transferred to CHCA from PHI, an affiliated nonprofit organization where he had completed similar work since 2001. Stu has a B.A. in economics and urban studies from Rutgers College.

Paula B. Voos, professor at the School of Management and Labor Relations at Rutgers University, was recently appointed a public member of New Jersey's Public Employment Relations Commission. She is a past president of the Labor and Employment Relations Association and editor of that association's 1994 research volume, *Contemporary Collective Bargaining in the United States*. Besides publishing extensively in the area of labor relations and public policy, Paula served on the Dunlop Commission in 1994. She came to Rutgers University from the University of Wisconsin in 1998, where she directed the Industrial Relations Research Institute.

Jacquelyn Yates, an associate professor at Kent State University, taught in the Political Science Department for 37 years, retiring from teaching in 2009. Since 1995, she has served as a researcher for the Ohio Employee Ownership Center and edited their semiannual newsmagazine, *Owners at Work*. She co-authored numerous papers and publications with John Logue. She was a National Merit Scholar and an NDEA fellow. A graduate of Chatham College and the University of Pittsburgh (Ph.D.), she is a member of Phi Beta Kappa.